ALSO BY CLAY RISEN

The Bill of the Century:
The Epic Battle for the Civil Rights Act

A Nation on Fire:
America in the Wake of the King Assassination

Single Malt:
A Guide to the Whiskies of Scotland

American Whiskey, Bourbon & Rye:
A Guide to the Nation's Favorite Spirit

THE
CROWDED
HOUR

THEODORE ROOSEVELT, THE ROUGH RIDERS, AND THE DAWN OF THE AMERICAN CENTURY

CLAY RISEN

SCRIBNER

New York London Toronto Sydney New Delhi

Scribner
An Imprint of Simon & Schuster, Inc.
1230 Avenue of the Americas
New York, NY 10020

First Scribner hardcover edition June 2019

SCRIBNER and design are registered trademarks of The Gale Group, Inc.,
used under license by Simon & Schuster, Inc., the publisher of this work.

For information about special discounts for bulk purchases,
please contact Simon & Schuster Special Sales at 1-866-506-1949
or business@simonandschuster.com.

The Simon & Schuster Speakers Bureau can bring authors to your live event.
For more information or to book an event, contact the Simon & Schuster Speakers Bureau
at 1-866-248-3049 or visit our website at www.simonspeakers.com.

Manufactured in the United States of America

1   3   5   7   9   10   8   6   4   2

Library of Congress Control Number: 2018053824

ISBN 978-1-5011-4399-1
ISBN 978-1-5011-4401-1 (ebook)

To My Mother

CONTENTS

THE COMPOSITION OF THE FIFTH CORPS, UNITED STATES ARMY

Maj. Gen. William R. Shafter, commanding

1st Division, Brig. Gen. Jacob F. Kent
    1st Brigade, Brig. Gen. Hamilton S. Hawkins
        6th U.S. Infantry
        16th U.S. Infantry
        71st New York Volunteer Infantry
    2nd Brigade, Col. Edward P. Pearson
        3rd U.S. Infantry
        10th U.S. Infantry
        21st U.S. Infantry
    3rd Brigade, Col. Charles A. Wikoff
        9th U.S. Infantry
        13th U.S. Infantry
        24th U.S. Infantry

2nd Division, Brig. Gen. Henry W. Lawton
    1st Brigade, Brig. Gen. William Ludlow
        8th U.S. Infantry
        22nd U.S. Infantry
        2nd Massachusetts Volunteer Infantry
    2nd Brigade, Col. Evan Miles
        1st U.S. Infantry
        4th U.S. Infantry
        25th U.S. Infantry

THE COMPOSITION OF THE FIFTH CORPS, UNITED STATES ARMY

3rd Brigade, Brig. Gen. Adna R. Chaffee
    7th U.S. Infantry
    12th U.S. Infantry
    17th U.S. Infantry

Cavalry Division, Maj. Gen. Joseph Wheeler
    1st Brigade, Brig. Gen. Samuel S. Sumner
        3rd U.S. Cavalry
        6th U.S. Cavalry
        9th U.S. Cavalry
    2nd Brigade, Brig. Gen. Samuel B. M. Young
        1st U.S. Cavalry
        10th U.S. Cavalry
        1st U.S. Volunteer Cavalry (the Rough Riders)

Troops A, C, D, and F of the 2nd Cavalry Regiment

Artillery Battalion
Independent Brigade (part of Fourth Army Corps, attached to
    Fifth Corps)
    3rd U.S. Infantry
    20th U.S. Infantry
Signal Corps
Siege Train
Hospital Corps
Engineers Battalion
Gatling Gun Detachment (13th U.S. Infantry)

Source: Correspondence Relating to the War with Spain (Washington, D.C.:
U.S. Government Printing Office, 1902).

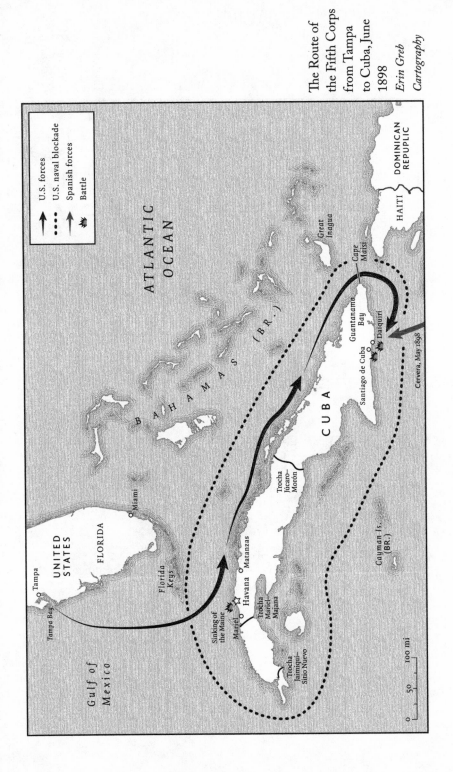

The Route of
the Fifth Corps
from Tampa
to Cuba, June
1898
*Erin Greb
Cartography*

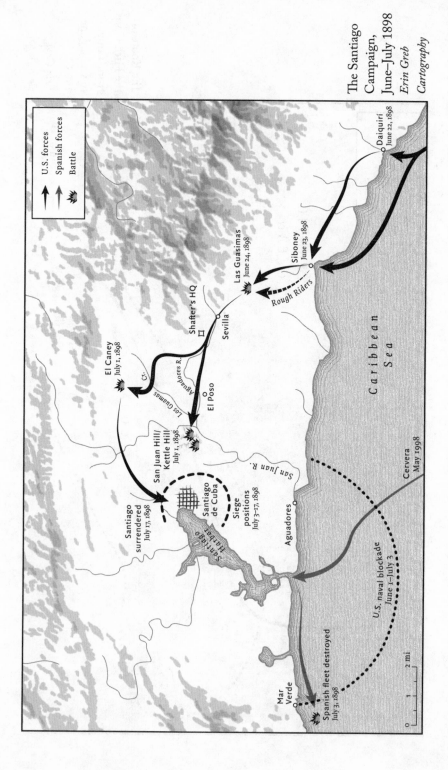

The Santiago Campaign, June–July 1898

Erin Greb
Cartography

Legend:
- U.S. forces
- Spanish forces
- Battle

Daiquiri
June 22, 1898

Siboney
June 23, 1898

Las Guasimas
June 24, 1898

Rough Riders

Shafter's HQ

Sevilla

El Caney
July 1, 1898

El Poso

Aguadores R.

Los Guamas

San Juan Hill/
Kettle Hill
July 1, 1898

San Juan R.

Santiago
surrendered
July 17, 1898

Santiago
de Cuba

Siege
positions
July 3–17, 1898

Santiago Harbor

Aguadores

Cervera
May 1998

U.S. naval blockade
June 1–July 3

Mar
Verde

Spanish fleet destroyed
July 3, 1898

Caribbean
Sea

0   1   2 mi

NEW YORK CITY, 1899

It was the grandest parade New York City had ever seen. It began with the ships—243 of them, battleships, cruisers, torpedo boats, armored yachts, practically every ship in the American Navy, alongside dozens of private craft, carrying 150,000 sailors and passengers, gathered in the early evening of September 29, 1899, off the eastern coast of Staten Island, to celebrate the American victory in the Spanish-American War a year before. As fireworks ripped into the sky from scores of sites around New York Harbor, the fleet sailed forth, cruising through the Narrows between Brooklyn and Staten Island. Under the glare of red, white, and blue starbursts, three and a half million people—two and a half million New Yorkers and another million visitors, who came from as far as California—watched along the harbor shorelines. To accompany the fireworks, the fleet beamed hundreds of spotlights on the crowds and buildings along the waterfront. "Wherever the eye turned, it was blinded by the magic light . . . and all the cities seemed to be bathed in harmless fire," wrote one observer. For two hours this went on, and there was more to come: The next day 30,000 soldiers, led by a 130-piece band conducted by John Philip Sousa, marched from Morningside Heights to Madison Square, in Manhattan, where artisans had erected a triumphal arch of lath and plaster, modeled on the Arch of Titus in Rome.[1]

In just a few months in 1898, the United States had defeated Spain and captured Cuba, Puerto Rico, and the Philippines; in a separate move, it had annexed the Hawaiian islands. The United States and Spain had signed a peace treaty at the end of the year, but it took nine more months to coordinate a celebration with so many men, and so many ships, some deployed halfway around the world, to meet in

New York. To the millions of avid onlookers, the delay was of little consequence. The celebration was less about the nation's recent past achievements than what those achievements foretold: a new, confident, global American empire. "Surely no Roman general, surely no Roman Emperor ever received such a tribute from the populace of the Eternal City," wrote the *New York Times*.[2]

Riding that day at the head of the New York State National Guard as it marched along the parade route was Theodore Roosevelt—naturalist, historian, war hero, and now governor of New York. Dressed in a frock coat, top hat, and kid gloves, he was the most powerful politician of this mighty state and a scion of the city's patrician class. But he was more than that: Perhaps no single person better embodied the excitement and national pride the war elicited, and the newfound martial fervor that followed. At the outbreak of the Spanish-American War, he had resigned from his job with the Department of the Navy to help lead the First United States Volunteer Cavalry—better known as the Rough Riders—during the invasion of Cuba. Roosevelt had trained the regiment, one of twenty-six in the invasion force and totaling nearly 1,000 men, then led them to Cuba and into battle, culminating in a desperate, riotous charge up a hill outside the city of Santiago, on the island's southeastern coast. He returned victorious and world-famous, an American Caesar who took Albany a few months after taking Santiago and now, everyone said, was poised to take the presidency, too. Though the parade's official man of honor was Admiral of the Navy George Dewey, who had defeated the Spanish Pacific fleet at Manila at the outbreak of the war, it was Roosevelt whom many in the crowd wanted to see that day. Halfway through the march, at 72nd Street, he paused to tip his hat to a reviewing stand. The crowd exploded, shouting "Teddy! Teddy!" and "Roosevelt for president!" Onlookers, trying to get close, pushed into the street; police had to hold them back. Aside from Dewey, the *Times* wrote, "the interest and admiration of the thronging people were expressed more uniformly and enthusiastically toward Governor Roosevelt than toward any one else."[3]

Roosevelt's experience as a wartime leader raised his national profile and changed him utterly. Until then, his career had included politics, ranching, history writing, and biology; he was good at most of these pursuits, frighteningly so, but he had struggled to unify them into a single intellectual project. A man with powerful friends, many people nevertheless dismissed him as a gadfly and a blowhard. By 1895, he worried that history had passed him by: "There will come a period in which I shall be whirled off into some eddy, and shall see the current sweep on, even if it sweeps in the right direction, without me," he wrote to a friend. He ended up, in early 1897, as the assistant secretary of the navy and an ardent advocate of war with Spain. When he quit that job to join the Army, his friends all said he was crazy—that even if he wasn't killed, he had cast off his career one time too many.[4]

Instead, he blossomed as a leader. He trained and led his men into battle, then watched over them during a grueling three-week siege outside Santiago, in which the bigger enemies, more so than the Spanish, were heat, disease, rats, and rainstorms. He kept his men in line, and he kept them loyal—years later, when Roosevelt was president, groups of Rough Riders would stop by the White House for a visit, and they were always allowed to skip past the crowd outside his office. It was these skills, as much as his charisma and unending appetite for work, that made Roosevelt such an effective public executive—as governor and, in 1901, as president.

Roosevelt blossomed intellectually as well. The experience with the Rough Riders, and his time at war, helped him hone his ideas about America, its place in the world, and his philosophy of the "strenuous life" that governed his approach to the presidency. It helped him clarify his complicated and flawed ideas about American unity—he embraced the notion of a country brought together by common values and a mission to bring those values to the world, even as he endorsed its exclusion of a large swath of its population behind disenfranchisement and Jim Crow. Roosevelt's time in Cuba also brought home for him the importance of what his generation called the manly virtues—the social Darwinian notions of competition, often violent, between men, and between nations. He did not discover these ideas on the battlefield, but the battlefield offered all the evidence he needed of their veracity, as well as the prestige to spread them among his adoring public. He became, wrote the historian Gail Bederman, "a walking advertisement for the imperialistic manhood he desired for the American race."[5]

The story of Roosevelt and the Rough Riders is not just a matter of presidential biography. The regiment, often dismissed by historians and pop culture as a cartoonish band of cowboys, in fact played a central role in the emergence of a new idea about American power, and in particular the military's role in projecting that power. It was unlike anything America had ever seen. Organized hastily to supplement the meager 28,000 men who comprised the Regular Army in 1898, the regiment brought together Westerners and Easterners, cowboys and college kids, New York City cops and frontier sheriffs, football stars and gold miners. They were men like Theodore Miller, the son of an Ohio industrial magnate and a promising New York law student who quit his studies to join the regiment. James McClintock was a journalist from California. Hamilton Fish was the product of a storied New York political family who had dropped out of Columbia University to work on a railroad. Bill Larned and Bob Wrenn were the first- and second-ranked professional tennis players in America; they both quit to go to war. So did Buckey O'Neill, the mayor of Prescott, Arizona.

Even if Roosevelt had stayed put in the Department of the Navy, these men would still have captured the national imagination, because to so many back home, they represented a quintessentially American story: ragtag, provisional, drawn from the country's vast distances and disparate communities, forged by patriotic fervor and sent out into the world to fight for what was right. As the journalist Jacob Riis wrote: "The Rough-Riders were the most composite lot that ever gathered under a regimental standard, but they were at the same time singularly typical of the spirit that conquered a continent in three generations, eminently American."[6]

Roosevelt made the Rough Riders, and the Rough Riders made Roosevelt. Together, they comprised one of the most storied, and most important, military units in American history. This book is an account of their story, and Roosevelt's story with them. It is also an account of the Spanish-American War: why it happened when it did, and how it shaped America at a crucial moment in its history. Roosevelt called his charge during the Battle of San Juan Heights, on July 1, 1898, his "crowded hour"—the brief span of time in which so much of his life came together, and from which, afterward, so much followed. Similarly, the Spanish-American War was America's own "crowded hour"—a relatively brief conflict that set in motion the wheels of myth-making, idealism, and national self-interest that would guide the country through the twentieth century.

John Hay, who started his career as Abraham Lincoln's personal secretary and ended it as Theodore Roosevelt's secretary of state, called the fight against the Spanish a "splendid little war." It was nothing of the kind. The Spanish-American War—more accurately, if less often and more awkwardly, known as the Spanish-American-Cuban-Filipino War—was certainly not "splendid" for the people involved. Though only a few thousand American soldiers died in combat in Cuba and the Philippines, thousands more died of disease, many of them volunteers awaiting orders in camps across the Southern states. It was even less "splendid" for Cuban and Filipino soldiers and civilians, whose total losses—many died of torture and in concentration camps at the hands of Spanish and American troops—are uncountable, but certainly range in the hundreds of thousands.

Nor was the war in any way "little." America's Cuban and Puerto Rican campaigns were indeed brief—less than six months from the Army's landing, in June 1898, at a beach called Daiquirí, on Cuba's southeastern coast, to the Spanish capitulation at San Juan, Puerto Rico, followed by a peace treaty with Madrid at the end of the year. But that was only one part of the war; by the time the Rough Riders arrived in Cuba, insurgents had been battling the Spanish colonial army for three years. And it does not include the American conflict in the Philippines, which went on for another four years. As a globe-spanning whole, the war lasted seven years, left at least 200,000 dead, destroyed the last of the Spanish Empire and opened the door to a century of American dominance.

The root cause of the war was the long decline of the Spanish Empire, which by 1898 was left clinging by its fingernails to its last two colonial holdings in the Western Hemisphere, Cuba and Puerto Rico. Cuba had come under Spanish control only a few decades after Isabella and Ferdinand conquered Granada—in other words, Spain had controlled Cuba for almost as long as Spain had been Spain. There had been Spanish citizens living in Cuba for over a century before the first English settlers landed on the east coast of what would become the United States. And history was just part of the reason for Madrid's tenacity; rich with sugar, tobacco, and minerals, Cuba was an economic bounty for the cash-strapped empire. Cuba allowed Spain to maintain its self-image as a global power—a fiction, but a vital one for the fragile Spanish state.

It had been a long time since anyone else had agreed with Spain's fantasies about its own power, once the greatest in Europe. Wars of independence had whittled away at its immense holdings in the Western Hemisphere, while it suffered chronic instability and persistent underdevelopment at home. Preoccupied, Spain let Cuba wallow in bureaucratic inefficiency, overbearing taxes, and the occasional burst of mindless, pointlessly oppressive violence. Eventually, the island exploded: first in a ten-year revolt that left 50,000 rebels, 100,000 civilians, and 85,000 Spanish soldiers dead, then in another, more brutal uprising, beginning in 1895, one that would shock America's conscience and propel the United States into its first major foreign conflict since the Mexican War in 1848.

The war broke out at a turning point in American history; arguably, it broke out *because* America was at a turning point. America in 1898 was growing at an unprecedented pace, absorbing millions of immigrants into its seemingly endless interior and converting their labor and the nation's natural bounty into a Mississippian flow of commerce. It was also recovering from a deep economic depression, which fed social and political unrest; that unrest, in turn, created what the historian Richard Hofstadter called the "psychic crisis" of the 1890s, a collective soul-searching about America's place in the world and each citizen's place within that quest. Populists were challenging the economic order of the fading Gilded Age, while Southern whites were fast erecting the apartheid regime known as Jim Crow.

At the same time, everyday Americans were beginning to look outward. For much of the nineteenth century, most had been content to have their country serve as a passive example for the world to follow—"a model of Christian charity," the Puritan leader John Winthrop had said in 1630, sitting aloof "as a city upon a hill." But by the

1890s a rapid process of civil war, territorial expansion, and a campaign of outright annihilation against Native Americans was largely completed—in 1898, Congress ended the primacy of tribal courts in Oklahoma, the last of their kind. With manifest destiny largely over at home, many Americans began to take an interest in the world. In 1885 alone, 100,000 Americans traveled abroad. Thousands of others went as missionaries. Their curiosity extended beyond tourist spots and saving souls; they also became interested in foreign affairs, and their nation's role in the world. As the economy grew, illiteracy plunged and the modern news media blossomed, and average citizens became more aware of the troubled world around them. When they read about massacres of Armenians by the Ottoman army, American editors and their readers were apoplectic, and demanded that the president threaten military action. They swooned over the underdog Greeks in their fights against the Turks. They called for war against Britain in a dispute with Venezuela over its border with British Guiana. And they flocked to the cause of "Cuba Libre": Thousands of Americans, including hundreds of Anglos, joined private military expeditions across the Straits of Florida; countless more donated to the network of pro-independence Cuban activists called the Junta; and millions kept up with events in the unending reams of newspapers that fed the minds of an increasingly urban, literate, middle-class country.[7]

Americans, especially younger ones, did not go to war with Spain reluctantly. They rushed in headlong. Freedom for Cuba had animated the 1896 American presidential campaign, and the question of what to do about it dominated the first year of William McKinley's administration, even if the president tried, at first, to avoid it. Newspapers, especially the so-called yellow press papers that trafficked in tragedy and rumors, hyped stories of mass execution and rape, but they weren't the only, or even the main, source of information. World-famous correspondents like Stephen Bonsal and Richard Harding Davis made extensive visits to the island, and brought back horror stories of their own, which they published in national magazines like *The Century* and *Scribner's*. Cuba was dying, they said, and America, as its neighbor and as the self-styled light of liberty, had to act. When it became clear that Spain was not going to cede the island on its own, intervention was just a matter of time.

Not everyone agreed with the rush to war, and all it implied about America's role in the world. The country had, many believed, been founded in opposition to the old ways of Europe, to the autocracies and bureaucracies and garrison societies that defined the continent's leading states. They detested the idea of a strong central government, and of a strong centralized military. Above all they detested colonies, for colonies required armies, and armies meant large state systems and coercive police powers and, in no short order, the end of the ideal of radical freedom that many nineteenth-century Americans held dear. Most telling was the way America treated its soldiers. At the end of the Civil War, the Union Army stood victorious, and enormous, with just over a million men under arms. Within a decade that number was brought down to about 28,000 officers and men, smaller than any major army in the Western Hemisphere—even Spain, that long-waning empire, had three times as many soldiers at home, and about five times as many in Cuba. As the *New York Times* editorialized in 1898, "We could offer no resistance on either coast to a first-class or second-class naval power. And two army corps could traverse the country as far as their commanders chose to take them without meeting any effectual opposition."[8]

And yet, as the century came to an end, two facts about America's place in the world stood clear. First, global economic power required comparable military power to protect it—from pirates, from hostile states—and to persuade difficult trading partners to come around. The United States had grown unchecked by foreign influence in large part thanks to its economic isolation, but its growth, and the geography-shrinking effects of technological progress, were bringing that isolation to an end.

But power, many Americans felt, could not be simply a matter of protecting material interests. This was the second fact: Theirs had never been just a country, in the eyes of its citizens and its admirers abroad; it was an idea, too. Every country likes to think it stands for something, but especially in the nineteenth-century era of realpolitik, that something was usually itself. America, by contrast, stood in the eyes of many for the universal values written into its founding documents, ideas about liberty and equality. These weren't vague notions bandied about in afternoon salons, either—millions of men had fought, and hundreds of thousands had died, over them during the Civil War. If America was going to be a world power, one that thrust itself and its armies into world affairs, how could it do so in a way that spoke to its values? Or, in a more cynical but no less realistic view, how could those values be used to justify the aggressive assertion of American interests onto the world?

Theodore Roosevelt and the Rough Riders offered an answer to both of those questions. At a time when the country was rapidly assuming the mantle of global influence yet deeply unsure about how to extend that power through military means, the sudden appearance of nearly 1,000 volunteer soldiers, drawn from all walks of life and all parts of the country, seemingly motivated not by money or servitude or anything other than a desire to do what they thought was right, offered a different way forward. Suddenly, the Army was not a corps of nameless, faceless social rejects and West Point martinets; it was men like Jesse Langdon, the son of a Dakota veterinarian who lied about his age to join the regiment, and Frank Knox, a Michigan boy who would go on to be Franklin Roosevelt's secretary of the navy—men whose lives seemed readily familiar and accessible, even if their decision to drop their civilian comforts and fight in a foreign land left those at home in awe. Writing on the eve of the Battle of San Juan Heights, outside Santiago, and just a few days after the Rough Riders' first engagement with the Spanish, at Las Guasimas, an editorialist for the *Philadelphia Inquirer* declared a sudden, newfound respect for the American military: "The American soldier is no machine. He is not drawn from the dregs of society. He is not drilled to the extent that he is an automaton. No, he is a patriot and a man of intelligence. When he fights it is for his country, and to love one's country is better than three years of service as a conscript." And it was the Rough Riders above all, he said, who showed that America could be both a military power and retain its ideals. "Whether Fifth Avenue millionaires or Western cowboys, they fought together and died together in Cuba for the great American principles of liberty, equality and humanity."[9]

Roosevelt and the Rough Riders were everything to everyone. They built on the myths about American history, and created new ones that would guide the country through the next century. The romance of the Wild West was already fast receding into history, yet here, suddenly, it was alive again, miraculously blended with the fin-de-siècle allure of Newport and Saratoga and the Social Register. (The very name "rough rider" was taken from Buffalo Bill's Wild West show, itself an act of myth-making.) The regiment brought together the sons of Confederate rebels and Yankee riflemen—proof, to many, that the country had finally overcome the still searing sectional divides wrought by the Civil War. Not coincidentally, there was never even the suggestion of including African American soldiers in the unit, despite the availability of thousands of black veterans who had fought in the Indian Wars. The Rough Riders were rich and poor, a suggestion, declared journalists and Sunday sermonists, that socialism and labor revolution were impossible in America—a concern that in 1898 felt all too real to the moneyed classes. And of course they were all men, a relief for those, like Roosevelt, who spent most of the 1890s fretting about the decline of the virile, Anglo-Saxon American male.

No surprise, then, that despite their being just one regiment within the Army's massive war effort, celebrity followed the Rough Riders wherever they went. The unit spawned fashion trends: In the fall of 1898, women in New York took to wearing the "Rough Rider," a roguish style of hat. Thousands of onlookers visited their camp in Texas, while thousands of others waited in the cities and small towns along their train route to Florida. Mothers gave them cakes and fresh milk; daughters asked for brass buttons from their uniforms as souvenirs. Dozens of reporters followed them closely, and hundreds of others dropped in and out of their retinue as they moved from their training grounds in dusty San Antonio to the Army's staging site at Tampa, to the beaches of Cuba, and finally to the hills east of the city of Santiago, where Roosevelt and his men won glory.

And yet for all their fame at the time, the Rough Riders remain obscure, hidden in plain sight from those who might know the name, but not much else. One reason may be a split among historical treatments of the regiment and the war. Books that discuss the Rough Riders at any length tend to be either biographies of Roosevelt, in which the regiment plays a colorful but passing role, or folksy adventure tales that ignore almost entirely the regiment's historical importance. In contrast, those books that do discuss the context—the small library's worth of mostly academic literature on the Spanish-American War—downplay the events of the war itself, including its most famous regiment. These books do an admirable job of answering questions about American imperialism, about the domestic politics behind the war, and about the consequences of America's rapid conquest of Spain's far-flung colonies. But rarely do they spend much time on the actual fighting, or the soldiers involved, or the public's reaction. Intentional or not, they give the impression that because the American war with Spain was so short—the hostilities lasted less than four months—its battles and personalities do not matter much.

Many Americans at the time saw things differently. They followed every development closely. They lauded heroes, and created them when heroes were not forthcoming. They wrote poetry and songs and consumed thousands of pages of newspaper and magazine reporting. And they saw, quite clearly, the central role that the Rough Riders played in this story. It may seem obvious, but the lack of scholarly attention demands it be said: To understand the impact that the war had on the American public and its attitudes about the world, one has to understand the war, and its most famous regiment, as well.

The public supported the American invasion of Cuba because they believed their country was engaged in a different kind of war, and a more noble use of power, than they were used to seeing play out in Europe. The Rough Riders put a name and a face to that belief, and seemed to promise that American power would always promote not just America's interests, but its values—a mission that the publisher Henry Luce characterized as the "American century."

It is only in hindsight that we can recognize how America's many subsequent interventions, almost always taken under the cover of promoting human rights and liberty, often hurt the country, and the world, as much as they helped (indeed, disgust at the Army's actions in the Philippines fueled a vocal anti-imperialist movement back home). We can recognize that the story of the Rough Riders became

11

one of the many myths that helped twentieth-century America build an empire yet deny that it had any intention of doing so. We can recognize that Roosevelt's talk about the Rough Riders as "American through and through" was an advertisement for a type of American "unity" that excluded blacks, Latinos, and women. We can recognize that the rhetoric of human rights and freedom abroad has often been abused by the powerful to promote their own interests. And yet in the Rough Riders' story, we can also recognize the best of America: citizens who set aside families, careers, wealth, and celebrity to fight and die for something other than themselves. We can recognize, above all, that the story of the American century is neither entirely heroic nor entirely tragic—rather, it is both.

CHAPTER 1

"THE PUERILITY
OF HIS SIMPLIFICATIONS"

O n January 13, 1898, John D. Long, the secretary of the navy, was sitting in his office in the State, War and Navy Building, a Second Empire jumble of columns and mansard roofs next to the Executive Mansion that Mark Twain had called the ugliest edifice in America. Long, fifty-nine, was a stoop-shouldered, gently cerebral former governor of Massachusetts whom President William McKinley had called out of private legal practice in Hingham, a coastal town south of Boston, to serve in his cabinet. He was an able administrator and politician, but he was happiest writing poetry and reading Latin; one of his proudest achievements was publishing a verse translation of *The Aeneid*.[1]

Long was, in other words, the exact opposite of Theodore Roosevelt, his assistant secretary, who at that minute burst into his boss's morning reverie. Roosevelt shut the door and, Long recalled, "Began in his usual emphatic and dead-in-earnest manner" to run through his latest efforts on the part of the department. Then, his face reddening, Roosevelt turned to Cuba, along with Puerto Rico the last remnant of the once vast Spanish Empire in the Western Hemisphere, and his certainty that Spain and the United States would soon come to blows over the island's struggle for independence. "He told me that, in case of war with Spain, he intends to abandon everything and go to the front," Long wrote.[2]

The cause of Roosevelt's eruption that day was an anti-American riot in Havana on January 12. The McKinley administration was putting diplomatic pressure on Spain to reach an end to its war in Cuba;

after rumors reached Havana that the government in Madrid had finally agreed to Washington's demands, Spanish loyalists and soldiers had rampaged across the center of the island's capital, attacking newspaper offices and the American consulate. Fitzhugh Lee, the consul general in Havana, cabled Washington with the news: While there was little damage to American property, the violence bode poorly for any hope of a negotiated settlement to the nearly three-year war, which had decimated the Cuban economy and killed well over 100,000 civilians, along with tens of thousands of Spanish soldiers and Cuban rebels.[3]

Long kept quiet as his assistant seethed. One didn't just listen to Roosevelt; one felt him. He seemed to have no inside voice. He expounded grandiloquently before crowds as small as one, in forums as intimate as the office of the secretary of the navy. He had a slightly high pitch to his voice and he spoke in rapid spurts, with long vowels and chopped-off consonants. He boomed, he hissed, he spat out words—"bully!," "delighted!"—like a Gatling gun. And he didn't speak merely with his mouth: His whole body shook in rhythm, his fists banging into his palms to drive home a point. But while he was often full of bluster, it wasn't hot air. Roosevelt was widely regarded as one of the most intelligent, well-read people in Washington, with a steel-trap of a mind and an ability to recall minor facts consumed years before. Even his detractors found Roosevelt's extemporaneous orations a thing to behold: He could speak off the cuff about everything from New England wildlife to German politics, whatever fit the moment.[4]

Still, it could be a lot to take in, and those who tolerated Roosevelt usually did so with resignation, rarely with enthusiasm. In the months since they had joined the department together, Long had learned to manage Roosevelt's energies, a full-time job in itself. When he wasn't preparing for war with Cuba, Roosevelt was ordering up new warships, or restructuring the department's procurement policy, or investigating mismanagement at the Brooklyn Navy Yard. "He bores me with plans of naval and military movement," Long wrote in his journal the night after Roosevelt barged into his office. "By tomorrow morning, he will have got half a dozen heads of bureaus together and have spoiled twenty pages of good writing paper, and lain awake half the night."[5]

"THE PUERILITY OF HIS SIMPLIFICATIONS"

Roosevelt had been thrust upon Long by President McKinley, and he in turn had been thrust upon McKinley by New York politics and Roosevelt's close friend Henry Cabot Lodge, a Republican senator from Massachusetts. Long appreciated Roosevelt for his energy, but he would have much preferred a quietly competent career naval officer as his second. Unlike Roosevelt, Long did not think war was coming. If anything, he was naive about the situation in Cuba and Spain's desire and ability to improve it. "My own notion is that Spain is not only doing the best it can, but is going very well in its present treatment of the island," Long wrote in his diary. "Our government certainly has nothing to complain of."[6]

More than temperament divided the two men. They came from different generations—both born on October 27, Long was exactly twenty years older than Roosevelt—and had vastly different ideas about America and its place in the world. Long's generation was both scarred and motivated by the experience of the Civil War; they knew what war was, and they believed that their achievements since— social stability, economic growth, industrialization, and the closing of the Western frontier—had made large-scale conflict unnecessary, at least as far as the United States was concerned. Minor wars might embroil Europe, but Europe was far away. Wise, sustained growth and a restrained, conservative foreign policy, the hallmarks of the Republican Party and its domination of national politics in the late nineteenth century, would ensure that America would never again face the horrors of war, domestic or otherwise. With no small amount of self-awareness, Long called a published edition of his diary *America of Yesterday*.

Roosevelt stood out even among his generation in taking exception to Long's vision of the world. He had grown up in the shadow of the Civil War and its veterans; he admired (and envied) their experience, but also questioned why, after such a searing war, they should be so afraid of another one that they refused even to prepare for it—an error that, Roosevelt believed, made another war more likely. Even more, it was America's responsibility, to its own interests as well as the world's, to use its growing power to shape foreign affairs. In his own autobiography, Roosevelt called the chapter on the Spanish-American War "The War of America the Unready."

15

• • •

Born in Manhattan in 1858 and called Teedie by his family, Roosevelt later described himself as a scrawny, sickly child, hindered by asthma and poor eyesight—"a great little home-boy," his sister Bamie said. To make up for his self-perceived deficiencies, he spent long hours as a boy exercising, hiking, and swimming. He kept daily records of his physical activity and subsequent gains in strength, weight, and stamina. He worked out alone when necessary, but he liked a partner because he favored violent sports, especially boxing. His love for the pugilistic arts continued long after he reached maturity, even after he returned from Cuba—as governor of New York, he had a ring installed in his mansion in Albany.[7]

Whatever physical ailments Roosevelt suffered, his greatest debilitation was his hero worship of his father, Theodore Roosevelt Sr. "My father was the best man I ever knew," Theodore Junior said. In letters and diary entries, he called his father "Greatheart," after the heroic giant-slayer in John Bunyan's *The Pilgrim's Progress*. Theodore Senior was born into wealth and proved a proficient if sometimes distracted businessman; he engaged with politics but resisted the opportunities that America's unbound postwar corruption offered. He cofounded New York institutions like the Metropolitan Museum of Art and the American Museum of Natural History. But he had also avoided service during the Civil War by hiring someone to go in his place—a legal, not uncommon avenue for wealthy Americans to get out of their martial obligations, but one that his son could never quite square with his faith in his father's courage. Nor was his father able to give him the paternal support his son needed; Roosevelt Senior loved his family deeply, but was also often absent from it, away on business. And then he died, of stomach cancer, when his Teedie was nineteen and a sophomore at Harvard. What this all amounted to, in the figure of Theodore Junior, was a man who burst with energy and intelligence, came from sufficient wealth to give him room to exploit his gifts, and carried an enormous chip on his shoulder. A man who had nothing to prove seemed to believe that he had everything to prove.

While still a teenager, Roosevelt climbed mountains in Maine and Switzerland, Germany and upstate New York. He taught himself taxidermy, and practiced it avidly, frequently emerging from his room covered in the blood of some animal he had killed on a weekend hunting trip. At Harvard he lifted himself from a middling B average as a freshman to Phi Beta Kappa; he was invited to join the Porcellian Club, the most exclusive undergraduate social organization on campus; and on the side wrote a book, *The Naval War of 1812*, that remained a standard text in college classrooms for decades. Along the way, he built himself from being "a youth in the kindergarten stage of physical development," as one classmate recalled, into a physical brute, strutting about the Yard, often shirtless, with gnarly mutton-chops bewhiskering his cheeks. He once rowed from Long Island to Connecticut, alone, in a single day, a full twenty-five miles. Some of the stories told about Roosevelt as a Harvard man later proved apocryphal, but like so much in his life, their veracity is beside the point: The myth is inextricable from the man. Roosevelt also developed a reputation as an ill-tempered, prudish elitist—uninterested in anyone not of the "gentleman-sort"—and as a result had few friends around Cambridge. In fact, what he disdained were the leisure classes. He admired those whom he judged, fairly or not, to come from hearty, hardy New England stock, whether they had used their brains and brawn to build wealth or simply earn a good day's pay. He had no time for those who took to the lighter side of life, who accepted the "gentleman's C," at Harvard or later as adults.[8]

As he neared the end of his studies, Roosevelt wasn't sure where to go next. Looking back, his career from graduation to inauguration as president—spanning just twenty-one years—seems to follow a straight line from achievement to achievement, from strength to strength. But in fact he often felt undirected and unwilling to commit to one single endeavor. He inherited a small fortune from his father, paying about $8,000 a year (a little under $200,000 in 2018), which allowed him to live comfortably without having to work for an income. His real love was science, especially what would later be called evolutionary biology, but was put off by the fact that serious graduate work, at the time, meant years studying in Germany, home to the world's best research institutions.[9]

Lacking a specific direction, Roosevelt went to law school, at Columbia. But he had already fallen into local politics, and left school in 1881 without graduating to run for, and win, election to the New York State Assembly. He proved an able and energetic politician, committed to the Republican Party but also willing to buck against its establishment in pushing reform bills. He led an anticorruption campaign against the railroad tycoon Jay Gould, and another campaign to ban the home manufacture of cigars. In all this he made no shortage of enemies, who called the twenty-three-year-old legislator "Young Squirt," "Weakling," and, most colorfully, "Jane-Daddy." Two years later, just as his political career was taking off, Roosevelt's wife, Alice, died from Bright's disease (kidney inflammation) soon after she had given birth to their daughter, and on the same day that his mother passed away, in the same house. Though he rarely spoke about his first wife again, Roosevelt was devastated. A few months afterward (and following the 1884 Republican National Convention in Chicago, where he tried, and failed, to block the nomination of James G. Blaine) he left political life and his daughter behind and moved to the Dakota Territory, where he intended to become a cattle rancher.[10]

Roosevelt had already spent time in the Dakotas, hunting deer and bison along the Little Missouri River. It was more than a hobby; his connection to the West was part of his self-identity: Almost immediately and for the rest of his life, he liked to tell crowds that he was "at heart as much a Westerner as an Easterner." Still, when he arrived in the town of Medora, near his new ranchstead, he was greeted skeptically, even derisively, on account of his thick glasses and unsullied clothing. He was, by appearance, a dude. As a group of cowhands watched, he dismounted and walked into the town's general store. While he was inside one of the men switched his saddle and bridle to a similar-looking, but very wild, bronco they called White-Faced Kid. Roosevelt came out of the store, mounted the horse—and the animal bucked him straight in the air.

The shopkeeper, Joe Ferris, came running out. "Are you hurt?" he asked.

"Not a bit," said Roosevelt. He remounted the horse, and once again went skyward.

"It's too bad I broke my glasses" was all he said, and he went inside for a new pair. And once again, he got back on the horse, who this time went flying off down the street with Roosevelt still in the saddle, dust clouds whirling behind them. The crowd grew worried; someone went looking for a doctor. But after a few minutes Roosevelt returned, shouting and grinning and trotting along on White-Faced Kid. "We took a shine to him from that very day," recalled one of the ranch hands, Fred Herrig, who years later would join Roosevelt as a Rough Rider in Cuba. "Any fellow who could ride White-Faced Kid at one trial and holler like that was the man for our money; except that we didn't have any money, until we'd hired out to Roosevelt."[11]

Despite his dramatic entrance, ranching proved one of the few failures of Roosevelt's life. He simply couldn't commit to the unending demands that came with being a cattle baron. He frequently returned to New York to see his daughter and keep his hand in state politics. On those trips he also began to court a childhood sweetheart, Edith Carow; the two were married in 1886. After a blizzard killed off most of his cattle, he conceded that one could not be a part-time rancher, like one could be a gentleman farmer back East, and sold his stock and property for a loss. It was inevitable, blizzard or not—his life was on the East Coast. In 1887 Edith gave birth to their first of five children, Theodore III (later known as "Junior," despite being third in the line), and Roosevelt began building a sprawling house for his new family in the village of Oyster Bay, on the North Shore of Long Island. He called his home Sagamore Hill. And as if politics and ranching and grieving and raising a family were not enough, he kept up a steady output of books—a series of memoirs and essay collections on hunting and the outdoors, biographies of Thomas Hart Benton and Gouverneur Morris, and the four-volume *The Winning of the West*. He also wrote a stream of magazine articles, on topics varying from machine politics to Civil War history to buffalo hunting, and cofounded the Boone and Crockett Club, the country's first organization of outdoorsmen dedicated to wildlife and wilderness conservation.

In 1889 President Benjamin Harrison, whom Roosevelt had stumped for in the 1888 campaign, appointed him to the United States Civil Service Commission, and he and Edith moved their family to Washington. The city was still small, in places verging on bucolic, with long trails winding through Rock Creek Park along which Roosevelt would hike or ride for hours. In the summers most of the population that could fled the city entirely, the better to avoid the malarial lowlands around the National Mall and the oppressive heat of the lower Potomac River basin. Roosevelt stayed. He joined a small social scene of like-minded Republicans, many of whom he knew already from New York and national party politics, like the writer Henry Adams, the diplomat John Hay, and the then-congressman Henry Cabot Lodge. Like Roosevelt, they were literary as well as political men, who loved nothing more than to argue into the night—Henry James called them "charming men, but exceedingly undesirable companions for any man not of strong nature"—and they would gather at Adams's house at 1603 H Street, on Lafayette Square, for long salons debating and eating and drinking (though Roosevelt himself rarely touched alcohol).[12]

The Civil Service Commission itself was something of a backwater, and though he made a typically Rooseveltian stab at energizing it, he made only moderate progress against the corrupt system of political patronage that drove much of American politics—and much of Washington's daily life. He held extensive hearings around the country, and eventually produced a masterfully crafted report, which hardly anyone read. And so it went, with Roosevelt writing his books, holding his committee hearings, and chatting away with his newfound circle in Washington, waiting for his next move. It appeared, for the moment, like Roosevelt's career had stalled.

Then, finally, opportunity arrived in the form of William Lafayette Strong, a reformist Republican who won the New York mayor's office in 1894, and offered Roosevelt a spot as president of the board of police commissioners. Roosevelt took it, and ran with it, remaking the city's police force in just a few years. He instituted physical and firearms exams, created merit-based awards, and eliminated political considerations from hiring and placement of officers. He became famous—or infamous, depending on which side of his favor one fell—for walking the city late at night in mufti, looking for wayward officers catching a nap. For company, he often took along reporters from the local papers, a habit that introduced him to rising-star journalists like Jacob Riis and Richard Harding Davis. Intentionally or not, that habit also won him praise in local newspapers and magazines, and he began his ascent as a national figure.[13]

But Roosevelt also had a unique capacity for angering the wrong people at the wrong moment. When he proved too conscientious as the head of the police board, enforcing Sunday closing laws that ran afoul of the commercial interests of New York's political establishment, Senator Thomas Platt, a backbencher in Washington but the most powerful politician in the state, arranged for the board to be shuttered. By 1896, Roosevelt's tenure at the top of the New York police force was rapidly coming to an end.

Roosevelt was happy to leave; he had had his fill of New York politics, for now, and he already had his sights set on a job with the incoming administration of William McKinley. Roosevelt had campaigned for him (and against the Democratic candidate, William Jennings Bryan, whom he detested), and he leaned on his friends in Washington—especially Lodge, now a senator—to find him his coveted spot: the assistant secretary (later known as the under secretary) of the navy. "I do not think the Assistant Secretaryship in the least below what I ought to have," Roosevelt wrote Lodge. McKinley, a Civil War veteran, was wary of the pugnacious young Roosevelt—"I am told your friend Theodore . . . is always getting into rows with everybody," he said to one of Roosevelt's advocates—but after considerable delay gave in to the multifront assault waged by Lodge and others (it helped that Platt, after considerable delay, endorsed Roosevelt as well, to get him out of New York).[14]

McKinley, a former governor of Ohio, entered office an avowed pacifist. When he said, in his inaugural address, that "war should never be entered upon until every agency of peace has failed; peace is preferable to war in almost every contingency," he was doing more than paying lip service to peace; he was expressing a deeply held belief that war was, in virtually every case, a losing proposition. McKinley did not spend much time thinking about foreign policy and what it might involve. In his address, he said nothing about military preparedness—Roosevelt's pet obsession—and nothing about international crises far-flung (Armenia, Greece) or near (Cuba).[15]

In this regard, McKinley was not unlike his post–Civil War prede-

21

cessors, Republican and Democrat, all of them veterans, all of whom abhorred the thought of sending American men to die in the national interest. This was not just antiwar idealism—antimilitarism was a guiding principle in American boardrooms, where "business pacifism" opposed military buildup because it meant higher taxes, more powerful government, and a good chance that a war would drain the country's economic and human capital. With the closing of the Western frontier, America was a country rich in natural and industrial resources, a place that could afford, many politicians believed, to ignore the rest of the world for generations to come.[16]

Unlike many in his party and their supporters on Wall Street, however, McKinley was amenable to economic and territorial expansion. Though he rarely said so in public, he was a strong believer in the need for the United States to add territory, directly or through economic dominance. As he told George Cortelyou, his personal secretary, "We need Hawaii just as much and a good deal more than we did California . . . it is manifest destiny." He understood that economic growth would inevitably involve the country in global affairs, and it was best to make moves now to be in a dominant position later. He believed that Hawaii, for example, was the gateway to Asia, and America should grab it—as long as it could do so without a fight. McKinley's was a nuanced, carefully forceful position, one that required the utmost discretion, with success to come through economic and diplomatic, not military, strength.[17]

Roosevelt had other plans. He had long believed that America's economic and diplomatic power meant nothing if it did not also improve its military power—and McKinley had put him in a position to do something about that. For several years already, the Navy had been recovering from its post–Civil War senescence. Spurred by a mix of commercial imperatives—the need to protect American shipping interests overseas—and an intellectual renaissance led by the historian Alfred Thayer Mahan, the department had undertaken an extensive expansion of its fleet, adding modern armored cruisers and plotting detailed strategies and plans for any conceivable contingency, from war with Germany in the South Pacific to a naval conflict with Spain in the Caribbean.

Roosevelt supported the Navy's reawakening—without it, he

feared a repetition of the country's early military mistakes. "There would have been no War in 1812 if, in the previous decade, America, instead of announcing that 'peace was her passion,' instead of acting on the theory that unpreparedness averts war, had been willing to go to the expense of providing a fleet of a score of ships of the line," he wrote in his autobiography. And yet the Navy's efforts to rebuild itself were still not enough, he felt, especially since they went unmatched by the Army. Roosevelt had watched, in the decades since the end of the Civil War, as the United States had let its military readiness slip—and it scared him. "A rich nation which is slothful, timid, or unwieldy is an easy prey for any people which still retains those most valuable of all qualities, the soldierly virtues," he said in a wildly popular address at the Naval War College, a combination think tank and officer graduate school in Newport, Rhode Island, in 1897, which was later printed in newspapers across the country.[18]

Roosevelt had pressured Long and, during the occasional presidential carriage ride around the city, McKinley himself to support his plans for naval construction: immediately, six new battleships, six cruisers, and seventy-five torpedo boats. McKinley and Long gave halfhearted consent, but that was all Roosevelt needed. Secretary Long was fond of taking vacations, and when he did, he left Roosevelt as acting secretary, a temporary position of which Roosevelt took full advantage. He ordered the Naval War College to update its Pacific and Caribbean war plans, and authorized summertime maneuvers for the North Atlantic Squadron, which he even joined for a few days to see the fleet's big guns at work (always keen on public promotion, he persuaded the artist Frederic Remington to come along and sketch the scene for later publication). Roosevelt launched a war on paperwork and investigated inefficiencies at the Brooklyn Navy Yard, one of the country's largest producers of naval vessels. And he maneuvered to have Commodore George Dewey, who had floated in and around his circle of hawks in Washington, named commander of the Navy's Asiatic Squadron.[19]

Roosevelt liked to talk about preparedness as an end in itself, as if war were something he opposed; in fact, it was something he desired. He often spouted off about going to war with Germany or Britain, even if it meant the sacking of an American city—an outcome he even welcomed, as long as it jolted the country out of its fin-de-siècle slumber. He would, John Hay said, "declare war himself . . . and wage it sole." During the 1890s Roosevelt's writing had become more forceful and bellicose. Gone were the long treatises on American history; in came the pointed essays on American character and manliness. Roosevelt bemoaned the decline of the American "spirit," by which he meant the individualistic, aggressive posturing he imagined his forefathers possessed, and that he imagined had defined the men he met during his sojourns in the West. He saw "grave signs of deterioration," a "lack of fighting edge" brought on by "oversentimentality" and "oversoftness. . . . Washiness and mushiness are the great dangers of this age and this people." A war every now and then, he argued, was a tonic for national well-being. "It was a good thing, a very good thing, to have a great mass of our people learn what it was to face death and endure trial together," he wrote of the Civil War.[20]

Reading them today, Roosevelt's essays from the 1890s are noteworthy for their racism and misogyny; though he used "race" loosely, as a synonym for nationality, he clearly thought much less of peoples not born of Anglo-Saxon stock, and feared what would happen if too many of them immigrated to the United States. And while he supported women's suffrage, he believed that the nation's future depended on its men, and he was wary of any move toward real gender equality. On both counts, Roosevelt was well within the mainstream of American thought at the time; still, his critics—and there were many—dismissed his essays as fatuous and self-righteous, focused more on attacking his purported enemies than laying out a constructive argument. His head was full of ideas, but he lacked the focus and experience to make them cohere. The novelist Henry James dismissed Roosevelt's work, saying it was "impaired for intelligible precept by the puerility of his simplifications."[21]

That bellicosity, however puerile, stood Roosevelt in good company upon his return to Washington, because Washington was becoming a bellicose town. Wall Street and the Republican Party elite might still cling to the idea of business pacifism, but in the nation's capital, jingoism was coming into fashion. The second administration of Grover Cleveland, from 1893 to 1897, had been aggressively anti-expansionist: Alongside rejecting all entreaties to declare the Cuban rebels equal belligerents on the island, Cleveland also rejected a congressional move to annex Hawaii. McKinley, at the outset and in public, did not seem to promise much different, and he continued his predecessor's policy of nonintervention in Cuba. But the tides were shifting, and regardless of who occupied the presidency, a new generation of thinkers and politicians and general officers were coming into leadership positions, and by and large they took a decidedly different attitude toward American power. At the center of this generation stood Theodore Roosevelt.

It seemed like fate that Roosevelt would arrive in Washington, in this job, at this moment. He soon reentered his old social circle of Adams, Hay, and Lodge; they lunched at the Metropolitan Club, then met again in the evening at Adams's home. They were, almost to a man, advocates of American expansion—their detractors called them "jingoes," and they embraced the term as a badge. Some jingoes advocated for outright, European-style imperialism, complete with colonies abroad and a massive navy and army to maintain them. Some were simply bruising for a war. Still others wore their imperialism more subtly, advocating for commercial and military alliances, not crass territorial grabs, and often cloaked their rhetoric in the language of liberty and freedom, American-made products ready for export. For most expansionists, it was a bit of all three. However dubious some of their conclusions, the question they raised was an important one: At the end of the nineteenth century, America stood unrivaled in its economic growth, and destined to soon overtake the rest of the world in sheer wealth. But how should America protect that wealth, and what should it do with it? As it became a world power, this was a moment when decisions were being made that would shape America's future for decades to come.

One evening at a dinner party, Roosevelt met President McKinley's personal doctor, an Army captain named Leonard Wood. Like Long and very much unlike Roosevelt, Wood was a reserved son of South Shore Massachusetts. Unlike Long and very much like Roosevelt, though, Wood was what a later generation would call an adventure junkie. As an Army surgeon, he spent years on the front lines of the Indian Wars; later, while stationed in Atlanta, he played with and coached for the Georgia Tech football team. After he cut his head open during a game, he sewed the wound shut himself. In September 1895 Wood moved to Washington to serve as President Cleveland's personal doctor (and frequent companion at the poker table); when McKinley took office, such was Wood's reputation that there was no question of replacing him—especially since Mrs. McKinley was frail and persistently ill. But even while Wood was tending to presidential ailments and making a name for himself on the Washington social scene, no one expected he was done with his martial aspirations. "If we ever have another war, you will be sure to hear of Wood," Henry Lawton, with whom Wood had tracked and captured the Apache leader Geronimo, said. Wood was, in short, everything Roosevelt admired in an American male. The two became fast friends.[22]

They hiked Rock Creek Park. They kicked footballs. They got in the boxing ring and punched each other in the face. During the winter they tried out cross-country skis that Roosevelt had ordered by mail. Wood was one of the few people Roosevelt had met, besides his father, who could push him beyond his physical limits. Roosevelt was smitten. In a letter dated January 11, 1898, he wrote to Wood: "Tomorrow (Wednesday) can you take a walk, or a football kick, or something vigorous? For ten days I have done nothing, and I am feeling as if I had been stewed; but I had a nice walk with the children on Sunday in spite of the rain, and only regretted that Leonard could not go." Wood engaged not only Roosevelt's obsession with physical exertion, but his imagination as well, at one point nearly persuading him to go to the Klondike in the middle of winter to locate stranded miners. Clearly, the two needed a project, a goal, for their intellectual and physical efforts. And soon they found one: Cuba.[23]

CHAPTER 2

"ONE DOES NOT MAKE WAR WITH BONBONS"

Spain had controlled Cuba since the beginning of its empire in the Western Hemisphere: Christopher Columbus landed there on his first voyage, in 1492. Just twenty-two years later Diego Velázquez de Cuéllar founded the city of Santiago, on the island's southeast coast. The Spanish brought sugarcane, from the Canary Islands; it grew like a weed in Cuba's loamy soil, with Santiago as one of the sugar industry's main ports—and the island's first colonial capital, before Havana. Cuba was also the place where Spain pioneered the genocidal approach to settlement that it and other colonial empires would employ against native populations for the next 350 years. Within a generation, Velázquez had so devastated the Ciboney, Guanahatabey, and Taino peoples that the Spanish turned to importing enslaved Africans to work the cane fields.

Over the next 200 years, Cuba became the beating heart of the Spanish Empire in the Western Hemisphere—Havana was one of the largest Spanish cities outside Spain. After the revolution in Haiti at the end of the eighteenth century shut down cane production in that country, European demand for Cuban sugar exploded, and the Spanish clamped down on dissent on the island for fear of meeting the same fate as the French colony to Cuba's immediate east. Spain also imported tens of thousands more slaves to feed the expanding sugar industry, which required even tighter control. As the rest of Spanish America fell to revolution and revolt, Spain's hold on Cuba closed even tighter, like a prized possession saved from a fire. Occasionally, politicians in the United States made moves to acquire the

27

island: In 1848, President James K. Polk authorized his minister in Spain to offer $100 million for it. Madrid replied that it would rather see Cuba sink into the ocean.[1]

Spain's desperate love for Cuba was not mutual, and rebellion finally erupted on the island in 1868. The response was swift and cruel. During the ensuing conflict, known as the Ten Years' War, the Spanish army laid waste to the rebels' stronghold in the rural, eastern half of the country, then dug a massive ditch—called the trocha—across the entire island, from Jucaro on the Caribbean to Morón, near the Atlantic coast. The Spanish posted guards and strung barbed wire along the trocha, a measure that did more to break up the movement of civilians than to impede the flow of rebels. Spanish authorities executed anyone over fifteen years old suspected of aiding the insurgency—more than 2,900 people in total—and they confiscated 13,000 Cuban estates, the proceeds from which allowed the colonial generals to return to Spain as millionaires. Eventually a new general, Arsenio Martínez Campos y Antón, arrived to make peace, and in 1878 the two sides did. The war had devastated the country: After ten years some 45,000 Cubans were dead; thousands more had been deported to Spanish penal colonies along the North African coast or on Fernando Po, an island in the Gulf of Guinea. Some 60,000 Spanish soldiers had died as well, mostly from tropical disease.[2]

With peace returning, the jungle overtook the trocha, and a sense of fraught normalcy overtook the island. The war and its aftermath created an investment boom: American dollars arrived looking for fortunes to be made in Cuba's sugarcane fields and copper mines, which had been abandoned by their Spanish owners. Investment reached $60 million in 1897 (about $1.8 billion in 2018 dollars). Thousands of Americans, both Anglos and Cuban Americans, lived in the country, or traveled between it and Florida and New York. If Cuba remained a Spanish colony in name, it was also growing much closer to the American orbit.[3]

The agreement to end the Ten Years' War was called the Pact of Zanjón, and it promised Cuba a constitution and an elected assembly. In practice, Spain thwarted even moderate reforms, while keeping taxes and tariffs high to cover the costs of fighting its own insurrectionary troubles at home. Spain also promised to abolish slavery on the island—which it did, beginning in 1886 and freeing the last slave in 1890. But because Spain had done little to rebuild the Cuban economy after a decade of fighting, and because American capital was consolidating sugar and mining operations—thereby reducing the need for labor on the island—the freedmen could not find work, and soon became part of a new army of dissension. And that was when things were good, when Americans had money to spend and workers to hire. Then came the Panic of 1893, at the time the worst economic depression in U.S. history.[4]

Largely the result of a bubble in the railroad industry, the panic shuttered thousands of businesses and sent millions of American workers into the streets. It also sent politicians scrambling for a response. One was the Wilson-Gorman Tariff Act, a package of free trade measures that, through the predictably opaque machinations of Washington, ended up raising tariff rates on a number of products, including a 40 percent tariff on cane sugar—which, by then, had become postwar Cuba's lone hope for economic development. Overnight, word of the new rates spread among the island's fields and villages, and despair set in. Anger was not far behind. When the tariff passed, one Spanish observer in Cuba recalled, "Youths, old men, women, and children cleaned off their machetes and their rusty rifles, waiting impatiently for the call to revolt."[5]

The tariffs went into effect in August 1894; almost exactly six months later, on February 24, 1895, a wealthy planter named Bartolomé Masó raised the one-starred Cuban flag above his plantation near Manzanillo, in southeastern Cuba; that same day uprisings sprang up in towns across the country. Masó, with his fortune and land, was an exception: The rebels mostly came from the middle and lower classes of Cuban society, and were emphatically multiracial. American reporters and filibusterers—men who traveled to Cuba to join the fight, against Washington's wishes—were often shocked to find black men serving as officers, with lighter-skinned conscripts following their orders.[6]

Within months after the insurrection began, the Cuban rebels had won a series of pivotal engagements and pushed into the Spanish-held west, nearly to the outskirts of Havana—before they ran out of ammunition. By the end of 1895, the war was at a stalemate: The

Cubans had the manpower, but not the gunpowder. And so they turned to the United States, and to the network of Cuban American activists known as the Junta. Based in New York but with chapters across the country, the Junta raised funds for the rebels and bought them weapons and supplies—but perhaps most important, it undertook a massive public relations campaign to turn the American public to the rebels' side. Pro-Cuban rallies filled Madison Square Garden, in New York, and touring tent speakers rivaled religious revival meetings in small towns from North Carolina to Kansas. Junta "sources" passed along information to reporters looking for juicy, bloody stories of Spanish atrocities; soon, fed with news, rumors, and outright falsehoods by Cuban activists, national magazines and newspapers were calling on readers to support the Cuban cause. In August 1895, an editor for *Cosmopolitan* wrote: "There is still a struggle going on for human liberty, and that almost at our very doors." Pro-independence plays, like James F. Milliken's *The Cuban Patriot* (1897), proliferated. So did middling poetry: "Arise! ye lovers of the right; / strike fast, O sons of liberty! / United in your purpose, smite, / and bleeding Cuba will be free!" read one poem, from December 1896. *Frank Leslie's Popular Monthly*, one of the widest-read periodicals of its time, published pro-Cuban articles aimed at young readers, like "Don Carlos's Raid: A Story of the War in Cuba," a fictional tale told through the eyes of two young rebels.[7]

The public answered, especially footloose young men in search of adventure. At any time, dozens of Anglo-Americans could be counted among the rebel ranks. One, Frederick Funston, had been turned on to the Cuban cause after attending an 1896 Junta rally in New York; after winning the trust of Junta organizers, he managed to slip by boat onto the Cuban shore along with four other "would-be Lafayettes and von Steubens," as he put it. Funston fought in two campaigns as an artillery officer, and was later wounded and captured by the Spanish. Somehow, he survived, and made it back to the United States—only to return as an officer in the American invasion and, after that, the American army of occupation in the Philippines.[8]

The cause of Cuban freedom in the latter half of the 1890s had appeal across classes and regions. Christian organizations poured out funds to help their coreligionists. Midwestern farmers and unemployed factory workers, beaten down by the depression, saw something of themselves, oppressed by distant moneyed interests, in the struggling Cuban peasants. African Americans flocked to the news that dark-skinned men were helping to lead the fight. Labor activists and socialists even saw the possibility of a revolt against capitalism on the island, the opportunity not only to overthrow the Spanish, but "wage slavery" itself (in this they were prescient, though by sixty years).[9]

Officially, the United States banned assistance to either side of the war, whether by the government or private citizens; in practice, the ban was impossible to implement, given the size of America's southern coast and the short passage across the Straits of Florida. Between 1895 and 1898, more than sixty ships, carrying guns, medical supplies, cannons, and men, set off from the United States; the Americans stopped twenty-three of them, Spain another two, and two more were lost at sea. But the rest got through with much needed men and supplies—most of the rebels' machetes were manufactured by a company in Providence, Rhode Island.[10]

Despite strong favor among the American public for Cuban independence, President Grover Cleveland, during his second term in office from 1893 to 1897, vowed to stay neutral. He was disgusted by the Cuban rebels—"the most barbarous and inhuman assassins in the world," he called them. Cleveland wasn't entirely off base. Something else set this rebellion apart from the Ten Years' War: This time, both sides pursued a scorched-earth strategy, and both insisted that there were no neutrals—every Cuban had to declare for or against the rebels. There was no right answer, and the wrong answer at the wrong time meant death. General Máximo Gómez, one of the rebel leaders, gave orders to execute any civilian who worked with the Spanish. To undermine the Spanish economy, he temporarily banned the processing of sugarcane, likewise punishable by death. In a strategy that later rebels and revolutionaries across the twentieth century would follow, Gómez both lived off the land and denied his enemy access to it. He insisted that anyone who sided with the rebels had to move east to the "free" provinces—in other words, turning the rest of the country into a free-fire zone. As he reportedly liked to say, "What even if the whole generation perish, when countless generations will benefit so greatly?"[11]

After a few months of fighting, the government in Madrid recalled its general in Cuba, Arsenio Martínez Campos, and replaced him with one of his former colonels, Valeriano Weyler y Nicolau. German by ancestry and born on the Mediterranean island of Majorca, Weyler had spent most of his career serving far from home—in Cuba during the Ten Years' War, then in the Canary Islands and the Philippines, with a brief return in between to Spain to fight in the Third Carlist War (1872–1876), in which far-right supporters of a conservative contender for the Spanish throne, Carlos VII, attempted to overthrow the country's constitutional monarchy. When Weyler finally returned to Spain again, as a general, he became something of an expert in squashing communists, anarchists, and various regional rebellions in Catalonia and along Spain's disruptive northern fringe. When the conservative government of Antonio Cánovas del Castillo decided to send Weyler to Cuba, patriotic Spanish cheered in the streets. Spain, it seemed, was done fooling around.[12]

Cánovas made Weyler both governor and general—essentially, a military dictator—and gave him wide latitude to suppress the rebellion. Weyler was a particularly close student of the American Civil War, and a great admirer of William Tecumseh Sherman and his March to the Sea campaign through Georgia. The doctrine of total war was, to Weyler, the only path to victory. He even had his own aphorism; where Sherman said, "War is hell," Weyler said, "One does not make war with bonbons." Like Sherman, he understood the relationship between an army and the land, and in Cuba and the Philippines he had seen how civilians and farms could sustain a rebel force. Even if a civilian didn't support the rebellion, his land might, by offering places to hide and a few chickens or ears of corn to steal at night. It wasn't enough, Weyler figured, to forbid civilians from siding with rebels. The two populations had to be separated, and the land between them destroyed.[13]

Weyler redug the trocha, then built another to the west of Havana, between Mariel, on the northern coast, and Playa Marjana, on the Caribbean. He thus split the country into thirds, each containing one of the leading rebel generals and his troops. Weyler threw "flying columns" of soldiers into rapid-fire raids on rebel camps and villages suspected of supporting the rebel cause. If rebels were not to be found, suspect civilians would do as an example, and a dozen or so men and older boys would be lined up and shot, or hung from a nearby ceiba tree. Thousands of other Cubans were exiled to Spain's African colonies.[14]

But Weyler still couldn't put down the rebellion. On October 21, 1896, he issued a declaration: Within eight days, all civilians who lived in villages and on farms had to move into a series of fortified towns, and "any individual found outside the lines in the country at the expiration of this period shall be considered a rebel and shall be dealt with as such." He outlawed the movement of food between towns and the grazing of cattle outside them. He surrounded the towns with barbed wire and armed guards, to keep rebels out but with orders to shoot anyone who tried to leave.[15]

These camps—the forerunner of those used a few years later and to similar ends during the Boer War and the American war in the Philippines, and a loose model for camps used for even darker purposes during the rest of the twentieth century—were not chosen because of their proximity to fertile soil or fresh water, but for their access to the rail lines and trunk roads the Spanish army used to move around the country. It wasn't long before the overcrowded towns began to run out of food and medical supplies, and people began to die. One correspondent, for *Leslie's Weekly* (a separate publication from *Leslie's Popular Monthly*), estimated that 100 people died a day in Havana, which had 25,000 so-called reconcentrados— the term for the people forced to live in the camps—living in pockets on its outskirts, in addition to its usual population. Clara Barton, who was in Cuba with the Red Cross, noted that by early 1898 more reconcentrados had died in the swelling, fortified town of Juraco than comprised its entire population before the war. Total deaths under Weyler's policy may never be countable; records were not maintained, and bodies were buried en masse. At the time, some claimed the death toll from Weyler's reconcentration policy was as high as 500,000. Even the most skeptical, latter-day analysis allows for at least 100,000.[16]

Weyler's strategy was brutal. And it worked. Within a few

months he had his guerrillas and volunteers acting as "beaters in," pushing the rebels into small sections of the country before attacking them with his regular troops. He made immense amounts of money on the side off confiscated property, but also kept his lieutenants' loyalty by lining their pockets, too. Concentrating most of his cruelty and firepower in the west, he managed to defeat the rebel generals who made forays past the trochas, killing one of the most respected and charismatic rebel leaders, Antonio Maceo, in the process. Though Weyler worked his men ferociously, he fed them well, and managed to keep them motivated. By early 1897, after fifteen months of no-quarter campaigning, he had beaten the rebels back—but the war remained at a standstill. The Spanish controlled large swaths of the west, and all the cities. But the rebels ruled everything else. Neither could move into the other's domain, and so they remained, hacking away at each other, day by day, while the civilians, caught between them, died by the cartload. The rebels were fighting a strategy of attrition; the Spanish, of atrocity. Weyler was unmoved by his critics. "This is war," he liked to reply.[17]

Weyler's campaign may have pushed back against the rebels, but it supercharged the American public's passion for Cuban independence. Within a few months of his reconcentration order, "Butcher" Weyler, as the yellow press nicknamed him, was perhaps the most infamous man in America. Descriptions of suffering reconcentrados filled page after page of American newsprint, as reporters in Cuba found new opportunities in purple prose. Stephen Bonsal, one of the better correspondents assigned to the Cuba beat, and one of the few to venture outside the Havana city limits, wrote: "I saw again the Eden of the New World as it now is—a mass of smoking ruins, a heap of ashes moistened with blood, and a gray, gaunt picture of hopeless despair." Junta propagandists touring the United States would open and close their stump speeches with tales of emaciated mothers trying to nurse dying infants and wide-eyed girls in search of a morsel to eat shot down while sneaking past the guards. Mobs burned Weyler in effigy. Far from bringing the war to an end, he hastened Spain's defeat by bringing the Americans closer to intervention.[18]

• • •

The American press played a particularly important, and not always admirable, role in pushing the public toward intervention in the .Cuban conflict. At a time when literacy rates and the middle class were growing, the market for news was endless—by 1900 there were 2,225 daily and weekly newspapers in America. New York residents had eight morning papers to choose from, and another seven every evening.[19]

The facts of the rebellion were bad enough to make for compelling copy. But readers had an insatiable demand for the next tale of blood and injustice at the hands of Spain, and publishers like William Randolph Hearst and Joseph Pulitzer were happy to give it to them—the more sensational, the better. And nothing in the late 1890s was more sensational than Cuba.

To feed that demand, a small army of reporters camped out in Key West, across the Straits of Florida from Havana. Ostensibly collecting information from American filibusterers and Cuban rebels moving surreptitiously between the island and the American mainland, they often simply rehashed rumors or made up stories completely, fed by sources acting for the Junta. These reporters, members of the reviled but widely read yellow press, told of ravenous Spanish brutes, moving village by village, burning homes, raping girls, executing boys, and throwing babies into the fire. Not content to let the war play out, they recounted fictional battles; when news was slow, they reported that, say, a Cuban rebel general had been killed— or, depending on their mood, that he had survived, and then overcome enormous odds to destroy a Spanish column. One of the few reporters who actually went to Cuba to get the story, George Bronson Rea of the *New York Herald*, wrote a lengthy book, *Facts and Fakes About Cuba*, debunking such Key West "dispatches," even singling out reporters and their articles for attack. "The great factories for 'war news,' situated in Florida," he wrote, "rivaled Baron Munchausen in the fertility and absurdity of their inventions."[20]

But the yellow press was not the only source of reporting in American papers. Several reporters, including Bonsal and Rea, made extensive trips across Cuba, meeting with rebel leaders and seeing the destruction firsthand. Their work appeared in daily newspapers, as well as in longer essays for magazines like *Scribner's* and *Harper's*. These reports, more so than the flotsam of the yellow press, were the real drivers in the news media pushing the American public toward intervention.

One of the most important such trips was made by Richard Harding Davis, at thirty-two years old already the most famous correspondent of his time. He had made his name as a crime reporter for the New York *Sun*, a beat that led him to cross paths with Theodore Roosevelt, then the chairman of the city's police board. Later, as a freelance journalist, he covered topics from the coronation of Nicholas II and his wife, Alexandra Feodorovna, in Moscow to the Harvard-Princeton football game, an assignment for which the news baron William Randolph Hearst paid him $500—about $12,000 in 2018 dollars. It was worth the cost: Hearst sold every newspaper he printed the next day.[21]

Davis stood six feet tall, with a square jaw and a dimpled chin, a full head of dark hair that he wore parted in the middle, and the body of an aging quarterback (he had played football for a year at Lehigh College, in Pennsylvania). Even before the days of mass photography, everyone in America knew his face, because the artist Charles Dana Gibson had used him as the model for the male counterpart of the Gibson Girl. Like her, Davis—or, rather, the Gibson Man—appeared in magazines and advertisements, on book covers and billboards across the country. Some credit the ubiquity of the clean-shaven Davis/Gibson Man image with the turn-of-the-century disappearance of beards in respectable society.[22]

In December 1896, Hearst paid Davis and the illustrator Frederic Remington $3,000 each (over $90,000 in 2018) to spend a month crisscrossing Cuba and reporting along the way. They arrived in early January, but after a week Remington decided to turn back. He had signed up for the trip expecting to confront death while still wading ashore on some desolate beach on a moonless night; instead, they had been greeted in Havana by General Weyler himself, and given a pass—and an escort—to travel the island. Remington telegraphed Hearst to tell him that there was no war, and there wasn't going to be one. "Everything is quiet. There is no trouble here. There will be no war. I wish to return," he wrote. The publisher allegedly, infamously, replied, "Please remain. You furnish the pictures and I'll furnish the war." In fact, it's unlikely Hearst wrote anything of the kind. There is no actual record of the telegram, and the only mention came second-hand, in a memoir published by the correspondent James Creelman. Hearst himself denied it. Whatever his reply, Remington ignored him, and left Cuba.[23]

Davis pressed on. Unlike Remington, he was convinced that there was fighting to be seen. Whether there was any truth to the stories about Spanish crimes was a different matter, and one he would set out, with Weyler's surprise blessing, to explore.[24]

At first, what Davis saw confirmed his skepticism. "I find myself growing to be the opposite of the 'alarmist,'" he wrote to his mother. "They show me the pueblo huddled together around the fortified towns living in palm huts, but I know that they have always lived in palm huts; the yellow kid reporters don't know that or consider it, but send off word that the conditions of the people is terrible that they have only leaves to cover them."[25]

But slowly, his impression of the war began to change. Over the next two weeks, Davis's travels took him across the island, nearly to Santiago on the southeastern coast. "Tonight I reached here after a six hours ride through blazing fields of sugar cane," he wrote on January 16, after traveling along the northern coast of Cuba, from Matanzas to Cárdenas. "I always imagined that houses were destroyed during a war because they got in the way of cannonballs or they were burned because the might offer shelter to the enemy, but here they are destroyed with the purpose of making the war hor-rible and hurrying up the end." The countryside was indeed beauti-ful, he wrote—"nothing out of the imagination can approach it in its great waterfalls and mossy rocks and grand plains and forests of white pillars with plumes waving above them." Though still in the Northern Hemisphere, he could see the constellation of the South-ern Cross, hanging low over the sky, a seeming promise from God to watch over the island. And perhaps the Lord would in fact pro-tect the island, Davis concluded, but not its inhabitants. "Only man is vile here."[26]

Davis ventured into seven fortified towns. There he saw the scenes he had long doubted, of suffering and disease and death on a massive scale. One of Davis's earliest achievements had been his coverage of the 1889 flood in Johnstown, Pennsylvania, in which a dam broke and the resulting wall of water killed more than 2,200 people. In that reporting, he focused on the human side of the destruction, the thousands of people left homeless and, soon, starving. But the misery he saw in Pennsylvania, he said, was nothing compared to what he found in Cuba: "Babies with the skin drawn so tightly over their little bodies that the bones showed through as plainly as the rings under a glove," he wrote. And this was during the dry season. "In April and May the rains will come, and the fever will thrive and spread, and cholera, yellow fever and small-pox will turn Cuba into one huge plague spot." Whatever skepticism Davis possessed had vanished by the time he reached Cienfuegos, on the southern coast. "There is no doubt that the process going on here is one of extermination and ruin," he wrote to his mother. "Wherever you look you see great heavy columns of smoke rising into the beautiful sky."[27]

After a few more weeks crisscrossing Cuba, Davis returned to Havana and sailed home. On board, he met a young woman named Clemencia Arango, who soon revealed that her brother ran guns for the insurgents. She was Davis's type, a Latina Gibson girl—upper-class, well-mannered, well-educated, and dressed as if she were headed to dinner at Delmonico's. She told him that before she boarded, a detail of Spanish police officers pulled her aside into an inspection house and had her strip-searched. She was searched again on board, as the ship was preparing to leave.[28]

When Davis arrived in Tampa, he sent a dispatch to Hearst, who put it on the front of the *Journal*, with an illustration by Remington. The drawing showed a naked Arango, her hair in a chignon, surrounded by leering Spanish officers. The headline read "Spaniards Search Women on American Steamers." When he saw it, Davis shot back to Hearst that he had never said Arango was searched by men, that in fact he knew she'd been searched by women. But it was too late—a reporter from Joseph Pulitzer's *New York World* found Arango in Tampa and conducted his own interview. The resulting exposé concluded that "Mr. Davis and Mr. Remington should be well quarantined before they are allowed to mingle again with reputable newspaper men." Davis was mortified, and vowed never to write for a Hearst paper again. Hearst, watching a headline war break out and his sales numbers rise, probably didn't care.[29]

Davis came back from his month in Cuba a changed man. "Personally it was the most beneficial trip I ever took—I feel five years older and it gave many things new values," he wrote his brother, Charles. He swung through Philadelphia and New York, and then headed to England to take up a roving correspondent job for *The Times* of London. And in his spare hours, he compiled a book, *Cuba in War Time*, which was published in the late spring of 1897. The dispatches collected in the book present a gripping, detailed portrait of a country in turmoil. The book is, moreover, an account of how Davis, an isolationist who had once looked at intervention in Cuba as a looming quagmire, became one of its most ardent advocates. When he arrived in the country, he wrote, "I refused for weeks to listen to tales of butcheries, because I did not believe in them and because there seemed to be no way of verifying them."[30]

But the more he saw and the more trusted sources he encountered, the more he changed his mind. He became, upon return, a fiercely pro-war hawk, and in the conclusion of his bestselling book, he framed the case for American intervention in the rebellion in a way that would not only persuade readers on Cuba, but in decades to come would win over the public to the cause of using American power to humanitarian ends:

Before I went to Cuba I was as much opposed to our interfering there as any other person equally ignorant concerning the situation could be, but since I have seen for myself I feel ashamed that we should have stood so long idle. We have been too considerate, too fearful that as a younger nation, we should appear to disregard the laws laid down by older nations. We have tolerated what no European power would have tolerated; we have been patient with men who have put back the hand of time for centuries, who lie to our representatives daily, who butcher innocent people, who gamble with the lives of their own soldiers in order to gain a few more stars and an extra stripe, who send American property to the air in flames and murder American prisoners.[31]

Davis was not the only reporter making this case. But he was the only one with the reach and the respect to draw in readers to his—and Cuba's—side. "Why should we not go a step farther and a step higher, and interfere in the name of humanity?" he wrote in *Cuba in War Time*. "Not because we are Americans, but because we are human beings.[32]

By early 1898, reporting like Davis's had convinced large swaths of the American public, and its leaders, that their country had to intervene to stop the fighting in Cuba. For Theodore Roosevelt and his circle, Cuba represented a perfect test, and opportunity, for America as an emergent world power—intervention would be "as righteous as it would be advantageous," Roosevelt wrote. His long talks with his new best friend, Leonard Wood, were similar to what people were saying across the country, over dinner tables, in debating societies, in bars, and in the halls of Congress. Politicians and ministers seemed to compete for the most excessive declaration of concern. "For more than three hundred years," wrote John James Ingalls, a former senator from Kansas, "a country nearly as large as England, with all the material conditions of opulent civilization, has been made a charnel house. Possessing all the elements of Eden, it has been turned into a hell."[33]

Added to the nation's humanitarian concerns was a long list of Spanish slights against America's people and reputation, going back to the 1873 execution of the crew of the *Virginius*, a filibuster carrying insurgents and supplies that the Spanish captured on its way to Cuba. Most recently, in February 1898, a scandalous memo from the Spanish consul in Washington, Enrique Depuy de Lôme, to the Foreign Ministry in Madrid had been intercepted by pro-Cuban activists and promptly published in Hearst's *New York Journal*. De Lôme had called McKinley a "weak," "low" president, and doubted whether the administration was smart and stalwart enough to win concessions from Spain. "Worst Insult to the United States in Its History," the

Journal headline had read. De Lôme was dismissed, but the scandal went down on the pro-interventionists' ledger.[34]

Others were interested less in where or why a war took place than simply that one did, soon. Labor and social unrest were simmering in the aftermath of the Panic of 1893 (and a second, smaller panic a few years later); elites feared not just unions, but populists, anarchists, and socialists, and not without reason. The candidacy of William Jennings Bryan in 1896, a populist Democrat, stoked concern among the urban middle and upper classes that the country was riven with class divisions and ripe for revolt. A war would unite the country, many believed, demonstrating the weakness of class warfare. In a similar vein, a war, by bringing together soldiers from Northern and Southern states, would demonstrate that the Civil War was over, and that sectional divisions had healed. Still others, echoing Roosevelt, wanted war as a cure, said Senator Albert Beveridge of Indiana, for "the intense materialism of the time" that "is palsying manhood, poisoning justice, driving faith from its throne." William James, the Harvard psychology and philosophy professor (and brother of the novelist and Roosevelt critic Henry James), believed that war was a "great preserver of our ideals of hardihood."[35]

A war would also announce to the world that the United States had arrived as a global power. Until the 1890s, much of Europe had looked at America as a hypertrophied child, with astounding economic growth and resources, but without the maturity to play a role in world affairs. They pointed to a dramatic, planned shrinkage of the United States Army after the Civil War as exhibit A. Some Europeans wrote paeans to America's natural beauty, and even some to its rough-and-tumble individualistic culture. But no one considered it a great power on the level of Britain or France or Germany, or even a fading empire like Spain's or the Ottoman Empire. For a time in the early 1890s, several European countries actually closed their embassies in Washington, as cost-cutting measures. Going to war would grab their attention, and victory over Spain would put Europe back on its heels.[36]

But if the reasons for action on Cuba were overwhelming, at first there was less agreement over what exactly was to be done. Some, like Senator Shelby Cullom of Illinois, wanted to invade and take possession of Cuba outright, the fulfillment of an even greater manifest destiny than America had been pursuing up to that point: "It is time some one woke up and realized the necessity of annexing some property. We want all this northern hemisphere." But outright annexationists were the minority. White Southerners—and most white Northerners—recoiled at the idea of adding several hundred thousand free black people to the citizenry. The business community feared that an American conquest of Cuba could be used to justify larger armies and state bureaucracies. And anti-imperialists worried that expansion would alter America's identity as a beacon for individual freedom and self-government.[37]

For decades, these competing cultural and intellectual strands—a minority in favor of continued expansion, with a majority opposed—had prevented America from venturing abroad. But the particulars of the Cuban crisis—starvation and death on a massive scale, combined with threats to American investments and the opportunity to profitably control the island's future, without having to conquer it outright—created a new and lasting justification for an activist American foreign policy. People referred to it in different ways, but most grouped it under the term "humanitarianism." It spoke to America's best ideas about itself; it tabled, for now, the difficult questions of outright territorial conquest; and it left open the possibility of a subtler but more pervasive form of empire. "The United States does not seek to control Cuba," wrote an editorialist for *Leslie's Weekly*. "It stands simply for the liberty of an oppressed people." Invading Cuba would be nothing short of a victory for "civilization over barbarism," declared Senator Ingalls of Kansas. "We are ministrars of that eternal justice for which every place should be a temple. We draw the sword to avenge the wrongs of the helpless. Our cannon speak for those who are voiceless. . . . Our victory will be the triumph of the nineteenth century over the Middle Ages; of democracy over absolutism; of self-government over tyranny; of faith over bigotry."[38]

This was not just war fever; it was a new way of thinking about war. During the 1890s, and with Cuba at the front of their minds, millions of Americans reimagined their national purpose—not just as a country that embodied liberty, but one that spread liberty to all the countries of the world, by force if necessary. It was the sort of militarism that everyone—Union and Confederate veterans, labor and business, socialists and evangelicals, hawks and doves—could rally behind. "The oppressed of all the nations of the earth are looking at America," intoned Pastor E. O. Eldridge of Waugh Methodist Episcopal Church in Washington, D.C. "We have a mission to all the nations of the world, as well as to the citizens of our own country." America already knew it was a powerful country. In the debate over Cuba, it had found a use for that power.[39]

President McKinley, Secretary Long, and others continued in early 1898 to hope that American power would not need to be tested, that Spain would come to its senses and end the war. But where McKinley and Long saw promising moves by Spain toward compromise, Roosevelt and Wood saw intransigence. In August 1897, an assassin killed Spain's conservative, hawkish prime minister, Antonio Cánovas; the queen replaced him with Práxedes Sagasta, a critic of Cánovas and General Weyler from the relatively progressive Liberal Party. Sagasta immediately recalled Weyler from Cuba, and announced that the Spanish colonial government would cede much of the control of Cuba's domestic politics—tariffs, public education, infrastructure—to the local forces, while retaining control over the island's military and foreign-facing capacities. Cubans would be allowed to elect representatives to a bicameral parliament, and take over control of local politics.

In fact, none of this happened. A Cuban cabinet did take office on January 1, 1898, but it had almost no power, even over the areas reserved to it on paper. And although he promised autonomy, Sagasta ramped up military pressure, sending 20,000 Spanish soldiers to reinforce the hundreds of thousands already there. He ordered Weyler's reconcentration program loosened, but not rescinded; in effect, it remained. He promised relief funds, but sent just $12,500, mere pennies per reconcentrado. (Real relief came when Sagasta permitted Clara Barton and the Central Cuban Relief Committee to enter the island in late January 1898.)[40]

McKinley had taken office after saying almost nothing about Cuba during the campaign, and for most of 1897 he committed himself to continuing Cleveland's noninterventionist policy, intercepting filibusterers and refusing congressional entreaties to at least recognize the rebels as belligerents, so they could buy American weapons. In the summer McKinley asked William J. Calhoun, a close adviser, to visit Cuba and report back on the situation. Like the many reporters who had already surveyed the island, Calhoun came back with stories about burning villages, ruined fields, and starving children—and a stalemated military situation that promised to drag out the crisis for years. Whichever side wins, he told McKinley, "is largely a matter of endurance."[41]

McKinley was hearing similar complaints from leaders in the business community, though they were less interested in the human suffering and more in the war's impact on their investments on the island: sugar, of course, but also tobacco, mining, and light manufacturing. Like McKinley, American businesses did not want war, and they did not care particularly about the outcome of the conflict, so long as peace returned, and along with it America's growing influence over the Cuban economy. By the time Sagasta took office, McKinley had already sent a series of letters to Madrid demanding that it find a way to peace on the island—but he offered no guidance, expressed no preference for what that would look like, and threatened no particular response if Spain did not follow suit. Not surprisingly, Spain opted to do nothing. After the initial burst of moderation under Sagasta, the Spanish and the rebels fell back into stalemate.[42]

Spain, it became clear, was not willing to leave the island, while the rebels would accept nothing less than complete independence. Domestic Spanish politics played a considerable role. For the previous seventy-five years, the government and the monarchy had teetered on the edge of collapse, threatened on the left by anarchists and other radicals, and on the right by ultraconservatives—the latter having dragged Madrid through the devastating Carlist Wars during the middle of the century. It would be one thing to lose a war to the rebels, or to American intervention—there would be little shame in noble defeat. But to give up Cuba voluntarily, or even cede it significant autonomy, would be a death warrant for the fragile monarchy. "They prefer the chances of war, with the certain loss of Cuba, to the overthrow of the Dynasty," as Stewart Woodford, the American minister to Spain, put it.[43]

For men like McKinley and Long, though, this was all part of the game of diplomacy, and any result would be preferable to war. To Roosevelt and Wood, the only possible answer to Spanish intransigence was war, and they expected that, eventually, McKinley would agree. In January 1898 they made plans to quit their respective jobs should war come and find positions as officers with one of their state militias (they dismissed outright the idea of joining a general's staff in the Regular Army, for fear that it would keep them from the action). Wood later recalled, in an interview with the writer Hermann Hagedorn, that while he was giving the president a checkup, or caring for the ailing first lady, McKinley would ask him: "Well, have you and Theodore declared war yet?" To which Wood replied, "No, Mr. President, we have not, but I think you will, sir."[44]

Even at the time, critics derided the humanitarian impulse as window dressing for old-fashioned imperialism. They ranged from literary figures like Mark Twain and William Dean Howells to labor leaders like Samuel Gompers to politicians like Grover Cleveland and his Republican predecessor, Benjamin Harrison. Thomas Brackett Reed, the speaker of the house and a former ally of Roosevelt and his fellow jingo Senator Lodge, denounced talk of intervention as "land hunger."[45]

The anti-imperialists were not wrong. For all the talk about humanitarian intervention and the spread of liberty, what was just as real, but much less explicit, were concerns over markets, and investments, and the need to find new outlets for social frustration and an expanding, restless population. The same urge that had driven white Americans to massacre Indians and take their land was now appearing in the rhetoric around Cuba—except this time, it was clothed in righteousness. Many clear-eyed Americans saw this. But events would soon unfold in a way that rendered them helpless to stop it.

CHAPTER 3

"A BURST OF THUNDER"

A t around 2 a.m. on February 16, 1898, Secretary Long was asleep at his house on N Street, in Washington, across from the British embassy. He had been up late at a reception with his daughter Helen, who had then gone off to an even later ball. He awoke to a knock on his door. It was Helen, who had just returned. She held a telegram in her hand. Something terrible had happened in Havana.[1]

Three weeks earlier, Long and McKinley had sent a battleship to pay a "friendly" visit to the city, a not-so-subtle demonstration of resolve after the anti-American riots that had so energized Roosevelt. That warship, the *Maine*, was one of the newest and best in the fleet: 324 feet long, with a complement of 374 officers and men, it bristled with Gatling guns, torpedo tubes, and four 10-inch cannons that could lob a 521-pound shell eleven miles. Although it was an impressive ship, the *Maine* was immediately overshadowed by more modern craft being built in Europe, and it was only marginally more powerful than some of the Spanish navy's best ships. Still, it was a steel-and-iron avatar for the Navy Department's renewed vigor.[2]

The *Maine* arrived on January 25 from Key West, where the Navy had already sent the bulk of the Atlantic Squadron to take part in what it was euphemistically calling "naval exercises," but were in fact a warning to Spain. Tensions had continued to rise that January; the *Maine*'s arrival came on the heels of the resignation by de Lôme, the disgraced Spanish minister to Washington. Nevertheless, the Spanish tolerated the ship's presence, and welcomed its sailors and officers in its cafés and other places of enticement whenever they came ashore for leave.

On the evening of February 15, most of those men were on board, and its captain, Charles Sigsbee, was sitting in his cabin writing his daily report. His dog Peggy curled up at his feet. Havana Harbor was a fetid, polluted body of water, but that evening a gentle breeze pushed most of the foul air out to sea. At 9 p.m., the ship's bell began to chime, and as it did a Marine bugler played taps, signaling lights-out. Forty minutes later, the *Maine* exploded.[3]

Onshore in her rented room, Clara Barton, who was in Havana with the Central Cuban Relief Committee, felt her desk shake, followed by "a burst of thunder" and the shattering of glass. "The air was filled with a blaze of light," she later wrote, "and this in turn filled with black specks like huge specters flying in all directions." Nearby, the windows of a waterfront café shattered all around the *New York Herald* correspondent Walter Scott Meriwether, who had just walked in the front door for a drink. Within minutes, bells were pealing and whistles blowing across the city, and it seemed as if every Spanish soldier in Cuba was rushing to the harbor.[4]

On board the *Maine*, Sigsbee had just pushed back his papers when he heard two explosions and felt the ship shudder, then jump into the air—a "bursting, rending, crashing sound or roar of immense volume," he later wrote his wife. He stumbled out of his cabin and onto the main deck as the ship settled and began to tip to its port side. Choking on fumes, he and a scrum of officers organized lifeboats, though scores of men had already jumped into the warm waters of the harbor. Sigsbee, holding Peggy (who had somehow found her way to his side), waited until all the men they could find were off the ship, then stepped into a lifeboat.[5]

Because the explosion occurred toward the front of the ship, most of the officers, whose cabins were to the rear, survived, but the overall loss was staggering—266 men, the worst naval disaster in American military history up to that point.[6]

Despite several official and private investigations, no one has ever determined what caused the *Maine* to explode. After a thorough study by Admiral Hyman Rickover in the 1970s, the consensus holds that it was some sort of accident, most likely caused by the spontaneous combustion of coal dust in one of the ship's fuel bins. What has not emerged is even a mote of evidence pointing to organized Spanish malfeasance, or the work of outside agitators—both common theories in 1898.[7]

The lack of evidence meant little at the time, and the news that Spain had sunk the *Maine* shot around the world. For William Randolph Hearst, it could mean only one thing: an act of war. Refusing to consider the possibility of an accident, he splashed "War!" and "Maine Destroyed by Spanish" in banner headlines across his papers. In London, Richard Harding Davis, the reporter, was just hours away from setting off on a trip to Belgrade, to report on fighting in Serbia and Bulgaria. He read the news in an afternoon paper and knew he had to come home, that war in Cuba was finally at hand. After his public embarrassment over the Arango affair, and his rebirth as a pro-intervention hawk, Davis saw a chance to both redeem himself as a reporter and elevate himself as a foreign-affairs intellectual. "If I do miss it, I shall be wild," he wrote to his family. And in Washington, Theodore Roosevelt grinned, and shouted, and declared that war with Spain had finally arrived. "The blood of the Cubans, the blood of women and children who have perished by the hundred thousand in hideous misery, lies at our door; and the blood of the murdered men of the Maine calls not for indemnity but for the full measure of atonement which can only come by driving the Spaniard from the new world," he wrote to his friend Brooks Adams.[8]

War had not, in fact, arrived. The morning after the *Maine* disaster, Leonard Wood was at the Executive Mansion giving President McKinley a routine checkup. While examining the president, the doctor offered his services as a soldier. The president shook his head. He was far from ready to declare war, and he needed time, he said, for "cool heads and cautious tongues."[9]

Next door, in the offices of the Department of the Navy, Long was likewise cautious. "My own judgment is, so far as any information has been received, that it was the result of an accident," he wrote in his diary. He was more worried that his assistant secretary might cause things to come to a crisis all on his own, thanks to his prodigious energies and lack of restraint. Roosevelt, wrote Long, "has come very near causing more of an explosion than happened to the *Maine*." Long was right to worry: Roosevelt had already ordered the Navy to start buying ships—supply ships domestically, and as many warships from foreign navies as his agents could find. He telegraphed Commodore Dewey, the head of the Asiatic Squadron in Hong Kong, telling him to keep his ships coaled in case orders arrived to sail on Manila, the capital of the Philippines, where Spain's Pacific fleet was based. And this was just in the first seventy-two hours. Calling Roosevelt "a bull in a China shop," Long wrote that he had chosen "the one course which is most discourteous to me, because it suggests that there had been a lack of attention which he was supplying. It shows how the best fellow in the world—and with splendid capacities—is worse than no use if he lack a cool head and careful discretion."[10]

Roosevelt also began to make plans to join the war on his own—though he didn't have much luck finding a spot for himself in a state militia regiment. In a letter to his friend William Sturgis Bigelow, he lamented that even if he found a unit to join, "The army may not be employed at all, and even if it is employed it will consist chiefly of regular troops. . . . I shall be eating out my heart." He was determined, though, not to stay behind at the State, War and Navy Building should war arrive. "My office is essentially a peace office," he told Bigelow. "The assistant secretary had properly nothing to do with military operations."[11]

The country's war fever began to cool off as Madrid went to every end to cooperate with the Navy's investigation. But then, on March 17, Redfield Proctor of Vermont walked to the floor of the Senate, in his hand a speech he had previewed for Roosevelt and Wood the day before at the Metropolitan Club.[12]

A Civil War colonel who made a fortune off his state's marble quarries, which he then parlayed into a turn in the governor's mansion in Montpelier and then a seat in Congress, Proctor had entered the year a committed skeptic of intervention in Cuba. He had a reputation as an unsentimental, unfriendly man, and for a politician he had few allies, let alone confidants. He came from a business background, and sided with business interests in Congress. Late that winter, he had accepted an opportunity from the president to visit Cuba to see for himself whether the horror stories had any bearing in fact.[13]

They did. "It is not peace, nor is it war," Proctor told his colleagues. "It is desolation and distress, misery and starvation." What Richard Harding Davis had documented a year before for Hearst, Proctor now verified for Congress: the trochas, the summary executions, the reconcentrados, the masses of starving innocents. "What I saw I

50

cannot tell so that others can see it," he said. "It must be seen with one's own eyes to be realized." He praised the work of Clara Barton and the Red Cross, and encouraged Americans to send them more money. But he also conceded that humanitarian aid alone was not enough. Intervention, diplomatic if possible but more likely by force, was the only solution. "When will the need for this help end?" he pleaded. "Not until peace comes and the reconcentrados can go back to their country, rebuild their homes, reclaim their tillage plots, which quickly run up to brush in that wonderful soil and clime, and until they can be free from danger of molestation in so doing."[14]

With Proctor's speech, a dam seemed to break in the remaining opposition to war. Said one observer, the address "was like the Roentgen ray, disclosing the hideous lesions of bigotry, cruelty, and misrule: the murder of the helpless, the starvation of the unoffending, the extermination of the innocent." Proctor was not a jingo. He was not an imperialist. For that reason, his speech won over previously skeptical corners of the American establishment, especially business interests. Proctor's address, the *Wall Street Journal* noted, "converted a great many people in Wall Street, who had heretofore taken the ground that the United States had no business to interfere in a revolution on Spanish soil."[15]

The following weeks saw a mounting hurricane of righteous interventionist sentiment. The country, wrote the *Sacramento Daily Record-Tribune*, "is about to enter upon a struggle, if the present portent does not change, which has for its justification on our side the cessation of a war that has been marked by brutality; and unparalleled offense against the humanity of the age; the freeing of a people who have the right to recognition in their effort to set up self-government; and to shake off the domination of a monarchical rule that has never made colonial control a success." Drawing on Proctor's address, editorialists, politicians, and preachers linked freedom for Cuba with a new, grand mission of an empowered, powerful America unleashed on the world. The *Scranton Tribune* declared: "One of the results of this war may be the acquisition of a dignity and importance in the eyes of people across the water that the United States has not enjoyed up to this time." Some even called intervention a religious obligation. "Sympathy with the insurgent Cubans had become the popular test of human kindness, and protest against war the unanswerable proof of Christian indifference," wrote Russell Alger, a lumber tycoon who was serving as McKinley's secretary of war.[16]

Not everyone agreed. The coterie of anti-imperialists in Washington and New York who had batted down campaigns to annex Hawaii and other expansionist enterprises—including the powerful speaker of the house, Thomas Brackett Reed, and the Republican Party fixer Carl Schurz—redoubled their opposition on the chamber floors of Capitol Hill and in the pages of the nation's leading magazines. Those who remembered America's last conflict warned that too many people leading the charge did not fully appreciate what they were calling for. Governor Edward Scofield of Wisconsin, a Civil War veteran who was taken prisoner by the Confederates during the Battle of the Wilderness in 1864, warned that "war is a terrible evil. It means destruction of life and property and untold misery and grief. It is brutal and savage in all its manifestations. Do those people who are talking war so freely know anything of its horrors?" Others argued that America should not become the world's policeman. "We cannot undertake to right the wrongs of the world," wrote the Stockton, California, *Independent*. "We have no occasion to declare war against Spain unless it is proven that Spain had designedly insulted us and then declines to make the usual amends." In Kansas City, a shoemaker hung black crepe across his storefront with the notice, "Closed in memory of a Christian nation that descends to the barbarity of war."[17]

But no one listened. Four days after Proctor's speech, a naval court of inquiry in Key West investigating the *Maine* disaster released its findings, which had been transported, under armed guard and secret courier, to the president. The explosion, it concluded, was caused by something outside the ship—a mine, most likely. The board did not affix blame; it left it to commentators to speculate whether the mine was placed intentionally or was a derelict device from the harbor's defenses. Nevertheless, coming so soon after Proctor's speech, the report was all the pro-war camp needed to make its final push for war. If Spain was at all complicit in the destruction of an American ship that Havana had welcomed into its harbor, what other proof did the antiwar camp need of Spanish perfidy?[18]

Roosevelt, once again, led the way. In between calling for military relief for suffering Cubans, he carried forth at every opportunity about American dignity and vengeance for the victims of the *Maine*. On March 27, he confronted Senator Mark Hanna, a leading dove and the mastermind behind McKinley's 1896 victory, at a party. Roosevelt was asked to give a speech after the meal. Rising to the occasion, he declared himself a member of a younger generation of Americans who, unlike Hanna and the president, "were anxious that the honor and dignity of the country should be preserved." Still standing, he turned to the seated Hanna and declared that while the business world might be paramount to the Senate, it was not to the American people. As applause rang out, one of Roosevelt's allies—unnamed in news reports—went in for the kill. "Now, senator," the man said to Hanna. "May we please have a war?"[19]

News of Roosevelt's dinnertime speech shot across the wires, and a transcript of it appeared the next day in papers nationwide. By the end of March, the public had turned on McKinley, too. In Durango, Colorado, a mob burned the president in effigy; one participant said they would use the ashes to pay back Spain for the gunpowder used on the *Maine*. The president came in for further, similar abuse in Richmond, Virginia, and Newport, Rhode Island. Privately, Roosevelt seethed. "McKinley has no more backbone than a chocolate eclair," he wrote.[20]

This wasn't entirely fair. McKinley cared about the plight of the Cubans: He arranged for Congress to spend $50,000 to aid Americans in Cuba, and he led a charity drive for the Red Cross that raised $200,000 by April 1898 (including his own, anonymous donation). He was determined to end the suffering in Cuba, and increasingly, he agreed with the hawks that for that to happen, Spain had to grant Cuba autonomy, if not outright independence. McKinley's first annual message to Congress, delivered on December 6, 1897 (by hand; it would be decades before presidents actually read their "state of the union" messages to the House and Senate), called Cuba "the most important problem" facing American foreign relations. He had made a clean break with Cleveland's noninterventionist policy, but, perhaps naively, McKinley held out hope that the Spanish would cave, that the newly seated Sagasta government, which he said was already taking "honorable" steps, would find a path to peace. But he also made it clear that if Spain did not follow through on its promises, he would not hesitate to intervene: "If it shall hereafter appear to be a duty imposed by our obligations to ourselves, to civilization and humanity to intervene with force, it shall be without fault on our part and only because the necessity for such action will be so clear as to command the support and approval of the civilized world."[21]

Still, McKinley remained deeply opposed to using force to achieve his goal. He had fought in the Civil War, had seen men bleed out on the battlefield at Antietam, had a horse shot from under him at Berryville. Even thirty-three years later, the memory of death, and the ripples of pain it had sent through his hometown of Canton, Ohio, remained fresh, and it guided him during those first early months of 1898. "I do not care for the property that will be destroyed, nor the money that will be expended," he told Senator Charles Fairbanks, "but the thought of human suffering that must enter many households almost overwhelms me."[22]

McKinley continued to have faith even as Spain rejected his entreaties to move beyond Sagasta's initial softening, even as those entreaties became more forceful demands. Spain countered one letter, sent on December 20, with an insistence that any further action on Madrid's part would come only after the United States cracked down on the pro-independence Junta network, which Spain believed was the life-support system for the rebellion. And McKinley continued to have faith, if not in Spain, then in the general ability of rational men to avoid an irrational war, even after the publication of the de Lôme letter, after more Spanish rejections, after the *Maine* settled to the bottom of Havana Harbor. "We must learn the truth and endeavor, if possible, to fix the responsibility," was all he would say.[23]

It was, simply, how McKinley operated. At a time when many Americans seemed to want passion, they had in their president a man who worshipped at the temple of dispassion, of biding time, of resisting pressure to act from all sides. McKinley, one aide told the *Washington Post* on February 27, "will not be jingoed into war, or act in anticipation of events which may never occur."[24]

Even after the *Maine* and the court of inquiry's report on its sinking, McKinley believed that he could appease the war hawks and pressure Spain to the bargaining table. On March 7 he called congressional leaders, Secretary Long, and Secretary of War Alger for a meeting in the Executive Mansion library. Turning to Representative Joe Cannon of Illinois, the chair of the House Appropriations Committee, the president said he needed supplemental funds for the military—$50 million for the Navy and the Army. Cannon slipped the request into the House hopper that afternoon; two days later, the bill was on McKinley's desk. Even before the money was spent, the very fact that America could toss around that sort of wealth stunned the world, and gave a preview of what a newly empowered, internationally aggressive America might look like. Impressing the world, and Spain, was McKinley's plan, anyway, and for a few weeks it worked.[25]

In late March Spain offered to enact real reforms, and said it would be willing to suspend hostilities if the rebels asked. But political crises often take on a life of their own, especially when war is involved, and in any case no one believed that Spain was sincere, or that the rebels would be willing to accept anything less than independence anyway. As spring flowered that late March, patriotic airs became popular programs at music halls and flags cropped up with the crocuses around front yards. Without McKinley saying much, by April 1 it became the national consensus that he would declare war within the month. In Congress, Senator John Morgan of Alabama submitted a declaration of war. Even Long, who sympathized with McKinley and admired his resolute rejection of the war party, wrote in his diary on April 5: "The country is so clamorous for action that the president cannot delay longer."[26]

As war approached, offers to fight, or to organize fighters, popped up around the country, like a precipitate emerging from a liquid. Young men who had grown up hearing stories of their fathers and grandfathers fighting at Gettysburg, or Chickamauga, or Veracruz, suddenly had a chance at their own adventure. And this time, they were motivated not by the desperation of national self-preservation, or the dubious logic of the Mexican-American War, but a moral compulsion to use the growing wealth they felt boiling up around them—in factories, in city streets, in railroads and street car lines and everything else that defined the newly prosperous, powerful America—to change the world.

Typical of this generation of war-happy young men was Theodore Miller, an 1897 graduate of Yale and a student at the newly opened New York Law School in Manhattan. The son of Lewis Miller, an Ohio industrial magnate, Theodore was of medium height, with wispy walnut hair, a broad chest and ropy arms that came from years rowing crew during the summer on Lake Chautauqua, New York (apart from his business career, Lewis Miller cofounded the Chautauqua Assembly, a wildly popular movement to bring intellectual life to Middle America). He was a studious, friendly young man who everyone said was going places. But in the spring of 1898, the only place Miller wanted to go was Cuba.[27]

Miller was living in a cramped apartment on Manhattan's Upper East Side with three friends from Yale, all students. Their abode—which they took to calling Poverty Flat—"was the resort of many '97 men who either came to town, or were living in the city," wrote his father's close friend John Heyl Vincent. "Many a night Theodore would sleep on the lounge or even on the floor, in order to make room for a welcome classmate or two from out of town." All anyone in Poverty Flat could talk about was the coming war. "There has been nothing exciting in here except the war but of course that is exciting enough for any patriotic citizen," Miller wrote to his sister Mina, who was married to the inventor Thomas Edison.[28]

Being in New York made the pressure to drop out of school and join the Army almost too hard to bear. Even before McKinley declared war, red, white, and blue bunting hung from every lamppost in every borough. The Cuban Junta sponsored soapbox speakers around the city, and newly formed militias paraded up and down Manhattan streets. Three hundred men in Flatbush, Brooklyn, declared their intention to go to war, despite any connection to the military hierarchy. A coalition of Wall Street firms offered to raise a regiment of 1,000 men.[29]

"What I want to do is to get into the scrap and be able to do something worth doing," Miller wrote in a letter to his father. "I may be too eager and ambitious, but that is what I want to do." Lewis Miller forbade it—ostensibly because he wanted his son to first finish the school year, but also, likely, because he had invested so much in his son's future. He had watched men of his own generation head off to the Civil War and not return; he knew what war could do to a family, to a community.[30]

But like any son anywhere, Theodore Miller would not countenance his father's wisdom. His letters to his family burst with righteous impatience. "I have been working solidly and find it mightily hard to with all this war news about," he wrote to Mina. Eventually, with war clouds gathering, Miller declared his own war, in a letter to his sister: "I am so sorry to worry mother about it but I don't see how to avoid it. I must go if there is a need and there is—and as soon as there is room."[31]

Miller's desire to fight was sincere; others' intentions were more whimsical, even bizarre. A group of "fashionable West End girls" in St. Louis offered to organize an all-female regiment, wearing "jaunty military caps" and carrying swords, to spur men to volunteer. A circus offered twenty-five elephants, in case the American Army needed to invade Cuba, Hannibal style. The New York *Sun* even reported that several hundred Kentucky "mountaineers" wanted to enlist en masse—"among them will be the representatives of every feud in Kentucky for fifty years."[32]

This was all fun and a bit tongue-in-cheek, but there was a real problem. After decades of neglect, America simply did not have the military manpower to send an army into Cuba, let alone to man the coastal defenses against a Spanish fleet in case of war. Aside from the Army's statutorily limited corps of about 28,000 men, there were tens of thousands more in state militias, but they were almost all paper soldiers; in most states, few men had even participated in a drill, or knew how to fire a rifle as part of a unit.

And so a few enterprising people, casting about, found a ready, novel solution: cowboys. Already by 1898, Americans had fantasized about harnessing the frontier prowess for violence and directing it outward. It sounds, looking back after a century of American military might, like an astoundingly stupid idea. But such was the need, and such was the hold that the frontier West had on the American mind, that at the time it made perfect sense to raise and equip a regiment of cowboys to go fight Spain alongside regular soldiers. Not surprisingly, Roosevelt had already thought of it: In 1886, hearing news of a clash along the Mexican border, he suggested raising "an entire regiment of cowboys" to Secretary of War William C. Endicott.[33]

Roosevelt was not alone. During a dinner in the spring of 1898 with General Nelson Miles, the top-ranking officer in the Army, Buffalo Bill Cody offered the services of the cowboys in his Wild West show. The Texas Rangers, suggested many a Lone Star voice, would be an excellent auxiliary. In late March, a man named George R. Shanton of Laramie, Wyoming, offered to raise "within ten days' notice a company of 50 rough riders and expert shots for service in the event of war." Melvin Grigsby, the attorney general of South Dakota, did the same, as did Porter J. Hand, an officer from Nebraska. Alexander Brodie, a veteran of the Southwest Indian Wars, enlisted the governor of the Arizona territory to telegraph McKinley directly, urging him to let Brodie raise a regiment of Southwestern miners, cowboys, and other frontier denizens for battle. On March 30, Senator Francis Warren, also from Wyoming, introduced a bill in Congress to authorize a "cowboy regiment." The bill went nowhere, but the idea was unleashed.[34]

By mid-April, it was clear that America was headed to war; the only question was the timing. On April 20, McKinley ordered a naval blockade around Cuba, an act of war by international standards. Four days later, he officially declared war on Spain—with congressional approval, he backdated it to April 20, to make the blockade legal. And as part of the declaration, the president announced the formation of three volunteer regiments, to be composed of cowboys and others with similar skills, like horsemanship and marksmanship. That same day, Alger offered command of one of the regiments to Roosevelt.[35]

Roosevelt, to everyone's surprise, demurred. He said he was sure that, with a few months training, he could develop enough expertise in tactics, maneuvers, and military operations. But in a few months, the war could be over, and he'd have missed his chance. And so he told Alger that he would only take a lieutenant colonelcy—second in command—and that the colonel slot should go to his friend Wood. Alger agreed immediately, and so did Wood.

Though there were three "cowboy" regiments formed during the Spanish-American War, only one seemed to matter to the public: the First United States Volunteer Cavalry, led by the president's personal physician and the charismatic assistant secretary of the navy. Even before they all met at their training site, in San Antonio, Texas, the unit was famous. Pen-and-ink renderings of Wood and Roosevelt graced full-page spreads about the regiment in papers from New York to San Francisco. Roosevelt was already a rising star after his days reforming the police in New York, and his decision to resign from the Department of the Navy and risk his life to bring liberty abroad captured the imagination of a young America starving for passionate, visionary heroes. In a typical dispatch, the *Washington Times* noted "a continent-wide interest and expectancy over assistant secretary Theodore Roosevelt's regiment of mounted riflemen."[36]

Friends and acquaintances, however, thought Roosevelt was making a mistake. "I really think he is going mad," wrote Henry Adams. "Roosevelt is wild to fight and hack and hew . . . of course this ends his political career." Members of the Union League Club and the Republican Club, friends and allies who had tied themselves to his political future, traveled from New York to Washington to persuade him to stay.[37]

One evening, a few nights before Roosevelt left Washington, he was walking with his friend John R. Proctor through Lafayette Square. Proctor had already made the case against leaving, and he pressed it one last time.

"My friends have been making me very miserable with their appeals during the last few weeks," Roosevelt replied.

"Yes and I suppose I have been the worst of all."

"Yes," Roosevelt conceded. He then stopped in the path, put his hands on Proctor's shoulder, looked him in his eyes, and said, "Proctor, I am going to Cuba. I will take all the chances of meeting death by yellow fever, smallpox or by a Spanish bullet just to see the Spanish flag once on a battlefield."

Proctor could only look at his friend in wonder. "His earnestness was almost terrible," he recalled.[38]

Roosevelt's boss, Secretary Long, should have leapt at the chance to get rid of Roosevelt. But the old Bostonian saw a certain method in his assistant secretary's madness. "He has lost his head to this unutterable folly of deserting the post where he is of the most service and running off to ride a horse and, probably, brush mosquitos from his neck on the Florida sands," Long wrote in his diary. "And yet how absurd all this will sound, if by some turn of fortune he should accomplish some great thing and strike a very high mark!"[39]

CHAPTER 4

"THE DAYS OF '61 HAVE INDEED COME AGAIN"

O n the morning of May 7, 1898, in a ceremony in his office at the State, War and Navy Building, Theodore Roosevelt was sworn in as a lieutenant colonel in the United States Army. He had already turned in his letter of resignation, but he had promised Secretary Long that he would remain in place until his successor arrived, so he was still holed up at the Department of the Navy. But he spent most of his days in late April and early May 1898 getting ready to leave for war.[1]

Outside dozens of reporters, onlookers, and applicants thronged in to join Roosevelt's volunteer regiment. Just two weeks old and still more idea than fact, the First United States Volunteer Cavalry was already the hottest story in Washington. On Roosevelt's desk towered a looming stack of letters from more would-be enlistees. More sat on the floor—in all, he received twenty-seven sacks of applications to join the regiment in the first few weeks of the war.[2]

Roosevelt took no small satisfaction in having the spotlight cast on him and his fledgling regiment, and that afternoon he showed off for reporters. The letter-writing supplicants, he told a reporter from the New York *Sun*, "are too late." President McKinley and Secretary of War Alger had already determined that most of the spots would be selected by the governors of the New Mexico, Arizona, and Oklahoma territories. Any additional applicants needed to have exceptional skills, Roosevelt said. He picked up a letter at random from the pile, to demonstrate. It was, to his surprise, from the grandson of the man who led the mounted riflemen at the Battle of King's Mountain during the Revolutionary War. Changing tack, Roosevelt decided to make an exception. "If anyone should have the chance, it is surely he. I will keep that."[3]

When not considering applicants, Roosevelt was arranging for equipment for the regiment—there was no guarantee that the Army would send it to them otherwise. "I have been rushing about all day making the lives of the Quartermaster General and the Chief of the Bureau of Ordnance a burden to them," he wrote to Wood, who had already left for San Antonio. He arranged with a supply depot in St. Louis to send uniforms and clothing to Wood by May 9; he contacted a supplier in Philadelphia to send flags and guidons. "I feel nearly crazy at my inability to hurry these ordnance stores and equipments faster; but all I can do I am doing."[4]

Though Roosevelt insisted Wood was in charge, the public and the media knew who the star was. Reporters couldn't wait until the actual fighting to look for heroes, and Roosevelt—acclaimed writer, noted outdoorsman, rising politician, a man who seemed to be risking it all to serve his country—was an obvious choice. The fact that he would be leading a band of cowboys into battle made the story of Roosevelt and his regiment irresistible. Almost immediately, the search was on for a nickname. "The First United States Volunteer Cavalry" was a mouthful, after all, and nicknames were something of a fixation for the turn-of-the-century press. Alliteration was important; so was a sense of familiarity, words that would render something as militaristically bureaucratic as a "volunteer cavalry regiment" into something tough but familiar. Reporters tried out "Teddy's Terrors"; for a while it stuck. But people soon settled on the nickname of one of Buffalo Bill Cody's touring troupes: the Rough Riders, which itself was a slang term for cowboys. It was a nickname Roosevelt detested, at first. "Please do not call us Rough Riders," he begged a journalist. "The name evokes a hippodrome." But no one listened, and Roosevelt was press-savvy enough not to fight too hard. Later, he adopted the nickname as the title for his memoir of the war.[5]

The Rough Riders were the stuff of romantic, nostalgic speculation. Unlike Regular Army units, made up of career soldiers, or militias, whose ranks were homogenous collections of small-town residents, the volunteer regiment drew from wide swaths of Americans from the country's semi-settled West. The golden age of the lawless frontier was already in the past, but the public, especially in the East, wanted to believe it survived, and reporters and their readers imbued this new unit with all their fantasies about the Wild West. "The biggest job will be to keep the cowboys in order," predicted the *Scranton Tribune* on April 28. In the entire regiment, predicted the *New York Tribune*, "There will not be a man who is not capable of riding anything with horsehair and four legs on it, from a cross country Corinthian hunter to a bucking bronco, and in addition to this every one will be able to hit a tent peg three times out of five with a Colt .45 from the back of a horse going at a full run." Decades later, the historian Richard Hofstadter would describe the 1890s as equally obsessed with Walt Whitman and Rudyard Kipling, the democrat and the militarist; in the Rough Riders, Americans found both in equal measure.[6]

The public adored the Rough Riders for their nostalgic appeal; the War Department wanted them because they filled a gaping hole. The American Army that Wood and Roosevelt joined was barely an army at all, and in the spring of 1898, with war declared, the department was forced to build one almost from scratch. Perhaps because of the terrible scope of the Civil War and the cruel ferocity of the Indian Wars, and because of the immense American military complex of the twentieth century, it is easy to imagine that the United States has always had a large, well-ordered Army and Navy. In fact, for much of the first 125 years of American independence, the country not only lacked a sizable fighting force, but it actively rejected the idea of maintaining one.

The history of the American military in the nineteenth century is largely defined by the tension between a voluntaristic, "Jacksonian" or "Jeffersonian" view, one that feared standing armies and relied on the inherent toughness of the American citizen, and a "Hamiltonian" view that promoted a standing army as a bulwark against enemies and a tool to project power abroad. The Jacksonians, inspired by the frontier fighting ethos of Andrew Jackson, believed that in times of crisis, private citizens would come together to fight, and that the rugged individualism bred into them by American society would make up for their lack of martial training. The Hamiltonians—inspired by the centralized-government visions of Alexander Hamilton, and of which Theodore Roosevelt was a leading voice—believed that the sort of military unpreparedness advocated by the Jacksonians made war more likely, and that especially in an industrializing age, with machine guns and motorized vehicles making wars shorter and bloodier, there wasn't time to raise and train an army every time war clouds gathered.[7]

For much of the nineteenth century, it wasn't even a contest—the Jacksonians prevailed. Standing armies, they believed, necessitated large, powerful, intrusive governments; and besides, America was isolated from the great-power conflicts that justified Europe's enormous armies. As a result, the American military complex of the nineteenth century was provisional, even haphazard, kept small by congressional decree and popular opposition. When wars did happen, the War Department would rush to recruit men to fill empty regiments, units that existed only on paper; when the fighting was done, they were mustered out, and the Army shrank. On the eve of the Civil War, there were just 16,367 men in the federal army. When it ended, there were over one million. Within a few years, the Department of War shrank the Army back toward its antebellum size, to just 50,000 soldiers.[8]

At first, the post–Civil War Army had a lot to do: deploy along the Southwestern border as a show of force against imperial French forces that had occupied Mexico, enforce Reconstruction in the postwar South, and fight countless small campaigns against Indians across the West. But within a decade the French were out of Mexico, Reconstruction was cut short, and federal forces began to gain the upper hand against Native Americans in the West. By the second half of the 1870s, the Army had lost much of its reason for being, and critics began calling for further cuts. Occasionally, the Army was deployed against striking workers, but after soldiers shot and killed five strikers in three different protests across the Midwest in the 1870s, active-duty troops were rarely used domestically. That left them with nothing to do but sit in one of hundreds of small outposts scattered across the West, or in cushy bureaucratic posts in Washington. In 1896 Johnson Hagood, a West Point–educated officer, said that serving in the military was "like a well trained fire department with no fires, and the firemen sitting out in front of the fire house playing checkers."[9]

It wasn't just that the Army, on the eve of the Spanish-American War, was smaller than it had been thirty years earlier; it had largely forgotten how to fight a war at all. During the Civil War, the military had operated on a vast organizational scale, with regiments of up to 800 men forming the building blocks of an integrated hierarchy of brigades (2,600 men), divisions (8,000 men), corps (26,000 men), and armies (80,000 men). Most regiments were composed of infantry, but they fought alongside cavalry regiments and artillery detachments in tightly choreographed combined operations. With the end of the war and the shrinking of the military, most regiments went back to being paper organizations, and those that remained (usually at half strength) were spread out across the frontier, fighting the Indian Wars or simply staffing far-flung outposts. Combined-arms tactics, the basics of an army's fighting doctrine, in which infantry worked with cavalry and artillery, became something taught at West Point and then quickly forgotten. And any semblance of cooperation between the Navy and the Army—at the time, two independent cabinet-level departments (the Marines being a small, specialized unit within the Navy)—faded, leaving the two arms of the American military machine to fight each other for the ever-smaller slices of funding distributed by Congress each year. By the time of the Spanish-American War, there were officers with decades of experience who had never participated in exercises or operations involving units larger than a regiment—and even rarely at that size.

The declining importance of the Army coincided with declining support from politicians and the public. For many Americans in the post–Civil War era, the sight of a man in uniform was a reminder of the horrors of combat, and a ready instrument that might lead some reckless politician to start another. Conservatives and business leaders believed that a large army was a requisite step toward a large government. Southerners hated the federal army because it was the instrument that had won the Civil War, and even more because it had enforced the terms of Southern capitulation—Reconstruction and civil rights for formerly enslaved people. In the event of a war, all of these constituencies held fast to their belief that the Jacksonian ideal of Americans as a ready-made fighting force, honed by rough living and motivated to fight for more than just a paycheck. They organized as local and state militias, civilians committed to fighting if called on, but nothing more. This was a virtue: Such volunteers, said one congressman, "are no mere hirelings, no mercenaries; they fight for the defense of home and country, for principle and glory, for liberty and the rights of man . . . they do not menace our liberties or the stability of our free institutions."[10]

In the 1870s, Congress limited the size of the Army to about 26,000 enlisted men and 2,000 officers, and steadily reduced its budget to just $40 million, barely enough to maintain the web of isolated coastal and Western outposts where most of the Army's men whiled away their careers. From time to time, congressmen would call for the abolition of the Army entirely. Between the end of the Civil War and the beginning of the Spanish-American War, the number of Americans doubled, but the size of the American Army shrank, as did the average soldier's pay. Only after war was declared against Spain did Congress authorize an increase in the size of the Regular Army— not counting volunteers—to 61,000, with a 20 percent wartime pay increase. But even then, the money that came with it was allocated mostly for coastal defense, and the additional troops were limited to a two-year period. In 1898, America had an army, but it could not fight a war.[11]

At first, President McKinley's plan for executing the Spanish-American War left the Army almost completely out of the picture. Perhaps because the only real thinking about a potential war with Spain had been undertaken by the staff at the Naval War College, the initial strategy relied almost entirely on America's Atlantic and Pacific-based naval squadrons. Even before he officially declared war, President McKinley ordered a blockade around Cuba and Puerto Rico, while Theodore Roosevelt, in one of his last official acts as the assistant secretary of the navy, ordered Commodore Dewey, whose Asiatic Squadron sat ready at Hong Kong, to steam immediately for Manila, the capital of Spain's vast colony in the Philippine Islands and home to its Pacific fleet. Dewey was to neutralize the Spanish fleet in the Pacific, so that it couldn't attack the American west coast, while the blockade of Cuba and the Philippines did the bloodless work of compelling the strapped, starving Spanish colonial government to sue for peace on the island. The Army would be sent to man the coastal defenses, and to be ready to occupy Cuba and Puerto Rico should Spain agree to leave altogether.

Dewey arrived at the Philippines on April 30, entered Manila Bay, and at 5:41 the next morning attacked the Spanish ships lying at anchor around the harbor. Within hours eight of Spain's thirteen ships had been sunk, and seventy-seven of its sailors killed; the Americans lost not a single ship, and suffered only one fatality, when an overheated sailor died of a heart attack. Dewey's victory sealed the fate of Spain in the Pacific, and gave a boost of confidence to an American war machine still gearing up. Whatever doubts America might have had about its ability to fight a war against Spain were dashed that morning in Manila Bay. Dewey became an overnight war hero of nearly unprecedented proportions: Without asking his permission—let alone his political leanings—both parties began talking about making him their candidate for president in 1900.[12]

Dewey's overnight success in the Philippines also changed the expectations that the American public and its leaders had for the war. Above all, it put pressure on the Atlantic Squadron to achieve something similar in Cuba and Puerto Rico—and on the Army to achieve its own spectacular military victory. Tens of thousands of volunteers were already coursing into militia armories and federal recruiting centers, and from there to one of the many staging camps being prepared around the Southeast—even though, at the time, no one knew what to do with them. And so, with the American public excited about the war and bloodthirsty for more victories like Dewey's in Manila, an immediate invasion of Cuba was fast becoming a fait accompli without a raison d'être.

The job of planning an invasion of Cuba fell to Russell Alger, William McKinley's gray-goateed secretary of war. Like many men in the president's cabinet, including McKinley himself, Alger had served with distinction in the Civil War—he enlisted as a private, in 1861, and in June 1865 was made a brevet (i.e., honorary) major general, even though he had already left the Army. He went on to make millions in timber and served as governor of Michigan from 1885 to

1887. Alger clearly had a head for business and politics; beyond his youthful experience, it was unclear whether he knew anything about war.

It was a question that didn't seem to concern McKinley—or Alger, for that matter. When war broke out, he, like the president, imagined that "a million men will spring to arms overnight," just like they did in 1861, forgetting the death and destruction that came from throwing regiments of half-trained farm boys against each other at Antietam and Shiloh. Against all evidence, Alger guaranteed the president that the Army could put 40,000 men in Cuba within ten days of declaring war.[13]

This was going to be a problem. It was true that modern armies could mobilize and move with lightning speed; in 1870, at the outset of the Franco-Prussian War, it took the Kingdom of Prussia and the North German Confederation less than three weeks to move nearly half a million men to the French border. But America was not Prussia. Not only was the entire Regular Army short of Russell's promised deployment by 14,000 men—assuming every single soldier was put on a boat to Cuba—but there was no mechanism for organizing and training additional troops. The Army lacked a general staff to plan the war, and it lacked the infrastructure to move thousands of men across the sea to land on a hostile shore. And no soldier under fifty years old had participated in a large, set-piece battle, with combined arms—coordinated cavalry, infantry, and artillery—against a similarly armed and prepared enemy. Alger was, simply, delusional.

But his delusion was instructive. Like many veterans of the Civil War, Alger had faith in the Jacksonian ideal of citizen-soldiers; he believed that pluck and patriotism would make up for a lack of planning and preparedness. In one sense, he was quickly proved right: Most Americans may not have countenanced a standing army, but countless men relished the chance to volunteer when the war with Spain began. The enthusiasm Roosevelt encountered around the Rough Riders was also a general phenomenon. McKinley, in his declaration of war, had called for 125,000 men; within weeks more than 100,000 had volunteered, a number that eventually rose to over a million. Boys just short of manhood begged their fathers to sign papers allowing them to join the fight; Civil War veterans pulled out their old uniforms and marched to their local recruiting stations.

In New York, Theodore Miller could hardly concentrate on his legal studies with all the parades and patriotism he encountered in the Manhattan streets. "Have been working pretty hard these two weeks in preparation for my exams but the war business has pushed everything else out of my head so I am terribly afraid I will flunk," he wrote to his sister, Mina Edison, in New Jersey. "I have the whole year's work hanging on a few hours."[14]

The nation's capital was similarly alive with activity, preparing for battle. McKinley had a war room installed on the second floor of the Executive Mansion, with maps of Cuba and the Philippines, and telegraph lines snaking across the carpet. Would-be officers flocked to the city, trying to buy favor with politicians who might win them a commission in their home state guard. Red, white, and blue bunting hung from every second-story railing. "The days of '61 have indeed come again in Washington," noted the New York *Sun*. William Allen White, who wielded outsize influence in national affairs as the editor of the Emporia, Kansas, *Gazette*, noticed the same fervor in the small towns on the plains. "In April, everywhere over this good, fair land, flags were flying," he wrote. "Trains carrying soldiers were hurrying . . . to the Southland, and . . . little children on fences greeted the soldiers with flapping scarfs."[15]

The reality of the soldiering life hit the volunteers soon enough. "During the early weeks of May," White went on, "many pert young militiamen came up from the inland towns who fancied they were soldiers because they could get across a level piece of ground without stepping on their own feet. But after the first four or five hours of hard work, the proud lines of the guardsmen began to sag and then to cave in." Thousands of would-be soldiers quickly dropped out, or were cut. By the end of June, 127,798 men had applied for enlistment, but only 29,521 had been accepted—meaning that 77 percent were deemed unfit to serve, an astounding rate for a country that prided itself on being able to muster citizen-soldiers in a time of need. The result was chaos: an undernourished, insular military was suddenly overrun with men who seemed more interested in playing soldier than being one.[16]

There was a further complication. The United States actually had many armies, each independent of the other: a single federal force, made up of career officers and enlisted men, and dozens of state militias and territorial defense forces. The militias, the forerunners of today's National Guard, were comprised of part-time, volunteer soldiers and officers, and existed at varying levels of preparedness and seriousness. State militias were supposed to provide the bulk of an American army, should the need arise. But by the 1880s most militias had devolved into social and professional clubs. In several states, they existed in name only; in 1898, only a quarter of the country's militiamen had any training whatsoever. What mattered to the members, and their communities, was the idea behind the militias: locally organized bands of citizens who saw in their own martial aspirations, however casual or pedestrian, a reflection of the Minutemen, the Green Mountain Boys, the Volunteers of '48, the Spirit of '61.

Though hundreds of thousands of men tried to join the fight against Spain, most wanted to do it within the familiar confines of their state militia, alongside and under the command of their neighbors. Joining a federal army, especially if it meant serving under an unfamiliar, West Point–trained officer, was simply unacceptable. In the spring of 1898, the state militias and their allies in Washington (many congressmen were active militia members as well) defeated a bill by Representative John A. T. Hull of Iowa to bolster the size of the federal army at the expense of state militias. Eventually, Congress and the War Department reached a compromise with the states: The militias would gather the volunteers, who would be sworn in as federal troops, but then be allowed to serve within state-designated regiments (the 71st New York Infantry, for example), with their own commanders.[17]

It was an imperfect solution to one problem; actually planning the campaign was another. McKinley had made a fundamental mistake: He had gone to war without a clear sense of what he was willing to do to achieve victory. He had declared war as a "neutral" force, to bring an end to the fighting without favoring Spain or the rebels. But realistically, that could only happen if Spain was forced off the island—and in any case, Congress was intent on achieving Cuban independence. If the blockade failed to bring Spain to the negotiating table, how quickly would McKinley be willing to invade? How many casualties was he prepared to accept? Would an invasion force merely support the Cuban rebels, or operate on its own? And when would it embark—immediately, before the rainy season brought misery and disease to the island, or much later in the year, when the climate was more amenable, but by which time the Spanish may have greatly reinforced their position?

McKinley lacked the answers, and the staff to come up with them. While the Department of the Navy, starting in the 1880s, had built an intellectual infrastructure to address these sorts of questions—by the time war broke out with Spain, the Naval War College had churned out scores of war plans dealing with every imaginable contingency—the Army had nothing of the kind. Instead, McKinley had to make do with his war room in the Executive Mansion and a small circle of logistically minded officers in the War Department next door. Those men—and lucky for McKinley they were smart, diligent men, like Henry Corbin, the adjutant general, the army's chief administrative officer—could not make up for the organizational chaos that spread out below them. The War Department did not even know, beyond a general sense, what Cuba looked like. Of course planners had access to maps, the same as the public—but as to the disposition of Spanish troops and rebel forces, or even street plans of smaller cities, they were at a loss, "no better informed than if their objective point had been the planet Mars," wrote the journalist Stephen Bonsal.[18]

During the first few weeks after Dewey's victory, a modest plan for Cuba emerged: With the blockade keeping out Spanish reinforcements, the Army would land a small force, maybe 5,000 men, in the center of Cuba, most likely on the southern coast of Las Tunas province, to bring supplies to the rebels and give the Spanish a taste of what might come if they refused to negotiate. Meanwhile, the blockade would do the real work, strangling the Spanish into submission. To command the landing force, the president chose General William Rufus Shafter.[19]

Long of body and short of legs, with blue eyes and an enormous waist, Shafter cut a much different figure from men like Nelson Miles, the commanding general of the army, or Leonard Wood, though all three had made their reputations as Indian fighters. He was born in Michigan, the son of a surveyor; he was a good student, but also a bully. He enlisted at the outbreak of the Civil War and was wounded in action at the Battle of Seven Pines, for which he received the Medal of Honor; later, he was put in charge of a "colored" (i.e., segregated) regiment. He was roundly disliked, but his men respected him because, unlike most white officers, Shafter did not treat black troops any worse than he did white troops—even if, in both cases, he treated them quite poorly.[20]

By the end of the war Shafter had developed a reputation as an effective regimental commander; afterward he was shipped to Texas to man the border against the French and, later, to police the Indian tribes the Army was in the process of subduing. Like Miles and Henry Lawton, rising-star officers he got to know in those years, he was an aggressive fighter who punished his troops with long marches through hot deserts, on several occasions pursuing bands of Native Americans into Mexico—he gained his nickname, Pecos Bill, for a long campaign he led near the Pecos River, in southeast New Mexico.[21] Later, he led expeditions to map the Southwest, an endeavor that paid off well for the military and for the Shafter family bank account—along his trips he kept track of potential mining spots, and when he returned to a city afterward he would invest in mining companies he had tipped off to the locations.[22]

Despite a career of solid achievements and adventures, time did not treat Shafter well. While life near the border seemed to harden men like Wood and Lawton, to chisel away at their bodies until they were made of oak, it softened Shafter, and greatly enlarged him— already a big man, by 1898 he weighed 300 pounds. He suffered from varicose veins and gout, for which he wore medical stockings. It didn't help that after living for so long in the Southwest, he transferred to a sedentary post in California. "Shafter couldn't walk two miles an hour, he was just beastly obese," wrote one reporter. Almost every criticism, from his fellow officers, foreign observers, or journalists, begins with and is seeded throughout with ad hominem attacks on his girth: "Gross beyond belief, over 25 stone in weight, and he had not glimpsed his feet for years," wrote Arthur Lee, a British Army attaché who was allowed to follow Shafter's army into Cuba.

Such ugly criticism might have gone unspoken had Shafter not been such a questionable choice to lead the invasion of Cuba—whatever he had achieved in the Indian Wars, he seemed singularly unprepared to lead tens of thousands of men in the invasion of a tropical island.[23]

While McKinley and Alger continued to cast about for a plan for Cuba, Roosevelt and Wood organized their regiment. Roosevelt, long an advocate for military preparedness, was stunned by what he found once he entered the ranks that spring. A few days before the declaration of war against Spain, he had visited a "top line general," expecting to find him working without sleep to catch up. Instead, he was holding a fashion show: Enlisted men paraded in front of him, demonstrating different variants of an updated uniform design. He motioned for Roosevelt to approach, and asked what he thought about the breast pocket placement. While Roosevelt stood there, stunned, an aide to the general recommended he get a uniform with black top boots, "explaining that they were very effective on hotel piazzas and in parlors." Roosevelt left, disgusted, and never purchased a dress uniform.[24]

Another officer tried to sell Roosevelt on the primacy of black powder over smokeless powder, despite the fact that virtually every modern army in the world, including Spain's, used smokeless powder. The officer noted, "with paternal indulgence," that no one knew what smokeless powder would do, and that the smoke would in fact conceal them from the enemy. The accuracy, or insanity, of the officer's arguments aside, Roosevelt knew that having smokeless powder, which was standard among the Regular Army regiments, would be vital in getting the Rough Riders considered as functionally equal to them—and therefore more likely to be sent to Cuba.[25]

Yet another time, a "very wealthy and influential man" called on Roosevelt to protest the Army's choice of Tampa as its embarkation point for sailing to Cuba, and to ask for it to be moved to another city in Florida. He made no point of concealing his motive: His railroad was under contract to haul soldiers and equipment for the Army, and he had investments elsewhere in the state—it was only fair, then, that he should get a cut of the money sloshing around. Such experiences made Roosevelt even more convinced of the importance of his new regiment—not just as a vehicle for his own glory, but as a model for the rest of the country. In the face of an inadequate, unprepared army and an energetic but hapless population, the Rough Riders stood out as an ideal for a newly empowered nation as it found its war footing, a bridge between the Jacksonian volunteerism of the nineteenth century and the Hamiltonian, if not Prussian, professional army that the country would need in order to compete on the world stage. They offered a country grappling with the implications and requirements of its new global power a vision for what that power might look like—spurs and all.[26]

Roosevelt and Wood knew that whatever chance they had of being sent to Cuba depended on being ready to fight alongside, and at the level of, fully trained soldiers in the federal army. With perhaps only a few weeks to prepare, they had to get creative, and select men who already had the skills needed to fight—even if they didn't know it. In early May Roosevelt learned that his regiment's size, the standard 800 enlistees and officers, had been expanded by about 200 slots above the allotments for Arizona, New Mexico, and Oklahoma, positions he could now fill with his own recruits. He moved immediately. He wrote a letter to Fred Herrig, the Alsatian immigrant whom he had gotten to know as a guide and tracker in the Dakotas, insisting that he drop everything and head to San Antonio (he did). Even before he learned of the additional spots, Roosevelt had written to his friend William Austin Wadsworth, asking if he could raise 100 men from New York's best clubs and New England's best colleges, assuming, not unreasonably, that these men would come with strong résumés as athletes and outdoorsmen. He also wrote to four current and former police officers he had known in New York, and asked them to join (all did; one died in combat).[27]

His most important letter went to Guy Murchie, in Cambridge, Massachusetts, asking him to raise a contingent from Harvard, Roosevelt's alma mater. Murchie had graduated from Harvard in 1892, and Harvard Law School after that, but remained on campus as a part-time football coach. He was a well-known figure around Cambridge, and he knew which students and recent graduates to tap for war. Roosevelt told him to gather a dozen men and head to Washington to be enlisted. Murchie did even better: Thanks to him forty-one men, about 5 percent of the entire regiment, were either students at or graduates of Harvard.[28]

J. Ogden Wells, one of Murchie's recruits, recalled the secrecy with which the Harvard men prepared to leave Cambridge. Murchie insisted no one could know about his recruiting drive, for fear that he would be deluged with the same scale of requests that had encumbered Roosevelt in Washington. They left Boston at midnight on May 2, with no one to see them off, and arrived in Washington the following afternoon. "Signs of the approaching war were to be seen on every hand," Wells wrote in his diary. "Officers in bright uniforms were to be seen constantly, while artillery now and then tumbled through the peaceful streets." The next morning they called on Roosevelt. He gave them a long speech and swore them in "for two years unless sooner discharged." Then their new lieutenant colonel told them to find their way west, and report to Colonel Wood, already in San Antonio, by May 9.[29]

Roosevelt also continued to consider individual applicants, and while he rejected almost everyone, a few got through. One who made it was a young Princeton graduate named James Robb Church, who had been trained as a doctor but had left medicine to work as a merchant mariner and miner in Alaska. During one of his adventures he had encountered Leonard Wood, and when the war was declared he wrote him for an introduction to Roosevelt. Wood told him to come along, and to head to Roosevelt's house on N Street, in Washington, to get a commission.

When Church arrived, he gave a servant his card, and waited. Eventually Roosevelt appeared. He looked at the card, then at Church, then back at the card.

"Do I know you?" Roosevelt asked.

Church rose from his seat and explained that Wood had already agreed to make him an assistant surgeon in the regiment. Roosevelt looked at him skeptically. Church handed him Wood's telegram.

Roosevelt lit up. "Well that makes it perfectly all right," he declared. "I am very glad that you are to go with us."

Like so many men before and after him, Church was astounded by Roosevelt's willingness to take him on at his friend's word. It was part of what made Roosevelt a great leader: his ability to identify people whose judgment he could rely on, then use that judgment to make quick decisions. "With a careful reading of a telegram and an inspection of me, he made his decision at once," Church told an interviewer years later.[30]

Roosevelt had other encounters with would-be Rough Riders. As he was leaving the Navy Department one day, a boy, not seventeen years old, accosted him on the building's front steps. His name was Jesse Langdon, and he had hoboed his way from Minnesota for a chance to join the unit. He had met Roosevelt as a boy, in fact; his father, a veterinarian in the Dakotas, had taken care of some of Roosevelt's sick cattle during his ranching phase. Roosevelt, impressed by the boy's pluck, looked young Langdon up and down, as he had Church, and asked if he could ride a horse.

"I can ride anything with hair," Langdon replied.

Roosevelt chuckled, and told him that if he could make it on his own to San Antonio, then he would make sure he was mustered into the Rough Riders, even if he was obviously too young by Army standards.[31]

If Roosevelt worried about the other two volunteer cavalry regiments being assembled, he never let on. Neither received anywhere close to the public attention basted upon the Rough Riders, and neither was anywhere close to their state of readiness. They seemed more like some of the state militias—interested in martial demonstrations more as an end in themselves than as practice for war. "There was another cavalry organization whose commander was at the War Department about this time, and we had been eyeing him with as much alertness as a rival," Roosevelt later wrote. "One day I asked him what his plans were about arming and drilling his troops, who were of precisely the type of our own men. He answered that he expected 'to give each of the boys two revolvers and a lariat, and then just turn them loose.' I reported the conversation to Wood, with the remark that we might feel ourselves safe from rivalry in that quarter; and safe we were."[32]

Roosevelt's success in standing up his regiment made him proud, but also worried. Things were moving fast. He wrote to Wood, pleading with him not to leave without him. At other times, he seemed to write off the possibility of seeing combat completely. "We're all fake heroes," he wrote to his sister Anna on May 8. "We sha'n't see any fighting to speak of." But he plugged away, swearing in new troops, shuffling papers, and dreaming of Cuba.[33]

Finally, on May 12, his desk duties squared away, Roosevelt was ready to go to San Antonio. Before he left, he ordered a uniform from Brooks Brothers—at the time, officers had to pay for their own clothing, and Brooks Brothers was famous for supplying uniforms and other matériel to the Union Army during the Civil War. Determined not to let his poor eyesight limit his readiness for combat, he bought a dozen pairs of pince-nez, and had pockets for them sewn into his clothing, even his hat. He made an appointment at a photography studio and had several portraits of himself taken; in his pose and demeanor he was every bit the military man he had longed to be. And then Roosevelt was off. He and his valet, Edward Marshall, an African American veteran of the segregated 10th Cavalry Regiment, left Washington on a 10 p.m. train.[34]

CHAPTER 5

"THIS UNTAILOR-MADE ROUGHNESS"

O n the afternoon of May 5, a reporter for the *Daily Light*, one of San Antonio's two newspapers, took a streetcar a few miles north from the center of town to Fort Sam Houston. There he found a tall, thin man with a thick brush mustache and sandy hair standing amid a herd of horses. He "looked every inch a soldier and the man who could lead a regiment to victory, but he did not look like a Westerner very much," the reporter wrote. The man was not, in fact, a Westerner, at least by birth. Leonard Wood—Colonel Wood, now, of the First United States Volunteer Cavalry Regiment—had arrived the day before, alone, and stayed at the Menger Hotel downtown. It was the last night he would spend in a proper bed for at least five months.[1]

Wood rose early and wasted no time getting to the fort; there was work to be done. It was a Thursday, and the first wave of volunteers for his regiment would arrive in two days, from Arizona. He had a long to-do list for the camp: establish sanitation protocol for nearly 1,000 men; write a daily schedule, from reveille to taps; find some way to get his men clothing and equipment; and figure out how to process them as they arrived, for they would be coming from all over the Southwest and beyond, often in large contingents, in other cases man by man.

But first came the horses. This was to be a cavalry regiment, so horses had to be purchased. Each man would need a mount; combined with several score of work horses, the regiment would require at least 1,200. Wood's demands were specific. In an advertisement sent to local ranches, he insisted that they stand "fourteen three to fifteen two hands high," be "four to eight years old," and weigh between 850 and 1,050 pounds. Wood did not yet have a uniform, so he stood surrounded by dust-kicking horses in a blue suit and a beat-up campaign hat, barking orders to the soldiers and horse traders around him. Just a few weeks earlier, he had been tending to the first lady and hobnobbing with politicians and the sort of preening-peacock officers who strutted around the Executive Mansion. In Texas, amid the dust and the soldiers and the horses, he was back in his element. The next few weeks would show whether he could make something of it.[2]

Wood's entire life had prepared him for this moment. The descendant of four passengers on the *Mayflower*, he was born in 1860, two years after Roosevelt, and grew up in Pocasset, Massachusetts, a whaling village at the armpit of Cape Cod. He sailed and swam and fished, his already fair hair sun-bleached to a snowy blond, which he kept closely trimmed above his wind-burned cheeks and gray-blue eyes. A reserved, even shy young man, Wood was a reader as well as an outdoorsman; one friend recalled him fishing with one hand and reading Plutarch's *Lives* with the other, the pages held down with stones. He had planned to attend the Naval Academy in Annapolis, but the beleaguered military, even the Navy, was a poor career choice for an ambitious young man in the late 1870s. His father's death in 1880, when Wood was twenty, sealed it: He would have to make enough money to support himself and his now widowed mother. He set aside his martial aspirations and went directly into Harvard Medical School (at the time, an undergraduate degree was optional).[3]

After a few unhappy years as a civilian doctor, in early 1885 Wood went to New York to take the exam for Army surgeons. He came in second out of fifty-nine, but passing the exam didn't guarantee a job; in fact there were none. The only opening was as a civilian contractor in the Southwest, where a long-simmering conflict with an Apache leader named Geronimo had broken out into open warfare, and doctors were needed to treat the wounded and the sun-struck. Wood didn't think twice. Two weeks later, he reported to Fort Whipple, an outpost near Prescott, Arizona.[4]

By the mid-1880s, the Indian Wars were all but over, with federal troops in command of vast expanses of land that less than a decade before, and for hundreds of years before that, had been the landscape of overlapping and shifting Indian nations. But Arizona, decades away from statehood, was still the frontier, where settlers and soldiers clashed with native tribes, and in particular the Chiricahua band of Apaches. In May 1885, two of their leaders, Natchez and Geronimo, assembled a group of warriors and their families and fled the San Carlos Reservation, where they had been restricted. A few weeks later, the *Silver City Enterprise*, in New Mexico, reported that thirty-three settlers had been killed by the war party. Geronimo and his band moved quietly, swiftly, crossing the border into Mexico and camping in the Sierra Madre, forbidding terrain they knew intimately. For almost a year, they eluded both Mexican forces and the United States Army.[5]

From Fort Whipple, Wood was forwarded to Fort Huachuca, deep in Indian Territory. He arrived just in time. The campaign against Geronimo had been taken over by General Nelson Miles, a decorated Civil War veteran—he was commandant of Fortress Monroe while Jefferson Davis was a prisoner there—who later made his reputation as a cruel and effective Indian fighter. Miles, in turn, gave day-to-day command to Captain Henry Lawton, another Civil War veteran; he was to set off immediately to find and capture if possible, and kill if necessary, Geronimo. Lawton told Wood to be ready to go the next morning, to act as his troop surgeon. Go where, he could not yet say.[6]

They did their best to track the raiders, but the Apaches on foot seemed to outpace—and outsmart—the soldiers on horseback. "A frightful country," Wood wrote in his diary. "The whole mountains are on fire . . . evidently set by the Indians." For weeks, they followed the Apaches less by their tracks than by where they struck—this settlement, that ranch, like vengeful ghosts they moved across the desert terrain. Wood went on foot, up ahead with the scouts most of the time.[7]

Eventually Lawton's dogged pursuit, and the intercession of a young officer, Charles Gatewood, who spoke some Apache, persuaded Geronimo and his men to surrender. Geronimo's campaign was one of the last great showings of Native American strength—they had not lost a single man to combat, though he and his party had killed hundreds. In a coincidence, Geronimo was taken to Fort Sam Houston, in San Antonio, and then sent to a series of prisons across the South before ending up in Oklahoma. In 1905 he pleaded with Theodore Roosevelt, by then in the White House, to be allowed to return to Arizona. The president refused. Geronimo died in Oklahoma in 1909, of pneumonia. Wood, for his effort in the fifteen-month campaign, received the Medal of Honor.[8]

The next several years took Wood around the country; prized for his combination of combat experience and medical knowledge, he went to the Presidio in San Francisco in 1889, then to Fort McPherson, outside Atlanta; finally, in 1895, Miles became the commanding general of the Army—the highest possible rank for a uniformed officer—and he arranged for Wood to come with him to Washington. In short order, he was caring for the president and his family as well as Miles. Two years later, he met Theodore Roosevelt.[9]

When the opportunity came to lead the Rough Riders, Wood wasted no time. Like Roosevelt, he understood what the war might actually involve—a lot of naval activity, with perhaps a brief show of force by the Army; Spain could very well surrender before troops even landed in Cuba. If they had any chance of seeing action, he and Roosevelt had to act fast. First, they needed men, and more importantly good officers to lead them. From his time out West, Wood knew a long list of veterans who could handle a regiment of green recruits. Within twenty-four hours of receiving his commission, he sent telegrams to several of them—Alexander Brodie (who had already volunteered to raise his own cowboy regiment), George Dunn, Allyn Capron—asking them to raise troops and join him in San Antonio.

Before leaving Washington, Wood stopped to see President McKinley. He understood that as the commander of a volunteer regiment, he would receive either the best equipment and treatment, or the worst—depending entirely on how many levers he managed to pull—and that the difference would decide whether they went to Cuba or languished in a dusty, hot staging camp somewhere stateside. He implored McKinley to make sure the Rough Riders received the best weaponry—Krag-Jorgensen .30-40 rifles, firing cartridges with smokeless powder, and the Model 1873 Colt Single Action Army revolver. These were the weapons the regular soldiers used; the state militias got old black-powder Springfields and Remingtons. His supplies secured, he hurried to San Antonio before the men arrived.[10]

Wood picked San Antonio for several reasons. It was close to Fort Sam Houston, across town and a good source of horses and supplies, should they need them (and it was good thinking, because they did). It was not far from the port of Galveston, from which they could easily embark for Cuba. And it was centrally located in the country, as good a place as any to receive and train hundreds of men arriving from all over to form themselves into a single fighting unit.

San Antonio was appropriate for symbolic and historic reasons as well, as it marked a high-water mark of Spain's holdings in the Western Hemisphere. By the start of the eighteenth century, the Spanish were firmly in control of Mexico—which, at the time, extended north to Colorado—but the French were beginning to expand westward from their colonial holdings along the southern stretch of the Mississippi River. To block their advance, in 1718 the Spanish chose a sandy plain alongside a lazy river in the northeastern province of Tejas to build a presidio and a string of missions; it quickly grew to be the largest settlement above the Río Bravo (the Mexican name for the Rio Grande). To the east, the settlement allowed the Spanish to project power against the French; to the west, it served as a check against incursions by Indian tribes, in particular the Apache. But the French threat receded after the French and Indian War decimated their North American territory, and therefore so did Spanish interest. For years the settlement languished. But soon in the place of Spanish soldiers arrived waves of Anglo settlers, invited by the Spanish to serve as a buffer between the Mexican heartland and another threat, the aggressive Apache and Comanche tribes to the north and west. The Spanish got more than they'd desired: By the 1830s the Anglos far outnumbered the Spanish, Mexican, and native population, and were agitating for independence.[11]

In 1821 Mexico gained its independence from Spanish rule, and fourteen years later Texas revolted against Mexican rule—a short but bloody fight punctuated by the siege at the Alamo, in central San Antonio. Once Texas split from Mexico and joined the United States, a new wave of immigrants arrived, this time from Germany, so many that by the eve of the American Civil War German had superseded Spanish as San Antonio's lingua franca (English being a distant third). Many of San Antonio's significant post-Spanish buildings were designed by Germans, including the Menger Hotel, whose bar, modeled on the pub inside Britain's House of Lords, was to become a favorite spot for the Rough Riders.[12]

San Antonio remained isolated until 1877 and the arrival of a rail connection from Houston; after that its population soared. By the time Wood arrived, it was not only the largest city in the entire Southwest, but a place whose history served as a perfect symbol for the war that he and his regiment were about to enter: from the rise and fall of Spain to the westward expansion of American civilization to the emergence, after the Civil War, of a multicultural nation struggling to find some semblance of unity as it assumed the mantle of global power.

Since Fort Sam Houston was already occupied by an infantry regiment, Wood chose to make camp at the city fairgrounds, 600 acres of open, dusty plain dotted with hackberry, pecan, cottonwood, and sycamore trees. In the center stood a massive, high-ceilinged exhibition hall, a Moorish fantasia peaked with garish onion domes. Just after dawn on May 7, Wood went to the small gate, or sally port, in the fencing that surrounded the fairgrounds. The first of his regiment, from Arizona, was about to arrive.[13]

The zeal with which Arizona rushed into war with Spain was typical of Western states and territories eager to prove themselves a part of the rapidly consolidating American republic. The territory's governor, Myron McCord, had been pressuring McKinley and Alger for permission to form a "cowboy regiment" of his own for two months; he was certain he could raise 1,000 men from Arizona alone, and he probably wasn't wrong. In the decade since Wood had tracked Geronimo in the territory's western expanses, Arizona's towns had begun to fill up and turn into small cities, full of men who had settled there after the fighting or were too young to have taken part. The Cuban Junta was active here as well; the week after the *Maine* disaster, two Cuban agents had visited Prescott, asking for support. Hundreds turned out to hear them.[14]

The War Department refused McCord's offer; worse, it said he could only send 170 men. But it offered the governor a consolation prize: He could choose the senior regimental major, in effect the

Rough Riders' third in command. That was an easy call—McCord chose Alexander Brodie, the Army veteran whom Wood had already been eying. A New York–born West Point graduate who, like Wood, had fought the Apaches, Brodie had then left the Army and settled down in Prescott, where he tried his hand at private life as a supervisor at a water storage company, then as county recorder and a mine manager. But his wife died in childbirth, and so did his child, and Brodie was eager to leave behind his pain by venturing to Cuba.[15]

The Arizona men left Prescott on May 4, riding in four passenger coaches. To see them off, the Prescott Brass Band played and Governor McCord gave a long and windy address. Members of the Women's Relief Corps of Phoenix and the women's auxiliary of the state's chapter of the Grand Army of the Republic gave them a huge, homemade American flag. Civil War veterans, the fire department, and scores of excited young boys swelled the crowd. The train cars were stocked with $500 in donated food fit for snacking along the ride— boiled ham, mutton, pig's feet. They finally departed at 7:15 p.m., one trooper recalled, to a "perfect sea of handkerchiefs and parasols."[16]

They came into San Antonio on the Southern Pacific, then transferred to the city's streetcars to get to the camp grounds. The men weren't the only creatures ambling into camp; the Arizonans brought a four-month-old mountain lion cub they dubbed Teddy; when they later learned it was female, they renamed her Josephine.[17]

Wood studied them as they went leaping off the cars, not waiting for them to stop. They were energetic and undisciplined; he thought they might be good for scouting duty, but not combat. That evening he sent fifteen of them to Fort Sam Houston to retrieve thirty half-broken horses. They went without saddles or bridles, just rope leads—not as a punishment, or a test; even though this was a cavalry regiment, their equipment had yet to arrive, and there were no saddles to be had. A while later, Wood watched with pleased surprise as all thirty horses arrived through the sally port; they bucked, but not a man was dismounted. He changed his mind. As serious cavalrymen, they might do.[18]

After the Arizona men arrived early on the 7th, new contingents rolled into camp almost every day. That afternoon a group from

85

Oklahoma showed up; three days later, 340 men under Major Henry Hersey arrived from New Mexico—the only contingent wearing their own, matching attire. Like the Arizona men, they had left their territory to great fanfare: After their swearing in at the governor's palace in Santa Fe, the New Mexicans had marched to the train station behind a carriage carrying a woman dressed as a "goddess of liberty," the crowd three deep on each side. The train, decked in bunting and signs reading "Remember the Maine," was loaded with flowers, candy, and cakes. That night in San Antonio more than 500 men camped out in the fairground's vast exhibition hall, tired but excited. At one point a shoe flew out of the darkness and hit a New Mexican recruit named Royal Prentice. "Having no immediate use for the shoe, I threw it back to the owner," he wrote years later, in an article for the *New Mexico Historical Review*. "But in the darkness aiming was bad, for it struck and aroused another sleeper and very soon the pavilion was a pandemonium of flying shoes, and everything else that could be thrown."[19]

Not all the men arrived as part of state contingents; such was the Rough Riders' instant celebrity that scores traveled individually to San Antonio for a chance to join, sometimes coming hundreds of miles. Arthur Cosby was a twenty-six-year-old lawyer with the Mutual Life Insurance Company in New York when he learned about the regiment. He wrote to Roosevelt, asking if there was still room. Roosevelt, who had followed Cosby's athletic exploits as a Harvard undergraduate, replied, "If you will come here and pass the physical examination, we will enlist you." Cosby quit his job the next morning. At 3 p.m. he was on a train to San Antonio.[20]

Another man, John Campbell Greenway, an engineering foreman at the Carnegie Steel Corporation in Duquesne, Pennsylvania, traveled all the way to San Antonio after hearing about the unit, without even bothering to seek out an introduction. He wasn't just another stranger off the train, though: The son of a Confederate veteran from Alabama who became a doctor in Arkansas, young Greenway had been an outstanding football and baseball player at Yale, and his senior year he was voted the most popular man on campus. Tall, lanky but muscular, Greenway was the sort of gentleman-athlete Roosevelt prized. He arrived and was made a second lieutenant on the spot.[21]

The men, whether individually or as part of the territorial contingents, came to San Antonio for different reasons. Some, like Frank Brito, a cowboy in New Mexico, went out of a patriotic duty—and because his father ordered him to. Others went for adventure, or to avenge the *Maine*. Many went out of a sense of duty to the Cubans. In 1894 a railroad signalman named Benjamin Colbert had even traveled to Guatemala, where he had heard a boatload of filibusters was preparing to leave for Cuba. But the American consul found out, arrested him, and had him sent back to the United States. Colbert was living in the Oklahoma Territory when he heard about the Rough Riders, and set out immediately to join. Sympathy for Cuba was especially strong in the Southwest, where memories were long and parents still told their children stories about the evils of Spanish rule. By the late nineteenth century, any town with more than a few hundred people had a daily newspaper that picked up stories from the Associated Press, and through it townsfolk and cowboys and farmers kept up with the latest news from Cuba. On the day McKinley ordered the blockade of Cuba, the front page of the *El Paso Daily Herald* declared: "The Edict Has Gone Forth from the Greatest of All Nations Proclaiming Cuba Libre! And Release a Suffering People from Spanish Barbarity."[22]

The Rough Riders were a cavalry regiment, so the unit used cavalry terminology: Wood arranged them in three "squadrons" of four "troops" each, with each troop composed of about eighty enlisted men. Each troop had different-colored horses: Troop A rode on bays, B had sorrels, C had browns, D had grays, and so on. For officers, Wood had himself and Roosevelt at the top of the organization chart, and under them three majors. He placed a lieutenant as adjutant—i.e., in charge of administration—and another as quartermaster, who oversaw supplies. There was a surgeon, two assistants, and three hospital stewards; a chaplain, two sergeants, a chief musician, a chief trumpeter, and two saddlers. But this was a bare-bones organization: there were no clerks, and no one to cook or handle the mess duties. For that, the men were on their own.[23]

The men who gathered in San Antonio were not, as the papers described them, all cowboys and ruffians. That was the romanticism of the West talking. Rather, they comprised a broad slice of America—white male America, at least—at the end of the nineteenth century, representatives of the emergent white-collar middle class in small but booming towns like Prescott and Las Vegas, New Mexico. James McClintock was a journalist. Thomas C. Grindell taught college in Tempe, Arizona. And while some of the men were indeed laborers in the nomadic animal trades, others were, as the regiment's first adjutant, Tom Hall, wrote, "Rich man, poor man, Indian chief, doctor, lawyer, not one thief. Merchant, sheriff, artist, clerk, clubman, quite unused to work, miner, ocean gondolier"—whatever that is—"broker, banker, engineer, cowboy, copper, actor, mayor, college athletes, men of prayer, champions of amateur sports, to boot." Decades later, whenever a reporter for their local paper came to interview them, the surviving Rough Riders would wax lyrically about the dangerous and uncivilized men who composed the bulk of their troop, but their stories read more like ex–fraternity brothers looking back with embellishment on their youth. It was an artifice some of the more perceptive reporters picked up on immediately. "The members of this so-called 'cowboy' regiment seem to have been recruited from the sort of cowboys that ranges up and down Washington Street, Phoenix," wrote an Arizona newspaper. "Many of them are not horsemen in the mildest construction, and as crack marksmen have yet to distinguish themselves."[24]

Yet the regiment did not lack for characters. By the time thirty-eight-year-old William O'Neill quit his job as the mayor of Prescott to join, he had already led enough life for two men: Born in Washington, D.C., and trained as a lawyer, in 1882 he had come out West seeking adventure. At various times, often at the same time, he had been a court reporter, a short story writer, a militia captain, a deputy marshal, and a judge; an adherent of the economic philosopher Henry George, he ran twice for Congress on the Populist ticket, losing both times. He was also an inveterate gambler, and earned the nickname "Buckey" for his tendency to "buck the tiger"—or go against the odds—in faro and other card games. His best friend, Tom Horn, had been an interpreter for the Army during Leonard Wood's hunt for Geronimo; he was later hanged for murder.[25]

One of the regiment's most popular enlisted men was Hamilton Fish Jr. He was the grandson of President Ulysses S. Grant's secretary of state, also named Hamilton Fish, and the scion of the New York establishment, whose family had been in Manhattan for centuries. An enormous man, Fish rowed crew for Columbia, but dropped out after three years and moved west, where he worked as a railroad brakeman. He returned to New York after he jammed an index finger into the coupling mechanism between two cars and had to have it removed. Fish was an ardent alcoholic, and several men reported him drunk for most of his time in San Antonio. He was also intensely loyal and, in his own way, kind. He loved to fight, but he also loved animals. One day he was walking through camp when he saw a crowd of men watching two dogs attack each other. He pushed his way through and pulled the two animals apart; cradling the smaller dog in his arms, he took it back to his tent, where he bandaged and nursed it. "Ham Fish was a curious combination of an aristocrat and a cruiser," one of his friends in the regiment told the historian Hermann Hagedorn. "A kind of Doctor Jekyll and Mr. Hyde; for all his wildness and brutality, at bottom a puritan and a reformer." Unsurprisingly, he became one of Roosevelt's favorites.[26]

Wood's assessment of the regiment on that first day with the Arizonans was to prove, at first, naive; the enlisted men were undisciplined, even unruly. Within a few days of arriving, they had located a set of loose boards in the fence around the camp, and that night a dozen or so men sneaked out and went to town. It happened again the next night, and soon members of the regiment were familiar faces in San Antonio's nightlife. Horse-drawn cabs waited a few hundred yards beyond camp to take them the five miles to the bars and gambling dens downtown. "It took but a few hours to empty pocketbooks, after which there was the long five mile walk over the railroad ties to camp," recalled Royal Prentice. They arrived home after midnight, slipping through the fence. Not all of them made it back: One enlisted man, from Arizona, was arrested and fined $100 after he chased people off a streetcar with a knife; when the police pursued him, he tried to overturn a buggy with two women in it. Another evening a band of Rough Riders and locals got into a fight in a bar on East Nueva Street, smashing bottles and firing their guns in the air.[27]

Apart from their nightly excursions, the men would also go into town during the day for sightseeing. For those who came from small towns and farms in New Mexico and Arizona, this was by far the largest and oldest city they had ever seen. By 1898, the Alamo was a national landmark, and they took note of the site where a previous generation of volunteers had fought in the name of liberty against a foreign adversary. Others took a swim at Scholz's natatorium—a swimming pool—in between stops at one of the town's general stores to buy Durham tobacco, paper, pencils, socks, and other items they expected to need in larger quantities than the Army was likely to provide. Benjamin Colbert went to a music store and asked to listen to a recording of "The Stars and Stripes Forever" by John Philip Sousa's Concert Band.[28]

Wood was wise enough not to enforce too much discipline too quickly; he was liberal with passes to town. Getting the regiment into some semblance of a fighting unit was his priority. The men were there for their skills as marksmen and outdoorsmen; Wood reckoned that their willingness to accept military regimentation would come later. One evening Wood was making his rounds and came across a man supposedly on sentry duty, but in fact on the ground itching at bug bites and swatting mosquitoes. The man saw Wood, paused, and resumed scratching and swatting. Wood remained, silent. Eventually the man stopped, looked up at him, and said, "Ain't they bad?"[29]

Those first few weeks especially, the camp was less like a military training facility and more like a slightly boozy Boy Scout ranch; several men played banjo, while others formed rival glee clubs. In their spare time, they organized baseball and football teams. For lack of tents and blankets, they slept in the exhibition hall. The food was bad and there was a lot of drudge work, but at least at first, a visitor could be forgiven for thinking the men were on a rustic retreat.[30]

Very quickly, San Antonio gave itself over to Rough Rider fever. Reporters from the two local papers hung around camp and reported on daily life, down to mundane details about drill routines: "The Rough Riders had a fatiguing time yesterday morning and a dull time in the afternoon," began a typical article in the *Daily Express*. When George Curry, a late solo arrival, came to town, he saw a man tacking a canvas sign onto a streetcar: "Take this car for the exposition Grounds where Roosevelt's famous Rough Riders are camped."

And, in fact, each day hundreds of onlookers—often led by Mayor Bryan Callaghan Jr.—took the streetcars out to the fairgrounds to see the Rough Riders in action. They came with cakes and meats and iced tea; young women took away brass buttons as souvenirs. A local band under the direction of "Professor" Carl Beck, a German immigrant, made regular visits, filling the afternoon air with bouncy waltzes. Every day they played what became the unofficial theme song of the regiment, and indeed the war, "There'll Be a Hot Time in the Old Town Tonight."[31]

Beck was at the center of the most infamous and widely reported incident involving the Rough Riders in San Antonio. On the evening of May 24, not long before they departed, he held a public concert in their honor. One of the pieces that night, a composition by Beck called "Cavalry Charge," required several pistols to fire off blanks. Beck had asked a few Rough Riders to oblige him. But when the time came, more than a few did—and, reportedly, they weren't firing blanks. Either by coincidence or errant bullet, the lights went out. "Men yelled, women screamed, and a frightened waiter dropped several glasses of beer," Hall wrote. Beck, who reportedly fought for the Germans in the Franco-Prussian War, said he had been as scared that night as he had ever been in battle.[32]

Events like the Beck concert were reported nationwide, with not a little hyperbole. Most of the troopers later denied that anyone had fired a weapon, and said that it had all been a misunderstanding. But the general idea—that the Rough Riders were a little rough—was more or less accurate. Wood forbade alcohol in camp, so bars popped up, mushroom-like, around its edges, claptrap structures that poured beer for 5 cents a pint—a steal for men accustomed to paying three times that in Arizona. The groundskeeper of the fairground opened a small diner adjacent to the camp, which the men nicknamed the Waldorf-Astoria. Troopers would stumble, bleary-eyed, to their morning formations, and spend nearly as much time thinking about how to slip out of camp as they did about how to prepare for battle. With the men still half equipped and half prepared, and with locals treating the camp less like a military facility and more like the fairground it otherwise was, Cuba, and the possibility that they might yet fight and die in it, seemed a long way off.[33]

Roosevelt's Easterners began to arrive on May 9. The local papers made them out to be caricatures of the rich city rube, spoiled and effete. "Ninety percent of them carry a large wad in their side pockets with which to play a little game of draw and large bank accounts behind them," wrote the *Daily Express*. "Some of them have their 'men' with them to care for their uniforms and top boots at a salary of $60 a month, also to cook at $100 a month." None of this was true. In fact, the Easterners were, in a way, disappointing. The Westerners were expecting dudes—inexperienced, arrogant city boys out for a bit of adventure before going back to their pampered lives. Rich they were, no doubt: Many took their last meals as civilians at the Menger Hotel, far beyond what the typical cowhand could afford, and several arrived at camp with valises full of suits and ties. But these the men gladly discarded when they realized they would not need them, and they quickly fell to work. They were all strong and well-disciplined, having been selected for their prowess in campus and amateur sports. Even more impressive, most of them could ride—Craig Wadsworth was one of the country's best steeplechase riders, and the other men were no slouches in a mount either, having grown up riding in the New York and Massachusetts countryside.[34]

The Easterners took to their new lifestyle immediately. That first night, after a dinner of boiled potatoes and coffee, they rolled out their blankets on the floor of the exhibition hall and were soon fast asleep alongside their new comrades. The next morning Woodbury Kane, a close friend of Roosevelt's from Harvard and a renowned yachtsman, was assigned to dig a ditch; he did it gladly. Wadsworth, who had also played varsity football at Harvard, was sent to collect firewood. Whatever skepticism the Westerners felt melted away. "I never will forget the time young [William] Tiffany, of New York, and myself . . . washed our clothes out and waited around exchanging little experiences we have passed through," recalled David L. Hughes of Tucson. The respect was mutual. "They are a splendid set of men, these Southwesterners—tall and sinewy, with resolute, weather beaten faces and eyes that look a man straight in the face without flinching," wrote J. Ogden Wells. Only Tiffany, a grand-nephew of Oliver Hazard Perry, complained—there was no hot water, he said, and the food was "nauseating." Tiffany came around in one respect, though; he and Kane used their own money to buy a pair of Colt machine guns for the regiment, which they set up behind Roosevelt's tent. The guns could fire 500 bullets a minute, and were effective to 2,000 yards.[35]

Despite their two famous commanders, the Rough Riders suffered from a lack of even basic military equipment—not as badly as many volunteer units, some of whom would never even receive rifles, but worse than the regulars, and at a level of want that cast a shadow over the military's ability to actually stand up a sufficient fighting force. They had arrived with little more than the clothes they wore, assuming, fairly, that uniforms, bedding, and other supplies would be provided. The men camped in the fairground's vast exhibition hall because they didn't have tents; many didn't even have blankets. For the first several days, they drilled with broomsticks in place of rifles. "The blunder and delay of the Ordnance Bureau defies belief," Roosevelt fumed in his diary. "They expense us stuff we don't need, and send us the rifles by slow freight!"[36]

Roosevelt and Wood had foreseen this risk, and ordered uniforms and other supplies ahead of time, even picking a less-common tan fabric, different from the dark blue of the regulars, because they thought the lower demand meant they'd receive it faster. What they hadn't counted on was the combined forces of the snarled American rail system and the even more gnarled military Quartermaster's Department, which was overwhelmed with demands for matériel, after decades of doing almost nothing. Though the uniforms for the enlisted men arrived eventually, the officers who had not already done so had to buy their own in San Antonio, or buy the fabric and have an outfit made for them. Decorations of rank were typically hand-made, by the officers themselves. "I am rather certain that Colonel Roosevelt himself wore more or less of this untailor-made roughness and was rather proud of it," Tom Hall recalled.[37]

In the meantime, they drew on the stores at Fort Sam Houston, where the Fifth Cavalry, the primary regiment garrisoned there, opened its doors. By coincidence, the fort had a large supply of everyday items that were set to be destroyed, either out of too much use or because no one wanted them: utensils, cups, plates, bedrolls, all the many things that few civilians think about when they contemplate war but that hungry, tired soldiers cannot do without. Even then, many men had to share a single plate, or drink from the same chipped cup, waiting for their own provisions to arrive by what was said to be an expedited supply train, but was in fact criminally slow.[38]

The uniforms finally arrived on May 13—in assorted lots, with no semblance of order or sense of the men who would be wearing them. Distribution was haphazard and slow. "The men would be issued a spoon and a pair of gloves one day, a coat and a mess pan the next, a tin cup and a cartridge belt the next," Hall wrote. Clothing was handed out with only rough appreciation for the man on the receiving end, and for the next few hours a new line would form, of men returning coats that couldn't meet in the middle to bottom or pants too big even to be belted around their waist. Hamilton Fish, one of the biggest men in the regiment, walked up and down a great line of shoes, looking in vain for a pair big enough to fit his outsize feet. Eventually, he gave up and settled for a still-huge pair that pinched his toes.[39]

Soon after reveille on Sunday, May 15, Leonard Wood emerged from his tent in a newly pressed brown suit with yellow trim, a new campaign hat, and freshly shined shoes—the first time anyone had seen him in uniform. He then ordered James Brown, the trumpeter for Troop D, to bring around a phaeton, a type of two-horse carriage, and drive the two of them to town. They stopped at the Western Union telegraph office and picked up the officers' messages and mail. Then, it was on to the Menger Hotel. "We had no more than stopped when a heavy set man with the broadest smile and wearing glasses came out of the hotel," Brown recalled. The man was dressed exactly like Wood, in a new khaki uniform. "They immediately embraced and both talking at the same time." Brown, a Kansas native, was "embarrassed" by the sight of two men hugging, "as that was not done where I came from." When he realized the stranger was Theodore Roosevelt, he relaxed a little—after all, he told himself, this must be how men did things back East.[40]

The entire regiment was waiting for the three when they returned. Roosevelt walked through the sally port with a wide grin on his face, like he was a boy headed off to camp. Right away, Major Brodie and Buckey O'Neill hurried over to shake his hand, but soon the lieutenant colonel was surrounded by greenhorn soldiers, who peppered him with questions about the war and their chances of getting into it. Roosevelt was sanguine: "The other fellows have reputations to make, but we seem to have one to sustain. It had been thrust upon us." A pair of men brought over a wooden box, and Roosevelt climbed atop it. "Men, in a few days we will be at the front and I promise you I shall spend your lives the same as I would spend my own," he shouted. Every man straightened up. "Up to that time it had been a lark for nearly all of us," one of them recalled. "But from that time on we all entered into the spirit of the adventure."[41]

Roosevelt spent the rest of the afternoon meeting with Wood, the other officers, and a retinue of local officials and onlookers who wanted a glimpse of the famous lieutenant colonel. That day, a Sunday, the *San Antonio Express* estimated that 15,000 people visited the camp, a sizable portion of the city's population. Eventually, it all became too much for Wood. He closed off the camp to visitors a few days later.[42]

Like several other men of means in the regiment, Roosevelt bought his own horses. One morning after breakfast, not long after he had arrived, he went into San Antonio, where he met Johnnie Moore, a friend with whom he had once hunted javelina in the Texas Hill Country. Moore had brought several horses, and Roosevelt rode them up and down St. Mary's Street, testing them out. Roosevelt picked two: one, a pony, he named Little Texas, the other, a larger steed, Rain-in-the-Face. He bought a new Stetson hat and had two pairs of glasses sewn into it. And he proudly displayed, attached to his belt, two weapons given to him before he left Washington: a revolver recovered from the *Maine*, a present from William Cowles, a Navy captain who was married to his sister Anna; and a German-made officer's saber with a sharkskin hilt, given to him by the staff back at the Department of the Navy.[43]

Another officer might have seen his wealth and fancy accoutrements as an obstacle to making a connection with his men—or, even, an excuse not to. But Roosevelt basked in the Western manhood around him, as if he were back in the Dakotas of his ranching days.

One day an Oklahoma cowboy named Billy McGinty showed him how to shoe a horse by tying its legs together above the knees, then tipping it over, so that its feet stuck out helpless. "Bully!" Roosevelt cried.[44] He reveled in their nicknames—Shoot 'em Up Bill, Smoky Moore, Happy Jack—and gave them new ones of his own devising. "The life histories of some of the men who joined our regiment would make many volumes of thrilling adventure," he wrote in his memoir of the war. He took quickly, especially, to Hamilton Fish and Buckey O'Neill, whom he overheard talking with James Church, the surgeon, about "Aryan word roots together, and then sliding off into a review of the novels of Balzac." Together, the regiment, in its manliness, its unruliness, and its determination, represented everything Roosevelt had wanted in life, for himself and for his country.[45]

These feelings were not, immediately, mutual. The men had all read about Roosevelt in the papers, and knew his reputation. So when the stout, bespectacled man stood before them, speaking in his loud, high voice, many were less than impressed. He struck them as a dude who liked to play cowboy but would never quite be one. But as they listened to what he said, and heard stories about his past exploits—it helped immensely that Fred Herrig was on hand to tell about Roosevelt's "bronco busting" adventure in the Dakotas—they began to change their minds. It wasn't his skill in the saddle and with a rifle that impressed them; it was his utter lack of pretension. The owners of the Menger Hotel offered Roosevelt a free room but he refused, preferring to sleep on the ground with his men. That first afternoon, to prove himself, Roosevelt picked up a lariat, threw it around a horse, then saddled the steed without help and took off. A trooper approached him later and said: "Well, colonel, I want to shake hands and say we're with you. We didn't know how we would like you fellars at first; but you're all right, and you know your business, and you mean business, and you can count on us every time!"[46]

Roosevelt and Wood settled into a division of labor that accorded with general military protocol but also their respective personalities. Roosevelt was to oversee drilling and practice, and to act as the regimental judge when a dispute or infraction arose. Wood was the planner and the point of contact to Washington. But the arrangement also reinforced the regiment's first impressions of the two—the men took to Roosevelt as a leader, but they regarded Wood with arm's-length respect, more as an administrator than an inspiration. Their camp was called Camp Wood, after the regiment's colonel, but the men—and the rest of the country—called the regiment "Roosevelt's Rough Riders."

A few days after he arrived Roosevelt assembled the men after breakfast mess for their first drill. He stood ramrod straight, lifted his chin, and shouted a command. Nothing happened. Roosevelt tried again. The men scrambled in confusion, eager to please but at a loss to understand. Major Brodie, standing beside him, tapped Roosevelt on the shoulder and whispered that his command was, while impressive, physically impossible to execute (the actual command went unrecorded). Roosevelt was taken aback; for a split second, he looked at a loss. But he recovered, and turned over the drill to Brodie. "As you were," the major said to the troops.[47]

It was the sort of mistake Roosevelt would not make twice. After a few late nights studying the slim "Drill Regulations for Cavalry, United States Army, 1896," he had the basics down, and within a few days had the men falling into the routine Wood had prescribed for them. Emil Cassi, a bugler, blew reveille at 6 a.m., followed by twenty minutes of working in the stables to rub and feed the horses. Then the men got breakfast themselves, followed by an hour and a half of mounted drills. After midday dinner, they had target practice and then a long march. The cowboys, so nimble in their mounts, found marching in step a challenge. Billy McGinty complained that he was having a hard time keeping pace on foot, but he was pretty sure he could keep in step on horseback. Still, wrote Arthur Cosby, "It was a thrilling sight to see these men marching their mounts in formation or launching in thundering gallops—all at quick response to the nasal, high-pitched commands of Colonel Roosevelt. I thought it was a miracle in a way—to see all these different kinds of men working so well together."[48]

Then it was back to the stables at four to wash and water the horses; the men cleaned themselves up the best they could, and gathered on the fairground for fifty minutes of dress parade. Supper came at seven, after which the enlisted men were free to relax while the officers gathered for "night school," where Wood and some of the seasoned veterans, like Brodie, walked them through the basics of military tactics and command. Cassi played taps at nine, after which the men were expected to stay in their tents—but often slipped through the fence and headed to town. If the creak of a swinging fence board reached their ears, Wood and Roosevelt said nothing. "Neither Wood nor Roosevelt had the least touch of that horrible freak known as the military martinet," recalled a trooper named Frank P. Hayes.[49]

Though it was still spring, the flatlands around San Antonio were boiling during the day. And just as the temperature dipped a bit in the evening, the mosquitoes emerged—"something terrible and wonderful," wrote Tom Hall, the regiment's adjutant. "The New Jersey mosquito is an amateur compared with his Texas cousin." The men grumbled, but they rarely complained out loud, because Roosevelt was always right with them—if they marched, he marched. "The men always do their best when he is out," wrote one Rough Rider, Kenneth Robinson, who was a cousin by marriage to Roosevelt's sister Corinne. "He would be amused indeed if he heard some of the adjectives and terms applied to him, meant to be most complimentary but hardly fit for the public."[50]

One afternoon, after an especially grueling march, Roosevelt brought his men past one of the saloons that had popped up outside the camp. He told the men they could drink all they wanted, and he would pay for it—but, he added, clenching his fist, "if any man drinks more beer than is good for him, I will cinch him."[51]

That evening Wood invited the officers of the regiment to dinner. While they ate, he gave them a long talk about drinking with the enlisted men—without naming Roosevelt, his entire speech was aimed directly at him. As Wood told the historian Hermann Hagedorn years later, he "ended up by saying that of course an officer who would go out with a large batch of men and drink with them was quite unfit to hold a commission." Soon after, Wood left for his tent. Roosevelt entered a few minutes later. "I would like to speak with the colonel," he said, staring ahead.

Wood looked at him silently.

"I want to talk with you, sir," Roosevelt went on. "I agree with every word you said. You are quite right, quite proper. I wish to tell you sir, that I took the squadron, without thinking about this question of officers drinking with their men, and I gave them all a schooner of beer. I wish to say, sir, that I agree with what you said. I consider myself the damnedest ass within ten miles of this camp. Good night." Then he left. A few days later, the beer hall owner, in a sign of gratitude, sent the regiment a few barrels of beer. When George Curry asked Roosevelt if they could drink it, the lieutenant colonel said, "Nothing doing," and threw his hands in the air. "Beer is a subject I do not want to hear about."[52]

Roosevelt and Wood continued to worry that all their efforts would come to nothing, and the war would end before they could leave San Antonio. Their concerns were misplaced: The war plans, inasmuch as they were plans at all, were taking on a life of their own, and growing grander by the day. Some 5,000 men were arriving daily in Tampa, the designated embarkation point for any invasion of Cuba, far more than the president intended to utilize (still more were gathering at Chickamauga, Georgia, and other camps along the Eastern Seaboard). Secretary Long, having shed his antiwar instincts, wanted to throw 50,000 men at Havana, immediately. In early May a convoy of American ships, including the Army-chartered sidewheeler steamer *Gussie*, set out from Tampa, intending to deliver weapons and supplies to the rebels; instead, the landing party, put ashore two miles from a Spanish fort, came under intense fire and had to retreat, their mission unaccomplished. Clearly a more substantial effort was needed. On May 8, General Miles, the head of the Army, was ordered to send 70,000 men to attack the Cuban capital directly—an unimaginable operation, even by Secretary of War Alger's unrealistic standards. Miles, who wanted to wait until after the end of the summer rain season before launching the campaign, fought back, to a standstill: no to Havana, yes to a major assault, as soon as possible. The lack of a firm plan in the face of immense pressure to do something against Cuba may have demonstrated the War Department's inability to control events. But it was welcome news to Roosevelt, Wood, and their men—it meant that they might have a shot at seeing action after all.[53]

On May 22, Wood gathered the men in the parade ground behind his tent to read them the Articles of War, which served to formally enlist them as volunteers in the fight against Spain. It was Sunday, and after reading the Articles he led the regiment in singing a hymn, "How Firm a Foundation." Some of the men wept. Wood wanted to say something else, too. At first, he told them, it had been rough; the men had no equipment or shelter, and they were undisciplined. But they had transformed into soldiers, thanks in no small part to Roosevelt, who he said was "working like a beaver from morning till night." Equipment and discipline had both arrived, as if by magic, after the first week. Somehow, through luck and effort, they had turned a disparate group of men gathered from around the country, most with no definable military skills, into something resembling a regiment in the United States Army.[54]

Wood said as much that evening, in a letter to the president. "I hope some time you may be able to see the men of this regiment," he wrote to McKinley, "as I am sure you will find them a most exceptionally fine body of men; they certainly far exceed my expectations; they are all intelligent, honest and full of enthusiasm. . . . Our men represent every phase of American life, presenting in their ranks ultra-fashionables from New York, men from the North, South, East and West, ranchmen, cowboys, miners, every profession, half-breeds from the Indian territory; in fact, pretty much every variety of American manhood."[55]

As May came to a close, and with most of the men wrapping up almost a month of training, there was still no official word on when the Rough Riders were to leave, or where they were to go—or, even, what they were to do if they should end up shipping off to Cuba. Some speculated that they were to act as a sort of special forces, contacting and organizing Cuban rebels in advance of the Regular Army. Others suspected they would be mounted scouts. But many, Roosevelt included, worried that they would be held in reserve, as the B team, should they even make it to the island.[56]

Wood ordered an increase in drilling, and set the morning exercise to begin an hour before dawn. Cavalry drills alone were to run six hours a day. The days were getting hotter, and it was an especially hot spring in Texas—punishing conditions for the men but excellent training for the near-tropical Cuban climate. "Troopers have fallen from their saddles and sentries have fainted while patrolling their posts or standing in line, from heat prostration," recalled one Arizona trooper, "but there is no grumbling and the man who would openly give expression to the wish that he had stayed home would speedily become the laughing stock of the regiment."[57]

Finally, on May 27, Wood received orders to move out. They were headed not for Galveston, as they had expected, but Tampa, several days away by train. When Wood read the telegram out loud, Roosevelt danced a jig. Two nights later, during the daily dress parade, Roosevelt addressed the men:

> Boys, as you know, we are breaking camp tonight and will start on our trip to Cuba; we are going to get close to the enemy, which means that a great many of us will be wounded, followed by much suffering and some of us will make the supreme sacrifice. I don't think we have, and we don't want, anyone to whine or complain as a result of these hardships, so now, if any one of you has a mother, wife or sweetheart that you feel you cannot afford to leave and take the chance of being lost to these dear ones, I want you to step forward, now, and you will be released, otherwise, I ask you to forever keep your peace.[58]

No one moved. They had experienced less than a month of training. The men were eager to leave for the war. Whether they were ready to fight was another matter.

CHAPTER 6

"A PERFECT WELTER OF CONFUSION"

The Rough Riders broke camp early in the morning on May 29.
They burned their garbage, packed their bags, and left behind
anything that couldn't fit in a blanket roll. Wood had determined that
the three squadrons should ride on three sets of trains and stagger
their departures, so that when one set stopped to feed and water its
horses the squadron behind it didn't get stuck waiting on the tracks.
The first squadron, under Major Brodie, left camp at 8:30 in the
morning, intending to be ready to board the train, with their horses
unsaddled and their baggage piled alongside the track, by 10 a.m.[1]

The ride on horseback from Camp Wood to the San Antonio
stockyards took a leisurely hour. But when they arrived, there was no
train. In what would become a pattern of mismanagement, the Quartermaster's Department had told the rail company not to send one
until that afternoon. And so the men in the first squadron waited,
which meant that the men in the second squadron also had to wait,
and the third behind them. After a while many of the men drifted off
to "the vile drinking booths around the stock-yards," in Roosevelt's
words. Finally, the first trains left at 3:45 p.m.—six day coaches, nine
baggage cars, one boxcar, six Pullmans, and twenty cars for the horses.
Hundreds of San Antonians showed up to see them off.[2]

That was just the first squadron. The rest of the men wouldn't leave
until well past midnight. As the men bedded down to nap under a
light rain, Roosevelt threw off his pack and fell asleep beside them.
Their trains arrived just before 1 a.m., and the second squadron
departed; the last squadron did not leave until the next afternoon. In
all the Rough Riders rode in seven trains, with Roosevelt in the last
in case anyone fell out of line along the way.[3]

Each train was self-contained, carrying entire troops and all their horses and equipment. The horses rode in stock cars, while their riders crammed into luggage cars and day coaches, often sitting several men to a bench seat or sprawling across a hill of baggage. They slept in the aisles and on the floor and used feedbags as pillows. The taller men would ride with their legs sticking out the open windows, which also helped circulate air, but they had to close them whenever hot ash from the engine flew in. The water coolers on the train didn't hold enough for all the men, so they had to quench their thirst with lukewarm coffee that the officers had sent back in regular intervals. Roosevelt stretched out in his berth and tried to make himself comfortable, reading *A Quoi Tient la Supériorité des Anglo-Saxons?*, a book by a Frenchman, Edmond Demolins, that purported to explain why the American and English education systems were better than the French. He later gave up his berth to a sick trooper, and bunked with the enlisted men. "I doubt if anyone who was on the trip will soon forget it," Roosevelt wrote.[4]

Going to Houston took the Rough Riders down out of the dry hills around San Antonio, into the lush country of southeastern Texas, past cane plantations and sugar refineries—"the country here is most beautiful, being prairie and forest," wrote one trooper, Guy Le Stourgeon, on May 31. The first trains passed through Houston without a problem, but the last few, with Roosevelt, sat at the stockyard for hours. Eventually, he lost his temper at the conductor. "Have this train, all trains, proceed at once, understand me," he yelled. "These are my orders, this delay is owing to your stupid inefficiency, and I don't propose to have my regiment suffer for other's sake!" The conductor, a burly, sunburnt man, got into Roosevelt's face and screamed: "This train don't go, damn you, until I get good and ready! I am running this caboose, not you, and you mind your own business, damn you, these are my orders! Who in the hell are you anyway?" Out of nowhere came Hamilton Fish and his fist; it crashed into the man's jaw and sent him reeling. "Do you know who you're talking to?" Fish screamed. The trains were moving a half hour later.[5]

Soon they were puttering along at twenty miles an hour through the cotton and cane fields of East Texas, and then into the thick forests and bayous of southern Louisiana. Every few hours they would stop to water and feed the horses, and each time a crowd would gather to ogle them. "All along the people have been most enthusiastic. They have given us flags, flowers, tobacco, cigarettes, liquor, cakes, vegetables," Le Stourgeon wrote from Lake Charles, Louisiana. "The girls have treated us fine and some have even offered to be our wives when we return." Within a few days every man wore a flower in each buttonhole or tucked into his hatband. Sometimes people in the crowd would call out for Rough Riders by name, especially the renowned athletes from the Eastern contingent, having read about them in the newspapers. "We would just point to any soldier standing on a train platform as the famous man the crowd sought," wrote Arthur Cosby.[6]

These were towns led by men who, in their younger days, had fought and killed federal soldiers. Now, over three decades later, those veterans were out with their wives, and children, and children's children to greet men from that same army. "The blood of the older men stirred to the distant breath of battle; the blood of the younger men leaped hot with eager desire to accompany us," Roosevelt wrote. "The older women, who remember the dreadful misery of war—the misery that presses its iron weight most heavily on the wives and the little ones—looked sadly at us. . . . We were told, half-laughingly, by grizzled ex-Confederates that they had never dreamed in the by-gone days of bitterness to greet the old flag as they now were greeting it." Among the war's many ulterior aims and ultimate achievements was reconciliation between the South and the North after the Civil War. "The cost of this war is amply repaid by seeing the old flag as one sees it today in the south," Wood wrote to his wife. "We are indeed once more a united country."[7]

It was good that so many people along the way were so generous, especially with food, since the Quartermaster's Department had underestimated how long it would take to move the regiment to Tampa, and only packed two days' worth of rations on board the trains. Even then, the Army's travel rations consisted mostly of hardtack, the scourge of hungry soldiers and sailors for centuries: Simple biscuits made of flour, water, and salt, hardtack was baked until it was bone dry; it keeps forever, but is almost impossible to eat. "Hardtack belongs in the ceramic group and is the best substitute for a durable bathroom tile yet discovered," joked one Army volunteer. At each stop several dozen men would hurry out to find better provisions; some almost got left behind when the feeding and watering finished up early. In other cases, men would hand out hardtack, stamped with "US" or "REMEMBER THE MAINE," as souvenirs to the gathered crowd of locals, in exchange for cakes or fruit.[8]

At a stop in New Iberia, in the Louisiana bayou, one of the troopers, John Avery McIlhenny, found his mother waiting for him. Beside her sat two lunch baskets, five kegs of beer, and two demijohns of champagne—to share with his mates, of course. McIlhenny's family lived on Avery Island, to the south, where they manufactured Tabasco sauce, which his father had developed using peppers from the family garden. When the war broke out J.A., as his family called him, had quit the company and tried to raise an infantry regiment in southern Louisiana; when he couldn't find enough men, he traveled to San Antonio and persuaded Roosevelt to let him join the Rough Riders.[9]

A few hours later they reached Algiers, across the river from New Orleans. The train cars were loaded onto paddlewheel boats and ferried across the river. Many of the men had never seen a body of water as large as the Mississippi, and they stood in awe as the boats moved across the river's half-mile, 200-foot-deep girth. On the other side a throng of people awaited. "There were cheers, music, beautiful women, many colored lights, etc., on all sides and coffee and tea were served us," Le Stourgeon wrote. "Also bananas, cigarettes, cigars, tobacco, ham sandwiches, deviled crabs, fried fish—never did I see such an ovation. A merchant gave us each a huge palm leaf fan." All of this was passed through the train windows, since for most of the layover only the officers were allowed off the trains. The enlisted men were locked inside, with guards posted at each end. Wood and Roosevelt trusted their men, but maybe a little less so in New Orleans.[10]

Theodore Miller, still in New York, was sure that he had missed the war. Bending to his father's demands, he stood down during McKinley's first call for troops, and focused, as much as he could, on his final exams. He was excelling at school, having been admitted to the New York Law School's prestigious Dwight Law Club, an honors association, and he had secured a clerkship with a Wall Street law firm. But he had stood by in silence while the 71st New York Volunteers had bulked up its ranks with volunteers, and one of his room-mates, from Vermont, had returned home to join his state militia. He remained silent when, on May 25, McKinley put out a second call for men. And he had watched as his friend and cousin David Goodrich, known as Dade, answered Roosevelt's invitation for additional men to join the Rough Riders—as did two of Miller's idols, Bob Wrenn and Bill Larned, two of the top-ranked tennis players in the country, who quit the professional circuit to join.[11]

The next day Miller met three of his college friends at Holland House, a fashionable hotel on Fifth Avenue, to commiserate over breakfast. One of them suggested that Miller at least see if Goodrich had advice. He thought that was a good idea, and that afternoon he sent his cousin a telegram, then headed to New Haven for "slap day," when undergraduates were inducted into Skull and Bones and the college's other secret societies. When he returned the next morning, there was a reply from Goodrich.[12]

The message said, simply, come along. Goodrich may have secured a spot for his cousin, or was simply hoping that Wood and Roosevelt would make room for him, should he make the journey to San Antonio. In either event, it was enough for Miller. That afternoon he went to Orange, New Jersey, to see his sister Mina Edison and her husband, Thomas; he returned the next morning and caught the 11 a.m. New York Central, bound for Texas. Though his train passed through northeast Ohio, Miller was so afraid of missing the Rough Riders that he didn't stop in Akron to see his family. Instead, he met his father in Cleveland, and the two headed south together. In St. Louis, Miller took time between connections to have a lawyer draw up a will.[13]

At some point between St. Louis and San Antonio—Miller's diary doesn't say exactly where or when—he met a traveler with some bad news: The Rough Riders had already left camp, and were fast on their way east, toward Tampa. They had passed through Houston, and were making their way to New Orleans. Immediately, Miller changed his ticket; he got "a shave, a shampoo, and a general refreshing," said goodbye to his father, and headed toward New Orleans on an overnight train. "My anxiety was at its height all night, as it was a chance for a prize I greatly coveted," he wrote.[14]

Miller got to Algiers at nine the next morning, and took a ferry across the Mississippi. When he arrived on the riverbank he asked about the Rough Riders; a passerby pointed him toward a spot several blocks away, and he sped off in a cab. "I almost yelled for joy when I saw the yellow canvas suits and the orderly appearance of many men getting on and off cars, for I felt sure I had caught the Rough Riders," he wrote. He poked through the scrums of soldiery until he found his cousin. Goodrich introduced Miller to Buckey O'Neill and his other new friends, then led him to Henry La Motte, the chief surgeon. With a clean bill of health, Miller was told that he would be mustered into the regiment when they reached Tampa. He settled into a bunk in the hospital car, the only space available. The train left at noon. Theodore Miller was a Rough Rider.[15]

The trains poked their way in a long black line across the Gulf Coast, through Mobile, Alabama, and Pensacola, Florida, on their way to Tallahassee. As they passed a pig farm in Alabama, one cowboy from Troop H threw a lariat around a large hog and hauled it on board—not to eat, but to enlist as a mascot, alongside the dog, mountain lion, and hawk that had already been added to the regiment's menagerie. Miller quickly made friends with Larned and Wrenn, the tennis players, and at one stop in the Florida Panhandle the three snuck into a town to buy milk and tomatoes, then into a nearby farm to steal a chicken, which they cooked and ate beside the train.[16] The regiment continued to find the crowds welcoming, even in the deepest of the Deep South, where the memories of the Civil War were at their rawest. "The mascots were the great attraction for the ladies and children, and they simply flocked about the car," Miller wrote in his diary. In other towns, La Motte, the surgeon, noticed a cooler reception than the regiment had received further west. When they reached Tallahassee, he found out why: A few days before, another trainload of soldiers came through and declared themselves "the only genuine Rough Riders," and had even warned residents of towns along the way that a group of impostors—circus performers pretending to be Roosevelt's famous regiment—was likely right behind them. (In fact, he later learned, the true impostors were civilian contractors, mostly mule packers and drivers.)[17]

The first train arrived on the outskirts of Tampa in the late afternoon of June 2; because there was just one track leading into town, and it was occupied by an endless chain of supply cars, they had to ride their horses the last eight miles and did not get to their campground until after dark. Along the way the men could make out the sleeping army camped in the darkness—endless lines of white tents, by far the largest collection of American military men in thirty years.[18]

The rest of the trains straggled in over the course of the next day. One of the last was delayed, not far from Tampa, for eighteen hours in the middle of a forest. Two miles away was a stockyard with water. George Curry, a captain, asked the conductor and engineer to move the train there. The men replied that the railroad company's orders forbid doing anything of the sort. Eager to get to Tampa, Curry placed the engineer and conductor under arrest, rounded up several soldiers who had worked on trains, put them in charge, and moved the train to the stockyard himself. They unloaded the saddles, left a guard on the train, mounted their horses, and rode to Tampa. The regimental adjutant, Tom Hall, livid at this breach of the law, wanted Curry punished, and told Roosevelt as much. Roosevelt approached Curry with a stern look, and Curry feared the worst. But then Roosevelt smiled. "Captain," he said, "why did you wait eighteen hours?"[19]

The campground assigned to the Rough Riders was a sandy plain, sloping off into swamp and framed by stands of pine. Under Wood's close direction, the men set up their tents in long rows, arranged by troops, with officers at each end. Along the ground, white strings coursed from stake to stake around the camp, delineating avenues and streets. In the following days, officers from the Regular Army would come around to see the famous Rough Riders and judge for themselves whether the motley crew was up to the task of a cavalry regiment. And, to be sure, in their mounted drills and military etiquette, the regiment was often found wanting. But no one could find a single thing to criticize about the camp. It was perfect.[20]

The Rough Riders' camp offered a sharp contrast with the general scene in Tampa. The city was "a perfect welter of confusion," Roosevelt said. First, there was Tampa itself. Located at the northern end of an oblong bay, the city straddled the Hillsborough River and consisted of street after sandy street of clapboard buildings. The entire city, Richard Harding Davis wrote in *Scribner's*, was mostly "derelict wooden houses drifting in an ocean of sand"—a frontier town not dissimilar, in ways, from the Southwestern outposts many of the Rough Riders had left behind. Tampa boasted a large cigar industry; the thousands of Cuban Americans who worked in Ybor City, then an eastern suburb, were a fountain of funds for the Cuban rebels during the Ten Years' War and then again since 1895. Western Florida was decades away from full-scale development, and cattle ranching and subsistence farming were still a big part of the local economy. Reached by a single rail line, the small city had little in the way of infrastructure to handle the influx of tens of thousands of troops, and even worse had no place to load such a large number onto ships to disembark. For that, they would have to ride the single rail line another nine miles down a peninsula to Port Tampa, where a narrow channel had been dug alongside a makeshift quay that could handle just two large ships at a time. And everywhere was sand, whipped up by the occasional strong wind, fast enough to lash a man's face or steadily wear the whitewash off a building. "Thriving and prosperous Tampa may be, but attractive or pleasing it certainly is not," wrote the correspondent George Kennan.[21]

There was no compelling military reason for collecting the army at Tampa. There were several natural, superior alternatives to Tampa as an embarkation point for an army of invasion: Mobile, New Orleans, and Galveston were all large, active ports with expansive loading facilities and well-served by a network of rail lines. They were a bit further away from Cuba, but only by a day or two. Tampa had none of these qualities. (Though it did have one distant historical resonance to its advantage: In 1539, at the dawn of the Spanish Empire in the Americas, the conquistador Hernando de Soto landed in Tampa Bay.) Instead, the military made its decision because of politics. A railroad tycoon named Henry Plant, who had invested heavily in the area's hotel real estate, lobbied the president to bring the Army to his city, largely as a way to elevate its reputation and give his holdings something to do in the summer months, after the tourist season ended. The Department of War, without considering the alternatives, agreed. By May 15, there were thousands of volunteers arriving daily, from all over the country. By the time the Rough Riders got there, the town of 15,000 was also the temporary home of a 30,000-man army.[22]

All of this should have been manageable by an able and efficient military. The problem was, the American Army was anything but efficient. To begin, it had two heads: The commanding general, who reported directly to the president, was in charge of the troops, while the secretary of war, who also reported to president, ran the Army's system of bureaus—including the commissary, which handled food, and the quartermaster, who handled equipment and supplies. The secretaries of war were nominally above the commanding generals, but they also came and went with administrations, while there had only been five commanding generals since the Civil War, from Ulysses S. Grant to the current occupant of the office, General Nelson Miles. More by accident than design, the secretary and the general stood in tension, and usually disliked each other personally; William Tecumseh Sherman, the commanding general under President Grant, so hated Secretary of War William Belknap that he moved his headquarters to St. Louis from Washington for two years. The clash between the two offices kept the Army working even less efficiently than Congress intended and the public desired. In times of peace, few noticed, or cared. But when the Spanish-American War began, it meant potential disaster.[23]

The secretaries of war had typically let each bureau operate independently, without much internal communication. When the Army suddenly needed to move tens of thousands of uniforms or rifles to Tampa, the quartermaster felt no obligation to inform the other bureaus, or General Shafter's staff. To make things worse, the war funding bill that McKinley won that spring forbade the Army from spending a penny until war was declared. Only then could it put in orders to arsenals for weapons or mills for clothing, which were quickly overwhelmed, and on back order for months. As a result, many of the volunteer regiments ended up fighting with old Springfield rifles with black-powder ammunition—if they were lucky. The 32nd Michigan arrived in Tampa with no weapons at all.[24]

Procuring supplies was one thing; delivering them to Tampa, and handling them once they arrived, was another. The Army lacked even a rudimentary system for logistics. Hundreds of train cars loaded

111

with supplies sat in the yards at Tampa, but no one had thought to attach bills of lading to the outside, so it was impossible to know what was inside. "I frequently saw officers and men of the Quartermaster's Department rushing frantically about, opening from fifty to one hundred cars, and parting open with crowbars the boxes that were in them, until they found the stores which were needed," wrote the correspondent Stephen Bonsal. Officers spent ten days looking for a car full of gun carriages, before finding it sitting on a rail siding. Only two or three trains were being unloaded a day; at one point the backup reached all the way to Georgia. When soldiers did find the right cars, they were often full of useless or out-of-date stores: heavy woolen uniforms better fit for the High Plains than the Cuban tropics; canned meat that had last seen light a decade prior; and not nearly enough ammunition for a major invasion of a hostile nation. "I had to buy 72 dollars worth of rations owning to the fact that it was absolutely impossible to get at our ration car or get anything out of the railroad people," Wood wrote in his diary in Tampa.[25]

Standing in contrast to all of this—the mobs of soldiers, the jumble of trains, the squalid, provisional character of the city itself—was the sprawling Tampa Bay Hotel, a place of immense luxury among the swamps of West Florida that in its strangeness was, oddly, the perfect setting for the headquarters of an equally strange, and equally massive, military undertaking. Henry Plant had opened the hotel in 1891 as a resort for tourists, who would then use his rail network to get to it. He was following a trend: Railroad and real estate developers were throwing up similarly enormous resorts in Key West, Miami, Jacksonville, and points in between. The Tampa Bay Hotel, at 511 rooms, was one of the largest.[26]

Plant spared no expense: The central rotunda was seventy feet square and twenty-three feet high, with mahogany doors opening and closing over carpets that Plant and his wife had bought in Europe. Designed by a New York architect, John A. Wood, and drawing on the same Moorish revival style that had influenced the exhibition hall in San Antonio, it boasted thirteen silver minarets with fluted domes, topped by crescent moons. Peacocks roamed the lawn. Richard Harding Davis, who arrived in Tampa in mid-May, was especially taken with the place. Writing in *Scribner's*, he celebrated its screens of climbing vines and mammoth clusters of red and yellow flowers, its gardens of flowers and palmettos in every shade of green, its "great porches as wide and as long as a village street." The Moorish architecture only added to its mystique, he wrote: "Someone said it was like a Turkish harem with the occupants left out." It was an oddity, but a convenient one for an army barely able to provide for its own soldiers. A saying went around the building: "Only God knows why Plant built a hotel here, but thank God he did."[27]

For the officers staying in the hotel, the weeks spent there were like a college reunion—indeed, many of the West Point graduates had not seen each other since receiving their commissions and heading to permanent posts out West. "One imaginative young officer compared it to the ball at Brussels on the night before Waterloo," Davis wrote. Adding to the continental feel was a squad of foreign military attachés who, as representatives of noncombatant countries, had been allowed to follow and observe the American military and report back home, a standard practice at the time. They were a diverse, cosmopolitan crew, with names like Major Clément de Grandpré of France, Lieutenant Saneyuki Akiyama of the Japanese Imperial Navy, and Arthur Lee of the British Army. The Americans, few of whom had ever left their home state, let alone their home shores, listened to the foreigners' stories like they were characters from a novel. "They were as familiar with the Kremlin as with the mosque of St. Sophia, with Kettner's Restaurant as with the Walls of Silence," Davis wrote. "They knew the love-story of every consul along the Malaysian Peninsula and the east coast of Africa."[28]

Davis called the weeks spent in Tampa "the rocking chair period of the war," and there was much truth in that. Dozens of officers were encamped at the hotel, and they spent as much time socializing as they did keeping their nervous soldiers in line. For weeks, every day word would go around the tables of men slowly sipping great glasses of iced tea that the orders had come through, and the Army was about to depart. And every day, a little later, the same people would whisper, with the same confidence, that the invasion had been delayed just another day or two. And so it went, on through May and into June. Rumors lived and died like mayflies; for a few hours, everyone was certain they were headed to Havana, then suddenly it was Cienfuegos. "There is no doubt now that we are to start for Porto Rico," Davis wrote his mother on June 1.[29]

The hotel let the Army's adjutants place a bulletin board in the lobby, where they would tack several telegrams an hour; at each new message a dozen men would rush forward to get the latest news. Over time, though, the officers began to relax. "Leggings and canvas shooting-coats gave way to white duck, fierce sombreros to innocent straw hats," Davis wrote, "and at last wives and daughters arrived on the scene of our inactivity, and men unstrapped their trunks and appeared in evening dress." On May 25, the officers threw a big dinner in honor of Queen Victoria's fiftieth anniversary of assuming the throne, but also in honor of Arthur Lee, the British Army attaché, whose wit and long career made him a favorite among reporters and bored officers hanging around the hotel.[30]

Lee may have been the man of the moment—"There was no one, from the generals to the enlisted men, who did not like Lee," Davis recalled—but Lee himself was taken with Roosevelt. The night he arrived, he saw a group of men gathered around a "stocky and bespectacled" colonel, "whose vigorous gestures and infectious spirits proclaimed him as someone out of the ordinary." Lee asked Davis who he was. "Good Heavens, don't you know Theodore Roosevelt?" Davis replied. "You must meet him this very minute. He is the biggest thing here and the most typical American living."[31]

Roosevelt and Wood both had rooms at the hotel, but they preferred to stay in camp with their men. One exception was a visit by Edith Roosevelt from June 2 to about June 7. She had given birth to their fifth child, Quentin, in November, and then been sick earlier in the year with an abscess in her psoas muscle. Though Roosevelt had found her a top doctor at Johns Hopkins, and seemed in his own way to care about her well-being, her condition seemed not to have given him even a second's pause before joining the war effort. "I would not allow even a death to stand in my way," he had confided to a friend. "It was my one chance to do something for my country and for my family and my one chance to cut my little notch on the stick that stands as a measuring rod in every family. I know now that I would have turned away from my wife's deathbed to have answered that call." If Edith had any private misgivings about her husband's choice, she kept them to herself: "Come back safe," she wrote him after he left Washington, "and we shall be happy, but it is quite right you should be where you are." Roosevelt put her up in his room—one of the hotel's sixteen suites—and he stayed with her at night. But he rose every morning at four to go the one and a quarter miles to camp in time for reveille.[32]

Some regiments kept a tight rein on their soldiers, but Wood and Roosevelt decided not to enforce discipline too strictly, a fact that Miller, Larned, Wrenn, and a few other late arrivals (who were, technically, not yet enlisted) took full advantage of. They went straight to the Tampa Bay Hotel, where they found a college friend of Miller's, Teddy Burke, who had arrived earlier and rented a room. They shaved and washed, and changed into new clothes—Miller wore blue trousers, a shirt loaned to him by brother-in-law Edison, patent leather shoes, a red bandanna, and a derby hat, a sartorial blend of Fifth Avenue and Rough Rider casual wear. Then they went to the dining room. "On our way down we met several celebrities," he wrote, including the artist Frederic Remington and Richard Harding Davis. Though still private citizens, they had the good sense not to insist on sitting in the main dining room, among the officers; instead, they got a back room. While eating, they wrote letters home over pitchers of sweet iced tea. They stayed in camp that night, but returned to the hotel the next day, Saturday, June 4, for a final meal—and this time they had the guts to sit a few tables away from Roosevelt, Wood, and Miles. That afternoon, Roosevelt enlisted them.[33]

The men slept two to a tent, often with their feet sticking out one end because the canvas sheets were too short. The tents came in two pieces, with each man carrying half. Decades later, veterans would look back fondly on their "bunky," or lament his death in battle. One morning Wells, one of the Harvard volunteers, went to the Tampa Bay Hotel for a shave; coming back, he fell in with a group of men from the 32nd Michigan Volunteer Infantry. He got to chatting with one of them, a man named Frank Knox. By then it was common knowledge that many of the volunteer regiments would be left behind on the first wave of ships, and Knox said he was eager to switch. Wells told Roosevelt about his encounter. He agreed to meet Knox—and was impressed with the man's intelligence. He added him to Troop D. Eventually, Knox shared a tent with Miller; decades later, after a long career as a newspaper executive, he became Franklin Roosevelt's secretary of the navy.[34]

Theodore Roosevelt was a nature lover, and there was much of it to love in Tampa. He sketched and jotted down the names of newfound species (to him) of birds, trees, and reptiles. "Here there are lots of funny little lizards that run about in the dusty roads very fast, and then stand still with their heads up," he wrote to his daughter Ethel. Others were less enamored with the local wildlife; several men were bitten by scorpions. Great herds of mosquitoes and blackflies clouded the air around the men, who swatted and swatted and eventually gave up. But most of all, they hated the sand—"nothing but sand, now red, now white, but all sand," Le Stourgeon wrote.[35]

As in San Antonio and along the route to Florida, locals flocked to see the Rough Riders in Tampa. By then, the country had gotten used to newspaper features about the famous and rich and exotic men who made up the regiment. As he had done in San Antonio, Wood had to set up guards to keep tourists from tramping through the camp, looking for souvenirs and knocking down tents. But Rough Rider fever infected Tampa nonetheless: Women and men wore gaudy handkerchiefs around their necks, like Roosevelt; local children cut out cardboard spurs to attach to their shoes, in imitation of the Rough Riders' signature footgear. Remington, the artist, came to the camp looking for some picturesque cowboys to sketch; to his disappointment, he found soldiers. "Why, you are nothing but a lot of cavalrymen!" he said.[36]

Onlookers especially liked to watch the regiment drill. Wood required them to keep a similar schedule as at San Antonio—reveille at 5 a.m., then breakfast and stable duties followed by two hours of mounted drill, with three more hours in the afternoon. At one point the entire cavalry division gathered for a drill with 2,000 horses spread out almost a mile wide, trotting across the sandy plain northeast of Tampa, cheering and waving their sabers and machetes. Though the men didn't know it, the drill marked the end of an era—the last mass cavalry demonstration ever put on by the American Army.[37]

From the moment they arrived, the Rough Riders had one espe-cially avid fan: Richard Harding Davis. Soon after McKinley declared war, Davis, in a pique of patriotism—and self-interested desire for adventure and acclaim—had applied for a position with the Massa-chusetts militia; while in Tampa, he received a commission as a cap-tain. "It's all very well to say you are doing more by writing, but are you?" he asked of himself, rhetorically, in a letter to his brother. "It's an easy game to look on and pat the other chaps on the back with a few paragraphs; that is cheap patriotism." But a few days later he was assigned a staff job as an assistant adjutant general, which would keep him stateside. Remington spent two hours in Davis's room in Tampa, talking him out of taking the post. He finally gave in—though it's hard to imagine he needed much convincing, knowing his choice was between going to Cuba as a reporter and sitting behind a desk as a soldier. Instead, he became an even more fanatical advocate for the Army, to the point where his reporting often blurred into propaganda. And no one did he advocate for more than the Rough Riders.[38]

Davis had known Roosevelt since their time rousting sleeping policemen in downtown New York, when Roosevelt was the head of the police board. Although Roosevelt was lukewarm about Davis (he thought his novels were salacious, and that Davis himself was a dandy), the lieutenant colonel recognized what Davis's martial, reportorial zeal could mean for the regiment. He invited Davis to see the camp, and tolerated it when Davis hobnobbed with the East-erners in the regiment, many of whom Davis had watched play in the Harvard-Yale game. The men knew a good thing when they saw it, too. "They use my bathroom continuously," Davis recalled, "and I never open the door without finding a heap of dirty canvas on the floor and a cheery voice splashing about in the tub calling out 'it's all right don't mind me. I'm one of Teddie's giants.' Then an utterly strange and utterly nude giant will appear from the bathroom."[39]

In between drills, the men in Shafter's army, organized into three divisions as the Fifth Corps, went to the beach. Some rode their horses; those who could, swam. Others went looking for alligators. Some stayed in camp and tried to learn Spanish. Still others went to Ybor City, the center of the area's Cuban community and the city's red-light district. Many of Tampa's bars had gone officially, temporarily dry under community pressure—residents didn't like the idea of thousands of drunken soldiers—but sold alcohol surreptitiously, with names like the General Robert E. Lee Milkshake or General Miles Grape Juice. It was in Ybor City that Frank Brito, a cowboy from New Mexico who had joined the Rough Riders, recalled his first and only experience with opium. "We laid down on some cots," he told the historian Dale Walker years later, "and a Chinaman brought in a pipe about three feet long and some black stuff that looked like coal tar. He worked the stuff into a ball and put it into the pipe and touched a candle flame to it while we sucked on the mouthpiece. I took about four puffs and that was enough. All of us were sick for a week."[40]

For other soldiers, who were there long before the Rough Riders arrived and who stayed long after they had left, Ybor City was more than just a place to blow off steam. With both black and white troops crammed into the camps, it was only a matter of time before the men, fueled by alcohol and sex, came to blows. Many of the 4,000 black soldiers camped in Tampa were Army regulars, men who had been raised outside the South and whose military experience consisted of life on the isolated plains, under the relatively egalitarian strictures of Army camp life. In Tampa, they faced both racist locals and hostile white soldiers, especially among the volunteers. By 1898, Jim Crow segregation was fast setting in across the South, and the black soldiers found service flat out refused to them at diners and bordellos—often for the first time in their lives. Whites especially resented seeing black men wearing the uniform of the United States Army, even though the federal forces were segregated, and there were only a handful of black officers. One black soldier wrote to a friend, "Prejudice reigns supreme here against the colored troops. Every little thing that is done here is chronicled as negro brazenness, outlawry, etc."[41]

Fights between black and white soldiers were common, sometimes man-to-man, often in large scrums. Already stoked on the rhetoric of national unity against a common, non-Anglo enemy, it was a short jump for Northern soldiers and reporters to side with Southern whites against black troops (though there is no evidence that any men from the Rough Riders participated in racial violence). This was the ugly side of the national reunification that Leonard Wood and the Rough Riders had celebrated during their trip along the Gulf Coast, the side that whites rarely considered or cared about. Reuniting North and South could only come at the expense of black equality, a deal that was forged in part during the Spanish-American War.

Typical of the Northern response to the scene in Tampa was a report about a race riot in the New York *Sun*. A group of black soldiers "went to the city and began drinking bad whiskey. In a short time they were hilarious and attempted to take the town. . . . Some of the white soldiers from the north, it is said, joined in with the colored regulars against the Southern boys, and a free fight was waged." Four black soldiers were killed. But this was not how the black soldiers reported the fight—in their telling, which appeared in black newspapers across the North, a bar owner refused to serve them, and a gang of drunken white soldiers had attacked them. "This is the kind of 'united country' we saw in the South," one black soldier wrote home.[42]

In a study of the Southern media coverage of the Tampa encampment, the historian Willard B. Gatewood Jr. found that in most cases, white violence—whether against property, civilians, or other soldiers—was dismissed in newspapers as rowdiness and steamblowing, while the same behavior by blacks was written up as "rackets" and "riots." The sight of uniformed, armed black men was a Southern nightmare, and a justification for further segregation. "Their presence in Florida contributed to the final capitulation of the white South to extreme racism," Gatewood concluded.[43]

On the morning of June 5, right after reveille, Wood announced a surprise inspection. As he had hoped and expected, the tents were perfectly spaced, the blankets were all folded precisely, and the picket ropes running around the camp were as straight as a shot. They had better be: General Joseph Wheeler, the commander of the cavalry division, was coming to visit.

Wheeler was a courtly Georgian of great stature but diminutive size—barely five feet tall, he had narrowly cleared the height requirement for West Point in 1854. When the Civil War broke out he joined the Confederate Army; when it ended, he was a cavalry gen-

119

eral, at just twenty-eight years old. He later served as a representative from Alabama, and though a Democrat—and therefore a member of a party that vociferously opposed the Army and its deployment—he had supported both the creep toward war with Spain and the president's cautious approach to actually declaring it. Once McKinley did, the president had called Wheeler to his office and asked him to command the cavalry division in Cuba. By then Wheeler was sixty-one years old, with a long white beard; there were younger, more adept generals in the Regular Army. But McKinley wanted Wheeler because of what he represented: sectional reconciliation.[44]

Wheeler relished his new job. More than anyone else in the Army, he took McKinley's directive about reuniting North and South to heart. At one point in Tampa, Stephen Bonsal wrote, someone asked Wheeler, "How does it feel, General, to wear the blue again?" Wheeler replied: "I feel as though I had been away on a three weeks' furlough, and had but just come back to my own colors." He also seemed to appreciate the way the Rough Riders deviated from the West Point playbook. "This is a mob of men," he said after watching the regiment drill. There was a long silence. Roosevelt looked on. "This is a mob of men I'm very glad and proud to command. I had just such another mob in Tennessee and the Yankees will tell you what that mob did. I'm glad to be with you."[45]

Despite the rapid influx of soldiers and the pressure to move on Cuba, General Shafter and his superiors in Washington refused to set sail for the island. There were many reasons for the delay—the lack of clear orders, the need to wait on more men and more supplies—but the primary concern was the Spanish Atlantic Squadron, under the command of Admiral Pascual Cervera y Topete. Reserved, cerebral, and opposed to the war, Cervera nevertheless knew how to follow commands, and had set sail from the Cape Verde Islands on April 29 with orders to defend Cuba from attack. American warships all along the Eastern Seaboard were put on alert, but Cervera ended up sailing into the harbor at Santiago de Cuba, on the southeastern coast, on May 19 without firing a shot. It took another week for the Americans to discover his hiding place, and on June 1 the cruisers *New York* and *Oregon* arrived to bottle him in. Two days later a Navy lieutenant named Richmond Hobson led a small crew on a near-suicide mission into the harbor, which snakes through a narrow channel before opening up into a bay just west of Santiago. Their boat was packed with explosives, and they aimed to detonate it in the middle of the channel, to stopper up the exit. This they did, but the ship drifted as it sank, and the channel remained free. Hobson and his men were picked out of the water by Spanish sailors and taken prisoner. Back in the United States, the crew became national celebrities overnight, and their misadventure underlined the importance of taking Santiago as soon as possible.[46]

The Navy faced a conundrum. As long as Cervera was at Santiago, the Americans had to maintain an extensive blockade around the harbor mouth, diverting nearly a dozen warships from their duty as part of the overall blockade of the island. But the harbor was so well-protected that it would be impossible to go into it for a naval attack. The only solution, concluded Admiral William T. Sampson, in charge of the fleet, was to capture the city by land, thereby capturing the Spanish ships as well. Conveniently, General Miles, commander of the Army, had already been assembling plans for Shafter's Fifth Corps to attack Santiago as an opening move in the assault on Cuba. Cervera's presence, and Hobson's capture, gave that plan a sudden urgency. Shafter received orders to sail for Santiago on May 29.[47]

There was a catch: Shafter did not have enough ships. There was no American merchant marine to speak of that could transport them. The Army and the Navy fell to squabbling. The Navy said the Army had never requested ships; the Army said the Navy refused to provide them. The Army had to scour Eastern ports for leasable ships, and even then came back with only enough to carry about 17,000 troops and a few hundred horses and mules. The rest would have to stay behind on the first wave.[48]

Each regiment had to make cuts. "The dreary hotel corridors were crowded with the anxious, expectant faces of those who were to go and of those who were to remain behind," Bonsal wrote. Some regiments made cuts man by man, but Wood and Roosevelt decided to leave four entire troops behind—C, H, I, and M—along with all but a few horses. Men wept; officers assigned to stay in Tampa pleaded with Wood to change his mind. Hamilton Fish, a sergeant in Troop I, resigned his commission so he could enlist as a private in a troop that was still going to Cuba; Allyn Capron, the West Point graduate and Army veteran in command of Troop L, immediately requested that Fish be added to his unit. Two particularly vocal troop captains, both from New Mexico, were George Curry of Troop H and Maximiliano Luna of Troop F. Wood called them to his tent. He told them he couldn't take both. Luna was the first to make his case. "He made the pleas that it was his right to go as a representative of his race," Roosevelt wrote. "He demanded the privilege of proving that his people were precisely as loyal as any others." Capron, standing nearby, suggested they flip a silver dollar. The two troop leaders assented. Luna won; Troop F would go to Cuba, and Curry and Troop H would stay.[49]

Less lucky were the soldiers, like Theodore Miller, who had joined late and didn't have all their equipment. At a troop review on the afternoon of June 6, his captain told him he would have to stay behind; among other things, Miller needed a rifle. "I almost broke down with disappointment, and did cry," he wrote. The next morning, though, his captain came up to him with a carbine and cartridge belt. The owner had been on guard duty and fallen asleep, and the captain had drummed him out. Miller was, he decided as he walked away with the gun, pretty lucky after all.[50]

Finally, on June 7, during his evening coffee, Shafter received a telegram from Washington, via Western Union: "You will sail immediately as you are needed at destination." He told the regiments to be ready to embark, at Port Tampa, the next morning. The men were camped mostly north of Tampa, but the port was nearly ten miles south, close to the mouth of what is today called Hillsborough Bay, and reachable by a single railroad track. Even then, the track ended fifty feet from the pier, the two points separated by loose sand in which even an unburdened man sank to his ankles—it would be much worse for soldiers and stevedores carrying fifty pounds or more of equipment.[51]

Once again, confusion reigned. There was no plan, or equipment, to actually move the regiments from their camps to the dock. "We were allowed to shove and hustle for our selves as best we could, on much the same principles that had governed our preparations hith-

erto," Roosevelt wrote. Wood and Roosevelt were ordered to have
their men at a nearby track at midnight, where there would be a train
to pick them up. They all drank a few cups of coffee, then set out. But
just as in San Antonio, at the start of their journey, no train materialized. The men dropped their packs and sacked out, there beside
the railroad track. "I never spent a night like that in my life, and felt
decidedly on the bum the next morning," Miller wrote. But there
was still no train, and Roosevelt and Wood began to worry they'd be
left behind. At one point they received orders to march to a different
track, but there was no train there, either. Finally at 6 a.m., a loco-
motive hauling coal bins came along, headed north; the two officers
persuaded the conductor not only to let the regiment pile into the
coal bins, but to go in reverse all the way to Port Tampa. The men
loaded in and held on as best they could, and the train jittered down
the track. At one point they passed a train full of men from the 71st
New York Volunteers, a regiment that, under slightly different circumstances, might have included Roosevelt, at the time one of the
country's most famous New Yorkers. "Hallo Teddy! Speech! Speech!
We—Want—Roosevelt!" the regiment cheered. Roosevelt demurred,
and the train moved on. By the time the Rough Riders arrived at Port
Tampa, they were covered in coal dust. One sergeant shouted: "Boys,
I guess we are rough riders now, all right!"[52]

The port itself was a hellscape, "a swarming ant-heap of humanity," according to Roosevelt: Tens of thousands of men, their horses,
and their supplies jostled for placement in the heat, and there was
no one there to direct them onto their assigned ships. While they
waited, many men, unable to find shade, simply sat fully clothed in
the muddy water to cool off. Henry Plant, who owned most of Port
Tampa, had built a smaller hotel here, an adjunct to the Tampa Bay
Hotel, but it was off limits to enlisted men. To make things more
difficult, the tycoon had refused to close off the rail line to civilian
trains, and thousands of sightseers competed with the Army for track
space, and for space on the quay when they arrived. A few enterprising locals had set up a row of temporary restaurants, whorehouses,
and bars nearby, and men with ready cash headed there to cool off.[53]

Shafter oversaw the loading from a makeshift desk beside the
quay—a packing case as a table and two cracker boxes as a chair.

Along with the handful of ships that could dock at the quay at a time, just six more could sit out in the twenty-one-foot-deep channel. The other twenty-five, along with the cruisers and destroyers and torpedo boats that would escort them, had to wait further down the bay. Despite the disarray, those who took a step back from it all were in awe of the moment. Clara Barton, who was then in Tampa, recalled standing at the quay, looking out over the bay: "The great ships gathered in the waters; the monitors, grim and terrible, seemed striving to hide their heads among the surging waves; the transports, with decks dark with human life, passing in and out, and the great monarchs of the sea held ever their commanding sway. It seemed a strange thing, this gathering for war. Thirty years of peace had made it strange to all save the veterans."[54]

While their men gathered on the quay, Roosevelt and Wood split up to find someone to direct them to a ship—none had been assigned to them yet. There was a colonel nominally in charge of the loading process, and they both found him at the same time. He pointed at a ship in the channel—the *Yucatan*, a 336-foot coastwise passenger ship that had been used to shuttle among New York, Havana, and points in between. It looked just big enough for the regiment to fit comfortably. Unfortunately, Roosevelt soon learned, two other regiments had been assigned to it as well. As soon as it docked, Roosevelt ran aboard, and Wood ordered Allyn Capron, who had been standing nearby, to rally the men to follow. As they were still walking up the gangplank, officers from the Second Regular Infantry and the 71st New York Volunteer Regiments arrived, a hair too late; the 71st went off in search of another ship, and four companies of the Second Regulars came aboard. Roosevelt, ever conscious of publicity, spied a two-man crew from the Vitagraph Company standing with their motion picture camera by the quay and shouted: "I can't take care of a regiment, but I might be able to handle two more." Secure in their berths, the Rough Riders spent the rest of the day and most of the night loading their equipment—which, in yet another moment of incompetence, had been unloaded at the far end of the quay.[55]

Unlike in the Civil War, soldiers in the Spanish-American War tended not to sit for photos. Especially in the North, it was common in the 1860s for men to have their image captured in a daguerreotype studio before heading to the front, giving later generations a rich record of the names and faces who fought. They often brought relatives or friends to sit with them, along with mementos and other visual clues about their loves, values, and hopes. Nothing like this exists for their children, the men who fought in Cuba and the Philippines at the end of the century. Perhaps, in 1898, no one expected the war to last very long; perhaps by then, photography was so commonplace that no one considered it necessary. But the result is that we lack that same rich visual archive.[56]

There is one photo, though, taken not in a studio but on a deck about the *Yucatan*, that stands out as a visual reminder of the sort of men who went to war in 1898. The photo is of Hamilton Fish. He wears a dark shirt, probably blue—though a close-up, it is grainy, and black and white. His sleeves are rolled up, above the elbow. His arms, thick as ropes, reach down to the gunwale, where his hands rest, large and sinewed. His face, framed by the shirt below and a broad-brimmed slouch hat above, is full and thick, but his skin is taut and leathered. It is the face of a young man who has already seen much, a face that has taken abuse at the expense of a will determined not to die without his share of scars. He has the nose of a pug, with thin lips wrapped around a wry smile. He is looking right at the camera. He is going to war.

The ships were expected to leave the next morning, and hundreds of Tampans gathered to see them off, with a band in tow. But as the men gathered on deck to wave goodbye to the crowd, word came that unidentified ships had been spotted in the Nicholas Channel, between Cuba and Florida. They would have to wait until the coast was, literally, clear. The crowd dispersed, the men's hearts sank. Though they didn't know it yet, it would be another six days before they sailed.

With so many men crammed into each ship, and so many ships crammed into the bay, the expedition went collectively stir-crazy. At one point the *Yucatan*, with 3,500 pounds of dynamite in its bow, barely avoided a collision with another transport ship, the *Matteawan*; the two vessels missed a head-on impact by less than ten feet. "As good as a mile," said Colonel Wood, wiping his brow in relief. The Rough Rider Woodbury Kane, standing next to him along the deck, replied, "I don't know, I think I'd have felt better if that confounded thing had been a mile away."[57]

The *Yucatan* was cramped and hot, and the men spent most of their time on deck, trying to find what shade they could. Some swam; those who couldn't, or were simply too much in awe of such an immense body of water, stood on deck with rifles in hand, watching for sharks, which rumor said were swimming nearby. The food was even worse than the meager rations they had eaten on the train. The core of each meal was "canned fresh beef," a stringy, stinky mass of meat that most of them refused to consume. At one point Charles Knoblauch, who had quit his job as a Wall Street stock trader to join the regiment, swam the half mile to shore with a wad of bills in his pocket, ate a big meal, and swam back. Theodore Miller, tasked with rowing Wood to the *Seguranca*, General Shafter's flagship, and other points around the bay, got lucky and managed to spend a few hours onshore. Among other items, he bought 35 cents worth of gum, which he sold for 70 cents back on board, "besides all I gave away and chewed myself."[58]

On June 13, the men on the ships learned the welcome but frustrating news that the "enemy" vessels were in fact a pair of civilian ships. Finally, they were allowed to leave. That morning thirty-one ships carrying 10 million pounds of rations, 2,295 horses and mules, 16 pieces of artillery, and 16,987 men—including 89 war correspondents and 11 foreign observers—slipped out of Hillsborough Bay toward the Gulf of Mexico. On the quay stood three women and a group of sweaty stevedores, the only goodbye party for the largest invasion force the United States had ever assembled.[59]

CHAPTER 7

"WHO WOULD NOT RISK HIS LIFE FOR A STAR?"

A s the fleet passed down through Tampa Bay and out into the
open Gulf, the water darkened from light blue to cerulean to
indigo, and the men cheered to be finally on their way to battle. Several ships had regimental bands aboard, and from any vessel a listener could hear strains of "Swanee River" and "Rock of Ages" and
the ever-popular "There'll Be a Hot Time in the Old Town Tonight"
carrying across the water from one ship to another, like seagoing
symphonies. "There is nothing so fine as the cheers and bands and
the sight of the thirty ships with their battleships guarding them,"
Davis wrote to his father. This wasn't just the largest amphibious
invasion ever mounted by an American army, and the first of any
note since General Winfield Scott landed 8,600 men at Veracruz
during the Mexican War. Despite the chaos leading up to its departure, the fleet was the largest foreign expedition anywhere since Britain set off for the Crimean War, forty-four years before. If America
needed to demonstrate its military prowess to the world, this was a
stunning debut. "We have scored the first great triumph in what will
be a world movement," Roosevelt wrote to his sister Corinne.[1]

From afar, the fleet must have struck quite an impression: thirty-one transport vessels, painted pitch-black, accompanied by fourteen
gray warships, all steaming along at eight knots in three columns,
each column led by a cruiser, a mass of ships altogether over half a
mile across and several miles long. Among the nearly 17,000 men
aboard the fleet, the transports carried 15,058 enlisted men, 819 officers, 30 civilian clerks, 272 teamsters and packers, and 107 steve-

dores. In the animal pens below huddled 2,295 horses and mules. The ships also held 114 six-mule wagons, 81 escort wagons, 16 light guns, four 7-inch howitzers, four 5-inch siege guns, a Hotchkiss revolving cannon, eight field mortars, four Gatling guns, and a pneumatic dynamite gun. Gunboats darted among the troopships, their captains barking orders by megaphone; at other times the ships communicated via colored rockets.[2]

The fleet looked different up close. For one thing, the troopships were not actually troopships. They were a motley collection of mostly cargo and cattle ships that had been hastily refitted in Tampa; the *Yucatan*, which carried the Rough Riders, had previously hauled mail and passengers for the Ward Line. And they were old: Two of the ships, the *Clinton* and the *Morgan*, were sidewheel steamers built for river and coastal use during the Civil War. One of the few ships of any modern provenance, the *Florida*, which carried a water-distilling plant, struck another craft while waiting in Tampa Bay and had to remain behind for repairs. The crews, all of them private commercial operators and none of them versed in sailing in formation, struggled to keep up and in their columns. Every day that healthy eight-knot clip slowed to seven, then six, and even then, transports lagged behind, fell out of line, had to be herded back in order by the martinet torpedo boats, "Like swift, keen-eyed intelligent collies rounding up a herd of bungling sheep," Davis wrote. One ship dropped behind by fifty miles before the fleet stopped to let it catch up. Every evening the fleet slowed to a crawl so that the stragglers could catch up and the torpedo boats could once again nudge the columns back into line. Still, Arthur Lee, the British Army attaché, wrote, "By daylight each morning all semblance of order in the columns had vanished." Officers on the escorting Navy ships recommended that the fleet split in two, with the faster ships moving on in a separate squad, but General Shafter, from his flagship, the *Seguranca*, refused. A voyage that should have taken two and a half days took over twice as long.[3]

The ships themselves were floating disasters—"suggestive," Roosevelt wrote to Senator Henry Cabot Lodge, "of the black hole of Calcutta." In the holds, contract crews had stripped out the stables and coal bins and cargo bulkheads and nailed together wooden bunks, with no consideration of personal space: On the *Yucatan*, the bunks stood four beds high, with about two feet between each of them. The wood used for the bunks was raw and unsanded; men got splinters just sitting on them. They found space where they could; Miller, Wrenn, Larned, and Teddy Burke located a small room in the stern, on the second deck, where the ship's crew had imprisoned a stowaway boy who had stabbed a sailor. They set up camp there, until they were kicked out to make room for a measles-quarantine ward. There were just a few water barrels on each ship for all personal needs, whether to drink or wash, and that water "smelled like a frog-pond or a stable-yard, and it tasted as it smelt," said Davis, who sailed with Shafter aboard the *Seguranca*. In Tampa, Colonel John Jacob Astor, an heir to the Astor fortune and a member of Shafter's staff, had offered to buy sufficient water for everyone, but Shafter refused—it was good enough for him, the general said, so it should be good for his men.[4]

Equine and fuel odors had already turned the air inside the ships revolting before the men boarded; after a few days at sea, it was hard to breathe anywhere belowdecks. The air was heavy with sweat and breath-stink. "I have often wondered how steerage passengers lived," Theodore Miller wrote in his diary. "Well, I found out, and experienced a much worse life." There were few lights; men found their way around with matches. After the first night, most of them dared court-martial and slept on the deck, so many that with the lights out, it was impossible to move topside without stepping on someone. It was worse for the animals, who had no choice but to stay crowded together in the suffocating holds, where spruce stanchions separated them into 2.5 foot by 8 foot pens. Dozens died, including 12 percent of the mules. The men tossed the carcasses overboard, letting them trail in their wake until being plowed under by the next ship in the line.[5]

In its haste to pack the ships with troops and horses, the Army had neglected to pack enough for either to eat. There was sufficient food for a quick trip from Tampa down to the Florida Keys and across the straits to Mariel or Matanzas, east of Havana, a daylong sail that had been part of the earlier plan of attack. No one had bothered to add more rations when the landing site shifted to Santiago, nearly 700 miles away, and on the opposite side of the island. Instead, the men ate whatever rations they had brought with them, and made them last as long as they could. Worse, the ships lacked cooking facilities for the enlisted men, so they had to eat cold food, mostly hardtack, a few cans of beans, and the ubiquitous, nauseating canned beef. In the semitropical heat, the cans would expand and pop when opened, recalled James Church, the Rough Riders' assistant surgeon, "with a kind of explosion effect, like a bottle of Mumm's extra dry; we would eye the contents in shuddering silence, while the bravest held their breath a while."[6]

When Alvin Ash, a Rough Rider from New Mexico, asked Roosevelt for something, anything else to eat, he handed a canned beef ration to him by way of explanation. "Are you complaining already?" Roosevelt said. "This is war, not pink tea. You've got to expect hardships."

"That's all right, colonel," Ash replied. "I've been used to hardships all my life, but I've always been fed right. And this canned carcass ain't right."

Roosevelt sniffed it, and agreed. He ordered all the canned beef tossed overboard.[7]

That didn't solve the lack of food. Some men had the foresight to stock up on pies and fruit from vendors at Port Tampa. Those who could procure some bacon from the galley, either by purchase or theft, would let it sit in the sun on a metal surface, and in less than an hour it was fried to a crisp. Some of the ships, including the *Yucatan*, also had a store of frozen beef, an experimental product sent south by a meatpacking company wrapped in burlap. But the men refused to touch it, let alone eat it; it had, said trooper Frank Hayes, "a bilious whitish green in color and a more or less cadaverous aroma"— derived, he concluded, from the application of formaldehyde. The cooks, who prepared food for the officers, made a fast side business selling meat sandwiches for 25 cents, a steep price that enlisted men were nonetheless eager to pay. Water was 5 cents a glass. The crews sold whiskey and beer as well—$20 a gallon for the former, 25 cents a pint for the latter. One cook reportedly made $1,100 during the five-and-a-half-day voyage.[8]

Theodore Miller had a different strategy. Posted to guard duty near the galley, he relied on his warm, loose smile and quick way with words to make friends with the cooks. "I worked it just right, so I could get fresh water and something to eat most any time I asked," he wrote. One cook, named Tony, often slipped him an entire dinner. Otherwise, "I should have certainly starved."[9]

When they weren't dreaming of food, many of the Rough Riders were bent over, seasick. The lack of healthy, sustaining sustenance and the close, stuffy quarters didn't help, and on top of seasickness, disease spread easily. Hamilton Fish had procured a basket of lemons at Port Tampa, and he dispensed them to stricken comrades, or made batches of lemonade, poured them into the troopers' tin cups and carried eight to ten at a time down to the ship's improvised sick bay, nervously stepping with the rolling of the decks. Those beyond the help of a few ounces of lemonade required a time-draining transfer to the *Olivette*, the hospital ship. "Every now and then some troopships would run up the ominous sick signal," wrote the *New York Times*, "whereupon the fleet would slow up and the sick would be brought aboard the Olivette"—which also carried most of the reporters.[10]

With all their fits and starts and confusion along the way, the ships made a ripe target for a Spanish attack. The fleet did not maintain a lights-out policy after dark, making things even easier for a courageous, or suicidal, Spanish captain. "At night when the ships were all lit up, it looked like a small town," wrote Billy McGinty, "with lights forming a village built on a hill because the ships ahead of us seemed to be higher than the others." A swift-running gunboat, dispatched from Havana or Matanzas or any of the ports along the northern Cuban coast, could have gotten close enough to fire off several torpedoes at the unarmed troopships before the American gunboats or cruisers could react. The fleet tried to remain alert to attack, and several times a day, having encountered a strange vessel, an American torpedo boat, which was normally towed by a larger warship to save fuel, "was slipped like a greyhound from the leash, and sped across the water toward it," Roosevelt recalled in his memoir. On every occasion, it was a false alarm. The Spanish knew the Americans were coming; it was sheer luck—and Spanish incompetence—that left the fleet unharried as it moved east.[11]

Roosevelt and Wood did their best to maintain order and discipline on board. They drilled the men in infantry tactics and held physical exercise sessions twice a day, at 7 a.m. and 4 p.m.; at night they continued the officers' school that had begun in San Antonio.

On Sunday, June 19, they held church service; Miller, an avid glee-clubber at Yale, sang in the choir next to Roosevelt. After everyone was asleep, Roosevelt stayed up, reading the manual of arms, cramming as much knowledge about tactics and military leadership into his head as he could before they landed. "Many nights I have waked up at 2 or 3 o'clock in the morning and I would find him with a piece of candle or an old smoky lantern, with bleary eyes, studying some military work," recalled one trooper, Sherrard Coleman. The next morning Roosevelt would pelt the regulars in the regiment with questions, especially Allyn Capron, a ramrod of a West Point graduate who, like so many of the veterans, had extensive experience as an Indian fighter. Roosevelt was especially curious about retreating, which to him was a venal sin but which the manual treated as just another tactical maneuver. In the face of overwhelming fire against infantry, the manual said the only smart thing to do was to pull back. Capron disagreed. Modern rifles were too accurate, he told Roosevelt; a full retreat, exposing your back, was suicide. "You had better impress on your men that the only way for them is to charge through it and to charge through it quickly," he said.[12]

Most of the men had never seen the ocean, and they stood at the railing and stared for hours at the multitudinous seas passing beneath them. Years later, Ash, from New Mexico, joked about the time his hat blew in the water: "I said, 'Oh Jesus, my hat's blowed into the creek.'" Another trooper was astonished when Roosevelt told him that, in fact, the ocean was not drinkable. The sailors seemed taken with the unworldliness of the American soldiers, and plied them with stories about Cuban wildlife: about boa constrictors hanging from trees, ready to drop on passersby, of the "accuracy by which gigantic monkeys could bean one with a coconut from the top of a palm tree," recalled the New Mexico trooper Royal Prentice.[13]

Life on board wasn't all bad; the four companies from the Second Infantry, which were on the *Yucatan* with the Rough Riders, had a regimental band, and when it played the Rough Riders' mascot mutt, Cuba, would run in circles howling on the *Yucatan*'s deck (the other two mascots, Josephine the mountain lion and Teddy the eagle, had been left in Tampa). With nothing else to do, the men sat and gawked at the flying fish and dolphins that popped out of the waves, or lay back and marveled at the expansiveness of the sky, picking out shapes in the cloud formations. To wash their clothes, they would tie them in a ball, attach a rope, and let them trail behind their ship—but haul them in before the current tore them to pieces. Alongside the clothing, several ships trailed fishing lines. And there were minor excitements: On at least one occasion, they encountered a water spout; when it got too close to the fleet, a warship fired a cannon at it, and when the shell broke the cyclone water showered down on the surrounding ships. A trade wind from the east kept the decks cool. The indigo waters were "as smooth as a mill pond," Wood wrote to his wife. On June 18, they caught their first glimpse of the Southern Cross, its vast cruciform sitting just above the horizon.[14]

It was along the railing, looking out at that pond-smooth water, that Roosevelt came to know Buckey O'Neill, the worldly lawyer-turned-sheriff-turned-mayor of Prescott, Arizona. Roosevelt enjoyed the men in the regiment, but he never shed his intellectual snobbery; as much as he liked to imagine himself a man of the West and its people, he lived off smart conversation and the play of ideas. He needed a witty interlocutor, and many of the men in the regiment were not that. O'Neill was different. Here was a man who seemed the mirror of Roosevelt: Raised in Washington, D.C., and formally educated, O'Neill had broken free of his Eastern confines and crafted a variegated life on the frontier, gambling and politicking and writing, the archetypal Rooseveltian hero. "Down at the bottom, what seemed to interest him most was the philosophy of life itself, of our understanding of it, and of the limitations set to that understanding," Roosevelt wrote. O'Neill had found sustenance in the military, finally, and he seemed intent on staying in after the war ended, and climbing the ranks. "Who would not risk his life for a star?" he asked Roosevelt, as the two of them stood on deck one evening.[15]

For days, the men were left to guess their first destination; most continued to believe they were headed to Puerto Rico. It was only when they passed the last of the Bahamas, Great Inagua Island, and turned south did they realize they might be headed for Santiago. As the fleet rounded Cape Maisí, on the southeastern corner of Cuba, a small sailboat approached. As the ships watched it warily, the sailor on board unfolded a large flag and ran it up his mast. It was the

Estrella Solitaria, the flag of Cuban independence. Cheers erupted from the ships.

The difficulties encountered by this underresourced army on a poorly planned expedition did not find their way back to the American public that June. Eventually they would; after the fall of Santiago, men would begin to rotate home and bring with them stories of mismanagement and incompetence and unnecessary death. In 1899 Congress would appoint Grenville Dodge, a former congressman and railroad executive, to hold hearings on the campaign and draw up a list of charges against the quartermaster's and transportation departments. Careers would be ended, reputations destroyed. But that was still long in the future.

For now, the Army enjoyed almost universal acclaim, before it had even fired a shot. It helped immensely that most of the 100 reporters who traveled with it to Cuba felt no special urge to reveal the ugly truth behind the expedition, though they all knew it privately. When one of them, Poultney Bigelow, an American writing for *The Times* of London, wrote about the "acephalous War Department in Washington, which had permitted the lack of supplies and logistical shortcomings in Tampa, Richard Harding Davis lashed out in the Army's defense. In a rebuttal published in the *New York Herald*, Davis said of Bigelow's reporting that it was "doubtful if anything has appeared in print since the beginning of the war, in even the yellow journals, so un-American, so untrue, or so calculated to give courage to the enemy." It was, in short, "treason." After that, few dared follow Bigelow's lead.[16]

Even still, it is hard to imagine a hundred reports like Bigelow's shaking the public's pro-war sentiment that June. This was an era long before public polling, but the tone of the country was set in its streets and in its daily newspapers and weekly and monthly magazines. Men continued to line up to volunteer, and the camps around the Southeast continued to swell with recruits. Patriotic, pro-war poetry filled newspapers and magazines, most of it doggerel. One representative example: "Go, at thy country's call./Whatever gentle bonds may hold thee here,/Whatever tender claims may seem more dear./Thy duty!—first of all." Newspaper ads incorporated aspects of the war into their product pitches, like one from the Herman Wise clothing store in Astoria, Oregon, that read: "Remember the Maine and Herman Wise when you are ready to buy a suit, a hat, a shirt, or anything else in that line."[17]

Calls for sectional and class reconciliation in the name of national unity during wartime got a boost as well. *Leslie's Weekly* wrote on April 28: "We have regained faith in ourselves as a nation; politics and quibbling and the dollar have been forgotten, and we have stood out loyal and strong. It has been a lesson showing the world that in a period of stress we have not lost ourselves in hysterics, but instead have been calm and self-held." That same issue included a short, crudely allegorical piece about two new fictional auxiliary cruisers, the *Dixie* and the *Yankee*, which "have not always fought together in the past, but in the future they will be inseparable on sea as well as land." Silly, but true: When the men of the 6th Massachusetts marched through Baltimore on their way to Florida, thousands of people turned out to greet them with flowers and flags; when the regiment had moved through that same city in April 1861 (albeit with an older generation of soldiers), pro-Southern militants had attacked them with bricks. Mobilization for the war, *Leslie's* wrote, "wiped away every vestige of the bitterest parts of the Civil War." Those prominent voices who might object that African Americans felt differently were few and far between, and never heeded in the rush to celebrate the new national harmony.[18]

Anti-imperialism, for the moment, was barely audible in the national conversation. Even the business leaders and editorialists and politicians who had railed against going to war now rallied behind the flag, or kept silent. Andrew Carnegie and Mark Twain, two prominent anti-imperialists, supported intervention once the war began. William Jennings Bryan, the "Boy Orator of the Platte" and the Democratic nominee for president in 1896, had strongly opposed intervention in 1897, but on the day McKinley declared war he wrote to the president, volunteering his services. Bryan joined a Nebraska volunteer regiment, traveled to Florida to await deployment, and promptly caught typhoid fever.[19]

To be fair to Bryan, Twain, Carnegie, and others, their advocacy for the war was not rooted in the jingoism of Senators Beveridge or

Lodge. They did not dream of American colonies, or even of American influence over nominally independent nations. Rather, they saw the war as McKinley and Roosevelt had painted it: as a humanitarian intervention, both to end the slaughter of Cuban civilians and to bring the American experience of liberty to a downtrodden people. Bryan had supported the Teller Amendment, which was tacked onto McKinley's war authorization and forbade the United States from annexing Cuba. In a speech delivered in February 1899, Bryan justified his support for the war in terms that would have rung very strange to his forebears in the Jeffersonian, Democratic tradition, but which would echo through practically every American military undertaking of the twentieth century: "Universal peace cannot come until justice is enthroned throughout the world. Until the right has triumphed in every land and love reigns in every heart, government must, as a last resort, appeal to force."[20]

Commodore Dewey's naval victory at Manila had set the tone for the rest of the war. Already, essayists were declaring it a turning point for the country, its debut on the world stage—and not as just another great power, but one with a mission, a vision, a set of ideas about a better world and how it could use its power to achieve it. This was partly propaganda, the fever dream of too many liberals in Congress and idealist editors at the nation's leading magazines. But it was also a deeply felt, and widely shared, sentiment. Walter Hines Page, the editor of *The Atlantic* and a cautious imperialist, argued that the war revealed a new turn in the American character, a willingness to shed its citizens' blood in order "to remove from our very doors this cruel and inefficient piece of medievalism." He worried, though, about the public's willingness to unify so quickly behind McKinley; though he called the war-born national unity "inspiring," he warned that it "puts a new responsibility on those leaders, and may put our institutions and our people themselves to a new test. A change in our national policy may change our very character; and we are now playing with the great forces that may shape the future of the world."[21]

The import of the war was immediately felt abroad. Europeans had watched for decades as America grew in numbers and economic power, and the perspicacious among them knew it was only a matter of time before those two strengths combined behind an assertive foreign policy. The only question was what form it would take. Now they had their answer. "One thing should be said at the beginning: it is predominantly the humanitarian instinct which has led 'the plain people of the United States'—to use Lincoln's phrase—to acquiesce in the war with Spain," wrote the *Manchester Guardian* on May 9. "The dominant aim of the American people is not to avenge the loss of the Maine, not to annex Cuba, but to do a bit of stern work in the interest of humanity." More cynically, the *Daily Telegraph* warned that the appeal to humanitarianism, combined with America's great demographic and industrial strength, invited in "the all-devouring militarism with which we in the old world are so well acquainted." What truly stunned observers, at home and abroad, was the speed with which Americans volunteered to fight, and what that speed demonstrated about the American character and about this new global power. It was this sense of idealistic, voluntaristic militarism that shook Europeans even more than the sheer size of the American industrial economy. "One grand use of this war," wrote the *London Spectator*, is to demonstrate that a great power could project its influence abroad "without wasting its toil upon the maintenance of armies."[22]

At the center of the acclaim were the Rough Riders. More than any other regiment, they represented the new American way of war. "The American has looked upon war as a disagreeable necessity, that comes along about once in a generation, and which is to be met, not by maintaining a large standing army, but by depending upon the bravery and the aptitude of our people for military service," wrote the *Philadelphia Inquirer*. The volunteer, the paper wrote, stood in contrast to the European conscript, "an automaton." And when Americans do go to war, they do so without regard to wealth or class. "Roosevelt's Rough Riders," the unsigned article concluded, "whether Fifth Avenue millionaires or Western cowboys," were off to fight "together in Cuba for the great American principles of liberty, equality and humanity."[23]

CHAPTER 8

"NO COUNTRY ON THE EARTH MORE BEAUTIFUL"

A fter rounding Cape Maisí and the eastern end of Cuba, the fleet passed Guantánamo Bay, where a few weeks earlier American Marines—at the time, a specialized section of the Navy used to support amphibious landings—had made the first land assault of the war, an effort to secure that pristine natural harbor for later use. The attack was a success, but twenty-nine Marines had been killed or wounded. By the time their comrades found their bodies, several had been mutilated, almost beyond recognition, their eyes and ears and large chunks of skin and muscle gone. American officials accused the Spanish of torture, and then, even worse, of disfiguring corpses, and said as much to reporters. But the culprits were not enemy soldiers, but something more revolting: vultures and land crabs. The latter could grow to a foot or more in diameter and lived mostly off scavenged meat, human or otherwise. The crabs—*Gecarcinus lateralis*, also known as blackbacks, for an inky splotch across the top of their shells—could be an ugly, unnerving sight, especially when they traveled in swarms, often thousands strong. Throughout the campaign they could be counted on to appear whenever there was bloodshed and fallen men. For all the man-made horrors the invading army encountered in Cuba, land crabs left the deepest, creepiest impression. "The sound they make in crawling over the twigs and dried leaves is enough to drive a healthy man to insanity," recalled one correspondent.[1]

The day before the fleet passed Guantánamo Bay one of the transports, the *City of Washington*—a leased civilian liner that, coincidentally, had been the closest American ship to the *Maine* when it exploded in Havana Harbor, four months before—began to lag behind, dragged by a barge it was towing. The *Yucatan*, with the Rough Riders aboard, was ordered to fall back to accompany it as it plugged along, and assist if needed. As the *Yucatan* finally passed the mouth of Guantánamo Bay, a high-speed launch came out to greet it. The ship carried only minor news; its officers' real reason for the mission was to meet Roosevelt, until recently their nominal boss in the Department of the Navy and a hero to naval officers worldwide for his reforms and advocacy of new ships and bigger budgets. From the boat's deck, a smart-looking naval officer shouted, "I want to speak to the assistant secretary of the navy, Colonel Roosevelt."

"Here I am," Roosevelt shouted. "What's the news?"

The officer told him about the recent fight, and assured him that everything was calm.

"Delighted to hear it. I hope we won't be too late ourselves."

The officer said the landing should be easy. But, he added, "We expect some very heavy fighting at Santiago de Cuba."[2]

The fleet arrived off Santiago, where the blockade ships stood at station, about five miles off the coast, on the morning of June 21. Rather than begin the landing, though, they idled offshore while the *Seguranca*, Shafter's flagship, sailed west, to a small coastal village called Aserradero, about thirty miles beyond the mouth of Santiago Harbor. He intended to find General Calixto García, the rebel leader in eastern Cuba. As the launch, which carried General Shafter, Admiral William Sampson, a few officers, Richard Harding Davis, and the British Army attaché, Arthur Lee—and no armed guard to speak of—neared the shore, a squad of Cubans onshore started cheering. Several of them stripped naked and waded into the surf to bring the boat in to land; a few of them lifted Shafter out of his seat and conveyed him to the dry beach on their shoulders. Lee was amazed, and a little dismayed, that Shafter would do something so brazen as come ashore, practically unarmed, so close to Santiago. "An enterprising Cavalry squadron could have captured the whole meeting without material risk," Lee wrote.[3]

After a trudge up a steep, rough trail, Shafter's party found García and his staff outside a hut, located within a grove of coconut trees.

The general bid them to sit down, and aides brought out mangoes, limes, pineapple, coconut milk, and coffee while they all examined a map of Santiago. The American officers were stunned to see that García's second in command, General Jesús Sablón Moreno, known by his nickname, Rabí, was a full-blooded Carib Indian, and that many of García's trusted inner circle were black. A segregated army from a segregated nation had come to Cuba to fight alongside an integrated, multiracial rebel army to free the island's people.[4]

General García himself cut a striking figure: Six foot four and wearing a white linen uniform, with white hair and a bushy, droopy white mustache and goatee, García looked, wrote a correspondent for the *San Francisco Call*, "like a Third Empire French marshal." In the center of his forehead was a hole that he kept stuffed with cotton gauze; during the Ten Years' War he had been on the brink of capture, and tried to defeat his would-be captors by shooting himself in the head. The bullet blew through his mouth and the front of his skull, somehow exiting without hitting a single major part of his brain. García told the Americans that Santiago and the surrounding towns held about 20,000 Spanish soldiers and volunteers, along with about 1,000 sailors and marines from the fleet (an exaggeration, or the result of poor intelligence; the total was closer to 12,000 Spaniards and pro-Spanish Cubans). Another several thousand were within a few days' march at Holguín. García's men, on the other hand, were brave and battle-hardened but also worn down by years of fighting and, more importantly, almost out of ammunition. With the Cuban rebels setting up a cordon around the west and north of the city to block reinforcements, García recommended that Shafter land troops on both sides of the opening to Santiago Harbor and then make a quick and relatively easy assault on the two fortresses that guarded each side of the entrance; once those fell, the American ships could sail into the harbor and capture the Spanish fleet—the overall objective of the campaign. But Shafter refused. He had been sent to capture the city, he said, and that is what he would do.[5]

Shafter conducted the Santiago campaign on two reasonable assumptions. The first grew out of his shipboard reading during the sail to Cuba: a history of the last time a foreign army tried to capture the city. In the summer of 1741, during the War of Jenkins' Ear,

English forces under Admiral Edward Vernon occupied Guantánamo Bay, but waited too long to assault Santiago. By the time he was ready it was the rainy season, and too many of Vernon's soldiers had died of disease; eventually he was forced to withdraw. Shafter was intent on avoiding a repeat performance, which meant attacking the city as fast as possible and then, once it was secure, sending as many soldiers as possible back to the United States, before the heat and disease of summer set in. That required, first, making an unimpeded landing, which would allow him to organize his assault without getting immediately bogged down in combat. "There is no more use in thinking that men can go into that climate at that season of the year and escape distress, than there is that you can put your hand in a fire and escape burning," he said. "I determined to rush it, and I did rush it."[6]

Shafter also believed that the American people's support for the war was superficial, and a difficult engagement with high casualty counts would rapidly turn them against the conflict. Shafter was no fool, at least in this regard—he had seen the imposing cliffs and massive stone fortress that towered over the entrance to Santiago, and knew that whatever García said, taking those heights would be a bloodbath. And so Shafter and his landing party returned to their ships, and the ships returned to the fleet, and preparations for the assault began.

On the afternoon of June 21, the fleet made a feint at Cabanas, two and a half miles west of Santiago Bay. Three small warships, the *Texas*, *Vixen*, and *Scorpion*, ran in close to shore and engaged the Spanish batteries, while ten transports, behind them, made exaggerated efforts to appear like they were preparing to land—dropping anchor, lowering boats, and so on. At the same time, 500 Cuban rebels attacked the Spanish line northwest of Santiago, as a ploy to divert attention from the Americans. Just before evening, the *Bancroft*, a gunboat, pulled up alongside the *Yucatan*. A young ensign came aboard and told a group of Rough Rider officers that the landing would commence in the morning. Roosevelt leapt with joy, sang "Shout hurrah, for Erin Go Bragh, and the Yankee Nation!" and danced a jig. Then, turning to Capron, who was watching his lieutenant colonel, mouth agape, Roosevelt said, "Come on, you old Quaker, let's go to supper." That night, tired of eating cold rations and feeling rebellious, several enlisted Rough Riders broke into the *Yucatan*'s galley and made biscuits, which they slathered with preserves they discovered in a cabinet.[7]

The actual landing took place the next morning at a tiny village called, grandly, Nueva Salamanca. But because it was also at the mouth of the Río Daiquirí, both Cubans and Americans called the landing site Daiquirí (many initial accounts referred to it as Baiquirí). The beach skirted a half-moon cove at the base of a string of low mountains centered on Mount Losiltires, a 1,000-foot cone. Shafter, recalling his days at the Presidio, compared it to the view across San Francisco Bay, to the Berkeley hills; Tom Hall, a New Jersey native, said the low mountains reminded him of the Catskills. Malcolm McDowell, a correspondent for the *Chicago Record*, wrote that Daiquirí itself "looks from a distance of a mile much like a Pennsylvania iron-mining town"—that is, until one noticed the dozens of Spanish forts and blockhouses that dotted the elevations behind it.[8]

Daiquirí was familiar to Richard Harding Davis. A decade earlier, at the very start of his career, he had accompanied an official from the Spanish-American Iron Company here. The company had ceased activity with the return of the war, but its facilities remained: a clutch of corrugated-zinc-roofed shacks on shore, and two piers—one for boats, the other, a forty-foot-high iron lattice, for loading ore into barges. On the latter that morning sat a pair of ore cars, in flames.[9]

The transports arranged themselves in a semicircle, five miles out, then moved in toward shore, hesitatingly. As they did, the warships undertook a thirty-minute bombardment. Yellow plumes of fire burst across the faces of the mountains in back and to the east of the site. "The marksmanship of the navy was fine and the way they put shells into a block house on a hill to the right of the town was wonderful," wrote Tom Hall, the adjutant. The barrage destroyed most of the buildings in Daiquirí, knocked down a sizable section of the forest alongside them, and churned up massive piles of dirt and sand. "Should a Cuban wish to plant in Daiquiri, in the near future, he will hardly have to plow the ground," one soldier said. The firing killed or wounded seven Cubans, but no Spanish; they had already largely withdrawn. The Americans could hear explosions from onshore— not the sound of Spanish cannons returning fire, as some thought initially, but of retreating Spanish soldiers demolishing bridges and buildings to impede the American advance. Eventually a lone Cuban rebel climbed out to the end of the iron pier, waving a white cloth to signal that the Spanish had left the scene.[10]

Shafter's invasion force, called the Fifth Corps, was organized into three divisions. The First and Second, both infantry divisions, contained three brigades each, and each brigade contained three regiments (together, the two divisions comprised 10,709 enlisted men and 561 officers). The last division, the cavalry, led by General Joseph Wheeler, contained two brigades of three regiments each, totaling 2,875 men and 159 officers. The Rough Riders were placed in the Second Brigade—though, since most of the horses had been left in Tampa, Wheeler's command was a cavalry division in name only, and the men fought on foot, just like the infantry divisions. The rest of the corps included artillery detachments, transportation units, and an "Independent Brigade" of two more regiments. On paper, it was all neat and tidy; as thousands of men tried to make their way ashore that morning, it was anything but.[11]

The landing began at 9:30 a.m. Immediately, there was a problem. During the voyage, a lighter and a barge, both of which were to take part in the landing, had been lost while being towed behind two transports; as a result, there were only enough boats to carry a quarter of the men at a time, and they piled into the craft until the water almost reached their gunwales. Soon, wrote the journalist Caspar Whitney, "The sea was literally alive with saucy little launches, carrying rapid-fire 1-pounders in their bow and the American ensign at their stern." There was no coordination to the effort: Landing craft went at their own speed, with no respect for or even awareness of an overarching plan. Sailors dug into their oars, with enough effort to remind the Eastern college boys of crew races along the Charles or the Schuylkill. Boats crowded around the pier, wrote Whitney, like "the scramble for elevated railway tickets after a big football game in New York." Things were more confusing onshore, where there was no one coordinating the landing or the disposition of supplies and equipment and men.[12]

One problem was the transport ships and their captains, who were responsible not to the Army but to their commercial owners, from whom the government was merely renting their services. The captains did not want to risk damage, so they remained three to twenty miles out from the coast—a decision, Davis wrote, "that should, early in the day, have led to their being placed in irons." He claimed to have been on six transports that day, and "on none of them did I find a captain who was, in his attitude toward the Government, anything but insolent, un-American, and mutinous, and when there was any firing of any sort on the shore they showed themselves to be the most abject cowards and put to the open sea, carrying the much-needed supplies with them." (To be fair, the Army had failed to take out insurance on the ships.)[13]

Davis assumed that he and the other correspondents would be allowed to land alongside the first waves of soldiers. But when the orders for disembarkation came around, they commanded that civilians stay aboard. Davis, standing on deck of the *Seguranca*, approached Shafter for an explanation. "General," he said, "I see the order for disembarkation directs that none but fighting men be allowed in the boats of the first landing party. This will keep back reporters." Shafter replied that it was for his own safety, and that there simply was not enough room for reporters to travel alongside the soldiers in the launches. Davis, apoplectic, replied that he was no mere reporter— he was a chronicler of history, a "descriptive writer." Shafter scoffed: "I do not care a damn what you are. I'll treat you all the same." Davis got to shore eventually that day, but he never dropped his grudge against the general.[14]

As Wood and Roosevelt pondered the task of rowing 600 men several miles to shore, a small ship pulled up alongside the *Yucatan*. On board was Roosevelt's former aide from the Department of the Navy, Lieutenant Alexander Sharp Jr., and alongside him stood a Cuban pilot whom Sharp said could get the *Yucatan* within a few hundred yards of shore. A few minutes later, as the boats approached land, Roosevelt marveled at their luck to be landing unopposed. "Five hundred resolute men could have prevented the disembarkation at very little cost to themselves," he wrote. The Spanish commander in charge in Santiago, Arsenio Linares y Pombo, had thousands of men under his command, but he had more than the Americans to defend against: to the north and west were hundreds if not thousands of

Cuban rebels, and the Spanish dared not take the risk of exposing the city to direct attack. Time and again during the campaign, this would be the story: The Spanish failed to take advantage of American weaknesses and mistakes, of which there was no shortage.[15]

To land, the men first had to lower themselves into bobbing, waiting launches and rowboats while carrying up to sixty pounds of gear. Hamilton Fish was the first of the Rough Riders to go, and timed his jump perfectly. The others followed suit, but getting into the boats was the easy part. The dock itself, where they disembarked, was deadly. Designed for larger boats, it was too high for the landing craft, except when a swell came along and lifted a boat, for just a second, high enough so that a few men could jump out. Because of the six-foot waves, the bow and stern ropes holding the boats to the dock had to be long, which meant that the boats pitched in and away as well as up and down. The men threw their gear onto the dock, then did their best to time their leaps. As one of the Rough Rider boats was disembarking at the dock, another, full of men from the 10th Cavalry, one of the segregated regiments, pulled up alongside. Suddenly an errant swell hit the two boats, and two of the men from the 10th, Corporal Edward Cobb and Private John English, fell into the water. Weighed down by their gear, they sank immediately. Buckey O'Neill and Charles Knoblauch, both excellent swimmers, dove in after them, fully clothed, but despite several attempts, couldn't find them. Already wet, O'Neill and Knoblauch spent the next hour diving beside the dock, gathering up equipment and weapons that other troopers had dropped.[16]

Among the first Rough Riders to land were Henry La Motte, the regimental surgeon; Sergeant Albert Wright, the color bearer; and Clay Platt, a trumpeter. They could see, atop a steep hill looming over the cove, an empty Spanish blockhouse. Platt, in his sack, held the territorial flag given to the Arizona contingent by the women of Phoenix, less than two months before. They knew what to do.[17]

"All the way up we encountered pieces of shells, traces of the navy's work of the morning," La Motte wrote. In the blockhouse atop the hill, the trio found half-full cups, dirty plates, stores of food, and, on a desk, an order by General Linares in Santiago to hold the fort. Alongside it, almost complete but never sent, lay an officer's reply, promising to singlehandedly push the Americans back to Florida. Soon the trio was joined by Edward Marshall, a correspondent for Hearst's *New York Journal*, who had somehow managed to evade Shafter's order to stay on the ships. He carried an American flag as well. After some effort, the three tied the two flags to a makeshift flagpole and mounted the pole on top of the blockhouse. A minute later, the sound of a ship's whistle rolled across the water, then two, then three, along with the faint but adamant roar of nearly 17,000 American soldiers.[18]

With the Spanish nowhere to be seen, the soldiers' focus turned to the Cuban rebels who greeted them. They were of mostly of African and indigenous background, and many had worked in the nearby mines and sugar plantations before the war. Their bodies and clothing showed the strain of three years of Weyler's war: A typical rebel wore only a loose pair of pants or just a thick thong; in either case, no one wore a shirt. Most were barefoot. For weapons some carried rusty Springfield rifles, though all of them had a machete tied with a string around their shoulders. Roosevelt called them "utter tatterdemalions." William Davidson, a sergeant with the Rough Riders, was even less kind: "So that's what we came to free? If the walking wasn't so bad, I'd go home right now."[19]

Not all the troopers were so dismissive of the Cubans. Several understood the rebels for what they were: a proud and accomplished but also exhausted force, men who had lost almost everything in their three years of fighting against a better-equipped but not better-skilled enemy. "These people, with the extreme odds against them, were putting up the most valiant fight for existence I have ever witnessed," recalled another Rough Rider, David Hughes. Even adjutant Tom Hall, a martinet not noted for his emotional intelligence, wrote that while the Cubans might not have looked like a crack fighting force, "they kept three hundred thousand Spaniards guessing for three years—no slight achievement." Frank Knox, the Michigan boy who had joined the regiment in Tampa, wrote in a letter to his family: "However disreputable their appearance may be the sacred flame of liberty must burn brightly in their breasts or they would have given up this uneven struggle long ago." They were, however, clearly malnourished—Hughes could see their thin arms and legs, and count their vertebrae: "Our men looked at these people with silent and set faces, knowing within them that the time had come when someone had to pay for these conditions."[20]

The Rough Riders, once ashore but not yet dried out, moved to a dusty flat plain at the back of the beach, where they made camp beside a bakery that had been blown in half by an American shell. The men had brought what they could carry on their backs; they left the rest of their equipment on the *Yucatan*, which they could already see sailing back to the protective clutch of warships, five miles out. Roosevelt only had the clothes he was wearing, a Mackintosh, and a toothbrush. Scores of the men sat on the beach, still reeling from the seasickness and vertigo of the voyage. They did find a cool mountain stream that ran into the cove nearby, and by nightfall hundreds of men had taken a bath, their first in over a week. A few of them caught a chicken and, with a few peppers found growing nearby, made soup. Hamilton Fish, never shy about his love for potent potables, ransacked the village looking for whiskey. He found a bottle of rum too strong even for him, but also several demijohns of Spanish sweet wine. He and Burr McIntosh, a correspondent (and, when he wasn't writing, a semifamous stage actor), drank a good part of the wine that night. By the end of the day 6,000 men had come ashore, and made camp with little regard to military protocol. For once, Wood didn't mind. "Everyone tumbled into his blankets in the most comfortable place he could find and slept as only tired soldiers can sleep," the colonel recalled.[21]

The next morning, the *Yucatan* returned, and a contingent of Rough Riders began hauling their equipment ashore. Cuban soldiers were teaching the rest how to make palm-frond lean-tos for shade. As the morning fog lifted, they could see the beach and much of the green valley that ran inland just west of Mount Losiltires, dotted with thousands of white tents. The bodies of Corporal Cobb and Private English, the two drowned soldiers from the 10th Cavalry, were found washed up on the beach, and given a hasty burial.[22]

There were no boats capable of ferrying horses and mules to shore. Instead, the crews used winches to pick them up and lower them into the water—or, lacking a winch, simply pushed them overboard—in the expectation that they would swim to shore. Many went the other way, until a trumpeter on the beach had the idea to play a few bars of drilling music, at which point the trained horses spun around and made a line for shore. One horse tried to swim back to the ship. "The transport had begun turning its screw to get steerage way," recalled Charles Post, a volunteer with the 71st New York. "The horse was caught in the slipstream; it plunged and splashed in the wake, and was swept into the stream of the following transport and brushed alongside until it vanished in a bloody cascade astern."[23]

Amazingly, only six animals were killed that day. One of them was Roosevelt's pony Rain-in-the-Face, which the crew had tried lowering into the water. As he hovered above the water, a breaker leapt up and dashed the animal against the side of the ship and pulled him into the sea, where he drowned. Roosevelt, who had returned to the ship, "split the air with one blasphemy after another to the indescribable terror of the young crewmen," recalled Albert E. Smith, a photographer with the Vitagraph Company. "Stop that goddamn animal torture!" the lieutenant colonel shouted. They took more care with Little Texas—too much care. For several minutes, the horse, held aloft by straps, was lowered haltingly overboard. "Before each pull at the hoist, pinions were exchanged and judgments rendered, until it seemed that if the animal did not collapse from the strain of sheer suspension it would sure die of starvation," Smith wrote. The crew finally cut Little Texas loose, and he swam almost a mile to shore.[24]

At 1 p.m. the 6,000 men already onshore received orders to march to the coastal village of Siboney, about eight miles to the west. Siboney, with a quarter mile of beach, was a better landing place; no one understood why, nevertheless, Shafter had chosen Daiquirí. Within twenty minutes the Rough Riders had struck camp, rolling their tent pieces into their sacks and putting out their fires. Many of the regiment's pack animals were still on the ships, and they only had eighteen to carry the heavier supplies. Wood rode up front, while Roosevelt took up the rear—mounted, at first, then on foot, like the enlisted men. Davis, who wore a tropical suit and a pith helmet, had long suffered from sciatica, and it flared up in the tropical heat. He had managed to procure a horse, and rode alongside the middle of the regiment, with Edward Marshall, the correspondent for the *Journal*, accompanying them.[25]

The path turned inland, slightly, weaving through war-torn, abandoned sugar estates that were already falling back into the arms of the encroaching forest, then back toward the coast, through a cathedral of embowering coconut palms, some of them 200 feet high. The men marched four across, but as the path narrowed around them, they shifted to two across, and eventually single file. "There is no country on the earth more beautiful than that through which we passed," Marshall wrote. The land was indeed stunning, but the day was scorchingly hot, and after two miles the regiment, to a man, looked like it had been dunked underwater, so heavily did the men sweat. The cowboys among them, not used to long marches on foot, took it especially hard. They were not alone in their suffering: The Rough Riders had not been the first regiment to set out, and along the way they passed wool jackets, packs, cans of meat, underclothes, and tent rolls, discarded by overheating soldiers ahead of them. Later they encountered dozens of men lying prostrate from the heat, their blue woolen uniforms wide open across their sweat-drenched chests. Soon, several Rough Riders fell out as well. "Our march was like a pipe organ, having many stops," quipped trooper J. Ogden Wells. They reached Siboney at dusk, after a five-hour march, with rain clouds looming to the west. Siboney was a proper town, though like Daiquirí it had been largely abandoned by soldiers and civilians. Nevertheless, the men were forbidden from bunking down inside the buildings, for fear of disease and vermin. Wood found his men a clear spot near the Siboney beach, lined them up in columns, and told them to camp where they stood. With rain imminent, they rushed to start fires to boil coffee and cook a meal—by then they had learned from the regulars how to fry bacon in a pan, then, keeping the drippings hot, drop in a few pieces of hardtack to soften them. Just as they finished cooking, the rains came.[26]

Theodore Miller had marched alongside his college friend Teddy Burke. They had met up in Tampa and been inseparable. But soon after landing, Burke grew ill, likely with malaria. Eventually Miller decided to leave him by the side of the path, figuring that eventually someone would take him back to a hospital ship. But about an hour after Miller arrived at Siboney, Burke came trudging into camp. He practically passed out where he fell, and slept even as the heavy rains pelted his body. Miller stretched out a rubber blanket over his friend, then went to look for water and a bit of wine, to revive Burke's spirit.[27]

Throughout the night, men trudged in from Daiquirí, while others began arriving in landing craft from the fleet, which had likewise shifted west. Soldiers, stripped to the waist, trudged through the surf to carry supplies onshore, while several ships threw their searchlights onto the beach. As Davis described it,

> It was one of the most weird and remarkable scenes of the war, probably of any war. An army was being landed on an enemy's coast at the dead of night, but with somewhat more of cheers and shrieks and laughter that rise from the bathers in the surf at Coney Island on a hot Sunday. It was a pandemonium of noises. The men still to be landed from the "prison hulks," as they called the transports, were singing in chorus, the men already on shore were dancing naked around the camp-fires on the beach, or shouting with delight as they plunged into the first bath that had been offered in seven days, and those in the launches as they were pitched headfirst at the soil of Cuba, signalized their arrival by howls of triumph.[28]

Siboney was located ten miles southeast of Santiago, though several lines of steep hills, bands of thick semitropical forest, and an unknown number of Spanish soldiers stood between the two. Around 11 p.m., in the middle of a drenching downpour, Wood went to meet with General Samuel B. M. Young, who commanded the Second Cavalry Brigade, and General Wheeler, who was in charge of the entire cavalry division. A Cuban detachment, led by General Demetrio Castillo Duany, had been marching north of Siboney earlier that day when it encountered several hundred Spanish troops, positioned about three miles inland at a crossroads known as Las Guasimas. The two sides fell into combat, and after several Cubans were shot, and one killed, they retreated. That evening, Young visited General Duany at his home in a nearby village, and the Cuban drew him a map of the Spanish line. Young returned and parleyed with Wheeler and the brigade and regimental commanders. There were about 1,500 Spanish located around Las Guasimas, Duany had told him.

Because Shafter was still on the *Seguranca*, Wheeler was the ranking officer onshore, with clear but open-ended orders to secure the beachhead and prepare to march for Santiago. Concerned that the Spanish might be grouping for an assault on the American beachhead, Wheeler decided to attack the next morning.[29]

Roosevelt, not part of the divisional inner circle, sat back among the men, soaking in the rain. His eyes scanned the regiment and fell on Capron and Fish, two of his favorites, deep in conversation. No doubt he saw something of himself in them, or wanted to see something. Capron had been a boxer at the Presidio. Fish rowed varsity crew. Like Roosevelt, they had both spent time out West, Capron as an Indian fighter, Fish as a railway brakeman. There were differences, of course: Both were terrible drunks. Civilian life simply did not fit them. At war, though, they glowed, and Roosevelt basked in their image. "Their frames seemed steep, to withstand all fatigue; they were flushed with health; in their eyes shone high resolve and fiery desire," Roosevelt later wrote.[30]

When Wood returned to the Rough Rider camp, he signaled Roosevelt to join him. They called over Capron and filled him in on the plan. They were to wake early the next morning, before dawn, and march up a limestone ridge toward the Spanish, while the main force under General Young took the Camino Real, which ran along a narrow valley toward Las Guasimas. Capron insisted that his troop, L, be allowed to take point. Wood consented. The regiment finally went to bed after midnight, for a few hours sleep.[31]

CHAPTER 9

"WE'RE LIABLE TO ALL BE KILLED TODAY"

T heodore Miller woke with a start. Nearby, a trumpeter was blowing reveille. It was not quite 4 a.m.

Mist hung over the beach as thousands of soldiers stirred from a night's sleep on the coral-strewn shore. Some had slept in their white canvas dog tents; others, including the Rough Riders, spent the night in the open, and were still damp from the previous evening's rain. Miller lay beside Teddy Burke, his sick friend, who was wet with sweat. Burke murmured about a polo match, how he'd been hurt but was ready to get back on his horse. Wood had ordered his captains not to tell their troops about the day's engagement, but somehow, through his foggy consciousness, Burke seemed to guess that the Rough Riders were about to go into battle.[1]

The village of Las Guasimas, their destination that morning, was little more than a crossroads, with a few houses and a distillery for aguardiente (a sort of rough, unaged rum). But it was a strategic point, located a few miles north of Siboney, at a dip between two ridges. Las Guasimas was perhaps the only place where the American troops could squeeze through the surrounding heights and mountains on their way to Santiago, which lay about eight miles to the west. If the Spanish were going to put up resistance, having done nothing of the sort at the landing sites, it would be there. With well-dug trenches and cleared fire lanes, a few hundred Spanish soldiers could have plugged up an American advance for days, even weeks. And weeks might have been enough—with summer would come malaria and yellow fever, and the Americans might face the same fate as the British did over 200 years before.

General Wheeler understood the importance of Las Guasimas and the urgent press of time. After he heard the reports about the Spanish forces that had ambushed General Duany's troops the day before, he decided not to risk the chance of an attack on the American beachhead, or give the Spanish time to solidify their hold on the ridges and passes that led from the beach to the eastern reaches of Santiago. His men were dog-tired and not yet recovered from the voyage, but he decided there was no choice. That morning, they had to take Las Guasimas.[2]

Miller was eager for his first firefight. But before he could go, he had to take care of his sick friend. He moved Burke, who was barely able to walk, into one of the empty houses (despite the ban on entering them), where he would be safe from the rain, and propped him on a bed. Burke whimpered with jealousy when Miller told him where he was going. Then Miller stepped outside and went to join his troop. There was no commissary or cook assigned to the Rough Riders, so each man was on his own to prepare breakfast from the meager rations the Army had provided. A few troops had pooled their food, and saved some items from the *Yucatan*—Troop L, which included Capron and Hamilton Fish, had collected several cans of tomatoes. Fish ordered them opened. "We're liable to all be killed today and we may as well have enough to eat," he said. Designated cooks, where they existed in other regiments, were standing around sputtering campfires, looking "like busy demons," recalled the correspondent Edward Marshall. Positioned near the head of the trail along which the Rough Riders would soon head out, Colonel Wood looked at his pocket watch, snapped it shut, and said, "We leave in five minutes! Anyone who isn't ready will be left behind!" It was 5:25 a.m.[3]

A contingent of about 470 men, drawn from the First Cavalry and the 10th Cavalry, a segregated regiment, had already left. They were to be the main column in the attack. They headed due north, along the relatively flat floor of a valley that led, gently upward, toward Las Guasimas. The Rough Riders were assigned to take a narrow path along a steep ridge that swung out to the west before going north toward Las Guasimas. If it all went as planned, the two lines would hit the Spanish forces at the same time. But for that to work, the Rough Riders had to move fast.[4]

To start, they climbed straight up a steeply graded path for almost half a mile, through thick woods and rising temperatures. Several reporters, including Davis, Marshall, and the reporter and short-story writer Stephen Crane, went along with them. Marshall recalled having to pull himself up along the path by grabbing bushes and boulders. Most of the march was single file, the route hemmed in by Spanish bayonet, a succulent plant with knifelike leaves. Looming around and over them were West Indian elm trees—or guácimas, the namesake of their destination—as well as ceibas, royal palms, and banyans, roped through with thick vines. Ahead, to the north-west, ran the Sierra Maestra, blanketed with dark green forests and topped by bare, rocky peaks. Roosevelt, ever the hunter, said the set-ting reminded him of deer country; Captain James McClintock, a former journalist who was born in Sacramento, said it reminded him of Southern California. Davis, riding on a mule because of his sci-atica, wrote: "To those who did not have to walk, it was not unlike a hunting excursion in our west; the scenery was beautiful and the view down the valley one of luxuriant peace." It was hard to believe that they were in hostile territory, that they were walking into what might be their first engagement of the war.[5]

Not that they lacked reminders. Within minutes, the Rough Rid-ers were high enough to look back over the cove at Siboney and the thousands of white tents scattered on its beach, punctuated by a few morning fires sending up thin wisps of smoke. They could see the dozens of transports and warships just offshore, which even at that early hour had already begun unloading men and matériel. But the ugliness of Siboney had melted away: "The squalor of the Cuban town at our feet was gilded into glory by the morning sun," Marshall wrote. They marched by abandoned plantation estates, places that not long ago had been teeming with activity but that were already "des-olate and overgrown with scrub and creepers," wrote Marshall, the victims of the "revolution."[6]

After a few hundred yards, they began to pass regulars from the

22nd Infantry on picket, or guard, duty, assigned by General Lawton's Second Division the night before. The pickets were surprised to see them: Lawton's men had arrived in Siboney ahead of Wheeler and the cavalry division, but Wheeler had left his fellow general out of his plans for that morning. One of the pickets, a captain named Nicholls, told Wood that he had heard crashing noises in the night, which he took to be Spanish defenders cutting down trees.[7]

After about twenty minutes, Wood ordered the sixty men in Allyn Capron's L Troop to the front, and told the captain to pick four men to lead on point. Fish volunteered. Duany, the Cuban commander who had briefed General Young the night before, had assigned two of his men to go along with the Rough Riders, and Wood placed them at the very front of the column, as scouts. The standard Army procedure for a march like this would be to assign several men to walk a few dozen yards to the right and left of the main column, to guard its flanks. But that was impossible—the forest was too thick. The Rough Riders would have to hope that they reached Las Guasimas without running into a Spanish ambush. Wood rode behind Capron's troop, with two men from Wheeler's headquarter staff, a Cuban officer, and Roosevelt, at the head of the next three troops; Major Alexander Brodie, the regiment's unofficial third in command, brought up the rear with his three troops.[8]

Down below, in the valley, the 470 men assigned to this main column, commanded by General Young, were as silent as the land around them. "No sound broke upon the still morning air," wrote the journalist Caspar Whitney, who traveled with them, "save the squash of feet in the mud and the occasional rattle of a canteen as it swung against the metal bayonet scabbard at the soldier's hip."[9]

Not so up on the ridge. The Rough Riders "wound along this narrow, winding path, babbling, joyously arguing, recounting, laughing; making more noise than a train going through a tunnel," wrote Stephen Crane. "Anyone could tell from the conformation of the country when we were liable to strike the enemy's outposts, but the clatter of tongues did not cease." Around them, birds cooed unseen, off in the woods. At one point they passed an abandoned Spanish blockhouse; inside, on the whitewashed walls, was a charcoal cartoon of a giant Uncle Sam with a long goatee running away from a smaller

Spanish soldier who was poking him with a bayonet. The artist had signed his name "Jose Cuenpagos."[10]

The day was growing hot. Several men later estimated it was well over 100 degrees by mid-morning. The entire regiment stopped to rest twice. Even then, within an hour of leaving Siboney, about seventy-five had dropped out, struck down by heat exhaustion and left to gather their wits by the side of the trail. Some caught up later, but most straggled back to Siboney. By the time the regiment closed in on the suspected Spanish position, there were fewer than 500 Rough Riders in the column, down from just over 600 who had landed two days before.[11]

After an hour and a half of marching, which put them about two miles beyond Siboney, Capron came running down the path toward Wood and Roosevelt. Fish's team, way out in front, had found a dead Cuban soldier in the path, his face already picked apart by land crabs. Relying on a bit of amateur forensic science, they concluded that this must be one of Duany's men, who had been killed in the engagement the day before—meaning the Spanish might still be close by. It was 7:10 a.m.[12]

Wood stopped the column, then rode up the trail to confer with his other officers. The rest of the men collapsed where they stood. They chewed grass and talked about their favorite things—beer, dogs—and their least—at the moment, the ill-fitting shoes they had spent a day and a half walking and standing in. They took off their slouch hats and fanned their faces. One man blew spit balls at his neighbors. Roosevelt turned to Marshall, the reporter, and chatted casually about the last time they'd seen each other, at a lunch with William Randolph Hearst at Astor House, in New York. Likely most of the men agreed with Davis's belief that the Spanish had probably already withdrawn: "I doubted that there were any Spaniards nearer than Santiago," he wrote.[13]

The trail to Las Guasimas ran along the side of the ridge. To the right, the forest was thinner, but sloped steeply downward. Beyond ran a barbed wire fence to the left, and a field rising gently upward toward a line of trees, "carpeted with grass almost as soft as the turf in the garden of an old English country house," Marshall wrote. Up ahead the trail turned sharply left, and disappeared back into the woods.[14]

Roosevelt, in between bits of conversation with Marshall, looked over at the barbed wire, the residue of an abandoned plantation. Something was off about it. He dismounted to get a closer look. "This wire has been cut today," he said.

"What makes you think so?" Marshall replied.

"The end is bright and there has been enough dew, even since sunrise, to put a light rust on it, had it not been lately cut."[15]

Up ahead, Capron told Wood he had a feeling that there were Spanish troops nearby. He asked permission to reconnoiter; Wood nodded. The colonel went back to the column and told Roosevelt to pass down the word: silence. Roosevelt took the opportunity to mention the rapid attrition of men from the heat. "Doctor La Motte reports that the pace is too fast for the men, and that over fifty have fallen out from exhaustion," he told Wood.

"I have no time to bother with sick men now," Wood replied.

"I merely repeated what the surgeon reported to me."

"I have no time for them now; I mean that we are in sight of the enemy."[16]

Most of the officers tied their horses to fence posts and ordered their men to ready their rifles. The line clicked with the sound of rounds being chambered. After about ten minutes, Wood ordered the men to spread out in a line. He sent three troops, under Roosevelt, down the hill to the right, to connect with Young's men in the column marching along the valley. Three more troops, under Major Brodie, spread to the left, over the fence and into the meadow beyond it. The rest would hold the center or stay in reserve.

As the troops were fanning out into their line, they heard the crack of a rifle. Tom Isbell, a trooper in Capron's L Troop who was on point with Hamilton Fish, had seen a Spanish soldier. He crept within sixty yards, and dropped him with a single shot. Isbell took the spent casing and put it in his pocket, as a keepsake. Seconds later, a line of Spanish rifles returned fire. Isbell was hit instantly; through the course of the fight he was shot six more times, and somehow managed to survive. "I don't know how many shots were fired at me," he later said, "but it seemed to me the entire Spanish army was shooting right at me."[17]

The sound of the Spanish bullets was very different from what the

Rough Riders were used to—though many of them were not used to the sound of any rifle fire at all. The Spanish carried, as their standard rifle, the M1893 Mauser, developed specifically for the Spanish army by a German weapons manufacturer. Unlike the lower-velocity fire of a Remington or Krag-Jorgensen carbine rifle, which the Rough Riders used, a Mauser bullet flew fast and straight, some 300 feet per second, making a high-pitched PHEWWW, rising and then falling in pitch as it as it sped past the ear, "like the sound of a very petty and mean person turned into sound," wrote Marshall. Roosevelt described it as "the humming of telephone wires."[18]

Back in the main column, Theodore Miller heard a few stray shots, then suddenly "volley after volley." Nine Rough Riders went down in the first nine minutes. Fire was coming in from up ahead, and over to the right. The Spanish had arranged about 1,000 men in a V-shaped formation and cut down trees to create fire fields through the woods, the source of the sounds that Captain Nicholls had heard the previous night. Later, Roosevelt and other Rough Riders concluded that the birds they thought they had heard cooing a few hours earlier were probably Spanish scouts, sending signals back to their line that the Americans were approaching.[19]

It was like the forest up ahead had exploded. "Bullets fell around me like hail stones," wrote one trooper. Leaves and bits of tree bark, spun off by bullets whizzing by, fell like snow across the battlefield. When the bullets hit a man's body, they made a flat, low "chug"—"not a pleasant sound," Marshall wrote, "for after one has heard it once, its significance becomes gruesome. It is not unlike the noise made by a stick when it strikes a carpet which is being beaten." The men fell silently. It is a myth that soldiers, when struck on the battlefield, always cry out. The shock and immediacy of the impact is often too quick to allow that; only later, when the pain sets in, do they find their voice. Instead, the only sound the falling Rough Riders made was a dull thud when hitting the ground, accompanied by a rustle of grass and the jingle of canteens hitting the metal of their guns.[20]

Colonel Wood had arranged the regiment so that most of the soldiers were arrayed along a long, thin line, perpendicular and mostly to the left of the trail; to the right the hill was steep and thick with trees. Wood stood in the middle of the line, walking up and down,

not flinching, leading his horse and yelling at his men to keep firing. One of the men from Capron's scouts, who were out ahead of
the main line of American soldiers, came back, his face bloody and
teary from a cartridge exploding prematurely in his rifle. He had
been nearly blinded, and cursed and screamed as he looked for help.
Wood marched up to him, put a hand on his shoulder and said, "Stop
that swearing. I don't want to hear any cursing today." If Wood was
concerned about how thin he had spread his line, he didn't show it.
But he was taking a risk: He wanted to block any attempt by the
Spanish to make an end run around the edge of the Rough Riders'
line and attack them from the rear. Wood's gambit was the sort of
gutsy move, taken without hesitation or fear, that earned him the
nickname "the Ice Box."[21]

William Tiffany, one of the wealthiest men in the regiment, had
taken care the night before to arrange for a mule team that could
carry one of the regiment's Colt machine guns, which he had helped
buy, up the hill. It would have come in handy, had the packer who was
in charge of leading the animals not decided to flee the scene, taking
with him one of the animals that happened to carry ammunition and
part of the gun; without a human master nearby, the rest of the mules
did as mules do and wandered away from the gunfire.[22]

The Spanish line was about 1,000 yards long and about 300 yards
in front of the Americans. By now all the Americans had dismounted,
but the officers mostly kept their horses close by. Roosevelt, leading
Little Texas and his troops, moved to the right of the main line, into
the woods; Wood had ordered him to support Capron's men, who
were still out in front, and to make visual contact with the left wing
of Young's forces, down in the valley. Davis ran after them, trying
to keep up on foot. As they moved forward, the Spanish fire grew
heavier. At one point a bullet hit a palm tree next to Roosevelt, sending splinters into his face. The oncoming fire did not faze him; Roosevelt seemed, to those around him, suddenly transformed into "the
most magnificent soldier I have ever seen," wrote Marshall. "It was as
if that barbed-wire strand had formed a dividing line in his life, and
that when he stepped across it he left behind him in the bridle path
all those unadmirable and conspicuous traits which have so often
caused him to be justly criticized in civic life, and found on the other

side of it, in that Cuban thicket, the coolness, the calm judgment, the towering heroism, which made him, perhaps, the most admired and best beloved of all Americans in Cuba."[23]

Meanwhile Major Brodie had led his troops over the barbed wire fence and into the field to the left of the trail, to extend the American line as far as possible. Men began to fall almost immediately, and in rapid succession. The Spanish fired in volleys, "the most perfectly executed that I ever heard," said trooper Royal Prentice, and at each volley another clutch of men fell, disappearing into the tall grass. "We had evidently stirred up a hornet's nest of a persistent mind not in accord with the then popular conception of Spanish quality in battle," wrote Caspar Whitney, the reporter, who was also following the regiment. At one point a bullet scorched Wood's wrist. He looked and saw two golden beans on the ground. Bending down, then looking at his sleeve, he realized they were irregular halves of a cuff link— split in two by a Spanish round.[24]

Davis, who had trailed Roosevelt, approached the lieutenant colonel with a pair of binoculars. He pointed out a row of Spanish slouch hats, several hundred yards away. "I can see them near that glade," he said. Roosevelt and Davis stood on the edge of a ravine. Down below, they could hear General Young's Hotchkiss machine gun, and two Spanish machine guns firing in response. The soldiers down in the valley had obviously joined the fight.[25]

Roosevelt took the binoculars and stared across. "It was Richard Harding Davis who gave us our first opportunity to shoot back with effect," he later wrote, full of praise for the reporter he had long disdained. "He was behaving precisely like my officers, being on the extreme front of the line, and taking every opportunity to study with his glasses the ground where we thought the Spanish were." Roosevelt called forward "three or four of our best shots" and ordered them to fire at the Spanish line. The first rounds were low, but soon they got the range, and the Spanish dashed out of their position.[26]

Roosevelt could see a much larger group of Spanish further on, and he called up the rest of his troops. They advanced haltingly; stopping to fire and take cover against the Spanish volleys. "To keep men from firing was almost impossible in the excitement, but it was amazing to see how cool our raw volunteers were," Theodore Miller wrote in his diary. Still, men fell. Roosevelt ordered the rest to keep moving, to leave their comrades behind. "It was hard to leave them there in the jungle, where they might not be found again until the vultures and land-crabs came, but war is a grim game and there was no choice," Roosevelt wrote in his memoir. One man who was shot, a trooper named Harry Heffner, asked his comrades to prop him up against a tree with his canteen and his rifle, so he could keep fighting. They did as he asked. When they returned after the fight, he was dead.[27]

As the Spanish left wing, opposite Roosevelt, disintegrated and the men melted back into the jungle, the scene became increasingly confused. Twice Roosevelt saw groups of men moving in the distance, but he could not tell if they were Spanish or American. Worried that they were friendly—and that they might fire at his men in the confusion—Roosevelt ordered a soldier to climb a nearby tree with the regiment's guidon, or pennant, to identify themselves. It was a dangerous task, but the man didn't hesitate. It worked: He waved the guidon; the men in Young's detachments waved theirs back. The right wing of the Rough Riders and the left wing of the soldiers in the valley were finally in contact.[28]

As Roosevelt and his men advanced, Davis fell behind, and suddenly found himself alone. He could hear the firing, and the shouting, but finding his way around the woods was "like breaking through the walls of a maze." He came across one soldier, already dead from a gunshot to the head. When he returned to the body two hours later, vultures had torn off the man's lips and plucked out his eyeballs. Davis then moved back, away from the danger, until he came to the spot where the regiment had first halted. It had since become the dressing station. A tall, thin young man was hurrying around the wounded, quickly tending to those he could save. "His head was bent, and by some surgeon's trick he was advancing rapidly with great strides, and at the same time carrying a wounded man much heavier than himself across his shoulders," Davis observed. "As I stepped out of the trail he raised his head, and smiled and nodded, and left me wondering where I had seen him before, smiling in the same cheery, confident way and moving in that same position."[29]

The man, who looked "like a kid who had gotten his hands and arms into a bucket of thick red paint, and had slopped it all over himself," wrote trooper Arthur Cosby, laid his charges in rough rows in the grassy field, and when he wasn't out collecting the freshly wounded, he was running among his charges, applying tourniquets. He was less punctilious about swearing than Wood was; they could curse all they wanted, he told the wounded men, as long as they didn't set the grass on fire. Davis finally realized who it was: James Church, the assistant surgeon. Davis had last seen him playing football at Princeton. Church was the same man who had presented himself at Roosevelt's house in Washington with the wild hopes of joining the regiment; now, with La Motte having stayed behind at Siboney, he was the only medical officer on the battlefield. "That so few of them died is greatly due to this young man who went down into the firing line and pulled them from it," Davis wrote. (Church received the Medal of Honor for his actions at Las Guasimas.)[30]

As Davis stood watching Church, a steward grabbed his arm and asked for help carrying a wounded trooper, Lieutenant John Thomas, of L Troop. The lieutenant had been shot through the lower leg, and despite a tourniquet, was losing blood rapidly, too rapidly to risk moving him back down the trail to the field hospital at Siboney. As Davis reached down to help lift him, Thomas shouted, "You're taking me to the front, aren't you? You said you would. They've killed my captain. Don't you understand? They've killed Captain Capron."[31]

It seemed impossible, Capron dead, but Davis knew instantly that it was true. He headed back up the trail until he saw Church, on his knees under a tree, with Capron's head propped on his lap. Church was tearing at Capron's tunic with a knife, trying to get to the hole in his chest. But he was already lost. "The skin, as white as a girl's, and the black open wound against it made the yellow stripes and the brass insignia of rank seem strangely mean and tawdry," Davis wrote.[32]

Capron's last words, according to another reporter, were, "How are the boys fighting?" Fred Beal, a trooper standing nearby, replied, "Like hell."

"Very well," Capron said. "I'm going to see this out." He closed his eyes, and was no more. It was his twenty-seventh birthday.[33]

Davis moved on. All around him, men were shooting, and crouching, and running, and dying. The air cracked with gunshots and screams; gun smoke mixed with the humid air to create a sticky, odorous haze. Though most men stuck to the line, others, wounded or dazed, stumbled about the battlefield. A few paces ahead of Capron, Davis found another soldier, mortally wounded; he had a bullet hole between his eyes, but somehow he was still breathing, short rapid pulls of air, his gaze already elsewhere. Davis lifted his head and tried to pour water into his mouth, but his teeth were clenched and it ran down his cheeks. In the man's breast pocket he found a small copy of the New Testament, inscribed with the name "Fielder Dawson, Nevada, Missouri." Just then another soldier, looking no older than fifteen, sat down on a rock next to Davis. "It is no use, the surgeon has seen him, he says he is just the same as dead," the young soldier said. "He is my bunkie, we only met two weeks ago at San Antonio, but he and me had got to be such good friends. But there's nothing I can do now."[34]

Up ahead Davis saw yet another body, in a sergeant's uniform, lying in the path. It was Hamilton Fish. He had been shot through the heart. A giant in life, to Davis he seemed, in death, to have shrunk, so that his uniform bulked around him, like a ready-made funeral shroud. Davis pulled out Fish's pocket watch. On it was inscribed "God Gives," the Fish family motto.[35]

Perhaps the sight of Fish's inert form made something click inside Davis. Ever since his public embarrassment at the hands of William Randolph Hearst, he had sought redemption. Compounding his shame and ambition was his deeply conflicted relationship with the war itself: Having encouraged America to begin it, Davis had struggled with his status as a noncombatant in America's first overseas war. Though war reporting was fast becoming a specialty among the world's correspondents, professional standards of objectivity and nonintervention were not quite where they would be a generation later. He grabbed a rifle from a wounded soldier and found L Troop. As they advanced toward the Spanish, Davis began to fire. "I knew every one of them, had played football, and all that sort of thing, with them," he wrote, "so I thought as an American I ought to help." In Davis's account, his firing was conservative; one might assume, in his telling, that the weapon was more for self-protection. Other accounts differ: Marshall, for example, says that Davis "was pumping wildly at the Spanish with a carbine." Davis made no mention, in his dispatches or later books, of the awkwardness of a correspondent fighting alongside soldiers while also reporting the scene.[36]

Marshall was likewise prepared to fight. He had procured smokeless revolver shells in Tampa, what he called "man stoppers," and he was intent on using them. Before he could, a Spanish bullet hit him in the back. The shot pierced his spine, and Marshall lay there in the grass, hoping someone would find him. Davis, after his shooting spree, had pulled back from the front line, where he found Stephen Crane, and the two of them soon found Marshall. "What can I do for you?" Crane asked.

"Well, you might file my dispatches," replied Marshall, as nonchalantly as he could manage, given the circumstances. "I don't mean file them ahead of your own, old man—but just file 'em if you find it handy."[37]

Crane figured Marshall was going to die—"No man could be so sublime in detail concerning the trade of journalism and not die," he wrote later—so he agreed to Marshall's request.[38]

But Marshall did not die. A while later a Rough Rider came by and moved him into the shade, where he waited over an hour for someone to help him get back to Siboney. It took three soldiers, each holding a corner of a dog tent, to carry him to the field hospital. Church "told me I was about to die," Marshall wrote. "The news was not pleasant, but it did not interest me particularly." He lay all afternoon in the sun; it was not until the evening that he could be moved back to Siboney.[39]

With the regiment's right wing solidified, Roosevelt took one of his troops back toward the center, where the fighting was still heavy. He had left his sword tied around his waist, and it threatened to trip him up each time he moved faster than a quick step. He found the main line of Rough Riders, with Wood still pacing behind them. "How Wood escaped being hit, I do not see, and still less how his horse escaped," Roosevelt said. Soon after Roosevelt arrived, Major Brodie, who was in charge of the men on the left side of the line, was shot in the wrist, and had to fall out; Wood ordered Roosevelt to take his place. As he did, he saw Theodore Miller and his cousin, Dade

Goodrich, tramping through the tall grass, keeping space between each other to avoid being hit by the same fire. Roosevelt ordered the men in the left wing to follow him further left, into the thick of the woods. They lost contact with Wood and the men in the center of the line, just as the Spanish fire was quickening again.[40]

Though it was still morning, the heat was overwhelming. The men had long since dropped their rolls and bags and other equipment; now they stripped off their blouses and undershirts, leaving just their canteens and cartridge belts to adorn their canvas pants. After an hour of constant shooting, the Spanish fire had slackened, and the Spanish line had pulled back, and the American line began to advance. They went slowly, moving through the thick grass a few feet at a time, "no more than a man covers in sliding for a base," wrote Davis, who was yet again near the front, having left Crane behind. They couldn't see the Spanish, their view blocked by the trees and grass, but they could hear them, or rather their rifles, the cracks reaching their ears simultaneously with the PHEWWW of the Mauser bullets. The Spanish fire tailed off, just a few shots a minute. Then, suddenly, it returned, hotter and faster and more concentrated than before. The Spanish had likely retreated, and regrouped. John Winter and William Erwin, two soldiers from San Antonio, were shuffling forward when a slash of blood hit Winter in the face. Erwin had been hit. "The breath left my body for the moment," he wrote in a letter to the *San Antonio Daily Light*, "as the whole top of his head flew up in the air, his skull blown to atoms by an explosive bullet."[41]

Roosevelt, at the head of a few dozen soldiers off to the left and now separated from Wood and the main body of Rough Riders, saw a pair of red-tiled buildings about 500 yards away. He decided the Spanish fire was now coming from there. He grabbed a rifle from a wounded man and fired back. As he did, from behind and to his right, he heard a cheering roar. In what the men would later call "Wood's Bluff," the colonel had called up his reserve troops and, with no backup, ordered a charge at the last of the Spanish. Almost 400 Rough Riders stood up and ran at full speed toward the clutch of buildings. They got within 200 yards before the firing from the opposite line halted; the last of the Spanish, it seemed, had fled. "When we arrived at the buildings, panting and out of breath," Roosevelt wrote, "they contained nothing but heaps of empty cartridge shells and two dead Spaniards, shot through the head."[42]

Roosevelt and the men around him began to cheer. But in the midst of their reverie, shocking news arrived: Wood had been shot during his charge at the Spanish line, most likely fatally. Roosevelt went silent, but just for a moment—then he began barking orders. He was now in charge of the Rough Riders.

The village of Las Guasimas was just a clutch of a half dozen buildings, including the distillery, at the intersection of several dirt roads. All around stood thick forest, interspersed with more abandoned farms. Roosevelt sent several of his men out in different directions, as guards. At the distillery a few other men found a pack mule loaded down with bags of beans; nearby they found an enormous barrel full of unaged rum, which the officers destroyed before their men could get ahold of it. Roosevelt sent others to fill canteens, and ordered the remainder to take cover, and rest, along a nearby sunken road. The wounded and heat-struck he ordered into one of the buildings. Roosevelt then went off in search of the rest of the men.

To his delight, he found Wood standing there among them, not even scratched, save for his broken cuff links.[43]

Las Guasimas was not a battle; it was little more than a skirmish, pitting rapidly advancing American forces against the rear guard of a retreating Spanish army (a fact later revealed by captured Spanish officers). Of the 964 Americans from the three regiments (the Rough Riders plus the units in the main column), 16 were killed and 52 wounded. Official American reports stated that 42 Spanish were killed (Roosevelt, in his memoir, argues that such a number was far too high). General Wheeler had expected the Spanish to make a stand at the crossroads. If they had, the American advance might have been halted, or even pushed back to the beach. Instead, the Spanish decided to pull back to Santiago, and cede the territory between them to the Americans. Like their failure to attack Shafter's convoy, or the American landing at Daiquiri, the failure to put up a bigger fight at Las Guasimas was another in a string of inexplicable decisions by the Spanish that made the American campaign significantly easier than it should have been.[44]

News of the engagement at Las Guasimas reached the United States by that night. The first dispatches worked off early, erroneous reports that the regiments had been ambushed and that scores were dead, including Colonel Wood. Even Davis, at first, reported that the Americans had walked into a Spanish trap. Later accounts corrected the most egregious errors, but the notion that the regiment had been ambushed persisted. "That the Spaniards were thoroughly posted as to the route to be taken by the Americans in their movement toward Sevilla was evident," the New York *Sun* wrote on June 27. In Washington, Representative John Hull, of Iowa, called for Roosevelt and Wood to be court-martialed—"Colonels Wood and Roosevelt needlessly led their men into the ambush. . . . It looks like a case of thoughtless, reckless, and impetuous disregard of orders," though it is not clear what Hull imagined those orders to be. Neither Wood nor Roosevelt planned the engagement or decided their plan of attack. For that, Hull would have to go after General Wheeler, who had overseen the attack on Las Guasimas. But Wheeler was also Hull's former colleague in Congress. Hull dropped the matter.[45]

Still, the question of whether Las Guasimas was an ambush dogged Roosevelt for years, especially during the 1904 presidential campaign. One could argue it was indeed a trap—the Spanish were ready and waiting, arrayed in a V-shape around the Americans' expected approach. On the other hand, the Americans had a strong sense of where the Spanish would be, and it was a Rough Rider, Tom Isbell, who fired the first shot. This was, in any case, the conclusion of the Dodge Commission, which was convened to examine the conduct of the war a year later. "The attack was opened by our own forces; there was no surprise, no ambuscade, no lack of definiteness as to plan, and no uncertainty as to purpose," it read. It helped, too, that Richard Harding Davis soon changed his mind and came to the Rough Riders' defense, first in his later newspaper dispatches and then in detailed, lengthy articles for *Scribner's*. This was no ambush, he declared: "There is a vast difference between blundering into an ambuscade and setting out with a full knowledge that you will find the enemy in ambush, and finding him there, and then driving him out of his ambush and before you for a mile and a half in full retreat."[46]

168

Not everyone appreciated Davis's reporting, or his access to Roosevelt and the regiment. Roosevelt's cultivation of the war correspondent continued: After the fight, he offered to make Davis an honorary officer in the regiment. Not surprisingly, as the campaign rolled on, Davis's dispatches focused more, and more glowingly, on Roosevelt and his men. "He had in his possession a very powerful pair of field-glasses," the reporter Burr McIntosh wrote, "which in no way could be adjudged neutral. Most people had to be looked at through these; consequently, when he gazed at General Shafter he looked through one end, and when he regarded Colonel Roosevelt, he looked through the other. The deeds of both were minimized or magnified accordingly." Back home, another satirist declared Davis to be Roosevelt's "brave and fluent body guard."[47]

The fact remains that the Rough Riders—despite losing over two dozen wounded and eight men killed, including Capron and Fish, two of their best soldiers—had shown that they could fire and maneuver as a unit, that they wouldn't break and run or shoot wildly under pressure. And they did so when most of the men in the regiment had never fired a weapon in anger before that day, let alone at unseen enemies. Add to that the triple-digit temperatures, the strange surroundings, and the seemingly invisible enemy, and their feat becomes even more impressive. More than that, observers wrote, the Rough Riders had shown that American gumption and guts could compensate greatly for a lack of formal military training. "Las Guasimas may have been only a skirmish," admitted Caspar Whitney, "but it cleared the road to Santiago and thoroughly tested the courage, determination, and marksmanship of the present generation of Americans from the lowest to the highest born, from the wage worker to the gentleman of fortune, and not one of them was found deficient on any count." In Washington, early criticism was replaced with talk of promoting Roosevelt to brigadier general; in New York, they talked of making him governor.[48]

The fight was not a victory for the Rough Riders alone. It was a victory for the entire cavalry division, including the two regiments that had fought down in the valley; they had reached the Spanish line about the same time as Wood and Roosevelt's men. In fact, were it not for the black soldiers in the segregated 10th Cavalry Regiment holding up the left wing of General Young's force, the Spanish might have managed to flank the Rough Riders on the right, where Roosevelt was in command. But no one could know that from the press coverage. The only thing any reporter wanted to talk about was the Rough Riders. "The Spaniards were no match for the Roosevelt fighters," wrote the *San Francisco Call*. "The western cowboys and Eastern dandies hammered the enemy from their path." (To his credit, Roosevelt titled the chapter in his memoir on Las Guasimas "General Young's Fight.")[49]

Though it was a minor engagement in a rural corner of a war-torn island, the Battle of Las Guasimas made banner headlines around the world—proof, for everyone to see, that America's way of warfare worked. "The Stuff That Americans Are Made Of," declared the *Daily Astorian*, in Oregon. "For the credit and the interests of the country, few things could have happened better at this juncture than just such a display of American ability at short notice to transform the quiet citizen into an effective self-reliant soldier, able to cope with the regular troops of an enemy, even at the disadvantage which marked the first engagement of Wood and Roosevelt's men," the *Washington Times* wrote. "It will exercise an immediate and marked effect upon European opinion of our ability to put a large army in the field at any time it may be required, and one not to be despised for its military qualities. The nation that can produce such troops in six weeks, from the cattle ranch, the university, the plow, bank parlor and club, and can scare up more than ten million of them, at a pinch, is to be respected and counted with in all the world problems of the future." And the Rough Riders, already famous, became celebrities. "The Rough Riders, the romantic figures in the American army, had aroused popular interest to a high pitch," wrote the *Los Angeles Herald* on June 26.[50]

Chauncey Depew, a lawyer for the railroad tycoon Cornelius Vanderbilt who would be elected senator from New York that fall, told of a trip he was taking aboard a German passenger liner, the *Kaiser Wilhelm der Grosse*, when news of Las Guasimas arrived. Immediately, the tone of conversation among the French and German passengers at his table turned to incredulity. "There had been a general belief that our ships were no good and our army, while being composed of good men, was gathered from the fields and had no experience or training," he wrote. "In place of what was expected it was discovered that our vessels were of the soundest construction, up to the most modern type of warship, with an armament unexcelled and manned and officered by skilled seamen and tacticians, while the army had displayed all the qualities of veteran troops."[51]

The reaction at home and abroad was put best by a Spanish prisoner captured at Las Guasimas and interviewed the next day by the reporter Stephen Bonsal. Speaking through a Cuban translator, he said, "When war was declared, we who knew the material wealth and prosperity of the Americans used to console ourselves by saying, 'Los Americans tienen canones, pero no corazones'"—the Americans have guns, but no hearts. "But after what we saw at La Guasimas, we changed our tune to saying, 'Los Americans no tienen canones, pero, por Dios! Tienen corazones.'"[52]

The battle over, Roosevelt dispatched Fred Herrig, the tracker he had first encountered at Joe Ferris's general store in Medora, to find the mules that had run off with the machine gun. Around dusk, Herrig found two sets of mule tracks in a ravine, but it was too dark to follow. He bunked down under a tree, caught a few hours of sleep, and was awake at 3 a.m. By sunup he was marching back into camp, the mules and the guns in tow. Roosevelt slapped his knee and said to Wood, "Didn't I tell you? Didn't I tell you, Wood? Fred would find those guns?"[53]

The Rough Riders spent the rest of the day on June 24 looking for wounded men—and dead men—in the forest and tall grass. Near the Spanish position, the spent casings were thick on the ground, so thick that the men, in their search, made a tinkling sound as they walked. Caspar Whitney, moving about the battlefield, tried to re-create the fight by looking for collections of shell casings, as a sign of where men had stopped to fire—nickel casings from the Americans, brass from the Spanish. Around him, soldiers gathered the fallen Spanish soldiers as well. They placed them into a long shallow trench, with little ceremony. Some of the men, at least, were struck by the small size and youthful faces of their enemy. Their Mauser rifles "looked about eight times too big for them," Whitney said.[54]

By the afternoon the Rough Riders had recovered eight American bodies, including those of Capron and Fish, and laid them out by the side of a road near the distillery. As the regiment regrouped, soldiers filed by to see them, as much out of respect for the dead as to prove to themselves that what they had just been through was real. Burr McIntosh, the reporter who had shared the purloined wine with Fish the evening they landed, happened to have a camera with him, and he took a picture of his fallen drinking buddy. "It seemed hard, very hard, to see the boy lying there in that far-off land, while the news of his death was speeding away to break the hearts of those to whom he was all the world," he wrote.[55]

Standing beside Roosevelt, looking down at the fallen men, Buckey O'Neill, the hyper-literate gambler from Prescott, said, "Colonel, isn't it Whitman who says of the vultures that 'they pluck the eyes of princes and tear the flesh of kings'?" Roosevelt shook his head and said he couldn't recall. This being Roosevelt, the question gnawed at him, until over a year later, when he was doing corrections on a later edition of his memoir *The Rough Riders*, he wrote: "It has been suggested to me that when Buckey O'Neill spoke of the vultures tearing our dead, he was thinking of no modern poet, but of the words of the prophet Ezekiel: 'Speak unto every feathered fowl . . . ye shall eat the flesh of the mighty and drink the blood of the princes of the earth.'"[56]

Capron's body was taken down to Siboney, so that his father, a captain in the artillery who was still helping unload the ships, might recover it; the rest lay there overnight, covered loosely with blankets, their comrades sleeping nearby. Or trying to sleep. Sherrard Coleman, a second lieutenant, lay near Fish's enormous body, which stuck out at the lower end, still wearing the boots he had dug out of the pile at San Antonio. "His feet were very large and they haunted me all night," Coleman told the historian Hermann Hagedorn. That night Wood ordered Troop L to be known, from then on, as "Capron's Troop."[57]

The next morning the regiment gathered around the distillery site. Henry Alfred Brown, the regimental chaplain, led the service. The remaining seven bodies lay beside a long trench. Trooper Frank Hayes wrote a few lines on a sheet of paper and slipped it into Fish's pocket. The paper read: "On Fame's eternal camping ground/their silent tents are spread,/and glory guards with solemn round/the bivouac of the dead"—lines from the poem "Bivouac of the Dead," written by the poet Theodore O'Hara to memorialize the fallen during the Mexican-American War. The men, heads bared, sang "Rock of Ages" and "Nearer My God to Thee," while Chaplain Brown led the Episcopalian burial service. While everyone's head was bowed, Roosevelt looked up and saw a swarm of vultures circling in the blue sky overhead. Each body was wrapped in a blanket with a name tag and placed in the trench. "There could be no more honorable burial than that of these men in a common grave—Indian and cow-boy, miner, packer, and college athlete—the man of unknown ancestry from the lonely Western plains, and the man who carried on his watch the crest of the Stuyvesants and the Fishes," Roosevelt wrote. Once the trench was shoveled full with dirt, a pair of Rough Riders built a small cairn to mark each body. "The bugle was blown as a parting salute, instead of firing, and the troops were dismounted," Theodore Miller wrote.[58]

At Siboney, the men who had accompanied Capron's body constructed a crude coffin out of spare wood slats they found up against one of the houses. They sent word to Capron's father, also named Allyn, but he was busy landing cannons at Daiquirí, where a few ships were still unloading. When he was finally located, he came hurrying to Siboney, though his son was already in the earth.

"Tell me about the boy's death," Allyn Capron Sr. asked one of the doctors at the field hospital. "I've heard nothing definite. How many times was he shot?"

"Twice," came the reply.

"He kept on, didn't he? He didn't quit after the first one, did he?"

"No! It was the second one!"

"That's good! That's good! I knew he'd die right."[59]

Nearby, at the field hospital, Marshall lay out in the open among dozens of men in various states of injury—some simply dehydrated or suffering heat exhaustion, while others had one or more Mauser holes blown into their bodies. Behind him lay McClintock, the officer and former journalist from California, whose leg had been shattered by a bullet. Surgeons, blood-spattered, moved among them, amputating limbs liberally. Land crabs crawled among them too,

173

picking at bloody rags and occasionally pinching recumbent bodies. Marshall was paralyzed from the neck down; he recovered slightly, but later had a leg amputated. As he contemplated his compromised future, he heard a low, off-key voice begin to sing: "My country 'tis of the, sweet land of liberty . . ." The voice sputtered and coughed, but then another picked up the verse. ". . . Of thee I sing." Then others joined in, until, within a few minutes, it seemed like the entire hospital there on the rocky Cuban shore was wheezing out: "From ev-er-ee mountain-side, le-et freedom ring."[60]

CHAPTER 10

"THE MONOTONY
OF CONTINUOUS BACON"

On Saturday, June 25, the day after the engagement at Las Guasimas, Roosevelt wrote just one word in his diary: "Rested."[1]
Following the burial service for Capron, Fish, and the rest, the men dispersed, mostly to find clean water for a bath and a shave—their first since leaving Tampa. Roosevelt's pack finally arrived from the *Yucatan*, and he was able to put on a change of clothes. Theodore Miller went back to the battlefield to find his gear, which he had dropped in the early stages of the fight; he recovered everything except his blanket and gloves. Almost alone among the regiment, Miller was in good spirits—after locating his equipment, he persuaded a grumpy Bob Wrenn to go swimming in a nearby pond. "He had talked me into so cheerful a frame of mind that I looked back on that afternoon as one of my pleasantest in Cuba," the tennis champ wrote in a letter to Miller's parents. When Miller got back to the campsite at Las Guasimas, he found Burke, his sick friend, asleep in a dog tent. Somehow, in the grip of a fever, he had made his way from Siboney to the front.[2]

The fight at Las Guasimas was not, technically, the first land battle of the Spanish-American War—that honor went to the Marines who had captured Guantánamo Bay on June 6. Nevertheless, it was significant: It solidified the American beachhead at Siboney and opened the path to Santiago. It gave the Americans a taste of victory, and the Rough Riders the confidence of more experienced soldiers. But instead of pressing his advantage, Shafter dawdled. Aside from his brief visit with General García at Aserradero, he had stayed on

175

his ship, the *Seguranca*, ostensibly directing the unloading process, but leaving his divisional generals, Wheeler and Lawton, to manage on their own (General Jacob Kent, in charge of the First Division, was still unloading at Siboney). Wheeler was, technically, the ranking officer, but Lawton was the more experienced, and likely resented being told what to do by a man who had shed his uniform thirty-three years before—and a Confederate uniform, at that. To compound the insult, Wheeler's men, bereft of their horses, were essentially just another infantry division, duplicative of, and competitive with, Lawton's own. Because Las Guasimas was a victory, Lawton had little room to criticize the white-bearded cavalryman; still, he threatened to resign if Wheeler went off on his own again.[3]

Over the next several days most of the nearly 17,000 men in the invasion force were ordered forward, to a position near Sevilla, roughly seven miles east of Santiago, where they would organize for an assault on the city. Sevilla sat on a sandy tableland behind a low range of hills, with expanses of guinea grass sliced through with tributaries of the San Juan River and pocked, here and there like outsize landmines, with Spanish bayonet and cacti of various shapes and sizes. The movement toward Santiago, and the selection of Sevilla as a staging point, was not a decision born of extensive analysis or thorough intelligence gathering; Shafter either did not think reconnaissance was necessary, or did not remember to consider it. He did not know how many Spanish troops were inside Santiago, how well armed they were, or how they were arrayed to defend against attack. He simply drew a line from Las Guasimas to Santiago, and ordered his men to march along it.

The next morning, the Rough Riders rose early, observed a brief Sunday service, and prepared to move to their new camp. Before they left, Miller took Burke to La Motte, the regimental surgeon, who diagnosed him with typhoid fever and ordered him back to Siboney. Though the rest of the regiment was headed west, Miller walked with his friend in the other direction, to the beach. When they arrived Miller found some bacon, hardtack, beans, and coffee, and made the two of them a proper meal, or as proper as one could get with cold, old rations. As they ate, they watched the thousands of men still disembarking from the ships, running their boats up to shore and unloading—without a dock at Siboney, the regiments were limited to whatever equipment they could fit in the launches, and whatever they could lift out of them. That meant no cannons, no wagons; all of that would have to wait until engineers could build a proper pier. The houses at Siboney were filling up, being converted into storehouses and hospital wards and headquarters, despite the proscription against entering them. Those men who weren't working were playing—swimming naked in the surf, lying on the rocky shore, as if Miller and the Rough Riders had not just fought and died in the first engagement of the campaign, barely two miles away. Miller was stunned, and jealous, and sad. He left Burke at the field hospital and marched toward the front.[4]

This time, marching through the valley instead of up along the ridge, it took Miller just an hour and fifteen minutes to get from Siboney to a point well past Las Guasimas, to where the Rough Riders had made camp. He had no want for company on this trip. Other regiments were streaming inland, up along the Camino Real. The "royal road" was just a cattle path, not wide enough for two wagons to pass each other, and in the heavy, cold rains that pelted Cuba every afternoon they became rivers of mud—"a simple stream of mud, with a spattering of huge rocks," Miller wrote. Later, soldiers and teamsters would try to improve the roads by throwing branches and logs across them as a rude corduroy, to tamp down the mud and give mules and wheels a purchase, but they usually just made the going tougher. Miller was spared the rain that afternoon, though. He found his regiment camped on a grassy plain just off the road, with a good breeze and a clear stream, the Aguadores River, alongside it. Apparently La Motte, the surgeon, had spread the word about Miller's selflessness in helping his sick friend back to camp, because Roosevelt bounded up to him as soon as he arrived, clapped him on the back, and said thank you.[5]

Life in Sevilla fell into a routine. The days were almost unbearably hot, even in the Rough Riders' camp, with its cross breeze and shade trees. And it rained, rain like nothing the men had ever seen—hard, piercing, painful rain, like the drops were not falling so much as being shot from a gun. "I never saw it rain harder for two hours consecutively," Miller wrote, though he added, "Perhaps that is exaggerated, considering our Chautauqua rains." The clouds passed quickly, and the nights were clear and cool. Those who stayed up late—not by choice, but usually because they pulled guard duty—counted the constellations that they had only read about in books: Scorpius, the Southern Cross. "The nights are beautiful, and I had the full benefit of their charm between one and three on this night," Miller wrote, peevishly, after a graveyard shift on guard.[6]

In their spare time, the men tried to write home, though they had to get creative with their writing implements and material. Especially paper—there was none to be had. Some took to writing on empty boxes of quinine pills. Others used the margins of the four-page daily newspaper that William Randolph Hearst, who had arrived in Siboney a few days earlier, distributed off a printing press he had brought with him on the *Sylvia*, his yacht. Lacking envelopes, the men sewed their letters shut and gave them to correspondents to mail from a temporary post office at Siboney, or to courier back home. "The letters could be considered curios in a dime museum from the ingenuity displayed," one correspondent wrote.[7]

There were other pleasures to being suddenly sedentary, but generally, the men suffered. Their tents provided only partial protection from the rain; they were not long enough to cover an average-size man's head and feet, and they had no floors, so the water that did not fall on them ran under them, and into the occupants' blanket and kit. As a defense against the torrents, the men dug trenches around their tents, but rarely deep enough. After an hour or so of deluge, dozens of men would be out in the rain, naked, frantically digging with whatever implements they had with them. Often they just used their hands, since their gear, aside from the officers', was still sitting at Siboney.

The men could not decide which was worse: the rain, or the wildlife of various sizes and aggression that came out when the rain stopped. There were, of course, the ubiquitous land crabs, "some of which are almost as big as rabbits," Roosevelt recorded. There were also tarantulas everywhere—Church, the assistant surgeon, made it his job to squash as many as he could find with his boot, pacing the camp in an undershirt and trousers. Men would wake up in their tents to find spiders, bigger than their hands, crawling on their chests. "I woke up the other morning with one seven inches long and as hairy as your head reposing on my pillow," Davis wrote to his father.[8]

Thomas J. Vivian, a journalist for Hearst, summed up a day in the camp life that summer:

The sultry air grew still sultrier. From the trampled, beaten, crushed, tropical undergrowth rose sickening odors and heavy miasmatic mists. As the heat grew fiercer, the odors and mists grew heavier. Every life-giving quality of the air seemed to be squeezed out of it, and even the myriad insects and crawling reptiles were quieted. Then, just as the sizzling heat reached a spot where it apparently could go no further and be bearable, a zigzag flash, a thunderclap, and a cataract of ice-cold rain came simultaneously, and every man was soaked and shivering. If the men were marching, they found themselves suddenly wading through swift running streams of cold muddy water. . . . If the men were in camp or the trenches, their fires were put out and every ditch became a mud pool. For two or three hours the icy mass of mud and leaves, and the muddy water in the trails had risen from sole to ankle and from ankle to legging top. Then, as suddenly as it had begun, the storm would come to an end, the sun came out hotter than ever, the wet ground steamed; horrible crawling, flying things filled the muggy air, and from shivering the men passed to gasping.[9]

Naturally, hygiene was a problem. Though the Aguadores River ran alongside the camp, it had to be kept clean for drinking water, and the men were forbidden to bathe or clean their clothes in it. They could either hike to another river, much further away, or devise makeshift baths by digging a hole, lining it with a poncho or rain-coat, and filling it with water. Rations were an issue, too. Because the unloading process at Siboney was going so slowly, and because there were only a few mule teams to pull a few wagons on the slow trip to the front, food that wasn't hardtack or bacon or beans was difficult to come by. At one point the men in camp saw four loaded six-mule wagons coming up the road; their minds went immediately to beans, rice, and meat, "to break the monotony of continuous bacon," Caspar Whitney wrote. But instead the wagon carried the deflated sac of an observation balloon.[10]

As with the thick blue wool uniforms the regular troopers wore, the commissary bureau had not planned for what a soldier in Cuba might want to eat. Heavy, fatty foods like salt pork, bacon, and hardtack were most likely not high on the list—"fitter for the Klondike than for Cuba," Roosevelt complained. The men did what they could to supplement their fatty diet with whatever they could scrounge locally. With the farms long abandoned, livestock and poultry were just a dream, but they had more than they could handle of coconuts, mangoes, and limes. Doctors had warned them not to eat coconuts or mangoes, believing that they would upset the stomachs of men raised on temperate-climate foods, but the soldiers did anyway—either straight from the tree or, in the case of mangoes, boiled and mashed with sugar into a sweet gruel. Trooper Allen McCurdy, whose brother was also in the regiment, became something of a specialist in preparing mangoes; he preferred to boil them down to a jelly, then either fry it or use it as a spread. (McCurdy, at least, loved the camp: "This is the garden spot of Cuba and a finer country I never saw.")[11]

Not only were the rations skimpy, but there wasn't much to prepare them with—no pots, few pans, and no utensils other than what the men carried. They had coffee, but the beans were whole, and green. George Hamner became one of the more popular men in the Rough Riders' camp after he devised a mortar and pestle out of an empty coconut shell, in which he ground up roasted beans. Missing among the rations was tobacco, which the men needed to calm nerves and sate hunger. Without it, they turned to less palatable alternatives: grass, roots, tea, even dried horse manure. For men raised in a rapidly growing, materially abundant society, this sudden deprivation was a shock. "In general, our army operated under Civil War conditions," Arthur Cosby wrote.[12]

After a few days, Roosevelt rounded up a squad of forty men, dragooned a wagon, and marched back to Siboney, where he found a clerk registering shipments of food. Roosevelt had heard that the commissary had large stocks of beans, and he wanted 1,100 pounds of them. "I'm sorry sir," the clerk replied, citing an obscure regulation stating that beans were for officers only. Roosevelt stormed out. But he returned a minute later and said he wanted 1,100 pounds of beans—for his officers.

Governor Theodore Roosevelt riding in the New York victory parade, September 30, 1899. Theodore Roosevelt Collection, Harvard College Library. (Citation No. 520.3, 560.3)

A bone pile comprised of the remains of Cuban civilians killed by the Spanish reconcentrado policy. Theodore Roosevelt Collection, Harvard College Library. (Citation No. 520.3, 560.3)

Reconciliation between the North and South was an important, barely concealed subtext in the push for war with Spain. Here, two men dressed in Union and Confederate uniforms are united by a young girl dressed as Cuban liberty. Library of Congress

The USS *Maine*.
Theodore Roosevelt Collection, Harvard College Library. (Citation No. 560.3)

Richard Harding Davis.
Library of Congress

Theodore Roosevelt, in his Rough
Rider uniform, before departing for San
Antonio.
Theodore Roosevelt Collection, Harvard
College Library. (Citation No. 520.3, 560.3)

An unidentified Rough Rider relaxing outside the exhibition hall at Camp Wood, San Antonio. Theodore Roosevelt Collection, Harvard College Library. (Citation No. 560.3)

Lieutenant Colonel Theodore Roosevelt and Colonel Leonard Wood in camp at San Antonio. Theodore Roosevelt Collection, Harvard College Library. (Citation No. 520.3, 560.3)

A group of Rough Riders pose behind the regiment's Colt machine guns. Theodore Roosevelt Collection, Harvard College Library. (Citation No. 520.3, 560.3)

Theodore Miller.
Courtesy of Mitch Schmidtke

Officers and journalists
gathered on the piazza o:
the Tampa Bay Hotel.
Theodore Roosevelt
Collection, Harvard College
Library. (Citation No. 560.3)

From left to right:
Major Alexander O. Brodie,
Major George M. Dunn,
Major General Joseph Wheeler,
Chaplian Henry A. Brown,
Colonel Leonard Wood,
and Lieutenant Colonel
Theodore Roosevelt.
Theodore Roosevelt Collection,
Harvard College Library. (Citation:
No. 520.3, 560.3)

Major General William R. Shafter overseeing the loading process at Port Tampa.
Theodore Roosevelt Collection, Harvard College Library. (Citation No. 560.3)

Hamilton Fish aboard the *Yucatan.*
Collection of the author

The landing at Daiquirí, Cuba.
Theodore Roosevelt Collection, Harvard College Library. (Citation No. 560.3)

A pair of Rough Riders prepare dinner at Daiquirí. Theodore Roosevelt Collection, Harvard College. (Citation No. 560.3)

A depiction of the Battle of Las Guasimas (misspelled as "La Quasina" in the caption) by Kurz & Allison. Library of Congress

Observation balloon at El Poso, Cuba. Theodore Roosevelt Collection, Harvard College Library. (Citation No. 560.3)

Soldiers lining up for the assault on San Juan Heights, July 1, 1898.
Theodore Roosevelt Collection, Harvard College Library. (Citation No. 560.3)

Captain Allyn Capron's battery firing on El Caney, July 1, 1898.
Theodore Roosevelt Collection, Harvard College Library. (Citation No. 560.3)

THE ROUGH RIDERS.
THEY ARE ROUGH ON THE SPANIARDS, WHETHER THEY RIDE OR WALK.

A cartoon, from the cover of *Puck* magazine, depicting Theodore Roosevelt leading the Rough Riders up Kettle Hill.
Library of Congress

Rough Riders cheering
at the news that the
Spanish had surrendered
Santiago, July 17, 1898.
Theodore Roosevelt
Collection, Harvard College
Library. (Citation No. 560.3)

A view of central Santiago soon
after the Spanish surrender.
Theodore Roosevelt Collection,
Harvard College Library. (Citation
No. 560.3)

Colonel Roosevelt
shakes hands with
the remaining Rough
Riders at Camp Wikoff,
Montauk, New York.
The regiment's gift to
Roosevelt, Remington's
The Bronco Buster, sits on
a table behind him.
Theodore Roosevelt
Collection, Harvard College
Library. (Citation No. 560.3)

"But your officers cannot eat eleven hundred pounds of beans," the clerk said.

"You don't know what appetites my officers have," Roosevelt replied.

He and his men returned to camp with the beans, and with a load of canned tomatoes, too. For most, it was the best meal of their lives.[13]

After his experiences at Las Guasimas, Richard Harding Davis was spending even more time with the Rough Riders. He probably felt a sort of soldierly comradeship with them, but he also saw them as a phenomenal news story in the making. Whatever might happen at Santiago, they were already great copy. Though Roosevelt had not yet followed through on his promise to make Davis an honorary member of the regiment, the reporter had insinuated himself deep into its routine—coming by at meals, chatting with the men about the campaign (and, depending on the man, about various social and athletic matters back in New York), taking notes all the while. Shafter had refused to offer billeting for the journalists, insisting that if they were resourceful enough as reporters, they should be able to scrounge food and shelter from a friendly regiment. Most units were happy to oblige. "We are very welcome," Davis wrote home, and by all accounts they were—Roosevelt wasn't the only member of the regiment to appreciate the sort of positive press that a reporter of Davis's stature could bestow on them, and what that press might bring. He was "our friend," wrote trooper Sam Weller, "so his accounts will do us full justice."[14]

Davis saw himself as a reporter above the fray—a "correspondent," he preferred to call himself. He had nothing but criticism for most of his fellow journalists: "The fault lies with the army people at Washington who give credentials to anyone who asks—to the independents and other periodicals—in no sense newspapers, and they give seven to one paper; consequently, we as a class are a pest to the officers and to each other." Davis reveled in his unparalleled access to Roosevelt and his regiment—at the top of one letter to his father, written on June 29, are the words "Headquarters, Wood's Rough Riders," a meaningless detail for the postal system, but a great point of pride for the writer. And he couldn't get enough of the regiment's comic mix of high and low, of seeing the sons of the elite roughing it on the front lines. He wrote home about seeing a sentry reading *As You Like It* while on duty. "It is very funny," he wrote to his father, "to see Larned the tennis champion, whose every movement at Newport was applauded by hundreds of young women, marching up and down in the wet grass."[15]

Davis was enough one of the boys to be an object of their occasional derision, too. Among Theodore Miller's duties at Sevilla was to build a new bench for the officers' mess. The next day around noon, Davis stopped by. When he saw the officers eating, he pulled out a plate and cup and sat down, "with a comfortable relaxation," as if he were just another major. Suddenly the bench collapsed under his weight. The officers laughed; Miller did not record Davis's reaction.[16]

It was little moments like this that helped the men forget what they had just been through, at Las Guasimas, and gird themselves for what might come. "I had felt great the last few days, in fact, never better in my life," Miller wrote. "Things to-day looked as though we were to stay here for weeks to come." Around a campfire one night, Buckey O'Neill, his coat off and his shirt unbuttoned, leaned back on his blanket roll and told his neighbor, "Anyone who wants to go back to the United States when this cruel war is over can go; for my, part, I plan to stay." Where others saw only destruction and poverty, he saw opportunity in Cuba's metal-ore mines and fertile fields. "We are going to have a new set of millionaires," O'Neill said, "and I am going to be one of them."[17]

Out on the water, General Shafter still sat on the *Seguranca*, even after most of his men had landed. The ship, like the others in the American fleet, did not use a stern anchor, so it swung back and forth in the tide and current, bumping against other ships. The situation was particularly fraught on June 27, when the *Seguranca* swung a little too closely between two other ships. The ship's master decided to move out to sea, but he forgot to raise the anchor; as the *Seguranca* steamed away at full speed, the cable drew taut and ripped out the windlass and riding bitts—the winch and posts at the other end of the cable. Now, bereft of an anchoring system, the *Seguranca* was forced to float several miles out at sea. Without any way to communicate easily with shore, Shafter decided, finally, to join his men.[18]

For over a century, historians of the Spanish-American War have debated Shafter's merits as a general. He was certainly the most despised officer in Cuba, by his men but even more so by the correspondents and foreign attachés who observed him, and felt free to condemn him widely and vociferously. Davis in particular disliked him: "His self complacency was so great that in spite of blunder after blunder, folly upon folly, and mistake upon mistake, he still believed himself infallible, still bullied his inferior officers, and still cursed from his cot." Not everyone demeaned Shafter. A reporter for the New York *Sun* wrote, "It is not hard to describe General Shafter: Bold, lion-headed, hero-eyed, massive as to body, a sort of human fortress in blue coat and flannel shirt." As historian J. P. Clark wrote, "It is a telling indicator of the state of the army in 1898 that historians can plausibly argue that Shafter was selected because he was either among the best or the worst of the available generals."[19]

The truth lay in the middle. Shafter possessed a keen mind and a tenacious temperament; he had demonstrated as much during his decades in the Indian Wars. He did not push for the Santiago campaign. When he accepted command at Tampa, it was to lead a small force into northern Cuba to deliver supplies to the rebels, or at most to capture coastal defenses that might otherwise threaten the naval blockade around the island. But like the rest of the country, Shafter had been swept up in the patriotic momentum. Dewey's victory at Manila demanded swift action in the Caribbean, and he would gladly deliver it.

But the fact remains: Shafter was utterly incapable of leading the Santiago campaign. He failed to empower officers to wrangle the chaos at Tampa, just as he failed to appoint someone to oversee the loading and unloading of his armada. He did not pack enough artillery, let alone the means to transport what he did have after landing in Cuba (later, he tried to pass off his mistake as wisdom, saying that artillery would have been useless at Santiago). And he refused to move decisively after landing at Siboney, let alone after the victory at Las Guasimas. He later failed to encircle Santiago, while his prejudice and pride prevented him from using the thousands of Cuban rebels at his service effectively.

But Shafter's litany of failures is as much an indictment of the

American military culture from which he came as it is of the man himself. Like the Army, after decades fighting the Indian Wars, far from the public spotlight, Shafter was suddenly thrust into it. Lacking firm leadership at home, he could only think of the domestic consequences of bloodshed or defeat. Like many of the general officers in the Army of 1898, men at the end of a career that began in the cauldron of the Civil War and was forged in sporadic, small-unit combat on the Great Plains and in the Southwest, he was an anachronism: fundamentally conservative, averse to risks and bold moves, but also incapable of managing his large forces so that, when the moment arrived, he could strike. If it were not for his fear of the oncoming malarial season, Shafter might have sat outside Santiago all summer, dawdling like McClellan after Antietam.

By June 27, the ships at Siboney and Daiquirí were unloaded, and the rest of the regiments began to move toward the burgeoning camp. The mule trains grew longer; some counted 100 animals pulling a dozen or more wagons. On more than one occasion, the rains and flash flooding were so severe that a pack train was stuck for the night along the way. Still, by June 29 the fields around Sevilla were full of soldiers, and several regiments were forced to camp along the Camino Real itself, even though, at that point, it was only about ten to twenty feet from one green-forested side to the other. "It was as though fifteen regiments were encamped along the sidewalks of Fifth Avenue," Davis wrote. "If Fifth Avenue were ten feet wide, one can imagine the confusion." In the mornings, the lifting mists were accompanied by the sound of trumpets blaring reveille and some 16,000 men clattering into shape; at night, the noise stopped abruptly at the sound of taps and "The Star-Spangled Banner."[20]

Every day columns of Cubans marched past the camp, their ranks of rags interspersed with bits of American-issued kit—a blue jacket, a canteen, a haversack, items they had either been given or simply taken from the battlefield. Whether they felt sympathy or disgust for the Cubans, the one thing most of the Americans did not do was talk to them—even though many of the men from New Mexico and Arizona spoke Spanish. If they had tried, they might have learned that the Cubans were not, in fact, overjoyed to see Shafter's army.

The Cubans had always been clear that what they wanted was American political recognition and military assistance in the form of guns, money, and above all ammunition—not an invasion.

Even after war was declared, the Cuban rebel leadership had assumed, based on communications with Washington, that the Americans would attack Puerto Rico, which was less well-defended, in order to relieve pressure on them. Naive, perhaps—but the Cubans were not the last group of freedom fighters to assume that Americans, arriving under the banner of humanitarian intervention, would let them set the terms of their own liberation. In fact, throughout the buildup to war and then the war itself, actual Cubans were almost completely absent from the American public eye. In their place came a series of caricatures that spoke volumes about America's ignorance of Cuba, and about its own self-image. Cuba, in the American mind, was a nation-as-damsel-in-distress, a place where all women were virtuous and virginal, and all men were chivalrous and self-sacrificing. For a country like the United States, and especially for a younger, wealthy, self-satisfied generation obsessed with finding ways to prove its manhood, the temptation to "rescue" Cuba was irresistible. "A failure to intervene," wrote historian Kristin L. Hoganson, "would reveal a lack of chivalry in American men." Those stereotypes flipped once the war began, though, and the realities of dealing with a nonwhite nation became clear. The Cuban rebels, suddenly, were written off as lazy and untrustworthy, and useless as soldiers. "It is now definitely known that little or no assistance from the vaunted 'armies of liberation' need be expected," wrote the *New York Tribune* on May 22.[21]

The Cubans, though wary of the arriving American forces, were also pragmatic, and welcomed them once their ships arrived off Daiquirí. General García, in a letter to General Nelson Miles in Washington in early June, pledged his complete support: "Your wishes are a command which I obey with great pleasure," he wrote, and offered to gather all his soldiers in eastern Cuba to place at General Shafter's disposal. In García's mind, he and his men would storm Santiago alongside the Americans.[22]

Shafter had other plans. The Cubans, where they were needed, would be used to dig trenches and carry equipment. Shafter did order several thousand Cuban soldiers to block the road north from Santiago, to interdict any Spanish relief columns (which they did, effectively if not completely; they blocked one swift-moving, so-called flying column, comprised of 5,000 men under General Luis Manuel de Pando y Sánchez, and delayed another, smaller force under Colonel Federico Escario). But as far as the Cuban forces camped alongside the Americans east of Santiago, they were to be "pack mules," as García complained, and nothing more.[23]

Shafter's neglect set off a downward spiral: Left with nothing to do, the Cubans sat around, which led American officers to assume they were lazy and undisciplined, which made it even less likely that they would be assigned any meaningful role in the campaign. "All day they sit in the shade of their palm-thatched camps and at night they smoke cigarettes and gorge on Uncle Sam's rations," wrote a correspondent for the Associated Press, "while in sight of them Uncle Sam's boys, with empty stomachs and not a bit of tobacco for their pipes, build roads all day under the blazing sun and sleep on their rifles under the starlight sky at night." Worse, in the press's eyes, the Cubans were savages— correspondents' accounts and soldiers' letters bubble with lurid stories of rebels taking command of captured Spanish soldiers and summarily beheading them with swift chops of their machetes.[24]

Some of this is undoubtedly true. Lacking any role in the campaign and facing deep distrust from their American "saviors," Cuban rebels probably did sit around, waiting for a task. Desperately poor and hungry, a few of them probably did occasionally swipe a ration or a canteen. And after three years of genocidal repression, it would be surprising if a Cuban rebel had not taken revenge on a Spanish soldier. The point is that no American, be it a soldier or a correspondent, ever stopped to wonder why.

If the Americans gave little thought to the Cubans, they were completely ignorant of the Spanish. Derogatory stereotypes ran rampant, as they always do in war—fed, in this conflict, by the long history of American anti-Catholic bigotry. The depiction of Spain, and especially its soldiers, as uniquely cruel, lazy, and intolerant, was prevalent across Europe and North America since at least the sixteenth century. Every Spanish soldier was a smaller, nastier version of "Butcher" Weyler—a serial rapist and child murderer. The disaster of the *Maine*, assumed by most soldiers to be the work of Spanish agents, if not the Spanish government itself, only reinforced this impression of diabolical deviance. A writer for the *Chicago Times-Herald*, in calling for American intervention, said that without it the war would continue until every Cuban was dead, because nothing else would sate "the thirst for blood inherent in the bull-fighting citizens of Spain." Representative Alexander Hardy, a Republican from Indiana, told his colleagues: "The Spanish soldiery at home and abroad have never hesitated to snatch the sucking babe from its mother's breast, dash its brains out, and then outrage the shrieking mother."[25]

Shafter and his officers onshore seemed little interested in learning much about the Spanish forces arrayed against them, or the conditions within Santiago—critical questions, one would think, for an army intent on laying siege to a large city. Even at the level of official intelligence, there was no assessment of the Spanish forces, no thought given to trying to understand their disposition, morale, motivation—anything that might help generals plan, the sort of questions that even a few decades later would be set upon by a large staff of clever young officers. A few competent officers, like Henry Lawton, the general in charge of the Second Division, sent out their own troops to reconnoiter the front. But there was no way for them to share that information with the rest of the corps, and no apparent interest from Shafter's staff in having them make the effort. Even after all the after-action reports and congressional investigations and books and magazine articles, it is hard to know exactly what Shafter expected to happen when he got to Santiago. Did he think the Spanish would simply surrender? If he drove at the city, would they part like curtains, or fight like demons?

What he did not know was that Santiago was living on borrowed time. Long before the Americans arrived on its outskirts, it was a city cut off from the rest of Cuba. Home to about 30,000 people, it was the largest on the island outside of Havana. It sits on the eastern side of a long narrow bay, along a slope that rises, often quite steeply, from the eastern waterfront to a series of ridges, which in turn are encircled by a line of hills, which are then hemmed in by the Sierra Maestra—a bowl within a bowl within a bowl. The blockade prevented most ships, of any nationality, from entering or leaving the harbor, while Cuban rebels had closed off the major roads leading out of the city. Even without an enemy at the gates, it was several days' march to the nearest city of any size, and the ravaged farmlands nearby had long since ceased to provide any sort of material sustenance. Already in late May, the Spanish army was growing desperate for food; on June 26, Frederick Ramsden, the British consul in Santiago, recorded that "to-day the military have taken possession of all the flour in town, and none will be left for the public; therefore, in another week, there will be no bread to be had, and the bakeries will be closed." Throughout June, those who could leave, did—but it was a long journey to the nearest town, and would-be refugees had to calculate whether the meager food they could scrape together would last them long enough to find shelter elsewhere. For most, staying put was the best option, best being relative: On June 18, Ramsden wrote: "People are now beginning to die in the streets of hunger, and the misery is frightful in spite of so many having gone to the woods." Plantains, wheat flour, and potatoes were all long gone. They had corn, and some rice; by grinding the two grains, Santiagoans could make a kind of bread, but it came out flat and hard as rock. "Living became almost impossible," wrote José Müller y Tejeiro, a Spanish officer in Santiago who later compiled an invaluable history of the campaign from the Spanish perspective. "Horses, dogs and other animals were dying from hunger in the streets and public places and the worst thing was that their carcasses were not removed."[26]

After the starvation came the bombardments. To soften up the city for Shafter's attack, the American Navy took to shelling the city several times a day—almost always without causing much damage, but adding to the general chaos and severe dislocation among Santiago's civilian population. As Müller y Tejeiro related,

There was hardly a day when gunshots were not heard at a greater or less distance, people were hearing them all the time; the falling of a chair, the closing of a door or window, the noise of carriage wheels in the distance, the crying of a child—everything was taken for gunshots, and gunshots was all that was being talked about. When they finally ceased, Santiago had become so identified with them that people almost missed them and were surprised to hear them no longer.[27]

The Spanish officer in charge at Santiago, Lieutenant General Arsenio Linares y Pombo, was in an impossible position. Like Shafter, he had failed to do much reconnaissance; he had simply no idea how many Americans there were coming from the east. And like the Americans, he shared with his men a cartoonish impression of the enemy—they were, in the words of a Spanish pamphleteer, "composed of the world's refuse . . . an immense agglomeration of men who had no military discipline, no love of the military, nor any love or respect for those who command." Linares, a proud patrician, could not even conceive of surrendering to such a force—even if, as it became increasingly clear, that force was much more powerful and disciplined than he thought.[28]

Linares had about 13,000 men under him in Santiago, though only about 9,000 of these were regular soldiers, the rest being a combination of volunteers, guerrillas, and sailors from the Spanish fleet bottled up in Santiago Harbor, whom Linares had demanded be disembarked and armed to defend the city. As for artillery, he was even worse off than Shafter—just six modern breech-loading guns; the rest were bronze and iron muzzleloaders, some over 100 years old, and most deployed at the Morro castle. Linares could also call on Cervera's fleet, anchored in the harbor, to lob shells at the Americans, but it was dangerous—it meant firing blindly over the city and the ridge, defended by Spanish troops, with the risk that an errant shot could fall into their own trenches, or hit a house. Even at the height of the American assault, Linares declined the opportunity (though rumors circulated around the city that, if the Americans got too close, he would have Admiral Cervera turn the fleets' guns on Santiago itself, destroying it instead of allowing the enemy to capture it).[29]

A brash rising nation like America, one that was asserting its newfound power abroad arrayed in the cloak of liberty and humanitarianism, could not have found a better enemy—both as a caricature to match its own self-mythologizing, and as a declining empire that, in its centuries-long claim to Cuba, much longer than white settlers could claim North America, revealed the artifice that underlay the oncoming American century. Spain was not evil, any more than America was good; its soldiers were not the infidels defending a Jerusalem on the Caribbean from the American crusaders. Spain

189

and America were simply global powers in passing, one on the way up, blinded by its own future, and one on the decline, gripping tenaciously its last vestiges of imperial property but knowing, all the while, it was doomed.

Around noon on June 30, General Shafter, who had made his way ashore and up to the front two days earlier, called a council of war. Sick with malaria and gout, he was carried to the front on a much suffering donkey, with a swollen foot wrapped in a gunny sack. They would attack the next day, he told his generals. The Second Division, led by General Lawton, backed by an artillery detachment, would move several miles north that night and, first thing in the morning, capture the small town of El Caney, where 500 Spanish soldiers were entrenched. Until the town was reduced, those Spanish troops presented a threat to the main assault against San Juan Heights, west of Sevilla, across a narrow river plain. Meanwhile, the 34th Michigan Volunteer Infantry Regiment would head south and make a "demonstration" of an attack at the village of Aguadores, near the coast, to throw off the Spanish. Once Lawton's men had engaged in fighting with the defenders at El Caney, the other two divisions—the First Division, under General Jacob Kent, and Wheeler's cavalry division—would emerge from a single trail leading down out of the jungle, ford the San Juan River, and assault the Spanish defenses arrayed along the heights. Throwing so many men at the defenses might result in a high casualty count, Shafter recognized, but it was preferable to watching them get sick and die in the squalid camps. Having waited this long, he had a new mantra: "To do it quick."[30]

There was another development: General Wheeler, in charge of the cavalry, and Samuel Young, in charge of Wheeler's Second Cavalry Brigade, were both sick. Samuel Sumner, Wheeler's second in command, was moved up to fill his place at the head of the cavalry division, and Wood took Young's place. That left Roosevelt in charge of the Rough Riders. The position he had been offered by Secretary of War Alger in April, and rejected, was finally his.[31]

At around three in the afternoon, just after a particularly heavy downpour, Roosevelt and his men received orders to break camp and move to the front. They were told to take their rifles, ammunition belts, and three days' worth of rations; everything else in their meager kit was to stay at their camp along the Aguadores River. They got on the move two hours later, and marched two and a half miles toward Santiago. Once again, confusion reigned. All that afternoon lines of men, hundreds long, jostled along the narrow Camino Real; one line would cut into the other, and men would suddenly find themselves marching in the wrong regiment, and have to double back. "Occasionally we came to gaps or open spaces, where some regiment was camped, and now and then one of these regiments, which apparently had been left out of its proper place, would file into the road, breaking up our line of march," Roosevelt wrote. "Once or twice we had to wade streams. Darkness came on, but we still had to march."[32]

"You could almost envy the ease with which the orange ball crossed the sky. It was all we could do to lift our muddy shoes," recalled trooper Arthur Crosby. The regiment arrived around 10 p.m., the night air cooling rapidly, the faint glow of the city haloing a far hill. They set up camp around an old building, with whitewashed walls and a red-tiled roof; it was, several of them surmised, an old monastery. It wasn't until nearly midnight that the various regiments were in place, and the thousands of American soldiers were bunked down, trying to get a few hours rest.[33]

The building sat on the slope of a squat, low elevation called El Poso. From the top, one could see a line of hills across the river valley and, beyond it, glimpses of Santiago itself. On June 27, Davis and a few Rough Riders had ventured up there to size up the Spanish defenses. What they saw shocked them: The Spanish, allegedly indolent and ignorant, were busy carving up the hills into defensive works, adding blockhouses, strips of barbed wire, and trenches like long yellow scars across the green landscape. By the time Shafter decided to begin an assault on Santiago's eastern defenses, the Spanish had dug over 4,000 yards of trenches, often three lines deep, interspersed, on the hilltops, with large blockhouses. Through his binoculars, Davis could see sombreros bobbing up and down, digging. "Rifle-pits were growing in length and in number, and in plain sight from the hill of El Poso," he wrote. "But no artillery was sent to El Poso hill to drop a shell among the busy men at work among the trenches." Worse, the Spanish had a good sense of where the Americans would attack—

the trails that descended from around El Poso onto the riverine plain between the two lines of hills—and had aimed their cannons and machine guns on them. "Of course the enemy knows where those two trails leave the wood," General Sumner, now in charge of the entire cavalry division, including the Rough Riders, told Davis on the night of June 30. "If our men leave the cover and reach the plain from those trails alone they will be piled up so high that they will block the road."[34]

Roosevelt and Wood, sticking close together despite their new, separated roles, camped with the Rough Riders, lying under their raincoats and over their saddle blankets. Davis was alongside them. After most of the regiment had fallen asleep, he got up and looked west from El Poso. "The attack on Santiago is to begin in a few hours—at 4 o'clock tomorrow," he wrote. "From this ridge we can see the lights of the city—street lamps shining across a sea of mist two miles wide and two miles long, which looks in the moonlight like a great lake in the basin of the hills." Another soldier—not a Rough Rider, but the author of an insightful memoir of the campaign—who went by the pseudonym Private St. Louis, said that the scene below El Poso looked "very similar to the floor of a theater, looking from the stage toward the back of the house." The next morning, the show would begin.[35]

CHAPTER 11

"AN AMPHITHEATER FOR THE BATTLE"

At about 4 a.m. on July 1, the nearly 17,000 men who comprised General Shafter's Fifth Corps crawled from under their blankets and out of their tents. There had been no bugle blasting reveille, so as not to warn the Spanish. Instead, sergeants went from man to man, shaking them awake. More than 10,000 soldiers were encamped around El Poso and Sevilla; the rest were already a few miles north, preparing for the assault on El Caney. If the men climbed the slopes of El Poso and peered hard enough, they could see the glow of central Santiago, seven miles away, framing San Juan Hill like a halo. Where they had time and inclination, they set small fires to boil coffee or fry some bacon. Most just ate a few pieces of hardtack and called it breakfast. No one spoke. Few had any illusion about what the day had in store for them. The night before, word had passed down—that morning, they were going to take the heights.[1]

On paper, the battle that unfolded that day paled in every way to the major engagements of the Civil War—Antietam and Gettysburg, of course, but also fights that have receded from common memory, like Malvern Hill and Perryville. And it was nothing like the weeks-long battles that would follow it in the twentieth century, like Belleau Wood and Iwo Jima and Hue. It was a one-day assault on the outer defenses of a provincial capital in the Caribbean, with a few hundred deaths on both sides. The Spanish defenses were formidable, but the landscape could not compare with the imposing escarpments that Union soldiers scaled at the Battle of Lookout Mountain, in 1863, or that Army Rangers climbed at Pointe du Hoc, on D-day.

And yet the Battle of San Juan Heights remains among the most important, celebrated, and contested engagements in American history. Numbers and topography tell us little about why the soldiers that morning, from Shafter to Roosevelt to the greenest volunteer private, felt in their bones the extraordinary significance of what they were about to undertake. For many it was to be their first experience of combat, and for most, their last. They were right to be afraid; by the end of the day, one out of every six of them would be dead or wounded. But there was something else, something collective and energizing and, in a way, much more daunting than the prospect of being shot by a Mauser bullet. If they carried the day, they would declare to the world that the United States Army could beat a European military power. And they were not just any army, but a small, untested force of enlisted regulars and barely trained volunteers, a force that most Europeans would dismiss as hardly an army at all.

Few Americans paused to think that Spain had long ceased being a first-rate empire, or that the soldiers arrayed against them had been dragooned into service, then physically weakened and emotionally demoralized by three years of counterinsurgency warfare. Few of the men in the invasion force considered that the numbers were in their favor, since General Arsenio Linares, in charge of the Spanish defenses, had deployed too many of his men on the city's northern and western sides, far away from Shafter's forces, resulting in nearly a 10-to-1 ratio in the Americans' favor along the eastern lines. (Nor, for that matter, did the rank and file grasp how many mistakes Shafter had made, and how those mistakes would come close to erasing whatever advantages the Americans held at the outset.) No one understood what would come next, if they won, or how they would recover, if they lost. Outside Shafter's inner circle, it is unlikely that anyone realized that, in either instance, there was no plan—no plan for victory, and no plan for defeat. One thing was sure, though: With dozens of correspondents and foreign attachés watching, news of their fight would spread around the world in nearly an instant, thanks to the telegraph and the presence of William Randolph Hearst, in person, watching the battle unfold from a nearby hill. That morning around the campfires, as the mists rose above El Poso and the San Juan River plain below them, there was only this: this valley, this hill, this fight.

Strictly speaking, there is no single San Juan Hill. It is merely one rise among many along a ridge that stood between the American forces and Santiago. The Spanish called it Los Cerros del Río San Juan; the locals called it Cerro Gordo or Cerro Alto. During peacetime, the slopes, long shorn of trees, were pastures for cattle and sheep. That morning the sheep were gone, and in their place ran rows of barbed wire and trenches, filled with soldiers in wide-brimmed sombreros. At the top was a stout blockhouse, with a ground floor studded with gun ports and a second, half-open floor that offered commanding views of the valley. In peacetime, no one would think much of the ridge; in battle, with the Spanish well-entrenched, to charge it was close to suicide.

On the eastern slope of El Poso, Roosevelt had already been awake for almost an hour. Arthur Cosby recalled that the first thing he saw, when he woke, was the new leader of the Rough Riders lathering his face with soap, for a shave. "It was a strangely reassuring sight," Cosby wrote. Roosevelt had dressed especially for the occasion: Along with his tan Rough Rider uniform, he wore bright yellow suspenders fastened with silver leaves, a blue polka-dot scarf tied around his sombrero, and a stand-up collar with the volunteer insignia on each point. He joined Colonel Wood for breakfast, and ate quickly—beans, bacon, hardtack, and coffee—and walked among the men who were still sleeping, prodding them awake with his boot. Then he summited the hill and scanned the field below. The sky was cloudless and deep blue. Like others, he found that the bowl-shaped valley lent a dramaturgical sheen to the day's coming events. "The lofty and beautiful mountains hemmed in the Santiago plain, making it an amphitheater for the battle," Roosevelt wrote.[2]

While the Rough Riders were still waking up, they heard a sound of squeaking wheels and of horses and mules and of men driving them. It was an artillery battery being pulled by a long team of horses, struggling along a rutted path toward the top of El Poso hill. Frederic Remington, standing nearby, sketched the scene, which he later painted as part of a pictorial history of the war for *Harper's*. "It was a fine sight to see the great horses straining under the lash as they whirled the guns up the hill and into position," Roosevelt wrote. That's putting a gloss on it: The weapons were pitifully insufficient for the task at hand, and far too few. The four pieces were all three-inch cannons, modern but small-bore weapons, capable of firing shells several thousand yards but using, that day, black powder, which would quickly give away their location. "They might as sensibly have been ordered to paint the rings in a target while a company was firing at a bull's eye," Davis wrote. Worse, there were only eight such artillery pieces available to the Americans that morning on the island—four at El Poso, four at El Caney—and a dozen or so more back at Siboney, fresh off the transports. Sixty more had been left at Tampa for lack of space on the ships. The only other thing larger than a rifle that day was a detachment of Gatling guns.[3]

The journalists and foreign attachés were given free rein of the American lines. To the latter, especially, Shafter's plan was madness. It ran against all the conventional wisdom they had learned in their careers, in much larger and better-trained armies than this one. A direct assault on entrenched troops along a ridge with barely any artillery support was sure to result in slaughter, and failure. Not only was Shafter throwing thousands of men against a well-defended position, but he had no idea how the Spanish might respond—for example, by flanking the Americans once the assault began. "It is scarcely conceivable, but none the less a fact," wrote Arthur Lee, the British attaché, that Shafter's forces "moved into this terra incognito without an advance guard, without flanking detachments, and with no military precautions save a 'point,' 100 yards in advance."[4]

Technically, it was no longer Shafter's battle to lead. At three o'clock that morning, his adjutant, Lieutenant Colonel E. J. McClernand, entered his tent to find the commander prostrate but awake, and groaning. Shafter said that he was ill from his exertions the previous day, having moved about on foot for hours in the hot sun, and that he would be unable to get up to El Poso in time for the attack. "He then asked if the staff officers understood the plan of battle, and upon being assured they did he directed me to establish Battle Headquarters at the El Pozo [sic] House and Hill, and said he would send staff officers to carry orders," McClernand recalled. Shafter would watch the battle from his camp on a hill a mile further east of El Poso. Though he kept in touch with McClernand via a telephone wire, the American side in the Battle of San Juan Heights would effectively be fought without a general.[5]

· · ·

196

About 5,400 men from the Second Division, under General Lawton, had marched the five miles north to El Caney the previous evening, and had gotten little rest before the attack (the remainder of the division had been kept back as a reserve). The village had been a summer retreat for Santiago's wealthier classes, who craved its slightly higher elevation and the way it caught the sea breeze heading inland. Several consuls, including the French, had homes there, but the residents were long gone. In their place were Spanish soldiers. There were only 520 men defending the town, either crouching in trenches arrayed in front of a steep-walled stone fort or huddled inside one of four log blockhouses, or in the steeple of the church that rose at the town center. At their head stood Joaquín Vara del Rey y Rubio, like General Weyler a veteran of the Carlist Wars and various regional uprisings in Spain. Lawton, backed by a four-cannon battery under Allyn Capron Sr., expected to have the town in American hands within two hours, and to meet up with the right flank of the main assault by noon.[6]

James Creelman, a correspondent for Hearst at the *Journal*, had crept up ahead of Lawton's front line, where he hid behind a strategically placed boulder to watch the battle play out. He could see the lines of American uniforms unspooling through the creek beds and tall grass at the foot of the hill. For almost half an hour, he watched as shells from Capron's battery slammed into the walls of the fort, after which the commanders of the Spanish would pop their heads up and, through field glasses, scan the tree line for an attack. Somehow, even in the middle of a barrage, a black hen poked its way around the front of the fort, oblivious.[7]

Just before 7 a.m., the assault began. Lines of men in blue plowed forward, then fell and fired, then ran a bit more, then fell and fired. In between shots, the Spanish responded, and every American surge forward included fewer men. Lieutenant General Adna Chaffee, a veteran of the Civil War and the Indian Wars who was in command of two regiments at El Caney that morning, ran up and down the line behind them, shouting, "Don't mind their fire, that's what you're here for. Keep her going!" Chaffee was remorseless; when one soldier was shot and fell, rolling down to crash into Chaffee's feet, he yelled, "Here! Someone! Take this man's rifle and get in on the line!" The hen, no longer able to ignore the shooting, dashed back and forth, flapping its wings in terror. "Poor creature!" Creelman wrote. "She escaped ten thousand bullets only to have her neck wrung by a hungry soldier that night."[8]

Chaffee and the hen were the only things doing much moving. After an hour of effort, the Americans had hardly advanced. The Spanish were too entrenched, too motivated, too well-trained to budge. Chafee tried to flank the main Spanish trench, but failed. Creelman, having temporarily abandoned his status as a correspondent, had picked up a gun and was moving forward with the soldiers. A few minutes later, he was hit. As he lay waiting for help, he could sense, through his pain-induced semiconsciousness, a figure standing over him. He opened his eyes to see his boss, Hearst himself, peering down, a straw hat on his head, a pistol on his belt, and a notebook and pen in his hand. "I'm sorry you're hurt," he said. "Wasn't it a splendid fight?" And then he dashed off to his boat, the *Sylvia*, to file a dispatch. Hearst, it seemed, had gotten his war. But Shafter's plan was unraveling.[9]

At 8 a.m., sure that the assault on El Caney was under way, McClernand ordered the battery of four cannons at El Poso to fire, and for the day's main event to begin. A voice rang out: "Number One, Load! Prime! Fire!" The first cannon jumped back eight feet. "Number Two, Load! Prime! Fire! Number Three, Load! Prime! Fire! Number Four, Load! Prime! Fire!" A cloud of white smoke soon drifted across the top of the hill, engulfing the Rough Riders who stood just behind the battery with a troop of Cuban soldiers to their left. Field glasses came out among the officers arrayed around the battery, and they watched for the shells to hit. The first landed far to the west. Wood, sitting next to Roosevelt nearby, leaned over and said that he wished the brigade had been ordered to wait somewhere else, away from the battery. The artillery men adjusted their range, and were preparing to fire again when they heard cracking sounds from across the valley. The Spanish were already returning fire. "Here it comes!" someone shouted.[10]

The Rough Riders heard a whistling crescendo, "like a bevy of quail rising," recalled La Motte, the surgeon. Several dozen soldiers were waiting for their orders in the yard of the monastery behind the cannons at El Poso. The first Spanish shell exploded in their midst; dozens were wounded, one had his leg blown off. Another shell hit the monastery. It collapsed the roof and blew men, mostly Cubans, out the windows. Two were killed in the Spanish counterfire, and more than a dozen wounded. Norman Trump, who had been assigned as a cook for one of the troops, was hit in the back and flew, face forward and arms outstretched as in a swan dive, onto the trail. Everyone thought he was dead. Then he stood, his back bruised and his tunic torn, but he was unbloodied, thanks to the backpack full of cooking gear he carried. Shrapnel from one of the shells hit Roosevelt in the hand, leaving a welt the size of a hickory nut. To make things worse, the Spanish cannons used smokeless powder, making it near impossible to pinpoint where that firing was coming from. "These casualties were utterly unnecessary," Davis wrote, "and were due to the stupidity of whoever placed the men within fifty yards of guns in action."[11]

The rapid return fire caught the Rough Riders by surprise. "I was quietly writing a few notes and thinking what a fine place I had to protect myself," reported Benjamin Colbert, who was sitting near the house. "I was just thinking 'just watch us lick 'em' when bang went a shell just over us." There was no doubt: The Spanish knew where the American forces were arrayed, and had their range. Chances were good, too, that the Spanish understood exactly where Shafter's regiments would deploy, knew about the narrow path out of the woods through which thousands of them would debouch—and had hundreds of guns trained on that spot.[12]

While the artillery detachment struggled with their cannons, McClernand gave the order to send forth the regiments. According to Shafter's orders, he was supposed to wait until word came that Lawton had captured El Caney. But after an hour, then two, nothing came. With the battle already engaged to the right, McClernand decided not to waste time.[13]

The American order of battle at San Juan Heights was comprised of two divisions: the First Division, made up of infantry, under General Jacob Kent, and Wheeler's (now Sumner's) division, made up of dismounted cavalry. The latter included two brigades, the First, under Colonel Henry Carroll (who had replaced Sumner), and the Second, now under Wood's command, which included the segregated 10th Cavalry, and, confusingly, both the First United States Cavalry and the First United States Volunteer Cavalry—the latter, of course, being better known as the Rough Riders. All told nearly 7,000 men were ordered forward (the rest were held in reserve).[14]

Despite the traffic jams the night before, no one had tried to address the fact that more than a dozen regiments were being directed to proceed along a jungle path barely ten feet wide. It took the regiments nearly three hours to mobilize, organize, and move down the trail. The disorder was obvious, but so, too, was the enormity of the undertaking. "It seemed as though every man in the United States was under arms and stumbling and slipping down the trail," Richard Harding Davis recalled. It wasn't until around 10 a.m. that Wood ordered Roosevelt to lead his regiment at the head of the Second Brigade, and directly behind the First Brigade, as it headed down the path, in columns of four. As the orders passed down the line to the Rough Riders, Theodore Miller wrote one last entry in his diary: "After constant bombardment, a skirmish took place. Must stop now. In line. Goodbye."[15]

As they moved along the wooded path past El Poso and toward the opening at the river, the men saw an oblong mass floating fifty feet above them. It was the observation balloon, which had been brought forward a few days before, now inflated and aloft, occupied by two intrepid observers. "It looked as though there might be a circus behind it," Cosby wrote. Such balloons had been a part of the American arsenal since the Civil War, and had made an appearance in European conflicts in the intervening years. But they were of limited use—good as an elevated platform of sorts well behind the lines and looking out toward a flat, treeless plain. But as mobile observation decks at the very front of a column in a hilly jungle, they were untested. Logic dictated that a fat target like an observation balloon would draw enemy fire, especially if the Spanish suspected, rightly, that its forward motion tracked with an advancing column of infantry below it.[16]

Shafter had ordered the regiments to divide up into two groups as they left the trail in front of San Juan Heights, infantry to the left and cavalry to the right. "Our orders had been of the vaguest kind, being simply to march to the right and connect with Lawton—with whom, of course, there was no chance of our connecting," Roosevelt said. They almost immediately had to ford the San Juan River, a broad, shallow stream that ran perpendicular to the trail. With the enemy beginning to open fire, the men made fast for the other side. "Close in to the right, men, at the next rush," shouted Buckey O'Neill to the men in his troop. "You will have a better chance there." It was too late for some—men fell almost as soon as they emerged from the water. A trooper named Henry Haywood, who had been a police officer in New York under Roosevelt, was just fifty feet ahead of Jesse Langdon when he was shot in the chest; Langdon recalled that "when he was hit it sounded like you hit your fist into a pillow." Surgeons and their assistants trudged through the muddy water, pulling wounded men off the banks and then, cradling them, hurried them to the other side. The location, as long as a city block, became known as the "Bloody Ford."[17]

Not long after fording the river, Roosevelt and his men looked up again at the balloon. At first, it had been pulled along on the ground by a wagon. But the road was too rough, and a gang of soldiers had taken over. It was already drawing fire from the Spanish cannons and rifles. A shell tore a hole in the side, then another flew through its middle. "The front had burst out with a roar like a brushfire," wrote Stephen Crane, who was observing from El Poso and later incorporated the scene into his short story "The Price of the Harness": "The balloon was dying, dying a gigantic public death before the eyes of two armies." It was not a total waste: while aloft the two men slung in a basket beneath it had spotted a hidden trail off to the left, and relayed their discovery to General Kent, at the head of the First Division, who immediately diverted his regiments along it, thereby relieving the congestion along the main path. But the discovery came at a high price: The balloon settled like a net in the tree branches along the Aguadores River, alongside the point where the path disgorged into the valley below the San Juan Heights. It became a giant marker for where the American troops were pouring onto the battlefield.[18]

McClernand had ordered the divisions to advance, but told them not to shoot until he gave a signal; as a result, the men waited nearly an hour under withering fire. They hid the best they could among the reeds and river brush along the banks. Some, in a daze, lapped up water from the river to sate their thirst. Some crept forward, to find shelter from Spanish fire along the sunken roads and earthen berms that striped the land around the river valley. But the grass was thick and high and blocked any possible breeze. Some men felt like they were suffocating and stood up, only to be cut down. The fire was coming in so hot and so relentless that a man couldn't put his finger in the air without getting it shot off, said one general. "I could hear the bullets whizzing through the grass as if they were mowing it down in front of us," wrote the Rough Rider Billy McGinty. "When I looked up I didn't find any grass missing, but some of the boys were." Enemy fire came from ahead, on the hill, but also occasionally from the side and even behind them: Spanish guerrillas had crept into the forest the night before and hid in trees, armed with their rifles, a bag of bullets, and a canteen. The casualty rates soared. Within ten minutes one regiment, the Sixth Infantry, had lost a quarter of its men. "There was not a single yard of ground for a mile to the rear, which was not inside the zone of fire," Davis said. "For a time it seemed as though every second man was either killed or wounded."[19]

Within minutes, casualties were pouring into the dressing station, located back up the trail. The surgeons in charge did their best to find places to shelter the wounded, but there was little solace, even in the forest, and on multiple occasions men came in limping, or carried by two comrades, only to fall dead from a new bullet hole in their back. Crane, wandering among the wounded, looked down to find, staring up at him, the familiar eyes of a former college classmate. "I had looked upon five hundred men with stolidity, or with a conscious indifference which filled me with amazement," he wrote. "But the apparition of Reuben McNab, the schoolmate, lying there in the mud, with a hole through his lung, awed me into stutterings, set me trembling with a sense of terrible intimacy with this war which heretofore I could have believed was a dream—almost."[20]

In their memoirs, men like Roosevelt painted pictures of their fellow soldiers as fearless Spartans. When they were shot, they fell silently, and gallantly. Davis had a different impression. They acted as soldiers, which is to say bravely and gallantly, but also nervously and afraid—often the same man went through the full range of emotions, torn in different directions by different instincts. "It was interesting to observe the pressure which men put upon their nerves suddenly slip from them, and to see them flying panic-stricken for a tree, or dropping on their knees and sliding along the ground," Davis wrote.

He observed one soldier who, whenever he would hear a shot nearby, "his nerves would refuse to support the strain any longer, and he would jump for the bushes and would sit there breathing heavily." Edward Marshall wrote that men "never failed to fall in little heaps with instantaneous flaccidity of muscles. There were no gradual droppings of one knee, no men who slowly fell while struggling to keep standing. There were no cries. The injured ones did not throw hands up and fall dramatically backward with strident cries and stiffened legs, as wounded heroes fall upon the stage. They fell like clods."[21]

The Rough Riders deployed near the far right of the American line, adjacent to the First Cavalry and the 10th Cavalry, the two other regiments in the Second Brigade. As they moved into position, they passed the 71st New York, the regiment that, were it not for the intercession of Russell Alger, the secretary of war, Roosevelt might yet be commanding. They cheered him along, to which he replied, "Don't cheer, but fight, now's the time to fight." That was easy to say, and harder to do—the 71st were volunteers, practically untrained, and armed with antiquated Remington rifles. Though they played no important part in the battle that day, the regiment had one of the highest casualty rates of the battle.[22]

Even the most veteran regular troops, however, lacked the sort of training in coordinated, large-scale combat that a battle like that day's required. Many of them, until then, had only rarely seen their entire regiment at once, let alone fought with it, having been deployed in smaller units at small, far-flung forts across the West. In Tampa they had trained together, finally, but even then their colonels and generals did a poor job of keeping order in a crowd, or communicating with other colonels and generals. And so, predictably, at the foot of San Juan Hill, with bullets and shells crashing around them, the men crouched and maneuvered for cover; the regiments mixed together, so that white and black, regular and volunteer soldiers came to compose one general mass of men.

The heat was almost as dangerous as the Spanish rifles. After a few hours, with the thermometer near 100 degrees and their canteens long since empty, soldiers began to pass out from dehydration and heat stroke. "Men gasped on their backs, like fishes in the bottom of a boat, their heads burning inside and out, their limbs too heavy to move," Davis wrote. "They had been rushed here and there wet with sweat and wet with fording the streams, under a sun that would have made moving a fan an effort."[23]

Frank Knox, the Michigan boy who had joined the Rough Riders at Tampa and befriended Theodore Miller, later wrote about the battle to his parents: "It is hard enough to face those ugly bullets with your own carbine smoking in your hand, but it becomes doubly hard when you lay under a hell of fire and can't fire a shot to reply." To keep his men calm, Buckey O'Neill was pacing above them as they crouched behind whatever cover they could find, smoking a cigarette and trying to act as unperturbed by the winging bullets as possible. Like Colonel Wood at Las Guasimas, he seemed to believe that it was his obligation as an officer to not show fear, even to invite death. His men begged O'Neill to get down, but he took the cigarette out of his mouth, blew a puff of smoke, looked down at one of them, and replied, "Sergeant, the Spanish bullet has not been made that will kill me." A moment later, a Spanish bullet hit O'Neill in the mouth, exiting the back of his head. There was very little blood, just a small spattering from his mouth. One of his men, Frank Frantz, ran over to help him, but he was too late. O'Neill was dead before he hit the ground.[24]

Most of the journalists and foreign attachés stayed at El Poso, where they could watch the battle unfold from relative safety. What they saw was a disaster in the making. "It was thoroughly evident that the Spaniards had the range of everything in the country," wrote Frederic Remington. Without sufficient artillery support, the men were pinned—it was, Davis wrote, "like going to a fire with a hook and ladder company and leaving the hose and the steam-engines in the engine house." The situation was growing desperate. There was no way to retreat, because thousands of men still clogged the trail, but without orders to attack, there was nothing any one man could do to relieve his situation. Charging the hill, if undertaken by a single regiment, would have been suicide against an entrenched enemy with modern weapons.[25]

It was now past noon, and Shafter, or his surrogates, had yet to order any sort of forward movement. Roosevelt sent back messengers to his commanders, seeking further orders. Finally a lieutenant colonel rode up with orders to "move forward and support the regulars in the assault on the hills in front." It was what Roosevelt had been waiting to hear. They were now to be in the first wave of the assault. "The instant I received the order I sprang on my horse," he wrote, "and my 'crowded hour' began."[26]

Roosevelt, still on horseback, rode down the line of Rough Riders, ordering them up and into a skirmish line. "Boys, this is the day we repeat what we have done before," he yelled from atop Little Texas. "You know we are surrounded by the regulars. They are around us thick and heavy." Ahead was a hill, slightly smaller and to the northeast of San Juan Hill, upon which sat a few small buildings and an immense iron pot, likely used to boil cane juice. The Americans called it Kettle Hill.[27]

Most of the men sprang up, but one Rough Rider, lying behind a bush, hesitated. The man, whose name went unrecorded, looked at Roosevelt confusedly, perhaps already suffering shell shock. Roosevelt urged him up, saying, "Are you afraid to stand up when I am on horseback?" As the man finally got on his knees to rise, he pitched forward on his face—a bullet had hit him in the head, and passed through him lengthwise. "I suppose the bullet had been aimed at me," Roosevelt said, "at any rate, I, who was on horseback in the open was unhurt, and the man lying flat on the ground in the cover was killed."[28]

Slowly, the mass of men around Roosevelt began to move forward. When the color sergeant from the Third Infantry Regiment was shot, a black soldier named George Berry, who carried the flag of the 10th Cavalry, stopped to pick up the guidon of the Third as well. "Dress on the colors, boys!" Berry yelled as they charged, calling on them to follow the flag. "Dress on the colors!"[29]

At first, Roosevelt stuck to the back of the regiment as it organized for its assault. But to get them moving, he rallied a group of nearby troopers, and a few men from other troops gathered beside them, and began to lead them forward, through the mass of soldiers. He then rode up to a captain from the Ninth Cavalry Regiment, Eugene Dimmick, whose men were taking cover behind a line of trees and barbed wire. Roosevelt said the Rough Riders had been ordered to join the battle in support of the regular regiments, and to let them pass. But Dimmick, fifty-seven years old and a veteran of the Civil

War, said he'd been told to stay by his colonel. Where is he? Roosevelt asked. I don't know, Dimmick replied. "Then I am the ranking officer here, and I give the order to charge." Dimmick had no choice; two of his men even volunteered to hold down the barbed wire so that Roosevelt could ride over it. Little Texas leapt over, and Roosevelt looked back at his men, waving his hat, and gave the order to charge.[30]

Back on El Poso, Richard Harding Davis heard someone shout and point to the right. "See those men rushing across that field?" the man yelled. "Look! Wheeler's brigade is charging that hill. There are the Stars and Stripes!" He watched as the cavalry regiments coursed up, fording another small river and then around a pond, some cutting left, while others, following Roosevelt's lead, went to the right. Davis recorded how "Roosevelt, mounted high on horseback, and charging the rifle-pits at a gallop and quite alone, made you feel that you would like to cheer. . . . It looked like foolhardiness, but as a matter of fact, he set the pace with his horse and inspired the men to follow."[31]

In a painting by Remington, who was watching the battle nearby, the Rough Riders run up the hill in an organized line, the force of their charge apparent in the strength of their stride and the determined look on their faces. The reporter Stephen Bonsal compared it to "a great wave sweeping slowly in from the sea." It is a testament to the errant power of collective memory that Remington and Bonsal, both correspondents, recalled a fact in great detail that is so far from the truth. The charge was not heroic, at least to watch it unfold. The men would run a bit, then take cover, or take aim, then run a little more. "We ran a few feet, fell flat, jumped up, ran, fell flat," Arthur Cosby recalled. Halfway up the hill he was hit; he was able to walk, so he made his way back to a first-aid station. The shot lodged in Cosby's chest but somehow missed his organs, and the bullet remained there the rest of his life.[32]

"I have seen many illustrations and pictures of this charge on the San Juan hills, but none of them seem to show it just as I remember it," Davis wrote.

In the pictures-papers the men are running up hill swiftly and gallantly, in regular formation, rank after rank, with flags flying, their eyes aflame, and their hair streaming, their bayonets fixed, in long, brilliant lines, an invincible, overpowering weight of numbers. Instead I think the thing which impressed one the most, when our men started from cover, was that they were so few. It seemed as if someone had made an awful and terrible mistake. One's instinct was to call them to come back. You felt that someone had blundered and that these few men were blindly following out some madman's mad order. It was not heroic then, it seemed merely terribly pathetic. The pity of it, the folly of such a sacrifice was what held you.[33]

No one bothered to fix their bayonets, and no officer thought to halt his men so they could fire at once, in concentrated volleys—it's unlikely any of the soldiers would have listened, had an officer tried. There was no order to the assault. They ran as fast as they could without drawing fire. "There was hardly a semblance of a line—simply a broad swarm," another reporter watching from El Poso, John Bigelow, wrote.[34]

Eventually the Rough Riders were joined by men from the Ninth, Third, Sixth, and 10th Cavalry Regiments. As they ran, they could see, off to their left, a wave of blue as the regular infantry begin to run up San Juan Hill at the same time, led by the white-maned General Hamilton Hawkins of the First Brigade, First Division, who knew something about gallant charges—as a young man, he had fought at the Battle of Gettysburg. "General Hawkins," Davis wrote, "with hair white as snow, and yet far in advance of men thirty years his junior, was so noble a sight that you felt inclined to pray for his safety; on the other hand, Roosevelt, mounted high on horseback and quite alone, made you feel that you would like to cheer." As his biographer Arthur Lubow points out, Davis was not shy about drawing the generational distinction between the two men, with Hawkins a noble relic and Roosevelt the dynamic future.[35]

It was a true skirmish—no ranks, no order, just a halting, furious run up the hill, cheering and jostling and falling along the way. "The whole line, tired of waiting, and eager to close with the enemy, was straining to go forward; and it seemed that different parts slipped the leash at almost the same time," Roosevelt recounted. He galloped back and forth, surging forward to urge the men on, then back to the sunken roads to direct more troops. He ordered Dade Goodrich, in charge of Troop D, to the right, and saw to it that another three troops followed them. Then he tore off uphill, where he found his personal orderly, Henry Bardshar, already in position, taking aim at Spanish troops who were pouring out of the small clay-colored house that sat at the top of the hill. The charge, said John Greenway, "was the grandest sight I ever saw."[36]

As the regiment got closer to the summit of the hill, they could hear American rifle fire plinking off the giant kettle on the top of the hill. The men stood to fire, and white puffs of smoke and dirt rose along the crest. One trooper, John Swetnam, knelt to fire and immediately fell over, a bullet hole in his forehead. "You couldn't place your finger more in the center of his forehead than that bullet that hit him was placed," said David Hughes, who was lying nearby. "He didn't even kick." About forty feet from the top, Roosevelt came to another barbed wire fence. Instead of trying to jump it, or wait for someone to hold it down, he dismounted, and was immediately attacked by two Spanish soldiers. Bardshar, Roosevelt's orderly, picked them off with his revolver. Wisely, this time Roosevelt had left his saber in camp, and he could run, unencumbered, the rest of the way up the hill.[37]

Who made it to the top first? In the confusion of the scrum, no one quite knew. By the time Roosevelt arrived after the first wave, there was already a fierce debate under way. The three New Mexico troops had all planted their guidons around the same time. But off to the other side of the hill, two troops from the Ninth Regiment claimed they were the first, and had their upright flags to prove it as well. "As for the individual men, each of whom honestly thought he was first on the summit," Roosevelt wrote, "their name was legion." With the Spanish in retreat from the hill and their gunfire lessened, Roosevelt ordered the dead, dying, and wounded moved to the side of the hill, away from the main body of men, so as not to demoralize them. While a detachment of soldiers handled their fallen comrades, others dove ravenously at a pot of hot rice they found still sitting over a fire. It might be poisoned, someone warned, but no one listened. "Poison or no poison we soon finished it up," said one trooper.[38]

The respite from Spanish gunfire did not last long. Within minutes, the few hundred men now gathered on the top of Kettle Hill were taking fire from the entrenched Spanish soldiers on San Juan Hill, less than a quarter mile to the south—not just rifle fire, but from small artillery, with timed fuses that exploded in starbursts of shrapnel above them. A few men took shelter behind the iron kettle; everyone took aim to return fire. Dade Goodrich remembered lying beside his cousin, Theodore Miller, and firing their Krags as fast as they could. "He seemed to be enjoying himself immensely," Goodrich recalled. They could just make out the blue jackets of the Spanish regulars in the San Juan Hill trenches, and the cousins smiled at each other whenever one would double over, or leap and fall back against the trench wall.[39]

The firefight went on for about ten minutes; from time to time a Rough Rider would drop, or roll on his side, dead or wounded. They were back where they had been at the bottom of the hill—exposed under fire, though this time much closer to the Spanish trenches. They could see, several hundred yards away, the American infantry still slowly making its way up the hill, but it was an even tougher climb than the Rough Riders had just completed. The noise of the carbines and the shouting of the men were intense, but above it all, Roosevelt could hear a quick, steady drumming. He paused, then realized—"It's the Gatlings, men, our Gatlings!" Lieutenant John W. Parker, the head of the Gatling detachment, had managed to pull up his battery of four machine guns to a flat open meadow to the left of the hill, and proceeded to pour fire on the Spanish positions. Under the cover of the rapid-fire guns, American infantry began to make their final push to the summit.[40]

Inside Santiago, the sounds of battle grew closer, though they remained muffled by the concentric lines of hills that surrounded the city. Müller y Tejeiro, the officer who would later be one of the few Spanish soldiers to recount his army's side of the battle, went walking around the empty Santiago streets—the soldiers were at the front, the civilian residents were in hiding. Over his head, shells fired by the Spanish ships, in the harbor, soared toward the far side of San Juan Heights. But without forward observers, there was no way to find the range; they were firing blind, and not hitting a thing. Müller y Tejeiro found General Linares, hurrying from one branch of his headquarters to another, shouting orders, insisting that he was on the verge of pushing the Americans back to Siboney.[41]

Finally Roosevelt could not wait any longer. His troops, watching the American infantry rush headlong toward the Spanish position, were in an excellent position to take on the enemy's flank. He stood and yelled for his men to follow him. He vaulted a barbed wire fence and ran out about 100 yards before realizing that only five soldiers had joined him. Immediately, two of them were shot. Roosevelt told the other three to find whatever cover they could, and he ran back to Kettle Hill. There he found his men more or less where he'd left them. "I taunted them bitterly for not having followed me," he said, before realizing that they simply hadn't heard him.[42]

This time Dade Goodrich and Theodore Miller rose up to follow Roosevelt, running down the gentle slope between Kettle Hill and San Juan Hill, joyous grins on their faces. Miller was hit almost immediately. Goodrich, steps ahead of his cousin, ran several more seconds before realizing something was wrong. Miller was on the ground, his chest heaving, his clothing soaking with blood. Goodrich tore open his shirt and saw the bullet had gone in through Miller's left shoulder and traveled, internally, across his upper body. Miller smiled and said he was okay. Leaving two men to guard him, Goodrich recalled, "I said goodbye to Thede and took a last look that he should be cared for . . . he was pale but perfectly calm and collected." But Miller was not okay. After Goodrich and the rest of the regiment had advanced, he looked up at one of the men, Harrison Jewell Holt, and said, "I'm going, Harry . . . but it's in a good cause, isn't it?"[43]

Missing from the assault were General Lawton and his men in the Second Division, who did not complete their assault on El Caney until nearly twelve hours after they had begun. Unlike the Spanish soldiers at San Juan Heights, those at El Caney seemed determined to fight to the death—inspired, perhaps, by the tenacity of their commander, Vara del Rey. He had been shot in both legs, but refused to remove himself or his soldiers. At 1:30 Shafter, via McClernand, ordered a retreat, so he could direct the Second Division to the south, but Lawton refused. The tide of battle only turned when Vara del Rey, still trying to stand on his bullet-riddled legs and still very much in charge of the Spanish defenses, was hit in the head, and killed instantly. (Two of his sons were killed that day at El Caney as well.)[44]

The Americans entered the fort at El Caney first. "The interior was a charnel house," wrote Secretary Alger, based on reports he had read from the field. "The remains of eighteen dead were lying about. The walls and floors were bespattered with blood." Only about 100 of the original 521 Spanish defenders escaped back to Santiago; 235 had been killed or wounded, the rest captured. Even after the fort fell, the Americans spent another hour in house-to-house combat. The Americans at El Caney lost more than 100 men, killed or wounded, scores more than Shafter had expected. Arthur Lee, writing later in *Scribner's*, said that the American dead were spread so thick across the hillside before El Caney "that one could only pass by stepping over them." General Lawton had completed his objective, but at enormous cost, and by the time he did it was too late to matter.[45]

In Alger's estimation, the delay at El Caney was a good thing—if Lawton had made quick work of it and then proceeded south to San Juan Heights, the three reunited divisions might have pressed on, by inertia, toward Santiago, tired but unstoppable. Had they made such an advance, Alger feared, the entire army might have pushed past the first line of Spanish defenses, atop San Juan Hill, but they would have been cut down once they reached better-defended Spanish positions closer to the city. "I shall always regard the unexpected delay experienced in taking Caney as one of the many incidents connected with the Santiago campaign in which the guiding hand of Providence seems to have interposed for America," he wrote. As it was, the two divisions assaulting Kettle Hill and San Juan Hill took more than 1,000 casualties that day.[46]

By the time Roosevelt and his men, now just over 490 in number, arrived at the top of San Juan Hill, dozens of the regular infantry were already there, and a close-order fight was under way. Many of the Spanish soldiers had already fled back toward Santiago, but hundreds more remained in the trenches and blockhouses. The trenches were nothing like the semipermanent affairs of the Western Front of World War I, two decades later. They were hastily dug, two feet wide and four feet deep, and one had to crouch inside them to gain any real protection. They were filled with Spanish bodies. American officers, armed with revolvers, stood picking off Spanish as they charged, or ran. Roosevelt, pulling out the pistol salvaged from the *Maine*, shot one man just a few feet from him. The man jumped back "like a jackrabbit," he bragged to Robert Ferguson, a second lieutenant in the Rough Riders and an old family friend—tellingly, almost the exact same phrase he had once used to describe killing a buck in the Dakotas, over a decade before. Roosevelt was overjoyed at being able to check off another of his life's carnal ambitions, to kill a man at close range, though his memoirs mention the incident only in clinical, passing terms. In the safety of hindsight, he was clearly ashamed of his bloodlust. But he made no attempt to hide his brutal joy that afternoon. "No hunting trip so far has ever equaled it in Theodore's eyes," wrote Ferguson in a letter to Edith Roosevelt. "T. was just reveling in victory and gore."[47]

Davis arrived on the hill a few minutes later. He found an undifferentiated mass of men; by this point there was no coherence to the regiments congregating on San Juan Hill—white, black, regular, volunteer, cavalry, and infantry stood side by side in the hot sun of July 1 in Cuba. The black soldiers had fought with particular courage, and white soldiers—even those used to bearing their prejudices openly—singled them out for praise. One Southern soldier told a reporter from the Associated Press: "I am not a negro lover. My father fought with Mosby's Rangers [a famous Confederate cavalry battalion], and I was born in the South, but the Negroes saved that fight, and the day will come when General Shafter will give them credit for their bravery." Roosevelt likewise praised the black soldiers, saying, in a letter to a friend, "I wish no better men beside me in battle than these colored troops showed themselves to be. Later on, when I come to write of the campaign, I shall have much to say about them." But in his memoir of the war, published in 1899, he was cooler. The black troops were brave, Roosevelt still agreed, but only as simple soldiers, who need white men to lead them: "Occasionally they produce non-commissioned officers who can take the initiative and accept responsibility precisely like the best class of whites; but this cannot be expected normally, nor is it fair to expect it." Roosevelt's revision of his own history set off a wave of consternation and disappointment in the black press, which had reprinted his earlier comments and generally looked with pride on the performance of the black regiments in the war.[48]

Those Spanish who had made it off the hill had regrouped and were firing at the Americans, so Roosevelt pointed at a few dozen men and ordered them to push further west, toward a line of palm trees behind which the new Spanish line had formed. It was not until they reached them, and saw, over a low crest of hills, Santiago itself, that they realized they were too far ahead of the main force, a few men suddenly exposed to a Spanish counterattack.[49]

What had been a pitched battle had turned into a rout, and a slaughter. Many of the Spanish dead had been shot by the Gatling guns while still in the trenches, which were filled with bloody, nearly headless bodies, their brains and skulls scattered against the hilltop. The dead men wore rope shoes, rotten and falling to pieces, and often too big for their small feet—they were, after all, conscripts in a war no one wanted to fight, which meant they were often taken from the ranks of the poor, the undernourished, and the young. The Rough Riders, among whom even the toughest had never seen more than a handful of men dead from gunfire at a time, were disgusted by the scene, and by themselves. "So help me God, they looked like kids about twelve years old. All of us boys kind of felt ashamed of ourselves, we really did," trooper Jesse Langdon said. "It was pitiful."[50]

The Spanish made two mistakes at the Battle of San Juan Heights. Even though it was clear for days that the American assault would come as a massive, pointed attack from the east, General Linares spread his forces in a semicircle around the city—fearing, ostensibly, the Cuban detachments arrayed to the north and west. The Cubans were a sizable force, but they had neither the ammunition nor the leadership necessary to pull off an assault on the city. As a result only 521 Spanish troops sat in the trenches at San Juan Hill, and just 137 at Kettle Hill, an order of magnitude fewer than the 7,000 American forces making the assault against them. Meanwhile there were 3,389 Spanish deployed around the rest of the city, and another 1,869 in reserve.[51]

The second mistake was even less excusable: Spanish engineers had designed the trenches so that they sat at the top of the hills, but not at the crest of the crown, the point on a hill where one can still see the bottom—in other words, they were too far toward the top of

213

the hill to be able, from inside a trench, to see down the entire slope. If the Spanish had been positioned correctly, the Rough Riders, as they advanced, would have faced much more fire from the Spanish trenches. "Had there been on the Spanish side any generalship worthy of the name, it is doubtful whether there would have been anything left of Shafter's army," wrote the historian Herbert H. Sargent, who fought in the battle and later wrote a three-volume history of the campaign.[52]

The Rough Riders suffered the highest casualties of any cavalry regiment that day: Out of the 490 men who made the assault up the hills, 13 were killed or would soon die of their wounds, and 76 more were wounded. Another 10 were wounded and four were killed in fighting the next day—in all a 19 percent casualty rate. But they didn't suffer alone—the entire cavalry division suffered heavy losses. "Some idea of the severity of the enemy's fire may be gained from the fact that of the five officers of the brigade staff four were killed or wounded and one exhausted by the extreme heat," Wood wrote in his after-action report.[53]

Acclaim for the Rough Riders began to appear almost immediately in the press back home. Davis's dispatches in particular were full of rich detail and focused on the achievements of Roosevelt's men that day; the lieutenant colonel's efforts to cultivate the correspondent were proving a wise investment. The charge up Kettle Hill "gave us such a thrill as can never stir us again," Davis wrote in *Scribner's*. It was "a miracle of self-sacrifice, a triumph of bull-dog courage, which one watched breathless with wonder." Other correspondents were equally in awe. "Wood, Roosevelt, the men who were killed and the men who survived at Sevilla all gave the world an object lesson in American bravery that will not soon be effaced from the tables," wrote one reporter. "By their reckless daring the Rough Riders set an example to the remainder of our armies which will undoubtedly tend to lift the standard of bravery."[54]

Almost instantly, the conversation back home turned from what America had done at San Juan Heights to what it would do now, with everything it has won—first the Philippines and now, it seemed, Cuba as well. The country was drunk on its feelings of national pride.

"The flags flying everywhere and the extra newspapers issued every hour or oftener remind us continually of the war, but in New York City the question of 'what will we do with this and that island when captured' seems to attract even more attention than the war," wrote one reporter.[55]

But of course the Americans had not yet won the war, or even the campaign. Santiago remained to be captured, and with it the Spanish fleet. Yet even this first major victory had come at significant cost. And so, in the coming weeks a backlash against Shafter began to form. Shafter had chosen to alienate reporters, and his mistake was a costly one. The casualty rate was unacceptable—overall 1,240 American soldiers had been killed, wounded, or gone missing, against 480 Spanish. Even more than the Spanish themselves, in the American press Shafter was the bad guy, and soon, by extension, were many of the other generals and civilian staff in Washington. Up until then, press coverage, and even personal reports from the front, were generally positive. But after the capture of San Juan Heights, a new twist emerged. The men and the line officers had won the fight—but in spite of, and not because of, the general officers' leadership. Davis and others were quick to blame Shafter for refusing to transfer command, because he was much too sick to be at the front. "So great the vanity and self-confidence of the man, that . . . he did not ask to be relieved of his command," Davis wrote. "It was not on account of Shafter, but in spite of Shafter, that the hills were taken."[56]

Roosevelt expressed similar sentiments in his correspondence. "Not since the campaign of Crassus against the Parthians has there been so criminally incompetent a General as Shafter," he wrote to Lodge four days later, "and not since the expedition against Walcheren has there been grosser mismanagement than in this. The battle simply fought itself." And whatever one thinks about Shafter's leadership up to that point, there's no debate that Davis and Roosevelt were right: Once the battle was joined, Shafter and his top generals left the stage, and the critical decisions about how and when to attack and maneuver on the field fell to the regimental officers. The nation's martial genius lay not in the generals or the planners in Washington, but in the troops at the front, the Everymen who made up in pluck and courage what they lacked in discipline. Said one general to Davis: "We had as little to do as the referee at a prize-fight who calls 'time.' We called 'time' and they did the fighting."[57]

There was one final question, which arose immediately and dogged Roosevelt for the rest of his life. Perhaps out of confusion, or just in search of good copy, the press back home conflated the sequence and arrangement of events during the assault, and within a few days it was an accepted consensus, among large swaths of the public, that Theodore Roosevelt had led the charge up San Juan Hill, and not just Kettle Hill. The fact that Roosevelt himself never made this claim mattered very little. Some of the blame rests with Davis, who later merged the two in his reporting. In any event, every so often during Roosevelt's political career in Albany, as governor, and then the presidency—and especially during the 1904 presidential campaign— some self-identified muckraking journalist would revisit the question, and declare that Roosevelt had lied about the whole thing. Had that person examined the record, and then looked at the facts of the charge up Kettle Hill, he would have seen that Roosevelt had nothing to lie about. The assault he did lead was more than enough glory for one man.

By the afternoon, the Americans were in command of San Juan Heights, and Shafter, who was feeling well enough to issue orders, decided to pause, rather than push on to Santiago. Even if Shafter had ordered the assault to continue, it is doubtful the men could have followed through. The day's fighting followed a week of debilitating, sweaty, malarial camp life, capped by an afternoon and evening and, for some, a late night of marching. Many men had eaten but a single piece of hardtack since waking up that morning. Most of them, even most of the regulars, had never experienced combat, let alone sustained, intense fighting like this. With the hilltops secured, the American soldiers regrouped their regiments, ferried the wounded back to dressing stations, ate what food they had, and began to dig in. That evening, just a few hundred men held the defenses at San Juan Heights. When darkness fell and the battlefield was quiet once again, one Rough Rider said, "never was night more welcome."[58]

CHAPTER 12

"HUMPTY-DUMPTY ON THE WALL"

On the afternoon of July 1, with the Spanish in retreat and the fighting at a lull, the American soldiers could pause to assess their position. Despite routing the Spanish from the San Juan Heights, their hold, Richard Harding Davis wrote, was "painfully suggestive of Humpty-Dumpty on the wall." Precious few soldiers faced thousands of Spanish still in Santiago, presumably planning a counterattack. There was no single American line; instead, clumps of soldiers crouched here and there, separated by as much as 200 yards of empty space. "They were so few in number," Davis added, "so utterly inadequate to the extent of the hills they had captured and were supposed to hold that their position was like that of a man clinging to a church steeple and unable, without breaking his neck, to slip down on any side; but who still proclaimed to the air about him, 'See how I hold this steeple!'" As Davis kneeled alongside them, Stephen Crane came crab-walking up to the front, sat down, sweating, and said, "Well, here we are."[1]

The Americans had not planned on laying siege to Santiago; in fact, they had not made any plans at all for what to do after taking the San Juan Heights. Shafter seems to have intended to capture the city in a single, massive assault, but if so he never explained how he meant to achieve it—where the Spanish weak spots were, where the best angles of attack on the city lay. Having not conducted the necessary reconnaissance, he and his officers would not have known where to start. At the same time, Shafter had made no plans for a siege—he left most of his heavy cannons in Tampa, and he did not bring enough shovels, telegraph cable, and other necessities for a long-term investment of a city the size of Santiago. But with thousands of Spanish troops well-defended inside the city, he had little choice.

Shafter did not receive much help from Washington. During the course of the siege, President McKinley, Secretary Alger, and General Miles would sour on General Shafter, but they offered no plan of their own—no plan for how to take Santiago, and no plan for how to move on from there to capture the rest of the island from the Spanish, who still controlled Cuba's major cities. And so, for much of July, the American campaign against Santiago became a siege by default, and a race against the heat and tropical diseases that were already eroding the American forces.

Of all the regiments, the Rough Riders' position was the most perilous. When Roosevelt halted his charge on San Juan Hill on July 1, he and about ninety men were 500 yards ahead of the main line of American troops along the heights, a skinny salient that would undoubtedly be the first point of assault when the Spanish counterattack began. They lay on the ground, propped on their elbows, panting, hungry. Almost immediately, Spanish artillery and small arms fire began to pour in from the second and third lines of trenches between the Americans and the city. One of the first artillery shots from the Spanish exploded directly over one of the Rough Riders' newly dug rifle pits, killing two men and wounding three.[2]

Shafter ordered Wheeler, who had recovered enough of his health to take nominal control of the cavalry division, to hold the hills at all cost. Roosevelt, with his 90 men out in front, was sandwiched between a complement of 10th Cavalry soldiers on the left and another band of Rough Riders to his right. Unwilling to wait for night to begin digging, he sent men to the Spanish blockhouses to look for entrenching tools. They returned with shovels, picks, and axes. Those without tools used empty cans, even their hands, to dig. They buried the dead Spanish in their east-facing trenches and spent the afternoon digging new ones, facing west toward Santiago. "Men who had never before handled pick or shovel, took hold with willing hands and labored side by side," recalled one trooper.[3]

While most of the regiment dug in, six men carried the wounded Theodore Miller toward the rear, in search of a field hospital. They improvised a stretcher by fastening a blanket between two poles. He winced with every movement and complained of the chills, despite the heat; they wrapped him in a blanket and kept moving. Miller's injuries took his friends by surprise—unaccustomed, as many still were, to the reality of combat. "Only a few minutes before two others had been shot by my side and had gone to the rear," one trooper recalled. "I thought his wound similar—not serious and I said 'Miller, I will come to you in a minute.' He replied in his kindly unselfish tone, 'That is all right . . . don't bother about me.'" The men eventually carried him all the way back to Siboney, nine miles on foot, unable to find a vehicle to take them. Wagons were in short supply, and the corps gave priority to moving supplies up to the toehold of a front that the Americans had won that day.[4]

That evening and all through the night the Rough Riders took turns digging and trying to sleep, if just for a few minutes. Joseph Crockett, a private, offered to make coffee for the regiment, and that evening doled out cup after cup of a strong brew he made from abandoned rations he found in one of the trenches. "All that night we worked like beavers digging rifle pits although we hadn't had a bite to eat since daylight," wrote trooper William Saunders. The men on the line had all left their gear at Sevilla or El Poso, and so most slept on the bare ground. A few found blankets in the blockhouses, including Henry Bardshar, Roosevelt's orderly, who gave his discovery to his boss—who, in turn, shared it with Dade Goodrich.[5]

At 3 a.m. there came the sound of a rifle shot, and the squeal of a dog, and then the Spanish line opened up. In the darkness, aim was nonexistent, on both sides. It was not until the morning that Roosevelt learned what had happened: A Rough Rider, seeing a dog but thinking it a lurking Spanish soldier, shot at it; he hit his mark, but gave away his position with his muzzle flash. The firing had lasted almost an hour, with little effect to either side except a loss of precious sleep.[6]

Though the regiment took fewer casualties on July 2, it was in some ways a harder and more perilous day than the previous. It rained without end, torrential buckets of cold, piercing rain. The men had very little food, and their personal supplies, including their tents, were at Sevilla, where they had camped before the assault on the San Juan Heights. Still they dug, and watched, and dug some more—it was now a race to entrench before the real counterattack began. They didn't have long to wait. Roosevelt was up early that morning, peering through his field glasses at the Spanish line. He saw movement among the Spanish soldiers, and seconds later they were shooting at him, and then the entire line was under fire from Spanish rifles and artillery. The American cannons, which had been brought up within 500 yards of the front the night before, began to fire in return, and in a moment thick clouds of white smoke hung over the heights, obscuring the regiments from each other. All morning and into the afternoon, the two sides traded shots and shells, but neither dared an assault. The Rough Riders, so far out front, were in a particularly tough spot—exposed to enemy fire in front, they also had to mind return fire from the other regiments behind them. Ten more were wounded that day, and four more killed.[7]

The trenches provided cover, but only barely. A single night of digging wasn't enough, and in most places they were just a few feet deep, forcing the men to crouch or curl or kneel for hours. "If anyone had discovered a more uncomfortable place to spend a hot day than in a four foot trench, I have yet to hear of it," wrote Frank Knox. "Oh, the misery of those ten hours I put in there I shall never forget." The situation was especially dire for about sixty Rough Riders who had been separated from the rest of the regiment during the fighting on July 1. The next morning Billy McGinty spotted them, near the Spanish line and crowded in a few shallow, hastily dug trenches. They were trying to crawl back, but they were pinned down. Roosevelt also saw them. "We've got to get them some food and drink," he said. McGinty volunteered to act as courier. Roosevelt immediately stepped forward and said he would go too. McGinty stared back—was Roosevelt fearless or a fool? He was in charge of the regiment, not an expendable member of the rank and file. Finally another trooper, Woodbury Kane, said he'd go in Roosevelt's place. "The whole regiment is depending on you, but no one is depending on us," he said. The men grabbed pails of water and cans of tomatoes—all that was on hand—and made a dash for it. The Spanish poured fire on them, but they made it safely. The cans didn't, though—the bundle in McGinty's hands was leaking red juice down his leg.[8]

By mid-afternoon the divisions had more or less re-formed, and arranged themselves on the line along San Juan Heights. General Jacob Kent's First Division, to the left, and General Henry Lawton's Second Division, which had hurried from El Caney overnight, to the right braced the cavalry division, of which the Rough Riders were the furthest out in front. Each regiment dug its own trenches and cossack posts—small pits in front of the line, large enough for a couple of men to act as an early-warning position against a Spanish attack—and maintained its own headquarters in the immediate rear, at the foot of San Juan Hill. Most, including the Rough Riders, didn't have time to dig communications trenches, which meant that moving from the rear to the front, and back again, involved a mad dash across open ground, vulnerable to any Spanish soldier with a rifle and half-decent aim.

Few correspondents ever take stock of a battlefield immediately after the fighting stops. Too often it is a cue for a writer to move to the abstract, to assess wins and losses. But what remains after the shooting also tells a story. While the Battle of San Juan Heights was undoubtedly an American victory, the cost was on full display in the roughly ten square miles between El Poso and the new American front line. Everything higher than a foot had a bullet hole in it, and most of the trees had been blown over by artillery. Small fires smoldered. Broad stains where men had bled out from their wounds darkened the soil. Armies of land crabs more numerous than the Fifth Corps clicked across the earth, and the sky was dark with vultures. Thousands of blanket rolls, canteens, cartridges, hats, boots, cups, half-eaten rations, empty cans, and tunics littered the ground. And the bodies—so many scattered around, many moving, others immobile and already bloating. One of the few to walk the battlefield afterward, the correspondent Caspar Whitney, wrote of "dead men lying beside the road, ghastly in their unstudied positions, men dying, men wounded, passing back to division hospital, some being carried, some limping, some sitting by the road-side, all strangely silent, bandaged and bloody."[9]

To handle the urgent cases, the corps had established a field hospital at the Aguadores River. Once stabilized, the wounded were sent to the rear, at Siboney. Set up for fifty men, the hospital soon had 400. Understaffed and undersupplied, it was more like a butcher's shop: a handful of surgeons reverting to Civil War methods—mostly amputation, with better antiseptic but without even mild anesthetic—in the face of the endless flow of bloodied and battered men. "They stood at the operating tables, wholly without sleep, and almost without rest or food, for twenty-one consecutive hours," wrote the correspondent George Kennan (uncle and namesake of the diplomat), who visited the hospital on July 2, "and yet, in spite of their tremendous exertions, hundreds of seriously or dangerously wounded men lay on the ground for hours." The few tents the medical officers had erected were already overflowing, and by noon dozens of patients were splayed outside, under the sun. No attendants came by with water or shelter, and so they boiled, adding heat stroke and dehydration to their long list of battlefield traumas. And after their surgeries, back they went, to wait for many more hours in the sun, or the chilling night air, for transportation to Siboney. Kennan estimated that by midnight on the 2nd, some 800 men lay in and around the field hospital. Many of those men would have died had it not been for Clara Barton and a team of Red Cross workers, who arrived that evening with blankets, tents, malted milk, and a nutrient-rich beverage they called "Red Cross Cider."[10]

That evening General Shafter called a war council. He was troubled. All day, reports had been coming in from officers on the front line, describing how tenuous their position was—one determined push from the Spanish, and it would collapse. The battle had been costlier than he'd expected, and there was now no chance of pressing on into the city, at least not for a few weeks, until fresh regiments and supplies arrived. At the same time, he guessed—wrongly—that Santiago was well-provisioned, with enough food, water, and ammunition to hold out until the rainy season, when tropical diseases would finish the job that the Spanish soldiers had begun on July 1. Shafter was still too weak to stand, or even sit; his aides found a wooden door and fashioned it into a bed on which he reclined, his generals arrayed around him. Shafter proposed that they withdraw from the line, to at least El Poso, and try again. There was murmuring of agreement, but also fierce dissent. General Wheeler, well on the mend from his illness or at least pretending to be, rose up and in all his five foot four inches of Southern indignation said he would rather die than see a single yard conceded. Some nodded their heads, but others stood resolute with Shafter. There were too few reinforcements; the men on the line were more or less all there was. Shafter said to give it a day, and dismissed the officers for the night.[11]

Hours later on July 2, lit by a bright moon, the Rough Riders came under a sudden barrage from the Spanish lines. The Spanish started by attacking one of the cossack posts, out in front of the line; the soldiers in the trenches behind it, convinced that they saw hordes of shadows advancing in the dark, opened fire. The enemy was haphazard and ill aimed in their shooting, and so was the return fire. Roosevelt, who had been down the hill in the Rough Rider camp, came running forward. He could see, in the distance, the flash of Spanish rifles, scores of them, but he could also tell that they were stationary. This was not an assault. He ran along the trenches, fully exposed to the enemy, yelling "Stop! Hold your fire!" The next day, with a short truce established for the Spanish to gather their dead, the Rough Riders watched as mules pulled away five cartloads. "Well boys," Roosevelt said, "looks to me as though you hadn't done so bad a job after all."[12]

At the Executive Mansion in Washington, the war cabinet—President McKinley, Secretary Alger, and Secretary Long—waited in the second-floor war room for news from Shafter. The general had been silent since July 1, and they were getting much of their information from newspapers. One of the striking things about war is how it brings into focus a society's most backward- and forward-looking qualities. In 1898, America was still fighting with a nineteenth-century mind-set, and in some cases with weapons and equipment held over from the Civil War. But it was also embracing technologies that would come to define the twentieth century: In New York, hundreds of automobiles already puttered down the street, frightening horses and pedestrians. The telegraph, though hardly new by 1898, enabled the transmission of information from the battlefield to Washington within minutes. Those men in the war room were now able to reach across thousands of miles, almost instantly, to communicate almost instantaneously with their officers in the field. Government officials were not the only ones using the undersea cables, which is why, in Shafter's silence, the newspapers were better sources of current information than their own general.[13]

Early on the morning of July 3, Alger sent Shafter a message: "I waited with the President until 4 o'clock this morning for news from you relative to Saturday's battle. Not a word was received, nor has there been up to this hour." Finally, several minutes later, the telegraph machine began to chatter. It was not what they wanted to read: "I am seriously considering withdrawing about five miles, and taking up a new position on the high ground between the San Juan River and Siboney." McKinley and, especially, Alger would have none of it. They wrote back insisting that Shafter stay in place.[14]

Unfortunately, word of Shafter's plan leaked out to the front line on the San Juan Heights, and officers and soldiers started to mutter mutinous thoughts under their breath. They called him "Fall Back Shafter." To mollify both Washington and the front line, later on July 3 Shafter sent an ultimatum to the Spanish, which he dictated to McClernand. It read: "I shall be obliged, unless you surrender, to shell Santiago de Cuba. Please inform the citizens of foreign countries, and all women and children, that they should leave the city before 10 o'clock to-morrow morning. Very respectfully, your obedient servant, William R. Shafter."[15]

However sincere Shafter's message, it was about to be rendered moot. "If I were to live a thousand years and a thousand centuries never should I forget that 3d day of July, 1898, nor do I believe that Spain will ever forget it," wrote José Müller y Tejeiro, the officer and chronicler of the Spanish defense of Santiago. The day, a Sunday, began normally enough. On the heights, the men continued digging. In Siboney, the sick and wounded continued to straggle into the hospital. And out to sea, Admiral Sampson decided that the blockade was tight enough, and the Spanish fleet docile enough, that he could send two of his ships to Guantánamo to refuel. Then he directed his flagship, the *New York*, to sail for Daiquirí, where he would land and then travel to meet with General Shafter at the front and press the general to make a final assault on the city. Two Rough Riders, Alexander Brodie and James McClintock, had come down with malaria and managed to board the *Olivette*, which was serving as a hospital ship and was floating just to the east of the squadron.[16]

The blockade was not as tight as Sampson had imagined. The eight remaining warships formed a semicircle around the mouth of Santiago Harbor, about eight miles out, like cats around a mousehole. Several had shut down some of their engines, to save fuel, and had allowed the tide to push them out of position. Only the cruiser *Oregon* had steam in its boilers; the rest would take at least twenty minutes to get moving. After a month of blockade duty, the days had fallen into a routine, and no one imagined that this day could bring anything different.[17]

Then, at 9:31, the unimaginable happened. The Spanish cruiser *Infanta María Teresa*, Admiral Cervera's flagship, its flags flying proudly, was coming out of the harbor mouth and steaming to the west. The day before, Cervera, after registering his formal opposition, had consented to Madrid's commands to take the fleet out of the harbor and make a dash for safety. Failing that, they were to engage with the American ships, and do as much damage as possible before they were destroyed. Cervera had never wanted war, had never wanted to sail from Spain in the first place, but he did as he was ordered, even if it meant his likely death. He thought the entire war was suicide, so what was one more, final push? There was something fatalistically poetic about it that may have appealed to Cervera, too: The destruction of the fleet could only herald the end of Spanish control of Cuba, and if this was the end of Spanish rule, better to go out with a bang. As one of his captains said later, "It was the signal that the history of four centuries of grandeur was at an end and that Spain was becoming a nation of the fourth class. Poor Spain!"[18]

On paper, Cervera and his fleet actually stood a decent chance against the Americans. Most of his ships were faster than the Americans', and he had the advantage of surprise. Had Cervera made a run for it at night or in a storm—as Sampson had feared he would—it might have worked, at least for the swiftest ships. But the Spanish hulls were fouled with barnacles, and their fastest ship, the *Cristóbal Colón*, was also the least armed. Their only hope was to slip through the space between the westernmost American ship, the *Brooklyn*, and the shore, before the blockade could get up steam.[19]

The Americans opened fire on the *Infanta María Teresa* immediately, even before their ships were in position. For ten brutal minutes, the cruiser was alone with the American fleet. Still stunned, the

American ships followed a preset battle plan: As they engaged their engines they converged on the harbor mouth, even as the *Infanta María Teresa* slipped westward. And they continued to press toward the harbor even as three more ships, the *Vizcaya*, the *Colón*, and the *Oquendo*, followed out of the harbor. (Two more, the gunboats *Plutón* and *Furor*, proceeded a few minutes later.) Shots from the American ships occasionally went high, flying over the hills and landing in the water of Santiago Harbor, close enough for the men on San Juan Heights to see.[20]

Despite being caught by surprise, over the next hour, the American fleet made quick work of Cervera's fleet. Eventually they tacked to the west, and gave pursuit of the fleeing Spanish. It became a running duel, with both sides firing rapid salvos, so much that the entire coastline, for miles out to sea, was blanketed with smoke. Temperatures inside the fire rooms rose far into the triple digits; men stripped to their underwear and still dozens were overcome with heatstroke. Remarkably, only one American died, a yeoman on board the *Brooklyn* named George H. Ellis. Ordered to visually estimate the range to the *Vizcaya*, he stood up on the forward deck and shouted "2,200 yards," and a Spanish shell took off his head.[21]

One by one Cervera's ships caught fire and, to save themselves from sinking, ran aground on the beaches west of Santiago. The *Infanta María Teresa* was out of commission within forty minutes of leaving the harbor. Fifteen minutes later the *Oquendo*, its decks aflame, beached as well. The *Vizcaya* went aground at Aserradero, where Shafter and Sampson had first gone ashore to meet García, not a month prior. The *Plutón* and the *Furor*, outgunned, surrendered quickly. The *Colón* almost got away, but alone, it bore the full brunt of the American fleet, and within a few hours it, too, had surrendered. Watching the ships burn, the sailors aboard the *Texas* let out a victory roar—to which the ship's captain, John Woodward Philip, replied with one of history's famous statements of battlefield empathy: "Don't cheer, boys! The poor devils are dying."[22]

The Americans spent the afternoon rescuing what men they could from the burning Spanish hulks. They plucked Admiral Cervera from the flame-broiled *Infanta María Teresa*; 1,813 others were saved and taken prisoner from the fleet, but another 323 perished. "Far from being depressed, the admiral was in high spirits," wrote Lieutenant Harry P. Huse, who had lunch with Cervera aboard the *Gloucester*. "He had done his duty to the utmost limits, and was relieved of the terrible burden of responsibility that had weighed upon him since leaving the Cape Verde Islands," over three months before.[23]

At two o'clock the next morning, walking home from the War Department, Secretary Alger encountered a newsboy hawking the extra edition: "Full Account of the Destruction of the Spanish Fleet!" Alger shook his head. Sampson had achieved his victory. Where was Shafter's?[24]

The American naval victory complicated matters for Shafter, who was now a man without a clear mission. The entire point of his campaign had been to assist the Navy in capturing the Spanish fleet; with that fleet destroyed, there was no purpose in taking the city. He could not retreat, even tactically. His men would mutiny. He could not go forward, because the Spanish defenses between San Juan Heights and the city were deadly in their density: barbed wire entanglements arrayed to funnel attacking soldiers into fire lanes, trenches, and booby traps, and towering barricades of sand-filled wine butts, behind which stood several thousand Spanish soldiers. But he could not, he was convinced, wait much longer—the Cubans joked that their greatest weapons against the Spanish were June, July, and August, the months of heavy rains and malaria, and now the Spanish hoped to extend the siege long enough that they could turn those same weapons against the Americans. Shafter had something else to worry about, too: The Cubans arrayed to the west had failed to stop a flying column of 3,300 Spanish soldiers from entering the city on the night of July 2.[25]

Shafter wanted to do whatever it took to get out of Cuba, even if it meant cutting a deal with the Spanish. The afternoon of the 3rd, he arranged a day-long truce with the Spanish, who were now led by General José Toral y Velázquez, after General Linares had been wounded on the 1st. Then, on July 4, while Americans celebrated both the naval victory and Independence Day, Shafter wrote Washington to say that he wanted to negotiate a compromise with the Spanish. The reply was once again unambiguous: "You will accept nothing but an unconditional surrender, and should take extra precautions to prevent the enemy's escape."[26]

The truce, while it did not relieve the men of their duties in the trenches, at least allowed them to stand up straight without worrying about being shot. "Everybody drew a long breath and thanked God," wrote John J. Pershing, a lieutenant with the segregated 10th Cavalry (the source of his derogatory nickname, Black Jack, which would stick with him for his entire career, even when he commanded the 1.2-million-strong American Expeditionary Force during World War I). Officers read a thank-you message from McKinley to their troops, bands played, and a contingent of Rough Riders sang "Fair Harvard." But there was tension in the moment. Only now, with the adrenaline no longer flowing, could the men stop to recognize how much they had lost, and what it would take to win the rest if the Spanish refused to surrender. "I went up to the top of the trenches and I could see the town's people moving about and the soldiers cooking their dinners," wrote Frank Knox. "Santiago is a pretty place. It seems a pity to lay it in ruins."[27]

To give the civilians of Santiago time to leave, Shafter extended the truce until noon of July 5. Just before the hour, the mayor of Santiago opened the gates to the city, and 12,000 children, women, and old men came trudging out, headed for El Caney. Many of the women had put on their finest clothing; emaciated and sickly, they marched in pastel dresses, carrying matching parasols. But nothing could mask the desperation of the procession, comprised of "mothers with little naked babies with their little ribs sticking out and their arms and legs like pipe-stems," wrote a correspondent for *Leslie's*. Soon a town built for 500 people was home, at least temporarily, to twenty-four times that number. By the end the campaign, there were 20,000 civilians camped in El Caney's bombed-out buildings and along its muddy, cobblestone streets.[28]

The Americans distributed what food they had to offer to the Cuban refugees, though for the most part they had nothing to give. The American soldiers were stunned by the tragic humanity of it all. Some had heard about recent refugee crises in Armenia and Greece, and of course some had read about similar crises in history books. But this was a magnitude and severity they were not prepared for. Later generations of American soldiers would learn, as part of their training, to deal with civilians as a matter of fighting a war. But in 1898, there was no protocol. "I shall never forget it," said the *Leslie's* correspondent. "It was the longest day I've lived."[29]

The regimental officers, on orders from Shafter and his staff, tried to prevent their men from coming close to the refugees, for fear of disease or, worse, Spanish guerrillas hidden in their midst. They said they would arrest them, and even court-martial them. But for the most part, the men didn't listen. They helped "carry their sick and decrepit and what little personal property they possessed and even carrying the little children for tired and overburdened mothers," wrote the *Leslie's* correspondent. They handed out spare rations— mostly hardtack, which the Cubans called "bisqueet"—but it was never enough. The hunger-induced barbarity of the crowd almost overwhelmed them. "The men pulled back women and children, and the strong got the food, the weak being shoved back," the correspondent wrote. "There was a struggling mass, waving cups, pans, baskets, bags and all sorts of receptacles, some hoisting them on sticks in the effort to get over the heads of the crowd in front."[30]

Eventually Roosevelt passed by and put a stop to it. "Boys, I did not think I could really love you more than I did but since witnessing what I have just seen I love you still more," he told his men, who were among the most eager in helping the refugees. "But you know these people have fever among them and my command at present is in fine condition and free from any malignant fevers and we all want to go to Puerto Rico, but should fever break out in the regiment that fact would debar us from joining the expedition, so you must not go near these people any more." Even the gentlest admonishment from Roosevelt achieved what the threat of arrest or court-martial could not.[31]

For a while, it looked like Theodore Miller would recover—not his full health; he was paralyzed from the neck down. But the cruel promise of a Mauser wound, because it was so clean, held that if you survived the first day or two, the wound was not going to be fatal, though any number of diseases might get you in the fetid hospital at Siboney. If a soldier could avoid those, he was going home. In fact, only thirteen men who arrived at the hospital with gunshots died from their wounds. The others, more than a hundred, survived (though hundreds of others died of diseases picked up along the way). And for a while, the doctors thought Miller might survive as well, and at least make it back to Ohio to convalesce. He was awake and dictating notes and chatting with friends, and making new ones.[32]

The hospital at Siboney comprised a few small buildings on a bluff above the beach. They were mostly used for administration—patients, in the main, slept in the same dog tents they had used throughout the campaign, which meant lying for hours, days even, on the hard ground with their lower limbs, at least up to their knees, exposed to the elements. Thomas Laird, a private, recalled: "The first night after the fight I tried to sleep near the field hospitals. I was kept awake by the awful shrieks and cries of the poor men lying in them." Two weeks after the Battle of San Juan Heights, there were more than 100 cases of yellow fever in the camp.[33]

Officers at the front, including Roosevelt, did everything they could to prevent their soldiers from being sent to Siboney. They knew that, however bad a man's wounds or illness, going back to the hospital was a death sentence—too many of them recovered from their battlefield injuries only to die of a disease picked up in the unsanitary hospital. The nine-mile trip alone was debilitating. Many men had to walk, or be carried by their comrades. At first there was no one to guide the wounded back to the coast, so they wandered, by the dozens, around the Cuban countryside. "For miles along the trail one has to wade through mud up to the knees, and the only variety in this experience is furnished when one gets to a stream of water," a reporter for the *Washington Times* wrote. "There the mud is not so thick." Occasionally a man would topple over, the victim of a Spanish sharpshooter who had worked his way behind the lines and sat picking off Americans from up a tree. Eventually squads of soldiers were dispatched to hunt them down. (The snipers were especially despised, not only because they targeted wounded men, but because they carried Remington rifles, which left a much nastier wound than the Mauser.)[34]

Those who did find transportation were only marginally better off, having to endure hours of bone shaking along the rutted, fetid half rivers of mud that constituted the main thoroughfares between the

front and the rear. There were no ambulances, which were fitted with
leather or spring shock absorbers. Those, like the artillery, had been
left in Tampa for want of space. If they were caught in a rainstorm,
the wounded might have to pause to wait for the resulting flash
floods to subside, and hope that they didn't wash out a stretch of the
route in the process. Men who died in transit were often buried, just
two feet under, without the dignity of a coffin, alongside the road. As
the rains washed away the paths and new trails had to be blazed, the
teamsters would occasionally encounter bodies half exhumed by the
rains. In the humidity, the smell of the rotting corpses and decom-
posing plant life that had been trampled underfoot made moving
along the routes nearly unbearable.[35]

With the truce in place, over the next few days the American toehold along the San Juan Heights grew; hastily dug trenches were
deepened and reinforced with sandbags arranged around the edges,
with loopholes for rifles. The Rough Riders brought forward their
Colts, which they put under command of Lieutenant John Parker,
who oversaw the Gatling detachment. They also brought up their
dynamite gun. Using it like a mortar, they intended to lob four-and-
a-half-pound Whitehead "torpedoes" into the Spanish trenches. And
they finally dug zigzag communication trenches to the rear. When
they were done, they had a well-armed, well-defended redoubt at
the front of the line, looking down toward Santiago. American flags
fluttered in the breeze. The Rough Riders called it Fort Roosevelt.[36]

Life along the front settled into a meager, tense existence. By the
end of July 4, just over 300 Rough Riders were left whole, out of
the 490 who had started at the Battle of San Juan Heights. Twenty-
three had been killed since the Battle of Las Guasimas, on June
24; the rest were wounded or sick. During the day the men sat in
their trenches or out in front in cossack posts, exposed to the sun
and the heat and the rain; they made what shelters they could in
the ground. They went around bare-chested, their shirts tied around
their heads as a make-do sun shade. They had little food and no
tobacco. "Some of them became delirious from the heat, and with
their tongues hanging out losing all sense or appreciation of danger,
would stand up and expose themselves as they looked around in the

hope of discovering water nearer than the creek, that was so distant," the reporter Stephen Bonsal wrote. One soldier told Bonsal, "I only wish the fighting would begin . . . for then we wouldn't have the time to think or feel how sick we are." Conditions were even worse for the black soldiers. After fighting alongside the white regiments as equals, they were relegated to menial duties, like digging communications trenches, or, paradoxically, going on the most brazen and dangerous missions.[37]

After days of marching and running and slogging through the mud, the soldiers' boots were in tatters, and they gained some respect for the Cuban rebels who, after three years in the field, wore little more than rags. "In the trenches a match was so precious a possession that, when you saw a man light his pipe instead of at the cook's fire, you felt as though you had seen him strike a child," Davis wrote. Lice flitted from man to man, so many of them that they developed a taxonomy for the bloodsuckers: the Rough Rider, the Gray Back, the Crab. (Somehow, though, Woodbury Kane, considered the dandiest of the Fifth Avenue Boys, always managed to appear every morning "clean-shaved and neatly groomed, shoes duly polished, neat khaki, fitting like a glove and brushed to perfection, nails polished, and hair parted as nicely as if he were dressed by his valet in his New York apartments," the novelist and reporter Frank Norris wrote.) As the pace of the fighting slowed, some men took the time to bathe. Lacking pails or nearby standing water, they would dig holes in the earth and line them with their ponchos; after the afternoon rains filled them with water, they took whatever ablution they could manage before it seeped away. They also built bombproofs—small caves burrowed into the side of the hill, essentially, that they covered with timber cut from coconut tree logs and, above that, four feet of soil. The bombproofing protected the men inside them, but they lent the front line a troglodytic quality.[38]

The Rough Riders' base camp was positioned safely behind the front line at the foot of San Juan Hill, underneath a twenty-foot tree. It was from this spot, during the weeks of siege that followed the fighting on July 1, that Roosevelt came into his own as a military leader. He had proven his mettle in battle, but it was only afterward, against the corrosive effects of disease, heat, enemy bullets, and

American bureaucracy daily threatening his troops that he proved his ability to lead and inspire. Sitting in his camp chair under the tree, working at a large wooden crate that he used as a desk, he pulled the levers of influence and paperwork to get his healthy men food and his sick men medical care. It was here that he adjudicated disputes among his men wrote long letters of condolence to the families of his fallen men, and it was from here that he left to inspect the lines, and go far behind them to retrieve food and organize water runs. Often Roosevelt paid for the supplies out of his own pocket, or else it came from one of the other wealthy troopers, like Woodbury Kane, who for all his dandy pretensions had a great affection for his comrades, and they for him—at one point he bought $85 (about $2,500 in 2018 dollars) worth of tobacco from the commissary at Siboney and distributed it to the men. Over several days Roosevelt built up a forty-eight-hour supply of hardtack and beans, in case of emergency.[39]

It was also during this time that the positive press around Roosevelt and the Rough Riders hit its stride. They were already famous, but now that they were stationary, captive even, reporters could come by daily to see their camp and their section of the line and write home with laudatory missives. Davis, who was practically living with the regiment along the front line, set the tone, and his friends and competitors did their best to match him. Over the coming months Americans poured into theaters to watch newsreels from the battle and its aftermath—though most of them, including those attributed to Smith and his Vitagraph crew, were inauthentic; one, "Raising Old Glory over Morro Castle," was staged by actors on a rooftop in New York. If audiences saw through the artifice, no one complained—the myth was what mattered. "The Rough Riders were the supreme of the elite; no regiment has ever received the newspaper space that was devoted to them," wrote a soldier in the 71st New York Infantry Regiment.[40]

Many of the most popular and oft-repeated stories at Rough Rider reunions came from this time. True or not, they illustrate the brazen humor and gumption that made the regiment so popular back home. An example: At one point Roosevelt sent the regimental chaplain, Henry Alfred Brown, to Siboney to buy food; he returned with a wagonful. Roosevelt asked how he got it. "God put it down there and kept it for me," the chaplain replied. "When I reached Siboney I found a great body of men packing supplies into a number of wagons. One wagon which was entirely loaded was without a driver. I supplied the deficiency and drove away. That was all."[41]

No American adventure story is complete without a heel, and the Rough Riders found one in their adjutant, Tom Hall. After fleeing to Siboney at the outset of the engagement at Las Guasimas, he returned to the regiment on July 3, acting as if nothing had happened. The men on the line welcomed him warily. But as soon as the Spanish trenches loosed a few volleys, he was off again. When Roosevelt heard, he told Bardshar, his ever-present orderly, "Take a gun and get that yellow dog and bring him to my tent."

Bardshar found him, loitering a few hundred yards away from the hill, and told Hall to come with him. Hall was indignant. "What do you mean stopping me in this way?" he protested. "Someone is exceeding his authority." Bardshar grabbed his tunic and roughly marched him to Roosevelt's tent. Hall, straightening himself, said that Bardshar should leave before the two of them discussed matters above his rank.

"I have no secrets from Trooper Bardshar," Roosevelt said. "And what I have to say to you, he or anybody else can hear. Get out—get out of the regiment and get out of Cuba. I hope I shall never have to see you again."

Hall began sobbing. He turned to James Church, the assistant surgeon, who was standing nearby, and asked him to intervene. Church turned away in silent refusal. The adjutant left for Siboney, and from there took the first ship home. (Hall would have something of a last laugh; the next year he published a best-selling, self-serving account of the regiment with the awkward title *The Fun and Fighting of the Rough Riders*.)[42]

On July 6, Roosevelt received a letter from his friend Senator Lodge. Enclosed was a clipping from the *Washington Times*, praising Roosevelt as one of if not the hero of the war. "I hear talk all the time about your being run for Governor and Congressman, and at this moment you could have pretty much anything you wanted," Lodge wrote. But the senator had more ominous news as well. He had been in the offices of the War Department a few days before. There was, as far as he could tell, no plan for what to do next—no plan, at the Executive Mansion at least, for how to make Santiago surrender, no plan for how to occupy it, no plan for how to move on from Santiago to the rest of the island, and above all no plan for what to do with the 16,000 men in Cuba, with more coming every day and the malaria season fast approaching. "A great deal of time is spent asking why the Navy does not do this, that and the other," Lodge wrote. "I have been filled with an anxiety about the Army in the last two or three days owning to the state of things at the department."[43]

For now, though, the siege held. The men suffered, and bent, but they did not break. The Americans could not go forward, but the Spanish could not get out. As July progressed, Shafter extended the line around Santiago, so that by the third week of the month he had the city completely surrounded. All he had to do—all he could do—was wait.

As with Roosevelt, the rigors of the siege were in some ways a better test of the Army than the battle that led up to it. Under appalling conditions made worse by the War Department's incompetence, the soldiers lacked all the essentials: food, water, clean clothes, shelter. And yet no one deserted, no one rebelled. The reporters noticed, and they told their readers, and the public standing of the Regular Army skyrocketed. "I had thought, and I believe it is the popular belief throughout the country, that the men of the regular regiments are to a very large extent the waifs and the derelicts of the great cities, together with a few country boys fired with a desire to do a little soldiering and see the world," Bonsal wrote. "This impression may have been the true one a few years ago, but it certainly is not now."[44]

What Senator Lodge did not know, and what Roosevelt knew only dimly, was that all the while, Shafter was negotiating with General Toral. On July 5 he persuaded the Spanish general to take back into Santiago some of the hundreds of wounded prisoners the Americans were holding in a makeshift hospital at El Caney. The next day he secured the release of Lieutenant Hobson and his crew, who had been in Spanish custody since being picked up from the sinking

Merrimac, over a month before. At noon that day, a group of American officers rode toward the Spanish line with three blindfolded prisoners. Hundreds of American soldiers stood up from their trenches, whatever they were doing, and watched. The blindfolded men were released to their comrades. After two hours, a clutch of figures materialized from the Spanish line. It was the men of the *Merrimac*. Suddenly the American soldiers stood at attention, every one of them. "Then there was a magnificent silence," wrote Stephen Crane, "broken only by the measured hoof-beats of the little company's horses as they rode through the gap. It was solemn, this splendid silent welcome of a brave man by men who stood on a hill which they had earned out of blood and death." Davis, standing near Crane, wrote that Hobson was the "first officer I'd seen saluted in six days."[45]

Shafter had told Toral that the truce would end an hour after Hobson's release, but again he postponed. That afternoon he told the Spanish that both the American Army and the Navy would begin bombarding Santiago at noon on July 9. Toral replied that he would surrender, but with conditions, specifically that he and all his men be allowed to retreat to Spanish-held territory to the west. Shafter was elated, but McKinley and Alger once again refused to accept anything but total capitulation. Shafter said as much to Toral, and extended the truce again, to noon on July 10. The sight of new truce flags was too much for the rank and file. "To the men in the pits, who knew nothing of the exigencies of diplomacy, those virgin flags were as offensive as those of red are to the bull," wrote Davis. Observing the table tennis of white flags passing back and forth between the lines in the valley below them, he added, "their watchfulness seemed wasted, their vigilance became a farce, and they mocked and scoffed at the white flags bitterly."[46]

Around July 7, Miller's friend Frank Knox arrived in Siboney, having come down with one of the tropical maladies sweeping through the American lines. Knox saw that Miller had begun to slip. He was having trouble breathing, and pain wracked his body. Still, Miller remained chatty. He told Knox about his parents, about his famous brother-in-law Thomas Edison, about how his father had founded the Chautauqua movement and how he was determined to get home to help run it. Knox, in a letter to Miller's parents that he later wrote from a quarantine ship docked outside New York, tried to put a gloss on their son's suffering. "All through those days of torture and pain he never uttered a complaining word but with a faint wan smile he would tell us he felt better," Knox wrote. "Not till the last did he suppose that his end was near."[47]

When Miller finally accepted that he was unlikely to leave Cuba alive, he asked Knox to make sure that his combat pay made it back to Akron. Then he fell asleep. "I sat by him the next day as long as I could sit up and then laid down on a cot near by (I was on the sick list myself) and fell into a doze and when I awoke he had left us," Knox wrote. "I went up and sat down and had a long look at his face. Around the corners of his mouth were the traces of that patient smile that he had worn so bravely through it all." Knox wept.[48]

That afternoon a detail from the 23rd Michigan Volunteers buried Miller in the graveyard adjacent to the hospital. Knox carved his friend's name and regiment number into a piece of wood and planted it as a makeshift headstone—enough of a marker, he hoped, to last until someone could come to claim the body.[49]

A few weeks after Miller died, his mother received a package in the mail. Inside was a small, weather-beaten book—his diary—and inside of that a letter. The package came from David V. McClure, a corporal in the Rough Riders, from Oklahoma City. The letter read: "Dear Mamma: A rather narrow escape but feel sure I will pull through all right. . . . Mr. Whitney offered to write to you but Mr. McClure had offered to do so before and so he is doing so. You must not worry about these things for Dr. Lesser is here now and is at the head of the Red Cross of America. He said I would come out all right soon. He said he was going to write to you himself. They are doing everything for me. I remain your most loving son and will be with you soon. Goodbye."[50]

Finally, at four in the afternoon on July 10, the Rough Riders were called to action: Toral had refused to surrender on Washington's terms, and the truce was over. They would fight again, and ignore, for the moment, the disease and thirst and heat. As soon as the Spanish flag of truce fell, their rifles and Gatlings and artillery opened up.

Even the dynamite gun managed to squeeze off a few rounds before it malfunctioned. From out in the Caribbean, the *Brooklyn* and the *Indiana* lobbed shells into the city. The Spanish replied weakly, and by dusk the American barrage petered off, with just a few casualties on each side. The two adversaries picked up their long-range duel the next morning, again with little effect. "The Spanish are more active to-day and we have suffered some loss from their shells,"wrote trooper J. Ogden Wells. "Our artillery seems to fire in a half-hearted sort of way." By then reinforcements had begun to arrive—not the reserves, held back during the battle almost two weeks earlier but otherwise just as beaten down by almost a month in the tropics, but men fresh from the mainland, including Nelson Miles himself, the commander of the entire Army, who had hurried to Cuba from Washington over concerns about Shafter's physical and mental stamina. And indeed Shafter was a sorry sight. Still laid up, his gout rendered his feet too swollen for boots, and he swaddled them in rags.[51]

The next day the Rough Riders were shifted a half mile north, to make room for fresh regiments from Florida coming onto the line, and to cover the road to El Caney. Life was getting marginally easier; tents were brought up, and Roosevelt had one with walls, tall enough that he could hang a hammock inside. That night it rained ferociously, and occasionally someone on the line would open fire, swearing that he had seen dark forms moving among the trees. The rain knocked down Roosevelt's tent and sent him soaking to the kitchen tent, where Bert Holderman, a Cherokee Indian from the Oklahoma Territory, was on duty. He gave Roosevelt some dry clothes, and let him sleep on a table that he had salvaged from a nearby house.[52]

On July 12 General Linares, likewise sick and bedridden, wired Madrid: "The situation is fatal; surrender inevitable."The Spanish plan to run out the clock had failed. But Shafter had no way of knowing how close he was to victory, how few cards his adversary held. The next morning, now with Miles's support, he wrote to Alger that he still did not think the Spanish, under the day-to-day leadership of General Toral, would surrender without concessions from the Americans: "If he fights, as we have reason to believe he may, it will be at fearful loss of life; and to stay here with disease threatening may be at great loss from that cause." But Alger and McKinley resisted, and the next day

Shafter and Miles met with Toral in person, at a spot between the lines. Miles told Toral that he was under orders not to accept anything except surrender or destruction of the Spanish force in Santiago, and that he and Shafter had enough fresh troops to achieve either goal. Miles offered to transport Toral's soldiers back to Spain, paid for by the American government. Toral asked for time to consult with Madrid, and when the trio met again the next day, he said he would accept America's terms, and surrender unconditionally, as long as the Americans would transport him and his soldiers home. Shafter, who had harbored little hope that his efforts at negotiation would work, was floored. "I was simply thunderstruck that, of their own free will, they should give me 12,000 men that were absolutely beyond my reach," Shafter later said.[53]

The surrender ceremony took place on July 17, a bright clear Sunday. That morning, two Spanish officers on horseback approached the American line, where they were met by a squad of cavalry. They passed through, and on to Shafter's tent. One carried a silver-encased sword, which he presented to the American general. Two hours later, Shafter and his officers sat on horseback under a ceiba tree, 200 yards forward of the American line. In the distance, they could see a Spanish cavalry column leave the city and make its way slowly toward them. At its head rode General Toral, erect and proper with a fine thin mustache; behind him a line of buglers sounded. Shafter, his feet wrapped in bandages and a pith helmet perched on his head, approached the general, and they spoke briefly through an interpreter. Then Shafter gave Toral back the sword, along with the sword and spurs of General Vara del Rey, which had been taken off his fallen body at El Caney. Over the next hour hundreds of unarmed Spanish soldiers marched along the same path their general had just ridden, and further still, to fields behind the American lines, where they would make camp as prisoners of war. "It was Appomattox again, and Mexico City and Yorktown," wrote Frank Norris, who watched the proceedings. "Tomorrow nearly a hundred million people the world round would read of this scene, and as many more, yet unborn, would read of it, but today you could sit in your saddle on the back of your little white bronco and view it as easily as a play."[54]

The Americans went the other direction, led by Shafter and Wheeler on horseback, filing through the barbed wire and abandoned barricades and into Santiago, down its narrow, steeply sloping cobblestone streets, its houses painted bright blues and yellows and pinks. The men, after so many weeks in the mud and the filth of the Cuban savannah, marveled at the interior courtyards, glimpsed through wrought iron lattices, full of green bowers and marble fountains. "It is exactly like a picture of Toledo, narrow streets, Moorish windows, steep hills and little two-wheeled carts that struggle up and down the steep and narrow lanes over the rough paved streets," Wood wrote home to his wife. "This town is just as strange and uncommon as some old place in Spain." Which is not to say it was pretty. Santiago had a reputation as the dirtiest city in the Caribbean, and a good part of that was well deserved. "Piles of mango skins, ashes, old bones, filthy rags, dung, and kitchen refuse of all sorts lay here and there on the broken and neglected pavements," wrote the correspondent George Kennan. "Every hole and crevice in the uneven pavement was filled with rotting organic matter washed down from the higher levels by the frequent rains, and when the sea breeze died away at night the whole atmosphere of the city seemed to be pervaded by a sickly, indescribable odor of corruption and decay."[55]

They kept on, marching until they reached the Plaza de Armas, the center point of the city, which sat on a bluff overlooking the harbor. While the accompanying enlisted men waited outside, the officers entered the governor's palace, where at 11 a.m. they were treated to lunch. Finally, at 11:45, the officers returned to the plaza, the men stood at attention, and a pair of soldiers attached an American flag to a pole in the center of the square. At noon, as soon as the bells of the nearby Catedral de Nuestra Señora de la Asunción had finished their peal, General Chambers McKibbin shouted, "Present arms!" The flag flew up the pole. An honor guard fired several volleys, and the entire assembly sang the National Anthem, then "Rally Round the Flag." After 384 years of Spanish rule, Santiago had fallen.[56]

Most of the Rough Riders had watched the surrender ceremony from afar, back in their position at San Juan Hill. They were miles away, but when they saw the flag go up through their field glasses, a great roar erupted along the line. The war would continue—the Spanish

240

still controlled most of Cuba, and all of Puerto Rico. But the Rough Riders' first campaign was over, and they had won.

Less enthused were the thousands of Cuban soldiers who were still maintaining the siege on the northern and western sides of the city. Their leaders had been excluded from the surrender ceremony, and they resented that the Americans treated the captured Spanish, who were their enemies, better than the Cubans, who were their allies. Armed rebels were not allowed to enter Santiago, even as thousands of Spanish soldiers were permitted to roam its streets freely. Worst of all, Shafter decided that the Spanish civilian government in Santiago would remain in charge—meaning that, for all of the Cubans' sacrifices, at least in the day-to-day life in the city, nothing much had changed. Frank Norris captured the mood in those first few arrogant days of American control: "There was no thought of humanitarian principles then, the war was not a 'crusade,' we were not fighting for Cubans just then, it was not for disinterested motives that we were there sabred and revolvered and carbined. Santiago was ours—was ours, ours, by the sword we had acquired, we, Americans, with no one to help."[57]

On July 17, a few hours after the surrender ceremony, General García, in command of the Cuban rebels around Santiago, resigned in protest. He had worked with and under Shafter for too long in the hopes that the result would be immediate Cuban independence. Now, with the Americans in charge and the Cubans pushed to the margins, he was convinced he had made a mistake. He later withdrew his resignation, and went on to lead a series of rebel assaults against the Spanish that summer, but his anger spoke for thousands. He also sent a letter of rebuke to Shafter. "I have not been honored with a single word from yourself informing me about the negotiations for peace or the terms of the capitulation by the Spaniards," he wrote. "I only know of both events by public reports." Did Shafter dismiss his men as "savages ignoring the rules of civilized warfare"? It was true, García conceded, that the Cuban rebels were "a poor, ragged army," but no worse off than "the heroes of Saratoga and Yorktown." Though his letter, published a few weeks later in American papers, set off a small storm of anti-Shafter protest, nothing came of it, and the American general never publicly responded to his Cuban counterpart.[58]

On Monday, July 18, the Rough Riders were ordered off the line
and up to a new camp in the foothills near El Caney, five miles away.
By then nearly half the regiment was dead or incapacitated, either
from wounds or, increasingly, disease. El Caney, despite being ravaged by battle and its aftereffects, was a welcome change from the
rigors of the line. There was a clean pond in which the men could
bathe. They camped in a nearby field, which was covered in green
grass and mango trees, and here and there with cocoa palms. Some
set up tents on the grounds of the Duerot mansion, the French consul's country home, with its terraced gardens and marble fountains.
The ruined buildings provided ample wood for fires, which had been
forbidden at the front. And after the surrender of Santiago, officers
could go into town for food, which was now flowing into the port.
One day Roosevelt went to Santiago with a team of men and a few
wagons and bought several hundred dollars' worth of rice, oatmeal,
potatoes, prunes, and tomatoes. Some of the men pooled their money
to buy beef cattle off a ship that had just arrived from South America, and shared the resulting steaks with the entire regiment. Another
welcome item was tobacco, which was finally, after almost a month,
arriving in reliable quantities. Kirk McCurdy, a trooper from Philadelphia whose brother Allen also served, formed a scavenging party
that found corn, lima beans, and cucumbers, the first fresh vegetables the men had seen since before Tampa. Roosevelt, at least, was
happy. "I am more than satisfied even though I could die of yellow
fever tomorrow, for at least I feel satisfied that I have done something
which enables me to leave a name to the children of which they can
rightly be proud and which will serve in some sense as a substitute for
not leaving them more money," he wrote to Henry Cabot Lodge on
July 19. Four days later, he wrote a letter to Alger, suggesting that the
regiment be sent immediately to join the next campaign, the invasion
of Puerto Rico—though he declined to mention that less than half of
the men were capable of going.[59]

Roosevelt didn't bother with drills during the two weeks the regiment spent at El Caney, but he tried to institute an exercise regime.
Several times a week, he would gather his healthiest men and go for
a hike in the Sierra Maestra foothills. Another time he swam out

to the *Merrimac* with one of his officers, ignoring the small sharks that joined them along the way. But whereas these efforts seemed to strengthen him, his men overexerted themselves. "The result was that half of the party were down with some kind of sickness the next day," Roosevelt wrote of his hikes. Despite the change in scenery, the men were getting sicker. They had been half starved for so long that many now overate, and suffered the consequences—which were bad enough on their own, but the resulting cramps and diarrhea weakened them to the point where serious disease began to course through the camp. Malaria and dysentery were common, though the real fear was of yellow fever. Roosevelt's orderly, Henry Bardshar, was among those afflicted; he recovered but lost eighty pounds in the process. By July 18 the regiment had just 275 healthy men, and the number was ticking down hourly.[60]

The camp grew increasingly unsanitary. The pond filled with dirt and scum; the grassy plain became a mudflat. It rained daily, and the fields had no drainage. "We attempted to keep reasonably clean by alternately washing our uniforms while wearing underclothes, and vice versa, but the humidity was so great that our clothing was soaking wet all the time," recalled trooper Royal Prentice. They each took a tablespoon of quinine a day, which seemed to help a bit but also made some men vomit or hallucinate. "We are having a terrible time just at present," wrote Ralph McFie, a private, to his cousin. "I am safe in saying that 4/5 of the men in our troop are sick and unfit for duty and they do not seem to recover as soon as they should. . . . We have the regular chills and fever and malaria, but most of us are attacked by spells of severe cramps and vomiting and are unable to eat or keep anything on our stomachs."[61]

Word of the worsening conditions began to appear in American papers, thanks in no small part to Richard Harding Davis. Up until then he had been a stalwart defender of the military effort. But he saw that Roosevelt was growing privately critical of the War Department's handling of the campaign, and that gave Davis the tacit permission to open his own attack. In a scathing article for the *Herald*, he described the conditions of the camps and the hospitals, pinning the blame less on Shafter than on the military's overall incompetence. "I do not see how men not made of iron can stand such a state of affairs much longer," he wrote. "The expedition was prepared in ignorance and conducted in a series of blunders." The article was read widely—allegedly all the way to Spain, where it was reprinted as evidence that Toral should have held out just a little longer.[62]

Santiago itself was slowly moving toward some semblance of stability. The refugees returned, and the remaining food stores were opened. For their hospital, American troops were using the Catedral de Nuestra Señora de la Asunción, underneath which lay the grave of Cuba's first governor, Diego Velázquez. Many of the Rough Riders spoke some Spanish from living in the Southwest, and when they traveled to town with Roosevelt or another officer to pick up supplies, they would flirt with the women, young and old, who hung out their second-story windows waving handkerchiefs at them. They enjoyed being able to sit in a café once again, and be served like regular customers. "We had coffee served in little cups that was as strong as lye and round, hard bread and rice with guava jelly," Royal Prentice wrote.[63]

Reporters took to hanging out at the Café Venus, on the Plaza de Armas, or the nearby Anglo-American Club. Roosevelt, during another visit, stopped by the club to brag about his regiment's performance in battle. "You may have heard a father talk like that when the boy had scored the winning touchdown in a big football game," said one correspondent, Ralph Paine. Roosevelt returned a few days later with the draft of a letter he wanted the gathered correspondents to review—and, without saying as much, to write about for their newspapers. He called it a "round robin," signed by all the top officers, and it indicted in detail the War Department's handling of the campaign. Among other things, it said, the department had failed to send sufficient medical supplies and staff, and now thousands of men were at risk of dying from disease. "If we are kept here it will in all human possibility mean an appalling disaster, for the surgeons here estimate that over half the army, if kept here during the sickly season, will die," the letter read. With Santiago fallen, there was no point in keeping them in Cuba any longer.[64]

"What do you boys think of it?" Roosevelt asked the reporters. "Have you any changes to suggest? . . . There is no more use for the army here, and it is dying on its feet, but the War Department refuses to listen." It was signed by most of the high-ranking officers in the Fifth Corps, but it identified Roosevelt as the author. "As a volunteer officer," Roosevelt told the reporters, "I am willing to be the scapegoat."[65]

There was more to the story than that. It began several days earlier, on August 2, when Secretary Alger had sent a cable to Shafter suggesting that he move the men inland, to higher and presumably drier climes, where they could rest and prepare to push westward toward Havana, which was still in Spanish hands. To Shafter, this would be suicide—whatever his skills or deficiencies as a general, he had a keen sense of a soldier's limits, and he knew that scores were already dying of disease in Siboney. Keeping them any longer in Cuba would destroy his army. Roosevelt agreed. Every time the men moved, they got sicker, and living off the land was proving impossible. "To have sent the troops there would have been simple butchery," Roosevelt wrote in his memoir. By then there were fewer than 175 Rough Riders on the active-duty roster.[66]

The next day Shafter called together his top officers—Roosevelt, Wood, seven generals, and the medical officers. Wood had since been appointed military governor of Santiago, and Roosevelt had been promoted to full colonel and put in Wood's place, in charge of the Second Brigade. The situation was untenable, Shafter told them, but Washington wasn't listening. Someone needed to talk to the press. The problem was that the generals and medical officers were all Regular Army men, and any sign of dissent would end their careers. But, Shafter went on, Roosevelt, being a famous public figure and a volunteer, could talk to a reporter, and the worst that could happen would be that he'd be on his way back to civilian life earlier than he'd expected. Roosevelt hesitated. He wanted to help his men get out of Cuba, but he suspected that if the source of the leak got out, Shafter might deny everything and leave Roosevelt to blame. But when Wood suggested he write a letter to Shafter that the general himself could then leak to the press—creating a paper trail that Shafter couldn't deny—he agreed.[67]

Later that day Roosevelt approached Bardshar with several rolls of paper. "I have a letter here I want you to type for me if you can," he said, and showed him to a typewriter he had recovered in Santiago. When Bardshar finished, he handed the pages to Roosevelt, adding,

"If you send it to the War Department, they will have you shot at sunrise." Roosevelt pared it back a little, but not by much. This was the draft he brought to the correspondents at the Anglo-American Club, and it was searing—a fearless indictment of Washington's handling of the campaign.[68]

He then pointed at a reporter from the Associated Press to come with him. The two went back to Shafter's tent, where the general was sitting by his camp desk. Roosevelt moved to hand the letter to Shafter, but the general waved his hand absently.[69]

"I don't want to take it; do whatever you wish with it," Shafter said.

But Roosevelt, worried that the general was clinging to the possibility that he could later deny any knowledge of the exchange, insisted that he at least touch the letter. Shafter relented, and the two of them, still each gripping a side of the paper, handed it to the reporter. Wood and the other officers also wrote their own statement, as did the medical officers. Those were also leaked to the press, and news of their existence spread rapidly. Three days later, the Army was ordered home.[70]

At eleven in the morning on July 28, 1898, hundreds of New York's most prominent residents—Harrimans, Stuyvesants, Stewarts—began to arrive at St. Mark's Protestant Episcopal Church, at Second Avenue and 10th Street in Manhattan, to pay their respects to Hamilton Fish. Edward Cooper, a former mayor, was there, and so was Thomas Platt, the power broker who had pushed Roosevelt out of his job as police commissioner. Several thousand more stood outside, peering through the wrought iron fence that surrounded the churchyard. All of New York had followed the exploits of the Rough Riders, and if they didn't know Hamilton Fish in life they now mourned him in death. As the service began the crowd outside pressed in closer, and dozens of police officers were needed to create a cordon around the church.[71]

St. Mark's was a fitting location: Fish's namesake, Alexander Hamilton, had helped incorporate the church, a century earlier, on land once belonging to one of Fish's maternal ancestors, Peter Stuyvesant. An honor guard drawn from Fish's Columbia fraternity, Delta Psi, carried his flag-draped casket into the sanctuary, past five massive wreaths of pond lilies and pink roses, on which small American flags were printed. The music was modern—"Asa's Death" by Edvard Grieg, the Funeral March from Richard Wagner's *Siegfried*. As a choir sang "Rock of Ages," seventy-five of Fish's Delta Psi brothers filed up to the casket, upon which they laid sprigs of evergreen.[72]

The service over, pallbearers carried Fish's casket outside; they mounted it on a hearse and then his family led the grieving hundreds up Second Avenue. Thousands lined the street for a glimpse of the procession as it made its way to Grand Central Terminal. The family and the casket rode together in a special train north along the Hudson River to the town of Garrison, where they put their son into the ground. Along with them went an honor guard of Rough Riders from Troop A, who had stayed behind in Tampa and traveled to New York for the funeral. At the graveside, they pointed their rifles at the sky and fired three volleys. Hamilton Fish, among the first Rough Riders killed in battle, was the first one home.[73]

CHAPTER 13

"THEY LOOK JUST LIKE OTHER MEN"

On August 4, the Rough Riders received orders to break camp and march to Santiago, and from there to board a ship for the United States. Three days later, just after noon, they left their dog tents standing and burned their clothing, their ponchos, everything but their packs and the clothes on their backs and walked a mile and a half to a railhead. Several dozen were too weak to go by foot and so rode in carts. Then they traveled the seven miles to the docks at Santiago, a fast twenty-minute ride, where they received two months pay and about two hours to explore the city. Most were too worn down to do much sightseeing, though a few had the energy to visit the Café Venus or buy shots of rum. That afternoon they filed on board the *Miami*, a converted civilian ship like the *Yucatan*, which had carried them down to Cuba. The Rough Riders had been in Cuba forty-five days. Of the 600 men who landed at Daiquirí, 23 had been killed in action, another 11 died of disease, and 104 were wounded. Scores more were stricken by malaria. "No other regiment in the Spanish-American War suffered as heavy a loss as the First United States Volunteer Cavalry," Roosevelt wrote.[1]

The regiment was leaving Cuba, but they were not leaving the war. Havana remained under blockade. General García, back in action, was moving inland with his columns, ready to invade the western part of Cuba and await the Americans' return that fall. General Miles was off to capture Puerto Rico; he met little resistance, and had the island in hand within a few weeks. (Richard Harding Davis went with him; in Miles he found the anti-Shafter, and wrote long, praiseful pieces about the general's conquest of the island.) Even with these rapid advances, the regiments that were heading north to the mainland might be needed yet—there was talk of attacking the Canary Islands, Spanish islands in the Atlantic, and even the Spanish mainland should Madrid refuse to capitulate. And so they were being sent to a holding camp, from which they could be put back in action should duty call.[2]

The *Miami* left Santiago at 7:30 on the morning of August 8; General Wheeler joined them on the voyage, as did a squadron from the Third Cavalry Regiment. So did Cuba, the dog that the Rough Riders had brought along as a mascot; somehow he survived the landing at Daiquirí, the march to El Poso, and the siege. A small band was there to see them off, playing "The Star-Spangled Banner" and "Yankee Doodle," with the now bustling port of Santiago behind them.[3]

As the ship slipped away from the dock and down through the harbor, the men crowded the starboard decks to gaze at the half-sunken hulk of the *Merrimac*, not 200 feet away. As the *Miami* turned east out of the harbor, they could see the irregular line of blackened and shell-beaten Spanish warships to the west, grounded just short of the beach. They passed Siboney, where a few transports still lingered and men laid out on the beach, relaxing. The hospital still overflowed with malaria patients. A few minutes later they passed Daiquirí, and then Guantánamo Bay. Then the *Miami* slipped north around Cape Maisí, and on toward the Gulf Stream, and in less than an hour Cuba was a memory.

The voyage north was as deceptively pacific as the trip down on the *Yucatan* had been. "The sea has been like a mill pond," one trooper wrote. But the ship itself was a pesthouse. The *Miami* had been used to carry animals before the Army leased it, stripped out the stalls, and erected narrow bunks of unfinished wood—"a chicken coop with bunks," Roosevelt wrote. There wasn't enough room, and men had to sleep on the metal floors belowdecks, or out on the deck, or on the roof of the cabin. Lacking the ballast of several hundred cattle, the *Miami* rolled constantly, even in the calmest waters. Scores of men were already ill when they boarded; even more developed symptoms once they left Santiago.[4]

Once again, the food was unappetizing, verging on nauseating— canned beef, hardtack, fatty bacon. The men sucked limes to ward off yellow fever, their great fear in such a confined place. The cooks and stewards aboard the *Miami* were even worse than those on the *Yucatan*. They charged a dollar for a loaf of bread, no exceptions. On August 11, Private George Walsh, a forty-three-year-old painter from San Francisco, died of dysentery, which Roosevelt blamed on the man's overindulgence in rum. He was accorded only the briefest of funerals. "The engine was stilled, and the great ship rocked on the waves unshaken by the screw, while the war-worn troopers clustered around with bare heads, to listen to Chaplain Brown read the funeral service, and to the band of the Third Cavalry as it played the funeral dirge," Roosevelt wrote. Walsh's body was wrapped in a hammock, and draped in an American flag. Then two of his comrades tied his ankles to a pair of iron grates, and dropped him into the sea. The *Miami* sailed on.[5]

As if the ship itself were not problem enough, the crew was drunk and mutinous, unhappy to be hauling several hundred malarial soldiers up the coast. Wheeler had ordered Roosevelt to oversee discipline on the ship, and Roosevelt ordered the crew to hand over their bottles. If they did, he said, he would return them when they got home—but if they did not, and he found them, he would toss them overboard. In all about seventy bottles and flasks came into his possession; Roosevelt found another twenty. That solved the drinking, but not the mutiny. "So I sent a detail of my men down to watch them and see that they did their work under the orders of the chief engineer," Roosevelt wrote. "I could easily have drawn from the regiment sufficient skilled men to fill every position in the entire ship's crew, from captain to stoker."[6]

As usual, Roosevelt was among the few to enjoy the hardship. "When we had become convinced that we would escape an epidemic of sickness the homeward voyage became very pleasant," he wrote. Somehow, while all the other men were sick or on the verge of descent into illness, Roosevelt was the picture of health—twenty pounds lighter, but the better for it. Every morning before breakfast he walked out to the deck, bare-naked. He then had two of his favorite troopers, John Greenway and Dade Goodrich, haul up buckets of cold seawater and drench him with it. "Bully! Bully!" he shouted as he splashed the freezing water in his face.[7]

And Roosevelt let loose, in his own way. He laid off drilling the troops, and allowed them to play cards. Mostly, he talked—and listened. For all of Roosevelt's loquacity, he was also a fabulous listener, especially when the stories came from the sort of strenuous lives he admired, and so desired. During those long bull sessions he heard of "voyages around Cape Horn, yacht races for the America's cup, experiences on foot-ball teams which are famous in the annals of college sport; more serious feats of desperate prowess in Indian fighting and in breaking up gangs of white outlaws; adventures in hunting big game, in breaking wild horses, in tending great herds of cattle, and in wandering winter and summer among the mountains and across the lonely plains." This, almost as much as the war itself, was what Roosevelt had been looking for. When he was ranching in the Dakotas or on long hunting trips out West, he was always in a position of paying for the comradeship of the rugged men he brought with him as guides and ranch hands. Here, on the *Miami*, he felt he had finally earned their respect and their friendship.[8]

It was a summer of discontent for Secretary of War Alger. What should have been a great achievement for him was turning into a public relations disaster. First came the newspaper articles, from Davis and others, describing the horrendous conditions in the camps and hospitals around Santiago. Then came Roosevelt's round robin and the other letters, which also appeared in the papers—"mischievous and wicked," Alger called them in his memoirs. The timing could not have been worse. With America's sympathy on the side of its soldiers, the country naturally turned against those who would do them harm. All the better if those malefactors turned out to be politicians located in Washington, D.C.[9]

News had spread fast. Within days after the Battle of San Juan Heights, wounded men were coming back home. The first arrived on July 5 in Key West, where they were to be quarantined. A crowd had gathered to greet them. But rather than seeing triumphant flag-waving soldiers emerge from the ship, they saw hollow-cheeked, weather-beaten faces, the men practically crawling down the gangplank. The crowd "received them in absolute silence as they limped by, clothed in the remnants of their ragged, blood-stained uniforms," *Leslie's Weekly* reported. From there the men dispersed—some back to Tampa to join the remnants of their regiments that had been left behind; others to Army hospitals strung along the Eastern Seaboard; still others back to their homes, to convalesce or die. As they did, they brought their own stories, and shared them with comrades, families, and local reporters around the country. Soon the patriotic joy over the victory at Santiago was tinged with horror, and then anger, at what the victors had been put through by their own Army to achieve it.[10]

At the time, and later in his memoirs, Secretary Alger tried to downplay the Army's mistakes. But each excuse only raised more questions about preparedness and priorities. The climate, he said, not the poor food or lack of supplies, was the problem. Yes, he admitted, Shafter had been sent off with too few hospitals, but it had been the right decision—space on the ships being limited. Yes, he said, the men suffered, but that's what soldiers did, and what the newspapers didn't understand. "The hardships of war were entirely new to them, and a large proportion of the reports in the daily press should have been read at the time with this understanding," Alger wrote. "A wave of indignation, caused by a misapprehension, swept over the United States, and every act of the War Department was interpreted from this distorted point of view." He even blamed the soldiers themselves, especially the volunteers: "The large amount of sickness among the volunteers was the result of their own inexperience and carelessness"—ignoring the high levels of disease among the regular troops as well.[11]

In his rage, Alger turned on Roosevelt as his scapegoat. A mid-level officer in a volunteer regiment had somehow become one of the biggest heroes of the war, vying even with Admiral George Dewey, the victor at Manila Bay. That itself offended Alger's great self-regard. Worse was Roosevelt's immense satisfaction with the Rough Riders, and the way in which the newspapers and the public seemed to view the entire campaign through the experience of this one "cowboy" regiment. Alger was especially galled by his request that the regiment be sent to Puerto Rico, along with the regular troops being sent under General Miles. Alger replied:

> Your letter is received. The regular army, the volunteer army, and the Rough Riders have done well, but I suggest that, unless you want to spoil the effects and glory of your victory, you make no invidious comparisons.

The Rough Riders are no better than other volunteers. They had
an advantage in their arms, for which they ought to be very grateful.

R. A. Alger

Secretary of War

Alger then released both Roosevelt's request and his reply to the
press.[12]

Apparently, he hoped that Roosevelt's arrogance would come
through, alongside his own courage in putting the upstart colonel in
his place. If that was his plan, it backfired. The *New York Times* called
the secretary's letter "just about the level of Algerian imagination . . .
to suppose that the publication of it would injure the author's pros-
pects." Alger was picking the wrong fight. Roosevelt was a war hero;
Alger was a politician with a losing hand. True enough that Roosevelt was arrogant and presumptuous and proud—but he was also
right, and the public was behind him. History renders its own verdict:
Roosevelt went on to be one of the nation's greatest presidents, while
Alger was remembered, briefly, as a synonym for incompetence and
corruption, before sinking beneath the waves of the past.[13]

The *Miami* steamed up the coast for Montauk, a village at the far
eastern end of Long Island. This was the site of the holding camp,
where the men would wait for drier, less malarial weather to reengage
in Cuba. The Army had chosen Montauk for its climate—cool in
the summer, with northeasterly breezes and relatively low humidity,
good conditions for men recovering from a summer fighting Spanish
soldiers and tropical maladies. The land, 4,000 acres on the northern
coast of Long Island's South Fork owned by the Long Island Rail
Road, was both isolated at the end of the island and a quick trip by
train to New York: It sat at the end of a rail line, the other end of
which terminated at Long Island City, a short ferry ride across the
East River from Midtown Manhattan.[14]

Once again, the War Department's incompetence nearly led to
disaster. Because Alger was late in deciding what to do with the soldiers in Cuba, the department was late in getting started on construction at Montauk. And it failed to appreciate just how isolated
Montauk was, and just how hard it would be to build a camp large

enough to handle nearly 30,000 soldiers (coming from both Cuba and various stateside staging camps), many of them ill, within a few weeks. The terminal facilities were too small to handle all the ships and trains arriving, first with material for building the camp, and then thousands of men for filling it. Wealthy New Yorkers chipped in to help—Helen Gould, the daughter of the railroad tycoon Jay Gould, who gave $100,000 to the federal Treasury at the start of the war, donated timber and nails to build floors for tents, but did not send along hammers or saws (if she figured the Army would provide them, she didn't know the Army). Then, on August 9, nearly all the carpenters went on strike. But the real trouble, quipped the *Detroit Free Press*, "was that the troops reached Montauk with embarrassing promptitude." For the first week, those soldiers unlucky enough to be in the early waves to arrive slept in dog tents, or out in the open, on the sandy ground, and ate little beyond a few pieces of hardtack a day.[15]

Still, by the time the Rough Riders neared, the camp was in some sense of order. From a small, sandy elevation just inland (which the regiments took to calling San Juan Hill), one could survey its entire expanse, dotted thickly with thousands of neatly ordered tents and interspersed with commissaries, mess tents, and hospitals. Out beyond, past a stretch of beach and shore grass along Fort Pond Bay, formed by a curve in Montauk's northern shore, stretched the stillness of Long Island Sound in August. The grounds were not quite as nice close up—covered in sand and coal dust, they were more like a boomtown out West than a convalescent camp outside New York City. But anything was a welcome change from Cuba.

The day the *Miami* left Santiago, Roosevelt had received a telegram with a single, cryptic word: "Peace." Nine days later, as the *Miami* sailed around the tip of Long Island and into Fort Pond Bay, a gunboat approached with good news. The Americans and the Spanish had declared a cease-fire on August 12. Spain would cede control of Cuba and Puerto Rico, and some, if not all, of the Philippines. The details would be worked out in Paris that fall; for now, though, it looked like the regiment was back in the United States to stay.[16]

More good news came on the morning of August 14, when, as the *Miami* approached shore, they got a closer look at their new digs: beaches, tall grass, cool breezes. "Why, it's just like the plains!" shouted one Rough Rider. Best of all, the Army had brought up the troops left behind at Tampa, and all their horses (as well as their other two mascots, Josephine the mountain lion and Teddy the golden eagle). "Say, boys, just look at the stock on the prairies back there," yelled another, up in the rigging. "Them's our ponies a switchin' of their tails sure enough, and we'll all go mounted again." A general cheer rose up, even from Roosevelt and Wheeler, who were sitting on the afterdeck.[17]

All morning the *Miami* lay at anchor, about four miles out into Long Island Sound, so that medical officers could come aboard and inspect for disease. Onshore a crowd had gathered—reporters, soldiers, onlookers of all sorts—to greet the Rough Riders, and especially their colonel, by now the most famous man in America. Just before noon, the *Miami*, pulled by a tug, coursed up to a pier, and dropped a gangplank. There was a band to greet them, playing many of the same songs they had heard from a similar band that saw them off in Santiago. As soon as the crowd caught sight of Roosevelt, they cheered "Hurrah for Teddy and the Rough Riders!"[18]

General Wheeler was the first to walk down onto American soil, and as he did a band struck up "The Battle Cry of Freedom"— ironically, a pro-Union, abolitionist anthem from the Civil War. Beaming, the ex-Confederate did not seem to mind. He wore a Spanish sword by his side and a white helmet on his head, which he doffed as soon as his first foot touched solid ground. Then came Roosevelt, trotting down the ramp in a new uniform. "When 'Teddy and his teeth' came down the gangplank, the last ultimate climax of the possibility of cheering was reached," wrote Edward Marshall, who after being shot at Las Guasimas and convalescing at Siboney had made his way north to New York, and now out to Montauk for the Rough Riders' return. At the bottom of the gangplank Roosevelt was rushed by reporters, who were less interested in his recent exploits in Cuba than his designs on Albany. One reporter, to break the ice, asked about his health. "I am disgracefully healthy," he told them. "I'm as strong as a moose. I'm way up. We had a fine trip and we've had a bully time all the way through."[19]

"Well colonel," replied a reporter, "most of us hope to have the chance to vote for you this fall."

Roosevelt did not take the bait. "I'm glad to have the chance to talk to you gentlemen about this regiment," he said, "but I want you all to bear witness that I have talked about nothing else." He tried to press on through the scrum, but the reporters hemmed him in. He pulled back, and then let loose with one of the stemwinder statements he was becoming famous for:

We have men from almost every state in the union—Maine, California, New York, Massachusetts, Texas, Louisiana, everywhere. It is a thoroughly American regiment. I think we have about every race and every religion of our people represented here, though 90 percent of the men are native born Americans. Of the last five promotions I recommended from the ranks to the grade of second lieutenant, one was a Jew, one a Catholic, two Protestant, and the religion of the other I know nothing about. We've got men from the east, west, Indians, half breeds, whites. We judge each man purely on his merits.[20]

This was not true. There were no black men in the regiment, or any regiment save the specially designated, segregated units. Roosevelt's impromptu speech revealed what passed for national unity in 1898, with its diversity rooted in shades of whiteness, and what would increasingly come to define "America" in the eyes of its white citizens.

Behind Roosevelt, the rest of the Rough Riders were filing down the gangplank. They did not trot, or run; they practically crawled. They were a motley sort: Some wore hats, and others wore towels or kerchiefs tied around their heads. Some had on coats, others just their tunics. They carried their belongings in whatever they had—some still had their Army-issue packs, while others toted their belongings in potato sacks. But it was their faces, and their bodies, that shocked. A woman in the crowd remarked, "Why they look just like other men," but in fact they did not look like other men, not most of them, not at that moment—sunburnt and emaciated, many had lost thirty pounds. A man shouted, "How are you, Sullivan?" To which Sullivan—there were two in the regiment, Patrick and William, and Edward Marshall, who recorded the event, doesn't say which—replied, "I'm well, thank God. But more than half of my troop were left behind among the dead and sick at Santiago."[21]

Arthur Cosby, who had been wounded on San Juan Heights and sent home early, was there to meet them, his arm in a sling. "It was a heartbreaking sight," he said. "The men had suffered from exhaustion, exposure, bad food and diseases like typhoid fever. They all looked depressed, thin and weak." Worse, mothers and fathers and girlfriends of men in the regiment were in the crowd, looking in vain for their loved ones. "At the end, the landing of the troops at Montauk had a tinge of sadness cast over it, in sharp contrast to the exuberant joy with which it had begun," Marshall wrote.[22]

Before they could enter the general camp, the Rough Riders, like every regiment brought into Montauk, had to spend five days in quarantine. To get there, they marched three miles up a hill; dozens fell out of line from exhaustion, and had to be carried the rest of the way. But once they arrived, they found rows of large, spacious tents that construction crews had rushed to erect for them—even working on a Sunday. Thousands of soldiers from other regiments were already there, some of whom had been in Cuba, others who were merely shifted north from Tampa. The food on offer was still terrible, but Roosevelt ordered a massive delivery of delicacies from the city: fresh fruit, eggs, milk, food of the sort that haunted their dreams in Cuba. Only after they were released from quarantine, on August 19, were they allowed to reunite with their fellow troopers from Tampa, and to mount their horses once again.[23]

Because the camp was only a few hours by train from New York, it was soon overrun with sightseers. By now the Rough Riders were used to the star treatment—the same had happened in San Antonio, in Tampa, and in every town they stopped at in between. This time, the visitors were welcome. They brought food and drinks; young women came to flirt; boys came to awe at the Rough Riders' uniforms and martial prowess, which they gladly demonstrated on the fields outside the camp, re-creating some of their battles and showing off their horse riding and marksmanship.[24]

Along with the crowds coming to see the Rough Riders came political suitors to see Roosevelt. Publicly, he abjured politics until the regiment mustered out. Privately, he was already scheming, and welcoming visitors who pitched him on his next move. Lemuel Quigg, an emissary from Senator Thomas Platt, the most powerful man in New York State politics, came to Montauk with a peace offering, and a proposal. Not two years earlier, Platt had engineered Roosevelt's ouster as head of the police board in New York City, a move that sent him to Washington, the Department of the Navy, and the Rough Riders. Now, recognizing that the colonel might be the Republicans' only chance to win the governor's mansion that fall, Platt was willing to set past differences aside—though he saw full well the consequences of his action. "If he becomes Governor of New York, sooner or later, with his personality, he will have to be President of the United States," Platt wrote. "I am afraid to start that thing going."[25]

Roosevelt had already received a visit from John Jay Chapman, of the reformist party known as the Independents, a fellow member of Harvard's Porcellian Club who encouraged him to seek the nomination of both his party and the Republicans. The Independents were mostly breakaway Republicans, sick of the Platt machine and eager to change state politics—a natural fit for Roosevelt. But the colonel was playing a longer game, and he needed the Platt Republicans and their ilk to climb higher still. Nevertheless, he endorsed Chapman's plan to nominate him, for the moment, and the next day he authorized the same from Quigg. Then he left for Sagamore Hill, his home in Oyster Bay, outside New York City, to see his family.[26]

Roosevelt arrived to find the entire town turned out to greet him, with banners and chants and a welcome-home bonfire. The next day, in between reading correspondence and roughhousing with his children, he entertained a long list of even more well-wishers. Among them was Robert Bridges, an editor from Charles Scribner's Sons. Scribner's was a New York publisher that, through its book and magazine arms, had already done much to publicize the latest writing about the Spanish-American War, including the work of Richard Harding Davis. Would Roosevelt write up his experiences in a book? In fact, Roosevelt said, he already had one blocked out in his mind. Scribner's, with its well-regarded magazine, was in a position to offer him a stellar deal: The book would first run serially, spread over six articles to run in the magazine, beginning in early 1899, for which he would be paid $1,000 each (more than $30,000 in 2018). They would then be rolled into a single book, which would come out a few months after the final installment. With all his free time between mustering out the regiment and running for governor—this was Roosevelt, after all—writing a memoir would not be a problem.[27]

The sprawling facility at Montauk was named Camp Wikoff, after Colonel Charles Wikoff of the 22nd Infantry, who was killed on San Juan Hill on July 1. Men continued to pour in; about 29,000 would pass through in its two months of operation. The tents, inviting at first, grew tattered and grimy with overuse. It resembled "a mushroom town of the frontier during a 'boom,' with a military post thrown in to account for the uniforms," wrote one trooper.[28]

The real problem was, as usual, the makeshift Army hospitals, where sanitation was close to nonexistent. Some 430 men were convalescing there at any one time. One of the assistant surgeons, a woman surnamed More, told a reporter for *Leslie's* about men lying in their own filth, their tent floors waxed with days-old vomit and feces. "She found men covered with vermin," the magazine wrote. "She found men fighting mad in delirium so desperate they would escape from the tents and run down the hill until pursued and brought back. She found ice wanting, milk wanting, and on some days, water wanting." The men had quinine, but no medicine for dysentery. In all, nine men, including two Rough Riders—Alfred Judson and Fred Gosling—died of disease in the camp (though their illnesses were likely contracted in Cuba, not in Montauk). Several others arrived ill in stateside hospitals, including Stanley Hollister and William Tiffany of the Rough Riders, both of whom died shortly after.[29]

Those who managed to stay out of the hospitals, happy to be back in temperate, relatively bullet-free climes, faced a different challenge: boredom. They ate eggs, oranges, vegetables, pastries, as much as they wanted, shipped in by thankful donors in New York, and they had all the tobacco they could smoke. They flirted with nurses and played in the water. Horses were easy to come by. Billy McGinty would take long rides out on the beach, between the camp and the lighthouse at the end of Long Island, about five miles away. One day, while riding back, he passed twin piles of clothing on a beach on the Atlantic Ocean called Ditch Plains, where the surf was especially strong. When he returned to camp, he heard that Wheeler's son, who had joined the Army and was likewise encamped at Montauk, and a friend were missing. McGinty rode back to the beach; the clothes were still there. That evening someone found their drowned bodies washed up on the shore nearby.[30]

On Tuesday, August 23, Theodore Miller was laid to rest in Akron's Glendale Cemetery. Three weeks earlier his brother John, an officer in the Navy stationed at Guantánamo Bay, had received permission to collect Theodore's remains and escort them home to Ohio. He caught a boat to Santiago, and then rode the recently reinstated train between Santiago and Siboney. When he arrived, he found a casket sent by his father. He also found the major in charge of handling burials, who led John up a steep, rough path to a small clearing in the brush, where eleven flat stakes marked eleven graves, not far from where Miller and the Rough Riders set out for Las Guasimas two months before.[31]

Miller's body was exhumed, and a detail of soldiers carried it back to the train and then to Santiago. The port city was busy with American soldiers and Cuban civilians and furloughed Spanish soldiers and Red Cross workers, all under the control of Leonard Wood. The next morning Miller's casket was placed on a barge and tugged out to *La Grande Duchesse*, a converted passenger liner already filling with 1,200 returning soldiers from the 71st New York Volunteers and the 16th Infantry. After hours spent floating alongside the giant ship, the casket came aboard, and stevedores nestled it in the far corner of a hold. A regimental band played the national anthem as the ship sailed away from Santiago, down the length of its narrow bay and between the zigzag passage it cut between two looming promontories before emptying into the Caribbean Sea. Above the forts that crowned each hilltop flew an American flag. His brother, on board, recalled: "Theodore, who lay quietly in death on board the ship, had done much in gaining this place for our flag, but could not join with the rest in enjoying the glorious result of his efforts and sufferings."[32]

They went first to Montauk, for quarantine, then to Jersey City, New Jersey, where John Miller met another brother, Ed. The two carried Theodore's casket onto a train and arrived in Akron at 7 a.m. on Sunday, August 21. "Thus in silence," John wrote, "Theodore returned home after a most pleasant and honored life among the heroic Rough Riders and after a glorious death in the land of the enemy and in the front ranks of our glorious army, fighting for his country, and for a cause in which he thoroughly believed in."[33]

Hundreds of Akron residents turned out for Theodore Miller's funeral two days later. A week earlier, Roosevelt, a great admirer of Lewis Miller's Chautauqua Assembly—he called it "the most American thing in America"—had written Lewis Miller expressing his condolences and his regrets that he could not attend. Miller's brother-in-law, Thomas Edison, and his sister Mina were there, despite Mina having given birth a month earlier—on the day, in fact, when a telegram arrived at the Edison home in Orange, New Jersey, with news of her brother's death. The Edisons had named their new son Theodore.[34]

When the masses of Akronites had settled into their pews, and the choir had sung its verses, Bishop John Heyl Vincent rose to the pulpit. Like his close friend Lewis Miller, Vincent had been born too early to serve in the Civil War, and like Miller had lived most of his adult life hoping, and then expecting, that he would never have to come so close to the tragic effects of combat again. And yet here he was, eulogizing the son of his best friend, who had died fighting a war against a foreign enemy in a foreign land.

Did Vincent rue the war? Did he wish Theodore had never volunteered? Did he worry that his country, having tasted victory in a foreign conflict, would seek out more? If he did, he hid those thoughts, and instead delivered a treatise on the new place of the soldier in American society, and the new place of America in the world that men like Miller and the Rough Riders had made possible.

Miller, Bishop Vincent said, was not just one man. In his life, and even more so in his death, he represented America itself: "When you look into his closed eyes you see constitutions, history, laws, rights, prerogatives, powers. When you touch his cold body you touch a sacred thing, and you hear drum-beat and bugle call and the thunder of armies."

Miller's death was just because the war was just, Vincent said, and the war was just because America was just. In a passage that could well be a blueprint for the opening of the American century, Vincent said:

> The war, across the black clouds of which the bow of peace now springs, has united the nation, north, south, east and west, in bonds stronger than any that have yet been woven or forged. It has given to the nations

of the Old World a larger knowledge of our power, progress, distinctive civilization, and approved our right to a voice in the affairs of the planet. It has increased the confidence of our people in our system of government. It has emphasized the radical bent of a civilization in which caste and priestcraft are dominant. It has brought the classes of society together, and aimed a blow at anarchism and socialism. It has taught the youth of today, the men and women of tomorrow, larger respect for national ideas. It has given notable lessons in religious fidelity, reverence, the knowledge of God, the value of sobriety. It has elevated into prominence young men, as distinguished for their humility and religious faith as for their heroism and their skill. It has brought out of the black blackness of despotism, millions of people who have for ventures been under the galling yoke of bondage.[35]

After the public service, the family and close friends retreated to Oak Place, the Millers' home in the West Hill neighborhood. They gathered in the library for a small, short ceremony. Then a squad of Theodore Miller's Yale classmates carried his casket outside to a horse-drawn hearse. A detachment of veterans from the Akron Grand Army of the Republic outpost led the mourners and the hearse a half a mile to Glendale Cemetery. They climbed up a steep hill, past the fields where young Theodore had played, through the wrought iron gate that marked the cemetery's entrance, past the neo-Gothic Civil War memorial chapel, to the Miller family plot. Theodore was placed into the ground near his sister Emily, who had died a year before, and near the spot where another sister, Jane, would be buried the following year. By the time she entered the ground, her father was already nearby. He died seven months and nine days after his beloved Theodore.[36]

Not long after Miller's death, the poet Meredith Nicholson published a short verse in his memory. It read, in part,

'Tis of such brain and brawn that God has made
A nation, setting wide its boundary bars
And to its banner giving the high aid
And courage of the stars.

He called his poem "A Rough Rider."[37]

263

• • •

Roosevelt, having barely settled in at Sagamore Hill, came rushing back to Montauk on August 25. He had heard that Russell Alger was paying the Rough Riders a visit. The secretary of war wanted to put a positive spin on what many in the press were calling yet another disaster in the making, this time at Montauk; three men died on the day he came to the camp. Still, Alger told the *New York Tribune* that "I did not find things in nearly so chaotic a condition as I expected, and by the time I left this afternoon I think the camp was pretty well organized." By the time Roosevelt arrived the secretary was gone, having promised to send medicine and better food.[38]

Alger also ordered camp officials to start dispensing passes to New York City, to relieve pressure on the facilities. Charles Knoblauch, who had been a wealthy stockbroker before joining the Rough Riders, got one of the first. "Boys, if there is anything of any thing that you want to eat, name it and we'll get it," he said as he left. More valuable than any victuals Knoblauch brought back were the words that he left with his rich and eager friends on Wall Street. He told them to send food, cigarettes, and whatever else they could think of to make his regiment's life easier. Within days whole trainloads of gifts were en route to Montauk for the Rough Riders.[39]

It was becoming clear that the regiment was unlikely to see combat again—after the armistice with Spain, thousands of troops had already been deployed from San Francisco to the Philippines, where a war with indigenous rebels would drag on several years and involve a level of cruelty and torture that mirrored many of the worst excesses of General Weyler's time in charge of the Spanish army in Cuba. Though some of the men from the Rough Riders ended up in the Philippines, the regiment, as a whole, was scheduled to be decommissioned.

The regiment's impending end did not dim its celebrity. Poetry about the Spanish-American War was commonplace that summer, and that August, America's would-be bards turned their talents to the Rough Riders. Newspapers and magazines overflowed with doggerel, song, and even short fiction about the regiment. On August 11 the *New York Times* featured "Song of the Rough Riders," sung to the tune of "The Irish Fusiliers," which included lines like "Rough Riders were we from the west, gallant gentlemen the rest, of colors the best; rallied to the flag at Roosevelt's behest to carve out way to glory." It continues like that for eleven verses.[40]

In New York, women flocked to Wanamaker's, a department store on Broadway, to snatch up the "Rough Rider," a hat available in black, pearl, and nutria—the pelt of a rodent-like animal that, coincidentally, was later introduced to the Louisiana swamps by Edward Avery McIlhenny, whose older brother John had joined the Rough Riders at San Antonio. Those who went out to see the regiment, and were lucky to come back with a pin or bullet casing from one of the troopers, were the envy of the town. "The picturesque character of the Roosevelt Rough Rider has appealed strongly to the fevered imagination of the small boy whose literature consists of dime novels, detective stories, etc.," wrote one correspondent. After men from the regiment arrived in the city, a father came up to one of them with his two children and said, "My boys have been nearly crazy to meet a Rough Rider." Another trooper was glancing absentmindedly in a shop window when a stranger approached, his hand outstretched. "I want to shake the hand of a Rough Rider," he said. "You are the only people in New York right now."[41]

As the troopers piled into the city, rumors spread that they were set to wreak havoc. "When the Rough Riders struck New York there was mischief to pay," reported *Leslie's Weekly*. And it's true that a few of the men went wild, drinking and carousing and having run-ins with the law. But mostly the soldiers behaved themselves—many never drank anything stronger than lemonade, and sat in bars and restaurants with infinite patience while mobs of onlookers crowded in. One reporter watched as six Rough Riders tried to walk down 23rd Street between Fifth Avenue and Broadway; eventually unable to part the crowd, they were pinned against the wall in front of the Second National Bank. It wasn't all torture, and the men were not exactly trying to avoid attention—they had dressed for the occasion, in full cartridge belts, revolvers, and even, hanging off one man's belt, a machete given him by a Cuban rebel.[42]

Wherever they went, no one would let them pay—for drinks, for food, for theater tickets. One night Kirk and Allen McCurdy, two troopers from Philadelphia, went to see a play, and asked at the box office for standing-room tickets, since they were already late. "Why standing room?" the teller asked.

"You told the man ahead of us there were no seats," Allen McCurdy replied.

"So I did. But you can't buy any seats. Here's a box, with the compliments of the theater."[43]

When they weren't sightseeing, they congregated at the Hoffman House, a hotel on the northern end of Madison Park. "They simply owned the place," wrote *Leslie's Weekly*. The hotel bar was famous as a hangout for Democratic politicians, and a popular watering hole for stockbrokers and wealthy out-of-towners. But for those days in August, the Rough Riders were the center of attention. "You could not get within two feet of the bar, for the Rough Riders and their friends."[44]

Stories like this, celebrating the guts and glory of the Rough Riders, fill the New York newspapers from August 1898, and for the most part they are true. But other, smaller, and more poignant stories are tucked into the papers as well. On August 10 the *Boston Globe* reported about an unnamed Rough Rider, who had not been sent to Cuba and so was already in town. He was invited to a Manhattan garden party; he arrived, stood around quietly for a few minutes, then wandered off. Passersby found him standing by one of the lakes in Central Park, confused and anxious. They asked him what was wrong and he simply stared at them. Another man, Harry De Vol, a private, went absent without leave from Camp Wikoff for almost two weeks; when he returned, he was arrested and put in a guardhouse. Somehow he got a gun and shot himself in the head. De Vol and his troop had been left behind in Tampa. Perhaps, as some speculated, he was despondent because he had missed the adventure.[45]

And then there were the men who never made it to Camp Wikoff. On August 29 Roosevelt and twelve of his troopers took a train to Newport, Rhode Island, for another Rough Rider funeral, this time for William Tiffany, who had died of a disease he contracted in Cuba, most likely yellow fever. Like Hamilton Fish, Tiffany was a flower of the New York elite. One of his uncles was the tycoon August Belmont, who was so rich he had his own subway train. As New York did for Fish, so Newport did for Tiffany: When Roosevelt and his men arrived in the town, they found all the flags at half-staff and the streets lined with people.[46]

By the end of August thousands of the men at Camp Wikoff had been furloughed or discharged. But it had one last famous guest to greet. On the afternoon of September 2, a small knot of onlookers stood at the ferry landing at Manhattan's 23rd Street, on the Hudson River. These were the only people in the entire city who turned out to greet President McKinley, a fraction of the number that had traveled out to see the Rough Riders in Montauk. After refreshing at the Manhattan Hotel, McKinley went to Camp Wikoff, arriving in the late evening. The vice president, Garret Hobart, was with him; and Secretary Alger was there, too, and the next morning the trio took a carriage ride around camp, trailing scores of reporters. When McKinley saw Roosevelt, on horseback, he leapt out of the vehicle and strode over to him. Roosevelt dismounted and fought to remove his glove, a whole fifteen awkward seconds; he finally pulled it off with his teeth. "Colonel Roosevelt, I'm glad to see you looking so well," McKinley said.

"Thank you, Mr. President, there isn't a healthier man in the camp than I am," Roosevelt responded. "I am delighted to see you down here, sir, and hope you will enjoy the trip. I do wish you to come see my boys while you're here."

"Oh I will, Colonel, I will" was the president's reply.

When McKinley's carriage returned, a few hours later, Roosevelt had arranged a riding demonstration by a few of the regiment's cowboys. They performed various tricks with lariats and pistols, then formed a line and, at Roosevelt's signal, charged across the field, right in front of the president.

"Mr. President, what do you think of my boys and my regiment?" Roosevelt asked when they were done.

His future running mate grinned. "Splendid, grand colonel."[47]

Roosevelt then raised the question of a parade for the Rough Riders—in recent days several New Yorkers from the business and municipal elite had been calling for one down Broadway. Roosevelt loved the idea, and had offered to pay the incidentals himself. "I think New York would like to see my men," he told a reporter from the

Boston Globe. Roosevelt even had a parade route mapped out, a loop around the neighborhoods just north of Union Square. But before McKinley could say anything, Alger interjected. He refused to allow it—the cost to the military would be too high, he said, and it wasn't fair to the other regiments. Plus, the Rough Riders were exhausted, and it would be wrong to put them through such an arduous march right before they mustered out. If Roosevelt and his men wanted to parade, they would have to do it as private citizens, in civilian attire and without their carbines or horses. Roosevelt, glaring at Alger, dropped the idea.[48]

Four days later Edith came out to visit with some of the Roosevelt family brood. Roosevelt had Billy McGinty take Ted and Kermit, ages ten and eight, on a horseback ride. McGinty was one of Roosevelt's favorites: The diminutive cowboy had shown him the fastest way to shoe a horse, all that time ago in San Antonio, and Roosevelt had yet to forget it. When the trio returned from their ride, they saw a group of reporters and political hangers-on around Roosevelt's tent. "I hope to be as great as my father some day," Theodore Jr. said.[49]

The day before the regiment was to muster out, Roosevelt was sitting in his tent, finishing some paperwork. The last few weeks had been busy ones. Along with his official duties, the colonel had been quietly inquiring about the financial health of his men, and of the families that his deceased soldiers had left behind. From his own funds, he would hand out small clumps of bills to the men directly; in other cases, using money sent to him by rich acquaintances in New York, he dispensed checks in the name of William Tiffany.[50]

There was a fluttering at the tent flap, and Major (now Colonel) Alexander Brodie, who had been the regiment's unofficial third in command in Cuba, put his head in and asked Roosevelt to step outside. Roosevelt pulled back the tent flap: 900 men—Rough Riders, plus several hundred from other regiments, plus reporters and a few civilian onlookers—stood in a neat hollow square around a table, upon which sat an object covered in a camp blanket. A private, William Murphy, a lawyer in his civilian life, approached and said they had all chipped in to buy their colonel "a very slight token of admiration, love and esteem." Then another man pulled back the blanket. Underneath it was a bronze cast of Frederic Remington's already iconic sculpture *The Bronco Buster*.[51]

Roosevelt smiled as he slowly caressed the artwork. He stumbled through tears to make a short speech:

> Officers and men, I really do not know what to say. Nothing could possibly happen that would touch and please me as this has. . . . I would have been most deeply touched if the officers had given me this testimonial, but coming from you, my men, I appreciate it tenfold. It comes to me from you who shared the hardships of the campaign with me, who gave me a piece of your hardtack when I had none, and who gave me your blankets when I had none to lie upon. To have such a gift come from this peculiarly American regiment touches me more than I can say. This is something I shall hand down to my children, and I shall value it more than the weapons I carried through the campaign.[52]

He had good words for the black regiments as well—men from the Ninth and 10th Cavalry Regiments stood in the crowd—and he singled them out for praise. "The Spaniards called them smoked Yankees but we came to know that they were an excellent breed of Yankees," he said. "I speak the sentiments of every officer and every trooper here, I believe, when I say that there is a tie between those two cavalry regiments." The men, who had been circled by visitors arriving to investigate the hubbub, exploded in cheers.[53]

Then Roosevelt asked the entire regiment to file past him, one by one. As they did, he had a compliment, a joke, or else some obscure but very personal anecdote for each of them. The men, with tears still in their eyes, walked off to be paid, receive their discharge papers, and leave the services of the United States Army. By the end of the next day, when the last man was handed his papers, the United States First Volunteer Cavalry had ceased to exist.[54]

CHAPTER 14

"THE STRENUOUS LIFE"

Most of the Rough Riders, their papers in hand, headed home after mustering out at Camp Wikoff. But about 100 remained in New York: Their colonel still needed them. Though the Republicans did not formally nominate Roosevelt for governor until October 4, his candidacy was an open secret, and he was already making plans to hit the campaign trail. And he could not have asked for a better booster club.

When the men returned to New York City, they found that Rough Rider fever had only grown stronger. With their now former colonel readying to run for the governor's mansion, they were received not just as war heroes, but as Roosevelt's praetorian guard. No longer in their uniforms, they played the part expected of them, dressing in slouch hats and cowboy duds, even when they went to the theater or dinner at the Waldorf-Astoria—all paid for by admirers.[1]

The Olive Tree Inn on East 23rd Street and a Red Cross center in Long Island City offered them free rooms. Not that they needed money—with five months pay, about $125, they were well-funded to take Manhattan. Newspapers reported on their daily movements: One group was seen trapshooting at Coney Island. Another visited the New York Stock Exchange, where the director brought them on the floor. Three men, walking along 28th Street, saw an automobile for the first time. The driver stopped and invited them along for the ride. They hopped in and waved their hats. "The driver seemed to enter into the spirit of the occasion and put on top speed" for six blocks, reported the *New York Times*. Others were seen in the Tenderloin, a block of town roughly between Madison Park and Bryant Park that was home to hundreds of bars, stages, and bordellos and

271

that "welcomed the famous cowboy heroes with open arms," reported the *Chicago Tribune*. As they moved around New York, they wore pins in their hats that read "Our Teddy for Governor."[2]

Once again the men made the Hoffman House their base camp, and could be found playing Mexican monte in the saloon. On the morning of September 17, several dozen Rough Riders gathered in the early morning; Roosevelt had sent word that he would be in the city, and wanted to see his men. Apparently news of his visit got out, because hundreds of well-wishers had packed into the bar along with them. The Rough Riders were not the only people Roosevelt wanted to see that day: Also waiting for him at the Hoffman House, though hiding away in a private room upstairs, was Senator Thomas Platt. Roosevelt arrived, with Lemuel Quigg, Platt's confidant, in a cab around three in the afternoon and went up to Platt's room by the "ladies' entrance" door. Platt wanted assurances that Roosevelt was not seeking an endorsement from the breakaway Independent Party, and that he would run for office—and hold it—as a loyal Republican. Realizing he was in a corner, Roosevelt agreed.

When he finished he walked downstairs to the bar. Before he could set foot on the floor, the Rough Riders charged him, jostling with a hundred other people trying to shake his hand. They had been waiting for two hours, and demanded he speak. Roosevelt began to oblige them: "I had a very pleasant conversation with Senator Platt and Mr. Odell—"

"Will you accept the nomination for governor?" someone demanded.

Roosevelt's face turned from confused to agitated to a broad smile. "Of course I will! What do you think I am here for?"[3]

The crowd went wild. The reunion with his men was not going to happen that day. "Boys, this is too much for me," he shouted over the din. "I cannot stand it any longer. You'll have to excuse me, and if I get a chance later I'll shake hands with all of you. I love you all. Good bye." Police officers, standing nearby, made a corridor for him out the front door to a waiting carriage. As he moved outside, he saw two Rough Riders at the curb. He asked how they were enjoying the city. "Colonel, this good time is killing us," one said. "It's worse than San Juan."[4]

Dozens of men agreed, and over the next week their ranks thinned further. "I ain't got no use for a place like this, where everybody is touchin' elbows and the air is full of smoke," one trooper told a reporter for the *Boston Globe*. Signs in Grand Central Terminal advertised "Half Rates for Rough Riders," and there was no shortage of takers. A few men, headed back West, made a stopover in Washington, to see McKinley. This being 1898, they were able to enter the Executive Mansion without an appointment (let alone a security check), and soon they were hobnobbing with the president of the United States.[5]

If there were any doubts about the centrality of his Cuban experience to Roosevelt's gubernatorial campaign that fall, a party at his home on Long Island on September 21 put that to rest. Some 2,000 people turned out to hear him give his first public speech since returning from Cuba; the streets of Oyster Bay were lined with flags and firemen and onlookers of all ages and sizes. As a local brass band played "Listen to the Mockingbird," Roosevelt mounted the dais in a black cutaway coat, wool trousers, a blue tie—and a giant cowboy hat. A man who had climbed a nearby tree for a better view shouted, "Three cheers for the old Rough Rider!"[6]

Roosevelt, ruddy-cheeked and full-bellied, having already put back some of the weight he'd lost in Cuba, thanked the crowd for the warm welcome, which he valued above nothing else save "the greeting of my own regiment." Then he compared his troopers to the New York electorate: "Our men were likewise from all walks of life, all standing precisely alike as far as the regiment was concerned. Standing shoulder to shoulder were the man who has a one-dollar a day job and the man born in wealth and reared in luxury; both good Americans and both anxious to show that this was not a rich man's war and a poor man's fight. . . . They showed in this war, as in all wars, that when the nation called for her sons they demanded the right to shed their blood for her."[7]

Roosevelt called up four Rough Riders and introduced them, one by one, before unrolling an extended run-through of the campaign— from San Antonio to Montauk, with references to the fallen, including Capron, Fish, and O'Neill. His disquisition might have been tedious were it not for Roosevelt's enthusiasm in delivering it, and the audience's eagerness to hear every word, whatever word, that came from his mouth. When he finished, and the applause died down, a chorus filed onto the dais beside him to sing a newly composed song, "The Brave Rough Riders."[8]

Two weeks later, at their state convention, the Republicans nominated Roosevelt for governor. Following tradition, he was not in attendance; a delegation of party leaders brought the news to him at Sagamore Hill. The next day he gave his first campaign address, in New York's Carnegie Hall. It sounded less like a gubernatorial stump speech and more like a declaration of a new American empire: "We cannot avoid facing the fact we occupy a new place among the people of the world, and have entered upon a new career . . . the guns of our warships in the tropic seas of the West and the remote East have awakened us to the knowledge of new duties. Our flag is a proud flag, and it stands for liberty and civilization. Where it has once floated, there must be no return to tyranny or savagery."[9]

And so he was off. With just weeks before the election, Roosevelt crisscrossed upstate New York, with a varying coterie of Rough Riders in tow, most often Albert Wright, the regiment's color sergeant—who often preceded the colonel to the stage, flag flying—and Emil Cassi, the trumpeter. On October 17 Roosevelt made seventeen stops along 212 miles of Hudson Valley railway. Like a comic who hits on a surefire bit and learns to work it into every show, Roosevelt realized that the crowds could take or leave talk of corruption and reform and infrastructure; what they wanted to hear were stories of the war. So that's what he gave them.[10]

Roosevelt understood that he was walking a narrow line—a reformer at heart, but running with the Platt machine's backing. On September 19 he had told Chapman, the head of the reformist Independents, that he could not accept his party's nomination, a decision that soon had Chapman and others attacking him in public as "a broken-backed half-good man" and a "standard-bearer of corruption." Roosevelt dodged such accusations by relying on his recent war record: The Rough Rider story, by now a household legend, let him run as something other than a politician. He was instead a soldier, back from the war, full of glory and stories.[11]

When Roosevelt did dip into policy during his campaign speeches, it was often to push for military expansion and reform. Above all, he wanted a larger Army to promote and protect America's growing foreign interests. "We don't need it for policy purposes at home; we don't need it to preserve order; for our people are quite able to preserve order themselves; but we do need it to protect our interests abroad," he told a crowd the day after he received the nomination.[12]

But mostly, he surrounded himself with the pomp and circumstance of his recent martial successes. At Port Jervis, New York, one of his former troopers, Buck Taylor, told the crowd: "I want to talk to you about my colonel. He kept every promise he made to us and he will to you . . . he told us we might meet wounds and death and we done it, but he was there in the midst of us, and when it came to the great day he led us up San Juan Hill like sheep to the slaughter and so will he lead you."[13]

Taylor's comments were bloody stuff, but the crowds loved it. On November 8, Roosevelt won the governor's mansion by 661,707 votes to 643,921 for his Democratic opponent, Augustus Van Wyck. Theodore Bacon, on the Independent ticket, won just 2,103 votes.[14]

On December 15, 1898, about six weeks after Roosevelt's victory in New York, President McKinley was in Atlanta. The Treaty of Paris, which formally ended the Spanish-American War, had been signed five days earlier. It ceded Puerto Rico and Guam to the United States outright; Spain also gave up the Philippines, in exchange for $20 million. Cuba was to receive its independence, but not yet—it would remain an American protectorate for three more years (and unofficially for many years after that). On top of all that, the United States had formally annexed the Hawaiian islands on July 7, while the Fifth Corps still laid siege to Santiago. There were complications: Tensions were growing between American and Filipino forces, and in a few months they would erupt into a full-scale conflict—the Philippine-American War—that lasted nearly four more years and resulted in the deaths of more than 16,000 Filipino fighters, 5,000 Americans, and tens of thousands of civilians. But as 1898 came to a close, it was a good time for some presidential stock-taking.

This sort of foreign engagement was precisely what McKinley had come into office promising to avoid. Yet that day in Atlanta, he embraced it. He praised his country's recent victory as the dawn of

275

a new era of enlightened American leadership. "We have so borne ourselves in the conflict and in our intercourse with the powers of the world as to escape complaint or complication and give universal confidence of our high purpose and unselfish sacrifices for struggling people," he told the audience at the city's auditorium.

America, despite having taken on a globe-spanning set of territories, was not following in Europe's imperial, colonial path. This had been, McKinley went on, a different kind of war. "At Bunker Hill liberty was at stake; at Gettysburg the Union was the issue; before Manila and Santiago our armies fought, not for gain or revenge, but for human rights," he said. Yes, he admitted, the resulting gain in territory was the same no matter the motive. But what was the alternative? "If we had blinded ourselves to the conditions so near our shores, and turned a deaf ear to our suffering neighbors, the issue of territorial expansion in the Antilles and the East Indies would not have been raised. But could we have justified such a course?"

"No!" shouted the crowd.

"Is there anyone who would now declare another to have been the better course?"

"No!"

The means, it seemed, justified the ends. America had no choice but to take on an empire, for the sake of the world. "With less humanity and less courage on our part, the Spanish flag, instead of the Stars and Stripes, would still be floating at Cavite, and Ponce, and at Santiago, and a 'chance in the race of life' would be wanting to millions of human beings who today call this nation noble, and who, I trust, will live to call it blessed," McKinley said. "Thus far we have done our supreme duty." American idealism and American empire were, in McKinley's speech, forged into one overarching national vision.

He went on. The war and its consequences were not just a victory for American military might and American values, McKinley thundered. It was a victory for American unity. "This government has proven itself invincible in the recent war, and out of it has come a nation which will remain indivisible forever more," he said, comments no doubt pleasing to his Georgia audience. "No worthier contributions have been made than by the Southern people." With the

276

country victorious and united, there was no choice, he concluded, except to embrace its new role, and new territories:

> Shall we now, when the victory won in war is written in the treaty of peace and the civilized world applauds and waits in expectation, turn timidly away from the duties imposed upon the country by its own great deeds, and when the mists fade and we see with clearer vision, may we not go forth rejoicing in a strength which has been employed solely for humanity and always been tempered with justice and mercy, confident of our ability to meet the exigencies which await, because confident that our course is one of duty and our cause that of right?[15]

McKinley's confident imperialism ignored the messy reality: not only the imminent fighting in the Philippines, or the tense occupation of Cuba, but an unfolding scandal around the Army's utter lack of preparedness, which would culminate in hearings by the Dodge Commission the following year. Still, the president's picture of the war as a selfless intervention in the name of humanity and Cuban liberty was widely shared at the time. "The war between the United States and Spain was, in brief, a war for humanity," wrote Alexander K. McClure and Charles Morris in their biography of McKinley, published in 1901. "America could no longer close her ears to the wails of the starving people who lay perishing, as may be said, on her very doorsteps. It was not for conquest or gain, nor was it revenge for the awful destruction of the *Maine*." In 1902 Woodrow Wilson, then the president of Princeton University, declared it a war "not for the material aggrandizement of the United States, but for the assertion of the right of the government to succor those who seemed hopelessly oppressed."[16]

Some historians would later depict the events of 1898 as an aberration, even a mistake—that America was not, at least for the time being, an imperial nation. And it's true that after the war in the Philippines, America did not try to acquire more territory, save for the Panama Canal Zone in 1903. But McKinley's speech in Atlanta makes clear that America was already, and permanently, set on a different path—one cloaked in idealistic rhetoric, one that would eschew the formal trappings of territorial conquest in favor of commercial power, political protectorates, and above all humanitarian intervention. In the coming years the United States solidified its control over the Caribbean, with repeated occupations and the opening of the Panama Canal. It extended its reach over the Pacific by building bases on far-flung islands. And it developed, under McKinley and his successor, Roosevelt, a rhetoric of American idealism and power that would change the world to a greater extent than guns and money ever could.

By the time he reached Albany, Theodore Roosevelt, who had turned forty less than two weeks before his campaign victory, had already led life enough for ten men—state assemblyman, bestselling author, rancher, police commissioner, and soldier; he had climbed European mountains and hunted javelina in the Texas brush. And he would go on to do much more—the vice presidency and presidency; a slew of progressive legislative achievements, including breaking up the trusts and mandating food and drug safety; the Nobel Peace Prize for negotiating the end of the Russo-Japanese War; and post-presidential adventures in Africa and the Amazon. But nothing matched the experience of leading the Rough Riders. He preferred, and often insisted, that he be called "Colonel" Roosevelt. "There are no four months of my life to which I look back with more pride and satisfaction," he wrote in his memoirs.[17]

In 1899 Roosevelt attended the first regimental reunion, in Las Vegas, New Mexico. His duties in Washington prevented him from attending subsequent gatherings, but men from the regiment were frequent visitors at the Executive Mansion (which Roosevelt took to calling the "White House"); official guests, on official business, sometimes found themselves waiting for an hour outside Roosevelt's office while he socialized with a few of his old comrades. He also campaigned for the Medal of Honor for himself, though the War Department declined to award it to him, a slight he would always ascribe to Secretary of War Alger and his allies. (He finally received the medal in 2001, eighty-two years after his death.)[18]

Three months after taking office as New York's governor, Roosevelt traveled to the all-male Hamilton Club in Chicago, where he gave a speech entitled "The Strenuous Life." Among the thousands of addresses, books, essays, and letters Roosevelt wrote during his life, nothing comes closer than this speech to defining his worldview, and explaining the impact that he had on American life at that critical moment, as the country moved into a dominant position on the world stage. If McKinley's address in Atlanta painted a picture of American imperial power as a peace-bringing, world-uniting force, Roosevelt's Chicago speech depicted a world of violent competition, one in which men and nations must be aggressively virile to survive.

The speech brings together so much of what Roosevelt had been thinking and saying for years, and yet it is hard to imagine it without his recent, searing experience in Cuba. In the early 1890s, Roosevelt wrote and spoke endlessly and vacuously about self-sacrifice, national honor, and a whole litany of aggressively virile themes that he saw as the American patrimony but that he feared his generation was at risk of squandering. But it was only after his time in Cuba that these themes congealed into a coherent philosophy, backed by the confident sense of moral superiority that came with having risked his own life for his beliefs.[19]

The strenuous life, Roosevelt told his audience, was "the life of toil and effort, of labor and strife"—and that applied as much to the individual as the nation. "If we are to be a really great people, we must strive in good faith to play a great part in the world," he said. America's newfound power meant that it would inevitably be drawn into foreign affairs; its long-standing values obligated it to play an active, even aggressive role in shaping them:

We cannot avoid meeting great issues. All that we can determine for ourselves is whether we shall meet them well or ill. Last year we could not help being brought face to face with the problem of war with Spain. All we could decide was whether we should shrink like cowards from the contest, or enter into it as beseemed a brave and high-spirited people; and; once in, whether failure or success should crown our banners. So it is now. We cannot avoid the responsibilities that confront us in Hawaii, Cuba, Porto Rico, and the Philippines.[20]

The speech is aggressive—Roosevelt attacked those who demanded peace in early 1898 or withdrawal from America's newfound possessions after the war as "weaklings," "sinister," "puerile," charges that he felt confident in making because he, unlike them, had been in battle. The speech is racist, calling for the conquest of "savage" peoples by civilized nations. But the speech also captured the spirit of a country that was suddenly feeling emboldened, united, ready to take on the world. "The Strenuous Life" was immediately hailed as a new definition of American values; it was reprinted in newspapers and magazines, and helped cement Roosevelt's position not just as a major American politician, but as an intellectual father of its new imperialism.

Roosevelt's vision, backed by his personal experience and sacrifice in battle, provided a model for the country, and at its best inspired generations of leaders to go beyond personal and national self-interest in the name of the common good. It also bequeathed a narrow, chauvinistic idea about what that common good meant—a set of values defined by the powerful, to be imposed on the powerless. And there is an obvious danger in Roosevelt's logic: If America's intentions are always good, and if America has an obligation to use its power to shape the world in its image, then soon every crisis, everywhere in the world, presents a challenge for American power. It is the sort of rhetoric that would later drive the country into Europe, the Pacific, Vietnam, Iraq, and dozens of other conflicts, at times to the benefit of humanity, but often at great cost. The inability to foresee those outcomes derives from a noble, blinkered view of American power—one that Roosevelt forged in his experience with the Rough Riders.

Looking back, it is possible to see the Spanish-American War for what it was: a half-baked, poorly executed, unnecessary conflict that pushed an immature military power onto the world stage—or, alternately, as a ham-handed land grab with a sugarcoating of idealism. But this was much less obvious at the time. The speed and élan with which the Americans won the field in Cuba—and above all the image of Roosevelt and his Rough Riders charging the hills outside Santiago—shocked and impressed the world. No one expected Spain to win the war, but no one expected the United States, with its puny Regular Army and hordes of half-trained volunteers, to achieve victory so quickly. "This war must in any event effect a profound change in the whole attitude and policy of the United States," wrote the London *Times*. "In the future America will play a part in the general affairs of the world such as she has never played before. When the American people realize this, and they realize novel situations with remarkable promptitude, they will not do things by halves."[21]

America was not just feeling empowered; it had found a new way of talking about power, one that drew on the country's best ideas of itself and used them to paper over its worst instincts. Standing on the podium in Atlanta, McKinley had nothing to say about the commercial and strategic interests behind the war, or the atavistic jingoism that motivated so many of its most adamant supporters. All of that was secondary to his embrace of a crusader ideal, intent on reshaping the world for the better—which is to say, in America's image and, not incidentally, to America's benefit. It was a 180-degree reversal of John Quincy Adams's admonition, uttered on Independence Day 1821, that America "goes not abroad, in search of monsters to destroy," that it remains "the well-wisher to the freedom and independence of all" but "the champion and vindicator only of her own." The majority of Americans had long opposed foreign intervention, and for that reason had opposed the maintenance of a standing army to execute one. But if that intervention could be packaged within the rhetoric of humanitarianism, then, it seemed, the public would get on board.

The war achieved something else as well. It set in motion a resolution between America's two competing traditions of militarism: the Jacksonian, which relied on the will of the people to rise up in times of need, and the Hamiltonian, which emphasized preparedness and a centralized, standing army. In this respect the story of the Rough Riders was absolutely central. They offered a bridge between the two, a way for the wary to become comfortable with the idea of a large, permanent federal military. They were something entirely different from the old stereotypes about military men: They were volunteers, but serving in the United States Army, not a state militia. They replaced the old image of carpetbagging, corrupt, dirty soldiers with a new ideal of an all-American force, drawn from all regions and classes, united behind a set of values, not glory or a paycheck. Time and again, it was the Rough Rider ideal of defending American values, not American interests, that drove thousands of men and women to enlist in the fight against Germany in World War I, to join the Marines landing at Da Nang in 1965, to volunteer to invade Iraq in 2003.

More immediately, the Rough Riders became an inspiration for the Army reforms that followed the war, and which laid down the basic outline of the twentieth-century American military. In August 1899 McKinley fired Alger as his secretary of war, replacing him with a close associate of Roosevelt's, the New York corporate lawyer Elihu Root (among other things, Root had helped Roosevelt avoid disaster during his gubernatorial run when it emerged that the candidate was not, technically, a resident of New York). With Congress—which in 1901 had already approved an increase in the size of the Regular Army, to almost 100,000, from 28,000 before the war—and public opinion behind him, Root rebuilt the Army, top to bottom. He replaced the position of commanding general with a general staff; he created the Army War College; and, most notably, he reorganized the state militia system into the National Guard, in which the states, in exchange for federal funds, agreed to let the federal government nationalize their units when it saw fit.[22]

Crucial to Root's plan was the public's willingness not just to go to war as a country, but to prepare for war in times of peace and to volunteer when the need arose. This form of "voluntaristic militarism" was very different from the massive conscript armies of nineteenth-century Europe, or the minuteman militias of eighteenth-century America. The goal, for Root, was a core standing army that could expand rapidly in wartime, without having to rely on untrained volunteers or poorly prepared militiamen; in other words, a combination of professional soldiers and permanent, trained citizens—the Jacksonian and Hamiltonian traditions in one. It is hard to imagine that Root did not have his friend Roosevelt's regiment in mind when he crafted these reforms.[23]

The story of the Rough Riders also pointed the way toward a new order at home. On September 18 the Reverend W. S. Crowe of the Church of the Eternal Hope, on Manhattan's Upper West Side, rose to the lectern to give a sermon on "some lessons of the war." After expounding on the now common themes of sectional reconciliation, liberty for Cuba, and a newfound purpose for American power, he alighted on the Rough Riders. "The experience of that picturesque and somewhat romantic band," he said, has put down a great deal of silly and mischievous comment on the strife between classes and masses in America. The wealth and culture of the East, the universities, the old and proud families, social exclusiveness, Newport and Bar Harbor, were liberally represented in that band of heroes, side by side with the frontiersmen. They ate and slept and fought and suffered and died together. The survivors have gone to their homes with a marvelous increased regard for manhood, whether it grew on the battle plains or in the drawing room. The entire country has witnessed a practical demonstration of manhood's equality. The wind is all taken out of the sails of the anarchist orator. . . . When the Arizona boys mingle with their old neighbors and cronies, and fill their old haunts with talk of the war, the Far West will conclude that what has been hated as the aristocratic East is quite worthy of confidence.[24]

If the 1890s were a decade of psychic crisis, in which a post-frontier America felt itself divided and frittering away its resources and willpower, especially among the young, then the Rough Riders showed a way out. At a time when regional, political, racial, and class differences threatened to rip the country apart, the regiment was able to unite Westerners and Easterners, ranch hands and star tennis players; the combination of so many different forms of contemporary manhood, deployed in the name of the national interest and national ideals, gave an entire generation of Americans a new sense of purpose. This was not an overnight change; anti-imperialist and isolationist crosscurrents continued to shape foreign policy as well. But as the twentieth century progressed, and as America asserted itself more confidently abroad, the Rough Rider ideal helped drive it forward.

There were limits to this newfound national unity. "America," like the Rough Riders, was diverse only within the confines of masculine whiteness; while the country contained multitudes, the idea of what it meant to be American at the turn of the century did not extend to African Americans or, fully, to women, and only on the margins to a few token Native Americans and Latinos. Even Roosevelt, who was quick to praise the segregated regiments in the first few months after the Santiago campaign, wrote in his memoir that black soldiers were only effective when led by white officers. Black veterans and journalists cried foul, but no one listened. If the Rough Riders defined "America" as the country moved into the twentieth century—and they most certainly did for that most ardent advocate of Americanism, Theodore Roosevelt—it was an America with a decidedly pale hue.

Roosevelt left the presidency in 1909, and although he ran a strong race as a third-party candidate in 1912, he never returned to public office. He did not retreat from public life, though: Alongside well-publicized hunting trips to Africa and an expedition up the Amazon, he continued to write books and articles, many of them criticizing the 1912 victor, Woodrow Wilson. And he continued to advocate for a military system that relied heavily on Rough Rider–style voluntarism, long after the realities of industrial-era warfare had made standing armies a necessity. The experience of the Spanish-American War, and Roosevelt's celebrated role within it, may have helped the country break from its allegiance to Jacksonian voluntarism, but the reforms and expansion they unleashed left Roosevelt behind. By the eve of World War I, he sounded as retrograde in his views on military affairs as the Civil War–era generals and politicians he had criticized in his youth. When the United States declared war on Germany in 1917, Roosevelt offered to raise Rough Rider–style units; Congress authorized up to four divisions, but Wilson rejected the plan. Roosevelt stayed home, though his son Quentin, a pilot, was shot down over German lines and died on July 14, 1918. Roosevelt died less than six months later, on January 6, 1919, of a pulmonary embolism at Sagamore Hill.[25]

Cuba finally achieved independence on May 20, 1902, after over three years of American control. For much of that time, Leonard Wood, who had started the war at the head of the Rough Riders, oversaw the entire American occupation as a military governor. He reformed the Cuban courts, rebuilt the railways, and got the economy back in working order. But in his reforms, he also greatly favored the interests of Spanish-born, urban peninsulares, as well as the members of the New York–based Junta who moved back to Cuba after the war, over the rebels and their provisional government. He wasn't alone: Immediately after the end of hostilities, American public and political opinion turned against Cuban independence. Poisoned by stories about ragtag rebel soldiers, the American public resented the rebels' alleged reliance on outside help, and repeated without question the racist stereotypes about lazy, untrustworthy Cubans found in the yellow press. The Cubans had soon sunk to the same level, in the American mind, as the Spanish. The journalist William Allen White, who had been a Cuba booster from his editorial perch in Kansas, wrote: "Both crowds are yellow-legged, garlic-eating, dagger-sticking, treacherous crowds. . . . It is folly to spill good Saxon blood for that kind of vermin."[26]

In 1901 Congress passed a bill to again enlarge the Army, alongside other early steps in Elihu Root's reforms. The bill included the Platt Amendment, after Senator Orville Platt of Connecticut, which placed severe limits on Cuban independence—among other things, the island's government could not take on additional debt, and it had to allow the United States to intervene again whenever it saw fit. Only by accepting those limits could the Cubans take over control of their own island. But they could not, really, rule a country that had no effective defense against its enormous northern neighbor—and, indeed, the United States invaded again, in 1906. Less concerning than outright intervention, though, was the economic and political control that the American government and American companies exerted on Cuba, influences that eventually fed another rebellion over fifty years later, this time led by communists under Fidel Castro.

This pattern of "intervene first, ask questions later" became a template for American foreign policy in the twentieth century. The need for prudent decisions based on informed understanding of a foreign country too often took a backseat to ideological claims about overthrowing tyranny and delivering freedom for the oppressed. American planners, whether in Korea, Vietnam, Iraq, or dozens of interventions through the subsequent century, ignored nuanced, and perhaps inconvenient, questions about a country's politics, demographics, and culture. Many of the journalistic accounts of the Santiago campaign, and especially the occupation that followed, could with a few minor changes have appeared in the 1960s to describe America's initial forays into South Vietnam, or in the early 2000s to describe the invasion of Iraq. In these cases and others, many Americans allowed appeals to "freedom" and "justice" to divert their attention from the difficult questions of how a country should be governed, by whom, and to what end. The Rough Riders set the template for how Americans would regard their military, and their militarism; the Spanish-American War set the template for how Americans would go out into the world in search of monsters to destroy.

The Rough Riders' fame endured long after Roosevelt won the governor's race and the rest of the regiment filtered back to their homes. Roosevelt's account of the war, *The Rough Riders*, was an overnight bestseller when it appeared in the spring of 1899. Tom Hall, whom Roosevelt had drummed out of the regiment during the siege of Santiago, had a similar success with his book, *The Fun and Fighting of the Rough Riders*, to the chagrin of his former comrades. The Rough Riders figured prominently in many of the dozens of books written by correspondents from the campaign, including Davis, Marshall, Kennan, and Creelman. And they were common base material for early movies: Along with multiple attempts to retell the regiment's story in Cuba (including several made by Thomas Edison), studios turned out a whole subgenre of films built around the notion of what the men might have done once they returned from the war—in 1939's *Rough Riders Round-Up*, for example, Roy Rogers stars as a soldier from the regiment who, back from the war, joins the United States Border Patrol.[27]

The regiment enjoyed acclaim and success away from the studio lot. When Dade Goodrich, Dudley Dean, and Charlie Bull, all alumni Harvard football team, went back to visit Cambridge, that day's practice was renamed "Rough Rider's Day."[28] A year after Theodore Miller died in Cuba, his friends and family endowed a memorial arch in his name at Yale, which still stands between Battell Chapel and Durfee Hall, just off the New Haven Green. Some men parlayed their newfound fame into political or business careers. Goodrich went to work for B. F. Goodrich, his family firm and one of the world's largest tire manufacturers, where he was chairman of the board for twenty-three years. John Greenway became a mining company executive, while Frank Knox became a newspaper publisher, first in Michigan and then in Chicago. In 1936 the Republican Alf

Landon chose him as his running mate against Franklin Roosevelt; FDR crushed them, but four years later he asked Knox to be his secretary of the navy. Others, including Billy McGinty and Tom Isbell, parlayed their renown into careers as traveling showmen. They and thirty-four other Rough Riders joined Buffalo Bill Cody's Wild West show, where they reenacted the charge up Kettle Hill—by now refashioned as the charge up San Juan Hill—hundreds of times, for tens of thousands of onlookers across the country.[29]

Bob Wrenn and Bill Larned, Theodore Miller's tennis-playing idols, went back to the sport. Larned won seven U.S. Open championships. Both ended their lives in tragedy: Wrenn killed a man with his car in 1914, and he died, broken, eleven years later, at age fifty-two. Larned, who contracted rheumatism in Cuba, became depressed after retiring from tennis, and despite a successful business career, shot himself in his private quarters at New York's Knickerbocker Club, in 1926. He was fifty-three.[30]

Richard Harding Davis, despite a career that ran for almost another two decades, never found a subject quite as compelling as Theodore Roosevelt or the Rough Riders. He certainly looked for one—he covered the Second Boer War; he was with the Japanese during the Russo-Japanese War; and he was in Greece, on the Salonika Front, during World War I. He continued to write for magazines, to write novels and plays as well, but his fame had plateaued. As his biographer Arthur Lubow argues, he was a man who caught the wrong wave; a modernist, even slightly avant-garde figure of the late Victorian era, by the 1910s he was a dinosaur, behind the times, someone who still believed that the ideal foreign correspondent was as much as participant as an observer. He died of a heart attack on April 11, 1916, just shy of his fifty-second birthday.[31]

The Rough Rider Reunion, held every other year in Las Vegas, New Mexico, also helped keep the regiment's story alive. An out-of-the-way place for many, Las Vegas was convenient for several of the most ardent veterans, who lived in Santa Fe and other nearby towns. And as a cattle town set amid the arid foothills of the Rockies, it helped maintain the image of the Rough Riders as a frontier, cowboy outfit. Roosevelt made the trip that first year, as did about 100 men from the regiment—and about 10,000 onlookers. The men kept coming back, but every year there were fewer and fewer, until eventually the event was tucked into Las Vegas's annual Cowboy Reunion, a tourist-centered celebration of another half-mythic artifact of America's recent past.[32]

As the years progressed, the stories the Rough Riders told, and that people told about the Rough Riders, morphed and expanded, became intertwined and distorted. If a Rough Rider veteran lived in a town, it was a sure thing that every few years a reporter for the local paper would come by for a visit. And each time the stories the man told grew a little bigger, and a little less accurate, and yet the editors printed them verbatim because they came from Rough Riders. Then there were the impostors—the City Museum of Las Vegas, New Mexico, maintains an extensive collection of clips, letters, and the museum's own investigations into men who falsely said they had fought alongside Roosevelt. Charles Howard, the owner of the racehorse Seabiscuit, claimed to have been a Rough Rider, as did a man named Warren McAlister, who boasted, long into the twentieth century, that he had boxed with Roosevelt in Cuba.[33]

In July 1970, Douglas Scott, a researcher from Columbia University, traveled to northern Westchester County, outside New York City, to interview Jesse Langdon. As a five-year-old boy Langdon had met Theodore Roosevelt in Medora, in the Dakotas; in 1898, when he was sixteen, he tramped to Washington to join the Rough Riders and, despite being underage, persuaded Roosevelt to enlist him. Seventy-two years later, he was one of the last three surviving Rough Riders, along with Frank Brito and George Hamner.[34]

Langdon had lived an eccentric's varied life. He performed in a traveling Wild West show; he fought in the Philippines, where he lost his right lung to disease; and he worked as a veterinarian for almost twenty years before quitting to become a full-time inventor. He claimed to hold 189 patents, "mostly valves," he told Scott, "because that's where I made the most money." For a while he lived in Brooklyn, where he and his wife, Marie Storey, put all their savings into the Langdon-Storey Foundation, which they created to promote something he called "taxless government." Set up as a nonprofit, he never received a single donation. When his wife died, he moved to

Lafayetteville, a hamlet in northern Westchester County, about ten miles east of the Hudson River.

Langdon's responses to Scott's questions were an equal mix of reliable fact, truth-tweaking, misremembering, and flat-out fabrication. He said Buckey O'Neill was killed on top of San Juan Heights, not the bottom, and that the regiment first charged San Juan Hill, not Kettle Hill. He claimed to have nearly died in a knife fight on the train to Tampa, eaten boa constrictor in Cuba, caught yellow fever in El Caney, boxed the British heavyweight champion in 1901, and made a fortune with his patents. Very little of what he said was even close to true.

It didn't matter. By then the Rough Riders had long since ceased to be purely historical figures. They became myths, as much an American legend as Daniel Boone and Davy Crockett. Langdon was among the last of a regiment that was famous as much for what it symbolized as for what it did—confident, idealistic American warriors, ready to take on the world.

Hamner and Brito both died in 1973. Langdon lived another two years, and died on June 29, 1975, less than two months after the fall of Saigon and the close of the Vietnam War. It was a fitting end to the Rough Riders. Conceived at the dawn of the American century, their last member survived to see the country's first defeat.[35]

ACKNOWLEDGMENTS

Whenever I embark on a book project, I say a prayer of thanks for the network of archives, research centers, and libraries—both online and in real life—that make work like this possible. In particular, I must thank the staff at the Houghton Library at Harvard University; the Albert and Shirley Small Special Collections Library at the University of Virginia; the Thomas A. Edison Papers at Rutgers University; the Columbia Center for Oral History; the Library of Congress; and the Fray Angélico Chávez History Library and the New Mexico State Records Center and Archives, both in Santa Fe. I extend special thanks to Michael Rebman at the City of Las Vegas Museum, who patiently walked me through the museum's extensive holdings on the Rough Riders, including its file on Rough Rider imposters. I would also like to thank Shane Bernard of the McIlhenny Company Archives in Avery Island, Louisiana, who shared with me material related to John McIlhenny.

Toward the end of my research, I made a brief but invaluable trip to Santiago de Cuba to see the sites of the Fifth Corps campaign. I could not have made it without the advice of Damien Cave and Hannah Berkeley Cohen. While there, I stayed at Roy's Terrace Inn; I recommend it to anyone passing through this lovely city.

Whatever one thinks of the introductory chapter, it would not be half as good as it is were it not for the input of James Goodman, David Greenberg, Jim Ledbetter, Michael Massing, Natalia Mehlman Petrzela, and James Traub. Thank you.

This book would not exist were it not for Kathy Belden, my editor at Scribner, who not only took a chance on my proposal, but took my gawky first draft and turned it into something worth reading. Kathy and her entire team deserves my sincere thanks. I will forever be in debt to Heather Schroder, my agent, who first gave me the opportunity to pursue book writing and has been with me ever since.

My wife, Joanna, and my children, Talia and Elliot, suffered greatly for this book, both from my long absences and my diminished attention at home. I love you all the more for putting up with me.

NOTES

Introduction: New York City, 1899

1 Moses King, *The Dewey Reception in New York City: Nine-Hundred and Eighty Views and Portraits* (New York: M. King, 1899), pp. 110–11.

2 *New York Times*, October 1, 1899, cited in Mike Wallace, *Greater Gotham: A History of New York City from 1898 to 1919* (New York: Oxford University Press, 2017), p. 38; King, p. 122.

3 *New York Times*, October 3, 1899.

4 Theodore Roosevelt, *The Letters of Theodore Roosevelt: The Years of Preparation.* Edited by Elting E. Morison. Cambridge: Harvard University Press, 1951, p. 495.

5 Gail Bederman, *Manliness and Civilization: A Cultural History of Gender and Race in the United States, 1880–1917* (Chicago: University of Chicago Press, 1996), p. 190.

6 Jacob A. Riis, *Theodore Roosevelt, the Citizen* (New York: Macmillan, 1904), p. 182.

7 Frank Ninkovich, *Global Dawn: The Cultural Foundation of American Internationalism, 1865–1890* (Cambridge: Harvard University Press, 2009), p. 39.

8 Edward M. Coffman, *The Regulars: The American Army, 1898–1941* (Cambridge: Harvard University Press, 2004), p. 4; J. P. Clark, *Preparing for War: The Emergence of the Modern U.S. Army, 1815–1917* (Cambridge: Harvard University Press, 2016), p. 116; *New York Times*, April 19, 1898.

9 Reprinted in the Cameron County, Pennsylvania, *Press,* June 30, 1898.

Chapter 1: "The Puerility of His Simplifications"

1 John D. Long, *America of Yesterday: The Diary of John D. Long*, ed. Lawrence Shaw Mayo (Boston: Atlantic Monthly Press, 1923), p. 139.

2 John D. Long, *The Journal of John D. Long*, ed. Margaret Long (Rindge, N.H.: Richard R. Smith Publisher, 1956), p. 212.

3 David F. Trask, *The War with Spain in 1898* (New York: Free Press, 1981), pp. 24–25.

4 For an unmatchable and quite enjoyable discussion of Roosevelt's speaking style,

NOTES

see Edmund Morris's prologue to *The Rise of Roosevelt*, especially pages xxv–xxvi (New York: Coward, McCann & Geoghegan, 1979; revised and expanded, 2001).

5 Long, *The Journal of John D. Long*, p. 213.

6 Ibid.

7 David McCullough, *Mornings on Horseback: The Story of an Extraordinary Family, a Vanished Way of Life, and the Unique Child Who Became Theodore Roosevelt* (New York: Simon & Schuster, 1981), pp. 111–12 and 162; Tim Egan, *The Big Burn: Teddy Roosevelt and the Fire That Saved America* (New York: Houghton Mifflin, 2009), p. 35.

8 Edmund Morris, *The Rise of Roosevelt*, pp. 58, 59, 73.

9 For details of Theodore Roosevelt Sr.'s will, see *New York Times*, February 17, 1878; McCullough, p. 126; Edmund Morris, *The Rise of Roosevelt*, p. 145.

10 McCullough, pp. 306–8; Edmund Morris, *The Rise of Roosevelt*, p. 143.

11 Ibid., p. 333; C. W. Guthrie, ed., *The First Ranger: Adventures of a Pioneer Forest Ranger* (Huson, Mont.: Redwing Publishing, 1995), pp. 26–28.

12 For a general introduction to the Hay-Adams circle, see Patricia O'Toole, *The Five of Hearts: An Intimate Portrait of Henry Adams and His Friends, 1880–1918* (New York: Clarkson Potter, 1990); Morris, p. 425.

13 For an overview of Roosevelt's time as police commissioner, see Richard Zachs, *Island of Vice: Theodore Roosevelt's Quest to Clean Up Sin-Loving New York* (New York: Anchor, 2012).

14 Edmund Morris, *The Rise of Roosevelt*, pp. 578, 584.

15 William McKinley, Inaugural Address, March 4, 1897, http://www.presidency. ucsb.edu/ws/index.php?pid=25827&st=inaugural&st1=, accessed May 30, 2018.

16 Samuel P. Huntington, *The Soldier and the State: The Theory and Politics of Civil-Military Relations* (Cambridge: Belknap Press of Harvard University Press, 1957), p. 222.

17 Margaret Leech, *In the Days of McKinley* (New York: Harper & Bros., 1959), p. 213.

18 Theodore Roosevelt, *An Autobiography* (New York: The Macmillan Company, 1913; rpt., Modern Library, 2004), p. 459; *Naval Institute Proceedings* 23, no. 3 (1897): 447.

19 Leech, p. 157; Michael Blow, *A Ship to Remember: The Maine and the Spanish-American War* (New York: William Morrow, 1992), pp. 20–21.

20 Hay cited in Edmund Morris, *The Rise of Roosevelt*, p. 455; David Healy, *U.S. Expansionism: The Imperialist Urge in the 1890s* (Madison: University of Wisconsin Press, 1970), pp. 115, 119.

21 Henry James, "Theodore Roosevelt and the National Consciousness," *Literature*, April 23, 1898, p. 484.

22 Chris Emmett, *In the Path of Events, with Colonel Martin Lalor Crimmins: Soldier—Naturalist—Historian* (Waco, Tex.: Jones & Morrison, 1959), p. 71; Hermann Hagedorn, *Leonard Wood: A Biography* (New York: Harper & Brothers, 1931), pp. 133–36.

23 Letter from Theodore Roosevelt to Leonard Wood, January 11, 1898, Box 26, Leonard Wood Papers, Library of Congress; Theodore Roosevelt, *The Rough Riders* (New York: Charles Scribner's Sons, 1899; rpt., Library of America, 2004), p. 14.

NOTES

Chapter 2: "One Does Not Make War with Bonbons"

1 John H. Latane, "Intervention of the United States in Cuba," *The North American Review* 166, no. 496 (March 1898): 350–61; George H. Gibson, "Opinion in North Carolina Regarding the Acquisition of Texas and Cuba, 1835–1855," *The North Carolina Historical Review* 37, no. 2 (April 1960): 185–201.

2 John Lawrence Tone, *War and Genocide in Cuba, 1895–1898* (Chapel Hill: University of North Carolina Press, 2006), pp. 1–3.

3 George C. Musgrave, *Under Three Flags in Cuba: A Personal Account of the Cuban Insurrection and Spanish-American War* (Boston: Little, Brown, & Co., 1899), p. 16.

4 *Forum*, February 1897, p. 659.

5 Tone, p. 28.

6 Musgrave, p. 19; Frederick Funston, *Memories of Two Wars: Cuban and Philippine Experiences* (London: Constable & Co., 1912), p. 64.

7 *The Cosmopolitan*, August 1895, p. 470; Philip S. Foner, *The Spanish-Cuban-American War and the Birth of American Imperialism, 1895–1902* (New York: Monthly Review Press, 1972), pp. 168fn, 169; *Frank Leslie's Popular Monthly*, February 1897, p. 28.

8 Funston, p. 19.

9 Foner, pp. 95, 174.

10 Funston, p. 32.

11 Tone, pp. 82, 155; Musgrave, p. 22.

12 Louis A. Pérez Jr., *Cuba Between Empires: 1878–1902* (Pittsburgh: University of Pittsburgh Press, 1983), pp. 53–55.

13 Tone, p. 164.

14 Stephen Bonsal, *The Real Condition of Cuba To-Day* (New York: Harper & Brothers, 1897), p. 139.

15 Ibid., p. 109.

16 *Leslie's Weekly*, March 24, 1898, p. 199; Clara Barton, "Our Work and Observations in Cuba," *North American Review*, May 1898, p. 552; Tone, pp. 223–24.

17 Musgrave, pp. 25, 29.

18 Bonsal, *The Real Condition of Cuba To-Day*, p. 149.

19 Charles H. Brown, *The Correspondents' War: Journalists in the Spanish-American War* (New York: Charles Scribner's Sons, 1967), p. 11.

20 Charles Bronson Rea, *Facts and Fakes About Cuba: A Review of the Various Stories Circulated in the United States Concerning the Present Insurrection* (New York: George Munro's Sons, 1897), p. 26.

21 Arthur Lubow, *The Reporter Who Would Be King: A Biography of Richard Harding Davis* (New York: Charles Scribner's Sons, 1992), p. 3.

22 Ibid., p. 68.

23 Douglas Allen, *Frederic Remington and the Spanish-American War* (New York: Crown, 1971), p. 11; David Nasaw, *The Chief: The Life of William Randolph Hearst* (New York: Houghton Mifflin, 2000), p. 127.

24 Letter from Richard Harding Davis to Rebecca Davis, n.d., Richard Harding Davis Papers, University of Virginia.

25 Letter from Richard Harding Davis to Rebecca Davis, January 16, 1897, Richard Harding Davis Papers, University of Virginia.

26 Ibid.

27 Davis, *Cuba in War Time*, pp. 53–54; Letter from Richard Harding Davis to Rebecca Davis, January 16, 1897, Richard Harding Davis Papers, University of Virginia.

28 Lubow, pp. 142–44.

29 *New York Journal*, February 12, 1897; Lubow, p. 143.

30 Letter from Richard Harding Davis to Charles Davis, n.d., Richard Harding Davis Papers, University of Virginia; Davis, *Cuba in War Time*, p. 104.

31 Davis, *Cuba in War Time*, p. 129.

32 Ibid., p. 133.

33 Roosevelt, *The Rough Riders*, p. 14; John J. Ingalls, *America's War for Humanity* (New York: N. D. Thompson Publishing Co., 1898), p. 18.

34 *New York Journal*, February 9, 1898.

35 Beveridge cited in Healy, p. 101; James cited in Healy, p. 104.

36 Ernest R. May, *Imperial Democracy: The Emergence of America as a Great Power* (New York: Harcourt Brace Jovanovich, 1961), pp. 3–5.

37 Cullom cited in Walter Millis, *The Martial Spirit: A Study of Our War with Spain* (Boston: Houghton Mifflin, 1931), p. 29.

38 *Leslie's Weekly*, March 24, 1898, p. 197; Ingalls, p. 20.

39 New York *Sun*, April 4, 1898.

40 Foner, pp. 130–31.

41 Ibid., pp. 210–14.

42 John L. Offner, *An Unwanted War: The Diplomacy of the United States and Spain over Cuba, 1895–1898* (Chapel Hill: University of North Carolina Press, 1992), pp. 86–100.

43 Trask, p. 32.

44 Roosevelt, *The Rough Riders*, p. 14; Leonard Wood, "Research Materials for the Rough Riders," Hermann Hagedorn Collection, Theodore Roosevelt Collection, Houghton Library, Harvard University.

45 Evan Thomas, *The War Lovers: Roosevelt, Lodge, Hearst, and the Rush to Empire, 1898* (New York: Little, Brown, 2010), p. 287.

Chapter 3: "A Burst of Thunder"

1 Long, *America of Yesterday*, p. 162.

2 *Final Report on Removing Wreck of Battleship "Maine" from Harbor of Habana, Cuba* (Washington, D.C.: U.S. Government Printing Office, 1913), p. 7.

3 Blow, p. 38.

4 Ibid., p. 93; Percy H. Epler, *The Life of Clara Barton* (New York: The Macmillan Co., 1915), p. 287.

5 Blow, pp. 96–101.

6 One could argue that the April 27, 1865, sinking of the *Sultana*, a paddlewheel steamer carrying former Union prisoners of war, killing 1,192, was a naval disaster. But the *Sultana* was a commercial vessel, and not all its passengers were military.

7   George Hyman Rickover, *How the Battleship Maine Was Destroyed* (Annapolis: Naval Institute Press, 1976), passim.

8   Davis letter cited in Lubow, p. 154; Roosevelt's letter to Adams cited in *Scribner's*, November 1919, p. 524.

9   Hagedorn, *Leonard Wood*, p. 141.

10 Long, *America of Yesterday*, pp. 163–70.

11 Theodore Roosevelt, *The Letters of Theodore Roosevelt*, pp. 801–3.

12 Mark Lee Gardner, *Rough Riders: Theodore Roosevelt, His Cowboy Regiment, and the Immortal Charge Up San Juan Hill* (New York: William Morrow, 2016), p. 14.

13 Michelle Bray Davis and Rollie W. Quimby, "Senator Proctor's Cuban Speech: Speculations on a Cause of the Spanish-American War," *Quarterly Journal of Speech* 55, no. 2 (1969): 131–41.

14 Speech by Senator Redfield Proctor on the Floor of the U.S. Senate on March 17, 1898, http://www.spanamwar.com/proctorspeech.htm, accessed September 25, 2018.

15 Ingalls, p. 17; *Wall Street Journal*, cited in Gerald F. Linderman, *The Mirror of War: American Society and the Spanish-American War* (Ann Arbor: University of Michigan Press, 1974), p. 42.

16 *Sacramento Daily Record-Tribune*, April 2, 1898; *Scranton Tribune*, April 28, 1898; R. A. Alger, *The Spanish-American War* (New York: Harper & Brothers, 1901), p. 2.

17 The *Independent* article was reprinted in the New York *Sun*, April 4, 1898; *Sacramento Daily Record-Tribune*, April 2, 1898; Millis, p. 161.

18 Official Report of the Naval Court of Inquiry into the Loss of the Battleship Maine, March 21, 1898, http://www.spanamwar.com/mainerpt.htm, accessed May 30, 2018.

19 *Cincinnati Inquirer*, March 28, 1898.

20 New York *Sun*, March 29, 1898; *Kansas City Journal*, March 31, 1898; Edmund Morris, *The Rise of Theodore Roosevelt*, p. 638.

21 William McKinley, First Annual Message, December 6, 1897, http://www.presidency.ucsb.edu/ws/index.php?pid=29538, accessed May 30, 2018

22 Linderman, p. 24; Trask, p. 58.

23 Robert W. Merry, *President McKinley: Architect of the American Century* (New York: Simon & Schuster, 2017), p. 260.

24 *Washington Post*, February 27, 1898.

25 Merry, p. 263.

26 Long, *America of Yesterday*, p. 176.

27 George E. Vincent, ed., *Theodore W. Miller, Rough Rider: His Diary as a Soldier Together with the Story of His Life* (Akron: Privately printed, 1899), pp. 3, 64–68.

28 Ibid., pp. 64, 68–69; "Letter from Theodore Westwood Miller to Mina Miller (Mrs. Thomas A.) Edison, April 22nd, 1898," Edison Papers Digital Edition, http://edison.rutgers.edu/digital/items/show/146758, accessed May 29, 2018.

29 *Sacramento Record-Union*, April 19, 1898.

30 "A Rough Rider from Chautauqua," *Chautauqua Daily*, August 18, 2016, http://chqdaily.com/2016/08/a-rough-rider-from-chautauqua, accessed May 29, 2018; Hendrick, p. 192.

31 "Letter from Theodore Westwood Miller to Mina Miller (Mrs. Thomas A.) Edison, April 22nd, 1898"; "Letter from Theodore Westwood Miller to Grace A. Miller, Mina Miller (Mrs. Thomas A.) Edison, April 26th, 1898," Edison Papers Digital Edition, http://edison.rutgers.edu/digital/items/show/146759, accessed May 29, 2018.

32 New York *Sun*, April 22, 1898; New York *Sun*, April 4, 1898; *Sacramento Daily Record-Union*, April 19, 1898; Hillsboro, Oregon, *News Herald*, April 28, 1898; New York *Sun*, April 26, 1898.

33 Edmund Morris, *The Rise of Theodore Roosevelt*, p. 336.

34 *New York Tribune*, April 19, 1898; *Topeka State Journal*, March 25, 1898; New York *Sun*, April 4, 1898; *Los Angeles Herald*, April 19, 1898.

35 *El Paso Daily Herald*, April 20, 1898.

36 *Washington Times*, May 1, 1898. For a thorough history of the other two regiments, see Clifford P. Westermeier, *Who Rush to Glory: The Cowboy Volunteers of 1898* (Caldwell, Idaho: Caxton Printers, 1958).

37 Edmund Morris, *The Rise of Theodore Roosevelt*, p. 641; *New York Tribune*, April 19, 1898.

38 *Des Moines Register*, July 10, 1898.

39 Long, *America of Yesterday*, p. 186.

Chapter 4: *"The Days of '61 Have Indeed Come Again"*

1 New York *Sun*, May 8, 1898.

2 Ibid.

3 Ibid.

4 Letter to Leonard Wood from Theodore Roosevelt, May 9, 1898, Leonard Wood Papers, Library of Congress.

5 Ibid.

6 *Scranton Tribune*, April 28, 1898; *New York Tribune*, May 1, 1898; Richard Hofstadter, *The Paranoid Style in American Politics* (New York: Alfred A. Knopf, 1965), pp. 158–59.

7 Huntington, pp. 222–30.

8 Edward M. Coffman, *The Old Army: A Portrait of the American Army in Peacetime, 1784–1898* (New York: Oxford University Press, 1986), p. 216.

9 Ibid., p. 404.

10 Graham A. Cosmas, *An Army for Empire: The United States Army in the Spanish-American War* (Columbia: University of Missouri Press, 1971), p. 88.

11 Alger, p. 7; Coffman, *The Old Army*, p. 5.

12 Trask, pp. 104–7.

13 A. C. M. Azoy, *Charge! The Story of the Battle of San Juan Hill* (New York: Longmans, Green, 1961), p. 26.

14 Alger, p. 7; "Letter from Theodore Westwood Miller to Mina Miller (Mrs. Thomas A.) Edison, April 22nd, 1898," Edison Papers Digital Edition, http://edison.rutgers.edu/digital/items/show/146758, accessed June 1, 2018; "Letter from Theodore Westwood Miller to Mina Miller (Mrs. Thomas A.) Edison,

May 12th, 1898," Edison Papers Digital Edition, http://edison.rutgers.edu/digital/items/show/146761, accessed June 1, 2018.

15 Lewis L. Gould, *The Spanish-American War and President McKinley* (Lawrence: University Press of Kansas, 1982), p. 12; New York *Sun*, April 22, 1898; White cited in Frank Freidel, *The Splendid Little War: The Dramatic Story of the Spanish-American War* (New York: Little, Brown, 1958), p. 27.

16 White cited in Freidel, p. 28; Alger, p. 16.

17 Clark, *Preparing for War*, p. 167.

18 Stephen Bonsal, *The Fight for Santiago: The Story of the Soldier in the Cuban Campaign from Tampa to the Surrender* (London: Doubleday & McClure, 1899), p. xix.

19 Alger, p. 44.

20 Paul H. Carlson, *"Pecos Bill": A Military Biography of William R. Shafter* (College Station: Texas A&M University Press, 1989), pp. 11–21.

21 Ibid., p. 80.

22 Ibid., pp. 7–30; 80–102.

23 Ibid., pp. 89–120, 163; Arthur Lee, *"A Good Innings": The Private Papers of Viscount Lee of Fareham*, ed. Alan Clark (London: William Clowes & Sons, 1974), p. 64.

24 Roosevelt, *An Autobiography*, pp. 475–76.

25 Ibid., p. 480.

26 Ibid., p. 476.

27 Roosevelt, *The Letters of Theodore Roosevelt*, p. 821.

28 Harvard Crimson, *Harvard Volunteers, 1898* (Cambridge: Harvard Crimson, 1898), p. 38.

29 Ibid.; J. O. Wells, *Diary of a Rough Rider* (St. Joseph, Mich.: A. B. Morse, n.d.), pp. 4–5.

30 James Church, "Research Materials for the Rough Riders," Hermann Hagedorn Collection, Theodore Roosevelt Collection, Houghton Library, Harvard University.

31 Reminiscences of Jesse Langdon, Oral History Collection, Columbia University.

32 Roosevelt, *An Autobiography*, p. 480.

33 Roosevelt, *The Letters of Theodore Roosevelt*, p. 829.

34 Dale L. Walker, *The Boys of '98: Theodore Roosevelt and the Rough Riders* (New York: Forge, 1998), p. 108; Roosevelt Diary entry, May 12, 1898, Hermann Hagedorn Collection, Theodore Roosevelt Collection, Houghton Library, Harvard University.

Chapter 5: "This Untailor-Made Roughness"

1 *San Antonio Daily Light*, May 6, 1898.

2 Ibid.

3 Hagedorn, *Leonard Wood*, pp. 25–27.

4 Ibid., p. 43.

5 Ibid., p. 52.

6 Paul Andrew Hutton, *The Apache Wars: The Hunt for Geronimo, the Apache Kid, and the Captive Boy Who Started the Longest War in American History* (New York: Crown, 2016), p. 346.

7 *Washington Herald*, May 10, 1914; Hagedorn, *Leonard Wood*, p. 71; Hutton, p. 77.

8 Hutton, pp. 419–20.

9 Hagedorn, *Leonard Wood*, p. 132.

10 Roosevelt, *The Rough Riders*, p. 18; Gardner, p. 26.

11 Lewis F. Fisher, *Saving San Antonio: The Preservation of a Heritage* (San Antonio: Maverick Books, 2016), p. 25.

12 Ibid., p. 26.

13 Emmett, p. 84.

14 Charles Herner, *The Arizona Rough Riders* (Prescott, Ariz.: Sharlot Hall Museum Press, 1998), pp. 10–12.

15 Ibid., pp. 12–14.

16 Ibid., pp. 34–40.

17 *Chicago Record, War Stories by Staff Correspondents in the Field* (Chicago: *Chicago Record*, 1898), p 150.

18 Ibid.

19 Herner, p. 41; "Biography of Alvin Ash," Alvin Ash Papers, Box 1, Fray Angélico Chávez History Library; Royal Prentice, "The Rough Riders," *New Mexico Historical Review* 26, no. 4 (October 1951): 266.

20 Arthur Cosby, "A Rough Rider Looks Back," p. 20. Unpublished copy available in the Hermann Hagedorn Collection, Theodore Roosevelt Collection, Houghton Library, Harvard University.

21 John Campbell Greenway, *It Was the Grandest Sight I Ever Saw: Experiences of a Rough Rider Recorded in the Letters of Lieutenant John Campbell Greenway*, ed. Charles Herner (Tucson: Arizona Historical Society, 2001), pp. 4–5.

22 *Las Vegas Daily Optic*, December 13, 1973; for examples of attitudes in the Southwest toward Cuba and Spain, see "A Rough Rider's Recollections of the Cuban Campaign After 50 Years," in Royal Prentice Papers, Fray Angélico Chávez History Library; *El Paso Daily Herald*, April 20, 1898.

23 *Arizona Republic*, May 19, 1898; Herner, p. 50.

24 Gardner, p. 23.

25 Dale Walker, "Arizona's Buckey O'Neill and the Rough Riders," *Montana: The Magazine of Western History* 21, no. 1 (Winter 1971): 60–71.

26 New York *Sun*, August 7, 1898; Thomas Ledwidge, "Research Materials for the Rough Riders," Hermann Hagedorn Collection, Theodore Roosevelt Collection, Houghton Library, Harvard University.

27 Herner, p. 68; "A Rough Rider's Recollections of the Cuban Campaign After 50 Years," in Royal Prentice Papers, Fray Angélico Chávez History Library; Emmett, p. 112.

28 *San Antonio Daily Light*, May 13, 1898; Gardner, p. 48.

29 John C. Rayburn, "The Rough Riders in San Antonio, 1898," *Arizona and the West* 3, no. 2 (Summer 1961): 125–26.

30 Ibid.

31 *San Antonio Daily Express*, May 26, 1898; George Curry, *George Curry, 1861–1947: An Autobiography*, ed. H. B. Hening (Albuquerque: University of New Mexico Press, 1958), p. 122. The chorus to the song went:

> When you hear
> Dem-a bells go ding, ling, ling
> All join round
> And sweetly you must sing.
> And when the verse am through
> In the chorus all join in,
> There'll be a hot time
> In the old town tonight.

32 Hall, p. 29; *San Antonio Daily Light*, May 25, 1898.

33 Curry, p. 122; Emmett, p. 87.

34 *San Antonio Daily Express*, May 11, 1898.

35 Wells, p. 7; Rayburn, pp. 118, 124.

36 Tom Hall, *The Fun and Fighting of the Rough Riders* (New York: Frederick A. Stokes Co., 1899), p. 8; Roosevelt Diary, May 21, 1898, Hermann Hagedorn Collection, Theodore Roosevelt Collection, Houghton Library, Harvard University.

37 Hall, p. 12.

38 Ibid., p. 11.

39 Ibid., p. 38.

40 Emmett, p. 80; James Brown, "Research Materials for the Rough Riders," Hermann Hagedorn Collection, Theodore Roosevelt Collection, Houghton Library, Harvard University.

41 *Chicago Record*, p. 152; Brown, "Research Materials for the Rough Riders."

42 *San Antonio Daily Express*, May 16, 1898.

43 Emmett, p. 107. The sword is on display at Sagamore Hill National Historic Site.

44 Billy McGinty, "Research Materials for the Rough Riders," Hermann Hagedorn Collection, Theodore Roosevelt Collection, Houghton Library, Harvard University.

45 Roosevelt, *The Rough Riders*, pp. 25, 39.

46 Ibid, p. 32.

47 Curry, p. 122.

48 Prentice, "The Rough Riders," p. 269; Cosby, p. 29.

49 Prentice, "The Rough Riders," p. 269; Frank P. Hayes, "Research Materials for the Rough Riders," Hermann Hagedorn Collection, Theodore Roosevelt Collection, Houghton Library, Harvard University.

50 Hall, p. 45; Corinne Roosevelt Robinson, *My Brother Theodore Roosevelt* (New York: Charles Scribner's Sons, 1921), p. 167.

51 Sherrard Coleman, "Research Materials for the Rough Riders," Hermann Hagedorn Collection, Theodore Roosevelt Collection, Houghton Library, Harvard University.

52 Leonard Wood, "Research Materials for the Rough Riders," Hermann Hage-dorn Collection, Theodore Roosevelt Collection, Houghton Library, Harvard University; Curry, p. 123.

53 Trask, pp. 162–71.

54 "Biography of Alvin Ash," Box 1, Alvin Ash Papers, Box 1, Fray Angélico Chávez History Library.

55 Letter from Leonard Wood to William McKinley, May 22, 1898, Leonard Wood Papers, Library of Congress.

56 Letter from Theodore Roosevelt to unknown addressee, May 8, 1898, Hermann Hagedorn Collection, Theodore Roosevelt Collection, Houghton Library, Harvard University.

57 Herner, p. 65.

58 Benjamin Colbert, "Research Materials for the Rough Riders," Hermann Hage-dorn Collection, Theodore Roosevelt Collection, Houghton Library, Harvard University.

Chapter 6: "A Perfect Welter of Confusion"

1 Roosevelt, *The Rough Riders*, p. 44.

2 Ibid, p. 45; *San Antonio Daily Express*, May 30, 1898.

3 Henry La Motte, "With the Rough Riders," *St. Nicholas*, July 1899, p. 730.

4 Douglas Brinkley, *The Wilderness Warrior: Theodore Roosevelt and the Crusade for America* (New York: HarperCollins, 2009), p. 317; Roosevelt, *The Rough Riders*, pp. 43–44.

5 Guy Le Stourgeon, *San Antonio Daily Light*, June 8, 1898; Frank P. Hayes, "Research Materials for the Rough Riders," Hermann Hagedorn Collection, Theodore Roosevelt Collection, Houghton Library, Harvard University.

6 Guy Le Stourgeon, *San Antonio Daily Light*, June 4, 1898; Cosby, p. 46.

7 Roosevelt, *The Rough Riders*, p. 46; Trask, p. 181.

8 Hall, p. 66; Charles Johnson Post, *The Little War of Private Post: The Spanish-American War Seen Up Close* (New York: Little, Brown, 1966; rpt., Bison Books, 1999), p. 15; Hall, p. 67.

9 "Rough Riders," *Country Roads Magazine*, February 22, 2017, http://country-roadsmagazine.com/art-and-culture/history/rough-riders-john-avery-mcilhen-ny-tabasco/, accessed April 4, 2018; Shane K. Bernard, *Tabasco: An Illustrated History* (Avery Island, La.: McIlhenny Company, 2007), pp. 68–74; Mary Eliza Avery McIlhenny, [Avery Island, La.], to Mrs. Sidney Bradford [Mary Avery McIlhenny Bradford], New Orleans, La., June 2, 1898, McIlhenny Company Archives, Avery Island, La.

10 Guy Le Stourgeon, *San Antonio Daily Light*, June 6, 1898.

11 Vincent, ed., pp. 69, 77.

12 Ibid.

13 Ibid, p. 78.

14 Ibid.

15 Ibid., pp. 79–80.

16 Ibid., pp. 81–82.

NOTES

17 La Motte, "With the Rough Riders," p. 730; Hall, p. 29.

18 Roosevelt, *The Rough Riders*, p. 47.

19 Curry, p. 123.

20 Roosevelt, *The Rough Riders*, p. 47.

21 Ibid.; George Kennan, *Campaigning in Cuba* (New York: The Century Co., 1899), p. 1; Richard Harding Davis, "The Rocking-Chair Period of the War," *Scribner's*, August 1898, p. 132; French Ensor Chadwick, *The Relations of the United States and Spain: The Spanish-American War* (New York: Charles Scribner's Sons, 1911), p. 3.

22 For an overview of the Tampa area and the buildup during the war, see "Florida and the Spanish-American War of 1898," https://www.floridamemory.com/onlineclassroom/spanish-american-war/, accessed September 28, 2018.

23 Cosmas, p. 14.

24 William H. Landon, *The U.S. Army's Deployment to the Spanish American War and Our Future Strategic Outlook* (Strategy Research Project: U.S. Army War College, 1998), p. 8.

25 Bonsal, *The Fight for Santiago*, p. 51; Edward Ranson, "British Military and Naval Observers in the Spanish-American War," *Journal of American Studies* 3, no. 1 (July 1969): 37; Diary, Box 2, Leonard Wood Papers, Library of Congress.

26 Susan R. Braden, *The Architecture of Leisure: The Florida Resort Hotels of Henry Flagler and Henry Plant* (Gainesville: University Press of Florida, 2002), pp. 258–60.

27 Ibid., pp. 13, 274–76; Davis, "The Rocking-Chair Period of the War," p. 132.

28 Richard Harding Davis, *The Cuban and Porto Rican Campaigns* (New York: Charles Scribner's Sons, 1898), pp. 58, 60; Ranson, "British Military and Naval Observers in the Spanish-American War," p. 33.

29 Letter from Richard Harding Davis to Rebecca Davis, June 1, 1898, Richard Harding Davis Papers, University of Virginia.

30 Davis, "The Rocking-Chair Period of the War," p. 133.

31 Davis, *The Cuban and Porto Rican Campaigns*, p. 56; Lee, p. 61.

32 Stacy A. Cordery, "The Precious Minutes Before the Crowded Hour: Edith and Theodore R in Tampa, 1898," *Theodore Roosevelt Association Journal* 31, no. 1–2 (Winter/Spring 2010): 22–31.

33 Vincent, ed., pp. 89–91.

34 Wells, p. 20.

35 Brinkley, p. 322; Guy Le Stourgeon, *San Antonio Daily Light*, June 12, 1898.

36 Cordery, p. 26; La Motte, "With the Rough Riders," p. 731.

37 Cosby, pp. 50, 56.

38 Richard Harding Davis, *Adventures and Letters of Richard Harding Davis* (New York: Charles Scribner's Sons, 1917), pp. 240–41.

39 Letter from Richard Harding Davis to Charles Davis, n.d., Richard Harding Davis Papers, University of Virginia.

40 Post, p. 58; Walker, p. 140.

41 Willard B. Gatewood Jr., "Negro Troops in Florida 1898," *The Florida Historical Quarterly* 49, no. 1 (July 1970): 4.

42 New York *Sun*, June 10, 1898; Edward A. Johnson, *History of Negro Soldiers in the Spanish-American War, and Other Items of Interest* (Raleigh, N.C.: Capital Printing Co., 1899); p. 23.

43 Gatewood, p. 15.

44 John P. Dyer, *From Shiloh to San Juan: The Life of "Fightin' Joe" Wheeler* (Baton Rouge: Louisiana State University Press, 1941), p. 220.

45 Bonsal, *The Fight for Santiago*, p. 57; Frank P. Hayes, "Research Materials for the Rough Riders," Hermann Hagedorn Collection, Theodore Roosevelt Collection, Houghton Library, Harvard University.

46 Trask, pp. 135–36.

47 Ibid.

48 Ibid.

49 Bonsal, *The Fight for Santiago*, p. 65; Cosmas, p. 185; Long, *America of Yesterday*, p. 192; Frank P. Hayes, "Research Materials for the Rough Riders," Hermann Hagedorn Collection, Theodore Roosevelt Collection, Houghton Library, Harvard University; Curry, p. 125; Roosevelt, *The Rough Riders*, p. 50.

50 Vincent, ed., pp. 94–95.

51 Edmund Morris, *The Rise of Theodore Roosevelt*, p. 657; Trask, p. 175.

52 Roosevelt, *The Rough Riders*, p. 50; Vincent, ed., p. 97; La Motte, "With the Rough Riders," p. 732.

53 Roosevelt, *The Rough Riders*, p. 50; Post, p. 85.

54 Landon, p, 17; Cosmas, p. 187; Clara Barton, *The Red Cross: In Peace and War* (Washington, D.C.: The American Historical Press, 1906), p. 552.

55 Roosevelt, *The Rough Riders*, p. 54; Report of the Commission Appointed by the President to Investigate the Conduct of the War Department in the War with Spain (Washington, D.C.: U.S. Government Printing Office, 1900), p. 3606; Trask, p. 659.

56 The photojournalist Ron Coddington has collected many of these photos in a series of books, including *Faces of the Civil War: An Album of Union Soldiers and Their Stories* (Baltimore: Johns Hopkins University Press, 2004).

57 *Chicago Record*, p. 100.

58 Vincent, ed., pp. 99–100; La Motte, "With the Rough Riders," p. 733.

59 Landon, p. 17; John David Miley, *In Cuba with Shafter* (New York: Charles Scribner's Sons, 1899), pp. 23, 44, 45; *Correspondence Relating to the War with Spain and Conditions Growing out of the Same, Including the Insurrection in the Philippine Islands and the China Expedition* (Washington, D.C.: U.S. Government Printing Office, 1902), p. 540.

Chapter 7: "Who Would Not Risk His Life for a Star?"

1 Letter from Richard Harding Davis to Lemuel Davis, n.d., Richard Harding Davis Papers, University of Virginia; Roosevelt, *The Letters of Theodore Roosevelt*, p. 843.

2 Freidel, p. 54.

3 Davis, *The Cuban and Port Rican Campaigns*, p. 91; Private St. Louis (Alfred Petty), *Forty Years After* (Boston: Chapman & Grimes, 1940), p. 27; Lee cited in Ranson, pp. 39–40; Freidel, pp. 56–57.

4 Roosevelt, *The Letters of Theodore Roosevelt*, p. 837; Vincent, ed., p. 99; Davis, *The Cuban and Porto Rican Campaigns*, p. 94.

5   Vincent, ed., p. 99; Report of the Commission Appointed by the President to Investigate the Conduct of the War Department in the War with Spain (Washington, D.C.: U.S. Government Printing Office, 1899), p. 499; Kennan, *Campaigning in Cuba*, p. 47.

6   James Church, "Research Materials for the Rough Riders," Hermann Hagedorn Collection, Theodore Roosevelt Collection, Houghton Library, Harvard University.

7   "Biography of Alvin Ash," Box 1, Ash Papers, Fray Angélico Chávez History Library.

8   Frank P. Hayes, "Research Materials for the Rough Riders," Hermann Hagedorn Collection, Theodore Roosevelt Collection, Houghton Library, Harvard University; John G. Wilner Jr., "Research Materials for the Rough Riders," ibid.; Trask, p. 195.

9   Vincent, ed., p. 101.

10 Frank P. Hayes, "Research Materials for the Rough Riders," Hermann Hagedorn Collection, Theodore Roosevelt Collection, Houghton Library, Harvard University; *New York Times*, June 29, 1898.

11 Billy McGinty, *Oklahoma Rough Rider: Bill McGinty's Own Story*, eds. Jim Fulbright and Albert Stehno (Norman: University of Oklahoma Press, 2008), p. 16; Roosevelt, *The Rough Riders*, p. 56.

12 Vincent, ed., p. 111; Sherrard Coleman, "Research Materials for the Rough Riders," Hermann Hagedorn Collection, Theodore Roosevelt Collection, Houghton Library, Harvard University; Capron cited in *Chicago Record*, p. 99.

13 "Biography of Alvin Ash," Box 1, Ash Papers, Fray Angélico Chávez History Library; Lubow, p. 55; "A Rough Rider's Recollections of the Cuban Campaign After 50 Years," Box 1, Royal Prentice Papers, Fray Angélico Chávez History Library.

14 Theodore Roosevelt, *Theodore Roosevelt's Letters to His Children*, ed. Joseph Bucklin Bishop (New York: Charles Scribner's Sons, 1919), p. 15; Post, p. 85; "Biography of Alvin Ash," Box 1, Ash Papers, Fray Angélico Chávez History Library; letter from Leonard Wood to Louise Condit Smith, Leonard Wood Papers, Library of Congress.

15 Roosevelt, *The Rough Riders*, pp. 58–60.

16 The dispute is described in Lubow, p. 164. Davis had likewise written a scathing piece about the war preparations, but he carefully limited his criticism to the non-Rooseveltian volunteers.

17 *Leslie's Weekly*, June 23, 1898, p. 23; *Daily Astorian*, July 2, 1898.

18 *Leslie's Weekly*, April 28, 1898, p. 260; *Leslie's Weekly*, June 16, 1898, p. 395.

19 Michael Kazin, *A Godly Hero: The Life of William Jennings Bryan* (New York: Anchor, 2007), p. 88.

20 William Jennings Bryan, *The Life and Speeches of the Honorable William Jennings Bryan* (Baltimore: R. H. Woodward, 1900), p. 59.

21 Walter Hines Page, "The War with Spain and After," *Atlantic Monthly*, June 1898, p. 725.

22 *Manchester Guardian*, May 9, 1898; *Daily Telegraph*, May 10, 1898; *London Spectator*, July 25, 1898.

23 Reprinted in the *Cameron County Press*, June 30, 1898.

NOTES

1 Harrie Irving Hancock, *What One Man Saw: Being the Personal Impressions of a War Correspondent in Cuba* (New York: Street & Smith, 1900), p. 26.
2 Frank P. Hayes, "Research Materials for the Rough Riders," Hermann Hagedorn Collection, Theodore Roosevelt Collection, Houghton Library, Harvard University.
3 Cited in Ranson, p. 42.
4 Foner, p. 349.
5 *San Francisco Call*, June 26, 1898; Foner, p. 350.
6 Cited in Freidel, p. 62.
7 *American Review of Reviews*, August 1898, p. 168; Roosevelt quoted in *Chicago Record*, p. 97; Prentice, "The Rough Riders," pp. 273–74.
8 *Chicago Record*, p. 54.
9 Ibid.
10 Hall, p. 110; Hancock, p. 5; Freidel, p. 64.
11 "US Order of Battle," http://www.spanamwar.com/usoob.htm, accessed September 28, 2018; Correspondence Related to the War with Spain (Washington, D.C.: Government Printing Office, 1902), p. 33.
12 Caspar Whitney, "The Santiago Campaign," *Harper's* 97, no. 581 (October 1898), p. 795; Cosmas, p. 210.
13 Davis, *The Cuban and Porto Rican Campaigns*, p. 127.
14 E. J. McClernand, "The Santiago Campaign," *Infantry Journal* 21 (1922): 284.
15 Roosevelt, *The Rough Riders*, pp. 62–65.
16 Sherrard Coleman, "Research Materials for the Rough Riders," Hermann Hagedorn Collection, Theodore Roosevelt Collection, Houghton Library, Harvard University; Roosevelt, *The Rough Riders*, p. 63.
17 La Motte, "With the Rough Riders," pp. 832–33.
18 Ibid.
19 Roosevelt, *The Rough Riders*, p. 65; Herner, p. 97.
20 David Hughes, "Research Materials for the Rough Riders," Hermann Hagedorn Collection, Theodore Roosevelt Collection, Houghton Library, Harvard University; Hall, p. 120; Letter from Frank Knox to his family, June 30, 1898, Box 2, Frank Knox Papers, Library of Congress.
21 Royal Prentice, "The Rough Riders—Concluded," *New Mexico Historical Review* 27, no. 1 (January 1952): 30; Leonard Wood, Diary, Box 2, Leonard Wood Papers, Library of Congress.
22 Herschel V. Cashin, *Under Fire with the Tenth U.S. Cavalry* (New York: F. T. Neely, 1899; rpt., Niwot: University Press of Colorado, 1993), p. 78.
23 Post, p. 110.
24 Albert E. Smith and Phil A. Khoury, *Two Reels and a Crank: From Nickelodeon to Picture Palaces* (New York: Doubleday, 1952), p. 59. The film historian Charles Musser calls into question whether Smith actually went to Cuba, though he provides no countervailing evidence, and Roosevelt, among others, attests to their presence. See Charles Musser, "The American Vitagraph, 1897 to 1901: Survival and Success in a Competitive Industry," in *Film Before Griffith*, ed. John Fell

(Berkeley: University of California Press, 1983), pp. 37-38. Thank you to David Greenberg for bringing Musser's article to my attention.

25 Edward Marshall, *The Story of the Rough Riders, 1st U.S. Volunteer Cavalry: The Regiment in Camp and on the Battle Field* (New York: G. W. Dillingham Co., 1899), pp. 78–81.

26 Ibid., p. 81; Wells cited in Trask, p. 217; Roosevelt, *The Rough Riders*, p. 78.

27 Vincent, ed., p. 116.

28 Davis, *The Cuban and Porto Rican Campaigns*, p. 137.

29 Ibid.

30 Roosevelt, *The Rough Riders*, p. 80.

31 Ibid.

Chapter 9: *"We're Liable to All Be Killed Today"*

1 Vincent, ed., p. 117.

2 Trask, p. 219.

3 *Hero Tales of the American Soldier and Sailor, as Told by the Heroes Themselves and Their Comrades* (Philadelphia: Century Manufacturing Co., 1899), p. 84; Marshall, *The Story of the Rough Riders*, p. 857; *Chicago Record*, p. 64.

4 Trask, pp. 219–21.

5 Roosevelt, *The Rough Riders*, p. 86; Richard Harding Davis, *Notes of a War Correspondent* (New York: Charles Scribner's Sons, 1911), p. 49.

6 Marshall, pp. 881, 905.

7 *Chicago Record*, p. 66.

8 Davis, *Notes of a War Correspondent*, pp. 48–49.

9 Whitney, "The Santiago Campaign," p. 795.

10 *Los Angeles Times*, July 24, 1898; *Chicago Record*, p. 66.

11 Richard Harding Davis, "The Rough Riders' Fight at Las Guasimas," *Scribner's*, October 1898, p. 259; George Hamner, account of fight at Las Guasimas, Rough Rider Collection, City of Las Vegas Museum.

12 Davis, "The Rough Riders' Fight at Las Guasimas," p. 261.

13 Edward Marshall, "A Wounded Correspondent's Recollections of Guasimas," *Scribner's*, September 1898; Edmund Morris, *The Rise of Theodore Roosevelt*, p. 672; Davis, "The Rough Riders' Fight at Las Guasimas," p. 261.

14 Marshall, "A Wounded Correspondent's Recollections of Guasimas," p. 263.

15 Marshall, *The Story of the Rough Riders*, p. 100.

16 Roosevelt, *The Rough Riders*, p. 236.

17 *Nevada State Journal*, September 13, 1899.

18 Marshall, "A Wounded Correspondent's Recollections," p. 273; Roosevelt, *The Rough Riders*, p. 75.

19 Vincent, ed., p. 117.

20 Dale Walker, "Last of the Rough Riders," *Montana: The Magazine of Western History* 23, no. 3 (Summer 1973); Marshall, *The Story of the Rough Riders*, pp. 119, 104.

21 Marshall, "A Wounded Correspondent's Recollections of Guasimas," p. 890.

NOTES

22 Roosevelt, *The Rough Riders*, p. 72.

23 Ibid., p. 77; Marshall, *The Story of the Rough Riders*, p. 104.

24 Whitney, "The Santiago Campaign," p. 798; "A Rough Rider's Recollections of the Cuban Campaign After 50 Years," Box 1, Royal Prentice Papers, Fray Angélico Sánchez History Library; Hagedorn, *Leonard Wood*, p. 165.

25 Roosevelt, *The Rough Riders*, pp. 75–76.

26 Ibid.

27 Vincent, p. 118; Roosevelt, *The Rough Riders*, p. 77.

28 Roosevelt, *The Rough Riders*, p. 77.

29 Davis, "The Rough Riders' Fight at Las Guasimas," p. 265; Lubow, p. 175.

30 Cosby, p. 87; Davis, "The Rough Riders' Fight at Las Guasimas," p. 267.

31 Davis, "The Rough Riders' Fight at Las Guasimas," p. 268.

32 Ibid.

33 *Washington Times*, June 29, 1898.

34 Davis, "The Rough Riders' Fight at Las Guasimas," p. 269.

35 Ibid.

36 Davis, *Adventures and Letters of Richard Harding Davis*, p. 255; Marshall, *The Story of the Rough Riders*, p. 116.

37 Stephen Crane, *Prose and Poetry* (New York: Library of America, 1984), pp. 999–1000.

38 Ibid.

39 Marshall, "A Wounded Correspondent's Recollections of Guasimas," p. 892.

40 Roosevelt, *The Rough Riders*, p. 80.

41 Davis, "The Rough Riders' Fight at Las Guasimas," p. 268; Roosevelt, *An Autobiography*, p. 491; *San Antonio Daily Light*, July 22, 1898.

42 Roosevelt, *The Rough Riders*, p. 82.

43 Ibid., p. 83.

44 Ibid., pp. 83–84.

45 New York *Sun*, June 27, 1898; *Florence Tribune*, July 2, 1898.

46 Report of the Commission, p. 226; Davis, "The Rough Riders' Fight at Las Guasimas," p. 270.

47 Burr McIntosh, *The Little I Saw of Cuba* (London: F. Tennyson Neely, 1899), p. 117; Lubow, p. 179.

48 Whitney, "The Santiago Campaign," p. 801; Edmund Morris, *The Rise of Theodore Roosevelt*, p. 676.

49 *San Francisco Call*, July 3, 1898.

50 *Daily Astorian*, June 26, 1898; *Washington Times*, June 25, 1898; *Los Angeles Herald*, June 26, 1898.

51 *Arizona Republic*, July 1, 1898.

52 Bonsal, *The Fight for Santiago*, p. 98.

53 Fred Herrig, "Research Materials for the Rough Riders," Hermann Hagedorn Collection, Theodore Roosevelt Collection, Houghton Library, Harvard University.

54 Frank P. Hayes, "Research Materials for the Rough Riders," Hermann Hagedorn Collection, Theodore Roosevelt Collection, Houghton Library, Harvard University.

55 McIntosh, p. 82.

56 Roosevelt, *The Rough Riders*, p. 230.
57 Sherrard Coleman, "Research Materials for the Rough Riders," Hermann Hagedorn Collection, Theodore Roosevelt Collection, Houghton Library, Harvard University; Bonsal, *The Fight for Santiago*, p. 98.
58 Frank P. Hayes, "Research Materials for the Rough Riders," Hermann Hagedorn Collection, Theodore Roosevelt Collection, Houghton Library, Harvard University; Roosevelt, *The Rough Riders*, p. 90; Vincent, ed., p. 122.
59 McIntosh, p. 98.
60 Marshall, "A Wounded Correspondent's Recollections of Guasimas."

Chapter 10: "The Monotony of Continuous Bacon"

1 Roosevelt Diary, Hermann Hagedorn Collection, Theodore Roosevelt Collection, Houghton Library, Harvard University.
2 Vincent, ed., pp. 123–24.
3 Whitney, "The Santiago Campaign," p. 796.
4 Vincent, ed., pp. 124–26.
5 Ibid., pp. 126–27.
6 Ibid., p. 128.
7 John C. Hemment, *Cannon and Camera: Sea and Land Battles of the Spanish-American War in Cuba* (New York; Appleton & Co., 1898), p. 133.
8 Roosevelt, *The Letters of Theodore Roosevelt*, p. 845; Richard Harding Davis letter to Lemuel Davis, June 29, Davis Papers, University of Virginia.
9 Vivian cited in Pérez, *Cuba Between Empires*, p. 207.
10 Whitney, "The Santiago Campaign," p. 797.
11 Roosevelt, *The Rough Riders*, p. 92; F. Allen McCurdy and J. Kirk McCurdy, *Two Rough Riders* (New York: F. Tennyson Neely, 1902), p. 11.
12 George Hamner file, City of Las Vegas Museum; Cosby, p. 88.
13 Roosevelt, *The Rough Riders*, p. 92; Report by the Commission, p. 2263.
14 Richard Harding Davis letter to Charles Davis, June 26, 1898, Davis Papers, University of Virginia; Weller cited in Gardner, p. 136.
15 Richard Harding Davis letter to Charles Davis, June 26, 1898; Richard Harding Davis letter to Lemuel Davis, June 29, 1898, Davis Papers, University of Virginia.
16 Vincent, ed., pp. 130–31.
17 Ibid., p. 131; *Chicago Record*, p 131.
18 Whitney, "The Santiago Campaign," p. 804.
19 Richard Harding Davis, "The Battle of San Juan," *Scribner's*, October 1898; New York *Sun*, June 30, 1898; Clark, p. 172.
20 Davis, *Notes of a War Correspondent*, p. 81.
21 Kristin L. Hoganson, *Fighting for American Manhood: How Gender Politics Provoked the Spanish-American and Philippine-American Wars* (New Haven: Yale University Press, 1998), p 11; *New York Tribune*, May 22, 1898.
22 Foner, p. 347.
23 Ibid., p. 356.
24 The Associated Press article appeared nationally; see, for example, the *Charlotte Observer*, June 28, 1898.

NOTES

25 *Chicago Times-Herald* cited in Tone, p. 218; Hardy cited in Hoganson, p. 50.

26 Frederick W. Ramsden, "Diary of the British Consul at Santiago During the Hostilities," *McClure's*, October 1898, p. 589; José Müller y Tejeiro, *Battles and Capitulation of Santiago de Cuba* (trans.) (Washington, D.C.: U.S. Government Printing Office, 1899), p. 33.

27 Müller y Tejeiro, p. 68.

28 Pamphlet cited in Tone, p. 254.

29 Müller y Tejeiro, pp. 80–84.

30 Leech, p. 249.

31 Roosevelt, *The Rough Riders*, p. 58.

32 Ibid., p. 94.

33 Cosby, pp. 96–97; Vincent, ed., p. 132.

34 Davis, *Notes of a War Correspondent*, p. 80; Davis, "The Battle of San Juan," p. 395.

35 *San Francisco Call*, July 3, 1898; Private St. Louis, p. 42.

Chapter 11: "An Amphitheater for the Battle"

1 Roosevelt, *The Rough Riders,* pp. 95–97; Davis, *The Cuban and Porto Rican Campaigns*, p. 193.

2 Cosby, p. 197; Roosevelt, *The Rough Riders*, p. 97.

3 Roosevelt, *The Rough Riders*, p. 95; Davis, "The Battle of San Juan," pp. 399–400.

4 Lee cited in Ranson, "British Military and Naval Observers in the Spanish-American War," p. 48.

5 McClernand, "The Santiago Campaign," p. 288.

6 Ibid.; Trask, p. 235.

7 James Creelman, *On the Great Highway: The Wanderings and Adventures of a Special Correspondent* (Boston: Lothrop Publishing Co., 1901), p. 198.

8 Ibid., pp. 200–202.

9 Nasaw, p. 139; Trask, pp. 235–38.

10 Whitney, "The Santiago Campaign," pp. 808–10; Roosevelt, *The Rough Riders*, p. 97.

11 La Motte, "With the Rough Riders," p. 830; George Hamner file, City of Las Vegas Museum; Lubow, p. 183; Davis, *Notes of a War Correspondent*, p. 86.

12 Colbert cited in Gardner, p. 149; Trask, pp. 238–39.

13 McClernand, p. 287.

14 Trask, pp. 233–36.

15 Davis, *Notes of a War Correspondent*, p. 82; *Chicago Record*, p. 78; Vincent, ed., p. 133.

16 Cosby, p. 103.

17 Roosevelt, *The Rough Riders*, p. 98; *Chicago Record*, p. 78; Jesse Langdon Oral History, Columbia University.

18 Crane, *Wounds in the Rain: War Stories* (New York: Frederick A. Stokes Co., 1899), p. 13; Trask, p. 240.

19 Davis, "The Battle of San Juan," p. 400; Alger, p. 139; McGinty, p. 29; Davis, *The Cuban and Porto Rican Campaigns*, pp. 204, 209.

310

20 Crane, *Wounds in the Rain*, p. 278.

21 Davis, *The Cuban and Porto Rican Campaigns*, p. 231; Marshall, *The Story of the Rough Riders*, p. 118.

22 Paul Grondahl, *I Rose Like a Rocket: The Political Education of Theodore Roosevelt* (New York: Free Press, 2004), p. 267.

23 Davis, "The Battle of San Juan," p. 400.

24 Knox cited in Freidel, p. 121; Roosevelt, *The Rough Riders*, pp. 101–2.

25 Frederic Remington, "With the Fifth Corps," *Harper's*, November 1898, p. 968; Davis, *The Cuban and Porto Rican Campaigns*, p. 199.

26 Roosevelt, *The Rough Riders*, p. 103.

27 Davis, "The Battle of San Juan," pp. 401–2; Hemment, p. 180.

28 Roosevelt, *The Rough Riders*, p. 104.

29 Ibid., p. 106.

30 *The Santiago Campaign: Reminiscences of the Operations for the Capture of Santiago de Cuba in the Spanish-American War, June and July 1898* (Richmond: Williams Printing Co., 1927), p. 422.

31 Davis, "The Battle of San Juan," p. 402; Lubow, p. 185.

32 Bonsal, *The Fight for Santiago*, p. 194; Cosby, p. 105.

33 Davis, *The Cuban and Porto Rican Campaigns*, p. 218.

34 John Bigelow, *Reminiscences of the Santiago Campaign* (New York: Harper & Brothers, 1899), p. 125.

35 Davis, "The Battle of San Juan," p. 402; Lubow, p. 187.

36 Roosevelt, *The Rough Riders*, p. 107; Greenway, p. 36.

37 Fred Herrig, "Research Materials for the Rough Riders," Hermann Hagedorn Collection, Theodore Roosevelt Collection, Houghton Library, Harvard University; David Hughes file, City of Las Vegas Museum; Roosevelt, *The Rough Riders*, p. 108.

38 Roosevelt, *The Rough Riders*, p. 108; Royal Prentice, "A Rough Rider's Recollections of the Cuban Campaign After 50 Years," Royal Prentice Papers, Fray Angélico Chávez History Library.

39 Letter from David Goodrich to Mary Miller, August 5, 1898, Theodore Roosevelt Collection, Houghton Library, Harvard University.

40 Roosevelt, *The Rough Riders*, p. 110.

41 Müller y Tejeiro, p. 86.

42 Roosevelt, *An Autobiography*, p. 497; Roosevelt, *The Rough Riders*, p. 111.

43 Letter from David Goodrich to Mary Miller, August 5, 1898; Vincent, ed., p. 135.

44 McClernand, "The Santiago Campaign," p. 298; Creelman, pp. 204–6; Trask, p. 236.

45 Alger, p. 140; Arthur Lee, "The Regulars at El Caney," *Scribner's*, October 1898, p. 407.

46 Alger, p. 149; *Copper County Evening News*, July 5, 1898; Trask, p. 245.

47 Roosevelt, *The Rough Riders*, p. 112; Sylvia Jukes Morris, *Edith Kermit Roosevelt: Portrait of a First Lady* (New York: Coward, McCann & Geoghegan, 1980), p. 181; Edmund Morris, *The Rise of Theodore Roosevelt*, pp. 264, 687.

48 Johnson, p. 59; Cashin, p. 147; Roosevelt, *The Rough Riders*, p. 116.

NOTES

49 Roosevelt, *The Rough Riders*, pp. 112–13.
50 Jesse Langdon Oral History, Columbia University.
51 Trask, p. 230.
52 Herbert H. Sargent, *The Campaign of Santiago de Cuba* (Chicago: A. C. McClurg & Co., 1907), p. 120.
53 Walker, p. 234; Roosevelt, *The Rough Riders*, pp. 126–27; Report from Leonard Wood to the Adjutant General of the Cavalry Division, 5th Army Corps, July 6, 1898, Box 26, Leonard Wood Papers, Library of Congress.
54 Davis, "The Battle of San Juan," p. 402; *York Gazette* (Pennsylvania), July 8, 1898.
55 *Mexico Weekly Ledger*, July 7, 1898.
56 Müller y Tejeiro, p. 86; Davis, *The Cuban and Porto Rican Campaigns*, p. 187.
57 Roosevelt, *The Letters of Theodore Roosevelt*, p. 849; Davis, *Notes of a War Correspondent*, p. 72.
58 Cosmas, p. 222; Wells, p. 52.

Chapter 12: "Humpty-Dumpty on the Wall"

1 Richard Harding Davis, "In the Rifle Pits," *Scribner's*, December 1898, p. 644.
2 Letter from William Sanders to Mrs. Sanders, July 19, 1898, Correspondence Concerning the Death of W. H. Sanders, Theodore Roosevelt Collection, Houghton Library, Harvard University.
3 George Hamner file, City of Las Vegas Museum.
4 Unidentified interviewee, "Research Materials for the Rough Riders," Hermann Hagedorn Collection, Theodore Roosevelt Collection, Houghton Library, Harvard University.
5 Joseph Wheeler, *The Santiago Campaign* (Boston: Lamson, Wolffe & Co., 1898), p. 274; George Hamner file, City of Las Vegas Museum; letter from William Sanders to Mrs. Sanders, July 19, 1898; Roosevelt, *The Rough Riders*, pp. 120–21.
6 Roosevelt, *The Rough Riders*, p. 124.
7 Ibid., pp. 183–219 (Appendix A: Muster Out Roll).
8 Knox cited in Freidel, p. 136; Billy McGinty file, City of Las Vegas Museum.
9 Whitney, "The Santiago Campaign," p. 814.
10 George Kennan, "George Kennan's Story of the War," *Outlook*, July 30, 1898.
11 Freidel, p. 144.
12 Lewis Maverick, "Research Materials for the Rough Riders," Hermann Hagedorn Collection, Theodore Roosevelt Collection, Houghton Library, Harvard University; Roosevelt, *The Rough Riders*, pp. 138–40.
13 "List of McKinley Firsts, Part 8: The Spanish-American War Was the First War to Be Managed from a White House War Room Connected to Military Headquarters in Washington, DC and the Field by Both Phone and Telegraph," www.mckinleybirthplacemuseum.org, accessed September 28, 2018.
14 Correspondence Related to the War with Spain, p. 72; Alger, p. 173.
15 Correspondence Related to the War with Spain, p. 79.
16 Müller y Tejeiro, p. 96; Herner, p. 168.
17 Trask, pp. 261–62.

NOTES

18 Captain Victor M. Concas y Palau, cited in Freidel, p. 151.

19 Chadwick, p. 138.

20 Trask, pp. 262–63; Müller y Tejeiro, pp. 102–4.

21 James Parker, *Rear-Admirals Schley, Sampson and Cervera: A Review of the Naval Campaign of 1898, in Pursuit and Destruction of the Spanish Fleet, Commanded by Real-Admiral Pascual Cervera* (New York: The Neale Publishing Co., 1910), pp. 192–93.

22 Ibid., p. 202.

23 Harry Huse, "On the Gloucester After the Battle," *The Century*, May 1899, pp. 115–16.

24 Freidel, p. 177.

25 Müller y Tejeiro, p. 70.

26 Alger, p. 194; Correspondence Related to the War with Spain, p. 116.

27 Freidel, p. 182; John Pershing, *My Life Before the World War, 1860–1917*, ed. John T. Greenwood (Lexington: University Press of Kentucky, 2013), p. 378; Knox cited in Freidel, p. 181.

28 *Leslie's Weekly*, August 18, 1898, p. 135.

29 Ibid.

30 Ibid.; George Hamner file, City of Las Vegas Museum.

31 George Hamner file, City of Las Vegas Museum.

32 Cosmas, p. 253; Vincent, ed., pp. 130–31.

33 Thomas Laird, "Research Materials for the Rough Riders," Hermann Hagedorn Collection, Theodore Roosevelt Collection, Houghton Library, Harvard University; Kennan, *Campaigning in Cuba*, p. 73.

34 *Washington Times*, July 15, 1898; Roosevelt, *The Rough Riders*, pp. 137–38.

35 *Leslie's Weekly*, December 8, 1898, p. 451.

36 Roosevelt, *The Rough Riders*, p. 150.

37 Casualty List, Rough Riders, July 1 to 3, 1898. Attachment to Report of Operations. Record Group 395, National Archives, https://catalog.archives.gov/id /301979, accessed June 2, 2018; Bonsal, *The Fight for Santiago*, p. 303.

38 Davis, "In the Rifle-Pits," p. 644; Post, p. 255; Frank Norris, *The Surrender of Santiago* (San Francisco: Paul Elder & Co., 1917), p. 181; George Hamner file, City of Las Vegas Museum.

39 Hall, p. 210; Roosevelt, *The Rough Riders*, p. 147.

40 David Greenberg, *The Republic of Spin: An Inside History of the American Presidency*. (New York: W. W. Norton, 2016), p. 15; Post, p. 203.

41 Henry Bardshar, "Research Materials for the Rough Riders," Hermann Hagedorn Collection, Theodore Roosevelt Collection, Houghton Library, Harvard University.

42 Ibid.

43 Letter from Henry Cabot Lodge to Theodore Roosevelt, July 6, 1898, Theodore Roosevelt Papers, Library of Congress.

44 Bonsal, *The Fight for Santiago*, p. 388.

45 Crane, *Wounds in the Rain*, p. 298; Davis, *The Cuban and Porto Rican Campaigns*, p. 270.

46 Davis, "In the Rifle Pits," p. 644.

47 Vincent, ed., p. 142.

48 Ibid.

49 Ibid., pp. 142–43.

50 Ibid.

51 Wells, p. 65.

52 Roosevelt, *The Rough Riders*, p. 155.

53 Bonsal, *The Fight for Santiago*, p. 518; Freidel, p. 194; Correspondence Relating to the War with Spain, p. 133; Shafter, speech to the annual banquet of the Los Angeles Chamber of Commerce, February 22, 1899, The Members' Annual Containing Information about the Los Angeles Chamber of Commerce, 1899, p. 39.

54 Norris, pp. 12–13.

55 Letter from Leonard Wood to Louise Condit-Smith, July 15, 1898, Box 190, Leonard Wood Papers, Library of Congress; Kennan, *Campaigning in Cuba*, p. 78.

56 Bonsal, *The Fight for Santiago*, p. 439.

57 Foner, p. 369; Norris, p. 19.

58 Foner, p. 370.

59 Roosevelt Diary, July 18, Hermann Hagedorn Collection, Theodore Roosevelt Collection, Houghton Library, Harvard University; David Hughes, "Research Materials for the Rough Riders," Hermann Hagedorn Collection, Theodore Roosevelt Collection, Houghton Library, Harvard University; Gardner, p. 216; Prentice, "The Rough Riders—Concluded," pp. 41–44; McCurdy, p. 30; Roosevelt, *The Letters of Theodore Roosevelt*, p. 851 [to Lodge], p. 859 [to Alger].

60 Edmund Morris, *The Rise of Theodore Roosevelt*, pp. 690–91; Roosevelt, *The Rough Riders*, 159–61. Morris writes that the officer who swam with Roosevelt to the *Merrimac* was John Greenway, but as Mark Lee Gardner demonstrates, there is no evidence that it was him.

61 Royal Prentice, "A Rough Rider's Recollections of the Cuban Campaign After 50 Years," Box 1, Fray Angélico Chávez History Library; letter from Ralph McFie to May Denier, July 25, 1898, Fray Angélico Chávez History Library.

62 *San Francisco Call*, July 7, 1898; Lubow, p. 189.

63 "Spanish-American War Journal," Box 1, Royal Prentice Papers, Fray Angélico Chávez History Library.

64 Ralph Paine, "Research Materials for the Rough Riders," Hermann Hagedorn Collection, Theodore Roosevelt Collection, Houghton Library, Harvard University; Roosevelt, *The Rough Riders*, p. 236.

65 Ralph Paine, "Research Materials for the Rough Riders," Hermann Hagedorn Collection, Theodore Roosevelt Collection, Houghton Library, Harvard University.

66 Roosevelt, *The Rough Riders*, p. 161.

67 Ibid., pp. 164–65.

68 Henry Bardshar, "Research Materials for the Rough Riders," Hermann Hagedorn Collection, Theodore Roosevelt Collection, Houghton Library, Harvard University.

69 Ibid.

70 Roosevelt, *An Autobiography*, p. 501.

71 *New York Times*, July 29, 1898.

72 Ibid.

73 Ibid.

Chapter 13: "They Look Just Like Other Men"

1 Wells, p. 74; Roosevelt, *The Rough Riders*, p. 219.

2 Trask, pp. 322, 336.

3 "A Rough Rider's Recollections of the Cuban Campaign After 50 Years," Box 1, Royal Prentice Papers, Fray Angélico Chávez History Library; Roosevelt, *The Rough Riders*, p. 165.

4 Greenway, p. 41; Roosevelt, *The Rough Riders*, p. 166.

5 Joseph W. Lee, "Research Materials for the Rough Riders," Hermann Hagedorn Collection, Theodore Roosevelt Collection, Houghton Library, Harvard University; Roosevelt, *The Rough Riders*, p. 167.

6 Ibid., p. 166.

7 Ibid., p. 168; Sherrard Coleman, "Research Materials for the Rough Riders," Hermann Hagedorn Collection, Theodore Roosevelt Collection, Houghton Library, Harvard University.

8 Roosevelt, *The Rough Riders*, p. 167.

9 Alger, p. 273.

10 *Leslie's Weekly*, August 4, 1898, p. 94.

11 Alger, pp. 283, 295, 429, 450.

12 *New York Times*, August 5, 1898.

13 *New York Times*, August 6, 1898. After he left the War Department, Alger was appointed by the governor of Michigan to the United States Senate, where he died in office, in 1907.

14 *New York Times*, May 17, 1998.

15 Leech, p. 194; Wilbur French, "Research Materials for the Rough Riders," Hermann Hagedorn Collection, Theodore Roosevelt Collection, Houghton Library, Harvard University; *Detroit Free Press*, August 21, 1898.

16 Roosevelt, *The Rough Riders*, pp. 167–68.

17 Edwin Emerson, "Life at Camp Wikoff," *Munsey's Magazine*, October 1898, pp. 256–72.

18 Edmund Morris, *The Rise of Theodore Roosevelt*, pp. 695–97; Emerson, "Life at Camp Wikoff."

19 Marshall, *The Story of the Rough Riders*, p. 240.

20 Ibid.

21 George Hamner file, City of Las Vegas Museum; Marshall, *The Story of the Rough Riders*, p. 241; *Boston Globe*, August 16, 1898.

22 Cosby, p. 139; Marshall, *The Story of the Rough Riders*, p. 240.

23 Emerson, "Life at Camp Wikoff"; Jeff Heatley, ed., *Bully! Colonel Theodore Roosevelt, the Rough Riders and Camp Wikoff—Montauk, New York, 1898* (Wainscott, N.Y.: Pushcart Press, 1998), p. 159.

24 Emerson, "Life at Camp Wikoff"; McGinty, pp. 65–66.

25 Edmund Morris, *The Rise of Theodore Roosevelt*, p. 699.

26 Ibid., pp. 700–701.

27 Edmund Morris, *The Rise of Theodore Roosevelt*, p. 703. Coincidentally, Scribner is also the publisher of this book.

28 Emerson, "Life at Camp Wikoff."

29 *Leslie's Weekly*, October 13, 1898, p. 286; Emerson, "Life at Camp Wikoff"; Roosevelt, *The Rough Riders*, pp. 183–219 (muster out roll); *Boston Globe*, August 20, 1898.

30 Emerson, "Life at Camp Wikoff"; McGinty, p. 66.

31 Vincent, ed., pp. 146–50.

32 Ibid., p. 152.

33 Ibid., pp. 154–55.

34 *Summit County Beacon* (Akron), August 25, 1898; Vincent, ed., p. 171; *Washington Times*, July 13, 1898.

35 Vincent, ed., pp. 160–68.

36 Ibid., p. 159.

37 Ibid., pp 169–70.

38 *New York Tribune*, August 27, 1898.

39 McGinty, p. 71.

40 *New York Times*, August 11, 1898.

41 New York *Sun*, August 31, 1898; *Leslie's Weekly*, October 13, 1898; *Austin Statesman*, August 26, 1898.

42 *Leslie's Weekly*, October 13, 1898, p. 287.

43 McCurdy, pp. 44–45.

44 *Leslie's Weekly*, October 13, 1898, p. 287.

45 *Boston Globe*, August 10, 1898; *Baltimore Sun*, August 29, 1898.

46 *Newport Mercury*, September 3, 1898; *New York Journal and Advertiser*, August 30, 1898.

47 Emerson, "Life at Camp Wikoff"; Edmund Morris, *The Rise of Theodore Roosevelt*, p. 705; New York *Sun*, September 4, 1898; Anthony Gavin, "Research Materials for the Rough Riders," Hermann Hagedorn Collection, Theodore Roosevelt Collection, Houghton Library, Harvard University.

48 *Boston Globe*, September 1, 1898; New York *Sun*, September 4, 1898.

49 McGinty, p. 72.

50 Roosevelt, *The Rough Riders*, p. 179.

51 Marshall, *The Story of the Rough Riders*, pp. 247–51; Roosevelt, *The Rough Riders*, p. 173.

52 Marshall, *The Story of the Rough Riders*, pp. 247–51.

53 *Chicago Tribune*, September 14, 1898.

54 Marshall, *The Story of the Rough Riders*, pp. 247–51.

Chapter 14: "The Strenuous Life"

1 *Chicago Tribune*, September 15, 1898.

2 Ibid.; *New York Times*, September 15, 16, 1898.

3 *New York Times*, September 18, 1898; Edmund Morris, *The Rise of Theodore Roosevelt*, p. 709.

NOTES

4   *New York Times*, September 18, 1898. Presumably, the trooper meant San Juan Hill.

5   *Boston Globe*, September 19, 1898; *New York Times*, September 19, 1898; *Chicago Tribune*, September 22, 1898.

6   *New York Times*, September 22, 1898.

7   Ibid.

8   Ibid.

9   Edmund Morris, *The Rise of Theodore Roosevelt*, p. 715.

10 Ibid., pp. 717, 719.

11 Ibid, p. 710.

12 *Washington Post*, October 6, 1898.

13 Edmund Morris, *The Rise of Theodore Roosevelt*, p. 720.

14 https://en.wikipedia.org/wiki/New_York_state_election,_1898, accessed June 2, 2018.

15 William McKinley, *The Speeches and Addresses of William McKinley: From March 1, 1897 to May 31, 1900* (New York: Doubleday & McClure Co., 1900), pp. 159–64.

16 McClure and Morris cited in Louis A. Pérez Jr., *The War of 1898: The United States and Cuba in History and Historiography* (Chapel Hill: University of North Carolina Press, 1998), p. 41; Woodrow Wilson, *A History of the American People* (New York: Harper & Bros., 1902), p. 274.

17 Roosevelt, *An Autobiography*, p. 507.

18 Mitchell Yockelson, "'I Am Entitled to the Medal of Honor and I Want It': Theodore Roosevelt and His Quest for Glory," *Prologue* 30, no. 1 (Spring 1998), https://www.archives.gov/publications/prologue/1998/spring/roosevelt-and-medal-of-honor-1.html, accessed September 28, 2018.

19 Theodore Roosevelt, *The Strenuous Life: Essays and Addresses* (New York: The Century Co., 1903), pp. 1–21.

20 Ibid.

21 Cited in May, *Imperial Democracy*, p. 221.

22 Leech, pp. 388–90; Cosmas, pp. 308–14; Russell F. Weigley, *History of the United States Army* (New York: Macmillan, 1967), p. 314.

23 Clark, p. 184.

24 *New York Times*, September 19, 1898.

25 Matthew Oyos, *In Command: Theodore Roosevelt and the American Military* (Lincoln: Potomac Books, 2018), pp. 77–78, 85; *New York Times*, May 19, 1917.

26 Cited in Pérez, *The War of 1898*, p. 221.

27 *Rough Riders' Round-Up* is available at https://www.youtube.com/watch?v=f87KSq2CFJU, accessed June 2, 2018.

28 *Boston Globe*, September 23, 1898.

29 "Frank Knox," https://www.history.navy.mil/our-collections/photography/us-people/k/knox-frank.html, accessed September 28, 2018; Kent Frates, "The Great McGinty," *True West*, November 14, 2014; McGinty, pp. 154–56.

30 *Cornell Magazine*, July/August 1998, pp. 6–13.

31 *New York Times*, April 12, 1916.

NOTES

32   Information about the Rough Rider reunions on display at the City of Las Vegas Museum, Las Vegas, New Mexico.

33   Impostors file, Rough Rider Collection, City of Las Vegas Museum.

34   Jesse Langdon Oral History, Columbia University.

35   *Poughkeepsie Journal*, June 30, 1975.

BIBLIOGRAPHY

Archives
City of Las Vegas Museum, Las Vegas, N.M.
    Rough Rider Memorial Collection
Columbia University Oral History Collection, New York, N.Y.
    Reminiscences of Jesse Langdon
Fray Angélico Chávez History Library, Santa Fe, N.M.
    Alvin Ash Papers
    Royal Prentice Papers
Harvard University, Cambridge, Mass.
    Theodore Roosevelt Collection
Library of Congress, Washington, D.C.
    Frank Knox Papers
    Theodore Roosevelt Papers
    Leonard Wood Papers
McIlhenny Company Archives, Avery Island, La.
New Mexico State Records Center and Archives, Santa Fe, N.M.
Rutgers University, New Brunswick, N.J.
    Thomas A. Edison Papers
University of Virginia, Charlottesville, Va.
    Richard Harding Davis Papers

Government Documents
Correspondence Relating to the War with Spain. Washington, D.C.: U.S. Government Printing Office, 1902.
Report of the Commission Appointed by the President to Investigate the Conduct of the War Department in the War with Spain. Washington, D.C.: U.S. Government Printing Office, 1900.
Spanish Diplomatic Correspondence and Documents, 1896–1900. Washington, D.C.: U.S. Government Printing Office, 1905.

Books
Abbott, Lawrence F. *Impressions of Theodore Roosevelt*. Garden City, N.Y.: Doubleday, Page & Company, 1919.
Abrahamson, James L. *America Arms for a New Century: The Making of a Great Military Power*. New York: Free Press, 1981.

BIBLIOGRAPHY

Alger, R. A. *The Spanish-American War*. New York: Harper & Brothers, 1901.

Allen, Douglas. *Frederic Remington and the Spanish-American War*. New York: Crown, 1971.

Azoy, A. C. M. *Charge! The Story of the Battle of San Juan Hill*. New York: Longmans, Green, 1961.

Ballou, Maturin M. *Due South; or, Cuba Past and Present*. Boston: Houghton, Mifflin & Co., 1885.

Barton, Clara. *The Red Cross: In Peace and War*. Washington, D.C.: The American Historical Press, 1906.

Bederman, Gail. *Manliness and Civilization: A Cultural History of Gender and Race in the United States, 1880–1917*. Chicago: University of Chicago Press, 1995.

Beisner, Robert L. *From the Old Diplomacy to the New: 1865–1900*. Wheeling, Ill.: Harland Davidson, 1975.

———. *Twelve Against Empire: The Anti-Imperialists, 1898–1900*. New York: McGraw-Hill, 1968.

Bernard, Shane K. *Tabasco: An Illustrated History*. Avery Island, La.: McIlhenny Company, 2007.

Bigelow, John. *Reminiscences of the Santiago Campaign*. New York: Harper & Brothers, 1899.

Blow, Michael. *A Ship to Remember: The Maine and the Spanish-American War*. New York: William Morrow, 1992.

Bonsal, Stephen. *The Fight for Santiago: The Story of the Soldier in the Cuban Campaign from Tampa to the Surrender*. London: Doubleday & McClure, 1899.

———. *The Real Condition of Cuba To-Day*. New York: Harper & Brothers Publishers, 1897.

Braden, Susan R. *The Architecture of Leisure: The Florida Resort Hotels of Henry Flagler and Henry Plant*. Gainesville: University Press of Florida, 2002.

Brands, H. W. *The Reckless Decade: America in the 1890s*. Chicago: University of Chicago Press, 1995.

Brinkley, Douglas. *The Wilderness Warrior: Theodore Roosevelt and the Crusade for America*. New York: HarperCollins, 2009.

Brooks, Van Wyck. *The Confident Years: 1885–1915*. New York: E. P. Dutton, 1952.

Brown, Charles H. *The Correspondents' War: Journalists in the Spanish-American War*. New York: Charles Scribner's Sons, 1967.

Bryan, William Jennings. *The Life and Speeches of the Honorable William Jennings Bryan*. Baltimore: R. H. Woodward, 1900.

Burrows, Edwin G., and Mike Wallace. *Gotham: A History of New York City to 1898*. New York: Oxford University Press, 1999.

Burton, David H. *Theodore Roosevelt: Confident Imperialist*. Philadelphia: University of Pennsylvania Press, 1968.

Carlson, Paul H. *"Pecos Bill": A Military Biography of William R. Shafter*. College Station: Texas A&M University Press, 1989.

Cashin, Herschel V. *Under Fire with the Tenth U.S. Cavalry*. New York: F. T. Neely, 1899; rpt., Niwot: University Press of Colorado, 1993.

Chadwick, French Ensor. *The Relations of the United States and Spain: The Spanish-American War*. New York: Charles Scribner's Sons, 1911.

Cheney, Albert Loren. *Personal Memoirs of the Home Life of the Late Theodore Roosevelt: As Soldier, Governor, Vice President, and President, in Relation to Oyster Bay.* Washington, D.C.: The Cheney Publishing Company, 1919.

Chicago Record. War Stories by Staff Correspondents in the Field. Chicago: *Chicago Record,* 1898.

Clark, J. P. *Preparing for War: The Emergence of the Modern U.S. Army, 1815–1917.* Cambridge: Harvard University Press, 2016.

Coffman, Edward M. *The Old Army: A Portrait of the American Army in Peacetime, 1784–1898.* New York: Oxford University Press, 1986.

———. *The Regulars: The American Army, 1898–1941.* Cambridge: Harvard University Press, 2004.

Cosby, Arthur. "A Rough Rider Looks Back." Unpublished copy available in the Hermann Hagedorn Collection, Theodore Roosevelt Collection, Harvard University.

Cosmas, Graham A. *An Army for Empire: The United States Army in the Spanish-American War.* Columbia: University of Missouri Press, 1971.

Crane, Stephen. *Prose and Poetry.* New York: Library of America, 1984.

———. *Wounds in the Rain: War Stories.* New York: Frederick A. Stokes Co., 1899.

Creelman, James. *On the Great Highway: The Wanderings and Adventures of a Special Correspondent.* Boston: Lothrop Publishing Co., 1901.

Curry, George. *George Curry, 1861–1947: An Autobiography.* Edited by H. B. Hening. Albuquerque: University of New Mexico Press, 1958.

Davis, Richard Harding. *Adventures and Letters of Richard Harding Davis.* New York: Charles Scribner's Sons, 1917.

———. *The Cuban and Porto Rican Campaigns.* New York: Charles Scribner's Sons, 1898.

———. *Cuba in War Time.* New York: R. H. Russell, 1897.

———. *Notes of a War Correspondent.* New York: Charles Scribner's Sons, 1911.

De Quesada, Alejandro. *Roosevelt's Rough Riders.* New York: Osprey, 2009.

Demolins, Edmond. *Anglo-Saxon Superiority: To What It Is Due.* Translated by Louis Lavigne. New York: Charles Scribner's Sons, 1898.

Dierks, Jack Cameron. *A Leap to Arms: The Cuban Campaign of 1898.* Philadelphia: J. B. Lippincott, 1970.

Downey, Fairfax. *Richard Harding Davis and His Day.* New York: Charles Scribner's Sons, 1933.

Draper, Andrew S. *The Rescue of Cuba, Marking an Epoch in the Growth of Free Government.* New York: Silver, Burdett & Co., 1899.

Dyer, John P. *From Shiloh to San Juan: The Life of "Fightin' Joe" Wheeler.* Baton Rouge: Louisiana State University Press, 1941.

Egan, Tim. *The Big Burn: Teddy Roosevelt and the Fire That Saved America.* New York: Houghton Mifflin, 2009.

Eisenhower, John S. D. *Teddy Roosevelt and Leonard Wood: Partners in Command.* Columbia: University of Missouri Press, 2014.

Emmett, Chris. *In the Path of Events, with Colonel Martin Lalor Crimmins: Soldier—Naturalist—Historian.* Waco, Tex.: Jones & Morrison, 1959.

Everett, Marshall, ed. *Exciting Experiences in Our Wars with Spain and the Filipinos.* Chicago: The Educational Company, 1901.

Ferrara, Orestes. *The Last Spanish War: Revelations in "Diplomacy."* New York: The Paisely Press, 1937.

Ferrer, Ada. *Insurgent Cuba: Race, Nation, and Revolution, 1868–1898.* Chapel Hill: University of North Carolina Press, 1999.

Fisher, Lewis F. *Saving San Antonio: The Preservation of a Heritage.* San Antonio: Maverick Books, 2016.

Foner, Philip S. *The Spanish-Cuban-American War and the Birth of American Imperialism, 1895–1902.* New York: Monthly Review Press, 1972.

Freidel, Frank. *The Splendid Little War: The Dramatic Story of the Spanish-American War.* New York: Little, Brown, 1958.

Funston, Frederick. *Memories of Two Wars: Cuban and Philippine Experiences.* London: Constable & Co., 1912.

Gardner, Mark Lee. *Rough Riders: Theodore Roosevelt, His Cowboy Regiment, and the Immortal Charge Up San Juan Hill.* New York: William Morrow, 2016.

Gauvreau, Charles F. *Reminiscences of the Spanish-American War in Cuba and the Philippines.* St. Albans, Vt.: Messenger Office Printers, 1912.

Gilman, Bradley. *Roosevelt: The Happy Warrior.* Boston: Little, Brown, & Company, 1921.

Gould, Lewis L. *The Spanish-American War and President McKinley.* Lawrence: University Press of Kansas, 1982.

Green, Constance McLaughlin. *Washington: A History of the Capital, 1800–1950.* Princeton: Princeton University Press, 1962.

Greenberg, David. *The Republic of Spin: An Inside History of the American Presidency.* New York: W. W. Norton, 2016.

Greenway, John Campbell. *It Was the Grandest Sight I Ever Saw: Experiences of a Rough Rider Recorded in the Letters of Lieutenant John Campbell Greenway.* Edited by Charles Herner. Tucson: Arizona Historical Society, 2001.

Grismer, Karl H. *Tampa: A History of the City of Tampa and the Tampa Bay Region of Florida.* St. Petersburg: St. Petersburg Printing Co., 1950.

Grondahl, Paul. *I Rose Like a Rocket: The Political Education of Theodore Roosevelt.* New York: Free Press, 2004.

Guthrie, C. W., ed. *The First Ranger: Adventures of a Pioneer Forest Ranger.* Huson, Mont.: Redwing Publishing, 1995.

Hagedorn, Hermann. *Leonard Wood: A Biography.* New York: Harper & Brothers, 1931.

———. *The Rough Riders.* New York: Harper & Brothers Publishers, 1927.

Hall, Tom. *The Fun and Fighting of the Rough Riders.* New York: Frederick A. Stokes Co., 1899.

Halstead, Murat. *Full Official History of the War with Spain.* New Haven: Butler, 1899.

Hancock, Harrie Irving. *What One Man Saw: Being the Personal Impressions of a War Correspondent in Cuba.* New York: Street & Smith, 1900.

Harvard Crimson. *Harvard Volunteers, 1898.* Cambridge: Harvard Crimson, 1898.

Healy, David. *U.S. Expansionism: The Imperialist Urge in the 1890s.* Madison: University of Wisconsin Press, 1970.

Heatley, Jeff, ed. *Bully! Colonel Theodore Roosevelt, the Rough Riders and Camp Wikoff—Montauk, New York, 1898.* Wainscott, N.Y.: Pushcart Press, 1998.

Hemment, John C. *Cannon and Camera: Sea and Land Battles of the Spanish-American War in Cuba*. New York: Appleton & Co., 1898.

Hendrick, Ellwood. *Lewis Miller, a Biographical Essay: A Life Developing the Chatauqua Idea*. New York: G. P. Putnam's Sons, 1925; rpt., Honesdale, Penn.: Boyds Mill Press, 2004.

Herner, Charles. *The Arizona Rough Riders*. Prescott, Ariz.: Sharlot Hall Museum Press, 1998.

Hero Tales of the American Soldier and Sailor, as Told by the Heroes Themselves and Their Comrades. Philadelphia: Century Manufacturing Co., 1899.

Hofstadter, Richard. *The Paranoid Style in American Politics*. New York: Alfred A. Knopf, 1965.

Hoganson, Kristin L. *Fighting for American Manhood: How Gender Politics Provoked the Spanish-American and Philippine-American Wars*. New Haven: Yale University Press, 1998.

Hopkins, A. G. *American Empire: A Global History*. Princeton: Princeton University Press, 2018.

Huntington, Samuel P. *The Soldier and the State: The Theory and Politics of Civil-Military Relations*. Cambridge: The Belknap Press of Harvard University Press, 1957.

Ingalls, John J. *America's War for Humanity*. New York: N. D. Thompson Publishing Co., 1898.

Jeffers, H. Paul. *Colonel Roosevelt: Theodore Roosevelt Goes to War, 1897–1898*. New York: John Wiley & Sons, 1998.

Johnson, Edward A. *History of Negro Soldiers in the Spanish-American War, and Other Items of Interest*. Raleigh, N.C.: Capital Printing Co., 1899.

Jones, Virgil Carrington. *Roosevelt's Rough Riders: The Saga of the Most Unusual American Regiment and Its Role in the Spanish-American War*. Garden City, N.Y.: Doubleday, 1971.

Kazin, Michael. *A Godly Hero: The Life of William Jennings Bryan*. New York: Anchor, 2007.

Kennan, George. *Campaigning in Cuba*. New York: The Century Co., 1899.

King, Moses. *The Dewey Reception in New York City: Nine-Hundred and Eighty Views and Portraits*. New York: M. King, 1899.

Knokey, Jon. *Theodore Roosevelt and the Making of American Leadership*. New York: Skyhorse Publishing, 2015.

Kreidberg, Marvin A., and Merton G. Henry. *History of Military Mobilization in the United States Army, 1775–1945*. Washington, D.C.: Department of the Army, 1955.

LaFeber, Walter. *The New Empire: An Interpretation of American Expansion, 1860–1898*. Ithaca, N.Y.: Cornell University Press, 1963; revised, 1998.

Landon, William H. *The U.S. Army's Deployment to the Spanish American War and Our Future Strategic Outlook*. Strategy Research Project: U.S. Army War College, 1998.

Lears, Jackson. *Rebirth of a Nation: The Making of Modern America, 1877–1920*. New York: Harper, 2009.

Lee, Arthur. *"A Good Innings": The Private Papers of Viscount Lee of Fareham*. Edited by Alan Clark. London: William Clowes & Sons, 1974.

Leech, Margaret. *In the Days of McKinley*. New York: Harper & Bros., 1959.

Linderman, Gerald F. *The Mirror of War: American Society and the Spanish-American War*. Ann Arbor: University of Michigan Press, 1974.

Long, John D. *America of Yesterday: The Diary of John D. Long*. Edited by Lawrence Shaw Mayo. Boston: The Atlantic Monthly Press, 1923.

———. *The Journal of John D. Long*. Edited by Margaret Long. Rindge, N.H.: Richard R. Smith Publisher, 1956.

Lubow, Arthur. *The Reporter Who Would Be King: A Biography of Richard Harding Davis*. New York: Charles Scribner's Sons, 1992.

Malin, James C. *Confounded Rot About Napoleon: Reflections upon Science and Technology, Nationalism, World Depression of the Eighteen-Nineties, and Afterwards*. Ann Arbor, Mich: Edwards Bros., 1961.

Marshall, Edward. *The Story of the Rough Riders, 1st U.S. Volunteer Cavalry: The Regiment in Camp and on the Battle Field*. New York: G. W. Dillingham Co., 1899.

May, Ernest R. *American Imperialism: A Speculative Essay*. New York: Atheneum, 1968.

———. *Imperial Democracy: The Emergence of America as a Great Power*. New York: Harcourt Brace Jovanovich, 1961.

McCaffery, James M. *Inside the Spanish-American War: A History Based on First-Person Accounts*. Jefferson, N.C.: McFarland, 2009.

McCallum, Jack. *Leonard Wood: Rough Rider, Surgeon, Architect of American Imperialism*. New York: New York University Press, 2006.

McCook, Henry C. *The Martial Graves of Our Fallen Heroes in Santiago de Cuba*. Philadelphia: George W. Jacobs & Co., 1899.

McCurdy, F. Allen, and J. Kirk McCurdy. *Two Rough Riders*. New York: F. Tennyson Neely, 1902.

McGinty, Billy. *Oklahoma Rough Rider: Bill McGinty's Own Story*. Edited by Jim Fulbright and Albert Stehno. Norman: University of Oklahoma Press, 2008.

McIntosh, Burr. *The Little I Saw of Cuba*. London: F. Tennyson Neely, 1899.

McCullough, David. *Mornings on Horseback: The Story of an Extraordinary Family, a Vanished Way of Life, and the Unique Child Who Became Theodore Roosevelt*. New York: Simon & Schuster, 1981.

McKinley, William. *The Speeches and Addresses of William McKinley: From March 1, 1897 to May 31, 1900*. New York: Doubleday & McClure Co., 1900.

Merry, Robert W. *President McKinley: Architect of the American Century*. New York: Simon & Schuster, 2017.

Miles, Nelson A. *Serving the Republic: Memoirs of the Civil and Military Life of Nelson A. Miles*. New York: Harper & Brothers Publishers, 1911.

Miley, John David. *In Cuba with Shafter*. New York: Charles Scribner's Sons, 1899.

Millis, Walter. *The Martial Spirit: A Study of Our War with Spain*. Boston: Houghton Mifflin Company, 1931.

Morris, Edmund. *The Rise of Theodore Roosevelt*. New York: Coward, McCann & Geoghegan, 1979; revised and expanded, 2001.

Morris, Sylvia Jukes. *Edith Kermit Roosevelt: Portrait of a First Lady*. New York: Coward, McCann & Geoghegan, 1980.

Müller y Tejeiro, José. *Battles and Capitulation of Santiago de Cuba* (trans.). Washington, D.C.: U.S. Government Printing Office, 1899.

BIBLIOGRAPHY

Musgrave, George C. *Under Three Flags in Cuba: A Personal Account of the Cuban Insurrection and Spanish-American War*. Boston: Little, Brown, & Co., 1899.

Musicant, Ivan. *Empire by Default: The Spanish-American War and the Dawn of the American Century*. New York: Henry Holt, 1998.

Nasaw, David. *The Chief: The Life of William Randolph Hearst*. New York: Houghton Mifflin, 2000.

Ninkovich, Frank. *Global Dawn: The Cultural Foundation of American International-ism, 1865–1890*. Cambridge: Harvard University Press, 2009.

Norris, Frank. *The Surrender of Santiago*. San Francisco: Paul Elder & Co., 1917.

Offner, John L. *An Unwanted War: The Diplomacy of the United States and Spain over Cuba, 1895–1898*. Chapel Hill: University of North Carolina Press, 1992.

Otis, James. *The Boys of '98*. Boston: Dana Estes & Co., 1898.

Oyos, Matthew. *In Command: Theodore Roosevelt and the American Military*. Lincoln: Potomac Books, 2018.

Parker, James. *Rear-Admirals Schley, Sampson and Cervera: A Review of the Naval Campaign of 1898, in Pursuit and Destruction of the Spanish Fleet, Commanded by Real-Admiral Pascual Cervera*. New York: The Neale Publishing Co., 1910.

Parker, John H. *The History of the Gatling Gun Detachment, Fifth Army Corps, at Santiago*. Kansas City: Hudson-Kimberly Publishing Co., 1898.

Pérez Jr., Louis A. *Cuba Between Empires: 1878–1902*. Pittsburgh: University of Pittsburgh Press, 1983.

————. *The War of 1898: The United States and Cuba in History and Historiography*. Chapel Hill: University of North Carolina Press, 1998.

Pershing, John. *My Life Before the World War, 1860–1917*. Edited by John T. Greenwood. Lexington: University Press of Kentucky, 2013.

Post, Charles Johnson. *The Little War of Private Post: The Spanish-American War Seen Up Close*. New York: Little, Brown, 1966; rpt., Bison Books, 1999.

Pratt, Julius W. *Expansionists of 1898: The Acquisition of Hawaii and the Spanish Islands*. Baltimore: Johns Hopkins University Press, 1936.

Private St. Louis. *Forty Years After*. Boston: Chapman & Grimes, 1940.

Rea, George Bronson. *Facts and Fakes About Cuba: A Review of the Various Stories Circulated in the United States Concerning the Present Insurrection*. New York: George Munro's Sons, 1897.

Rickover, George Hyman. *How the Battleship Maine Was Destroyed*. Annapolis: Naval Institute Press, 1976.

Riis, Jacob A. *Theodore Roosevelt, the Citizen*. New York: Macmillan, 1904.

Robinson, Corinne Roosevelt. *My Brother Theodore Roosevelt*. New York: Charles Scribner's Sons, 1921.

Roosevelt, Theodore. *An Autobiography*. New York: The Macmillan Company, 1913; rpt., Library of America, 2004.

————. *The Letters of Theodore Roosevelt: The Years of Preparation*. Edited by Elting E. Morison. Cambridge: Harvard University Press, 1951.

————. *The Rough Riders*. New York: Charles Scribner's Sons, 1899; rpt., Library of America, 2004.

————. *Selections from the Correspondence of Theodore Roosevelt and Henry Cabot Lodge, 1884–1918*. New York: Charles Scribner's Sons, 1925.

————. *The Strenuous Life: Essays and Addresses*. New York: The Century Co., 1903.

————. *Theodore Roosevelt's Letters to His Children.* Edited by Joseph Bucklin Bishop. New York: Charles Scribner's Sons, 1919.

Rotundo, E. Anthony. *American Manhood: Transformations in Masculinity from the Revolution to the Modern Era.* New York: Basic Books, 1993.

Samuels, Peggy, and Harold Samuels. *Teddy Roosevelt at San Juan: The Making of a President.* College Station: Texas A&M University Press, 1997.

The Santiago Campaign: Reminiscences of the Operations for the Capture of Santiago de Cuba in the Spanish-American War, June and July 1898. Richmond: Williams Printing Co., 1927.

Sargent, Herbert H. *The Campaign of Santiago de Cuba.* Chicago: A. C. McClurg & Co., 1907.

Schake, Kori. *Safe Passage: The Transition from British to American Hegemony.* Cambridge: Harvard University Press, 2017.

Schlereth, Thomas J. *Victorian America: Transformations in Everyday Life, 1876–1915.* New York: HarperCollins, 1991.

Sexton, Jay. *The Monroe Doctrine: Empire and Nation in Nineteenth-Century America.* New York: Hill & Wang, 2011.

Slotkin, Richard. *Gunfighter Nation: The Myth of the Frontier in Twentieth-Century America.* Norman: University of Oklahoma Press, 1998.

Smith, Albert E., and Phil A. Khoury. *Two Reels and a Crank: From Nickelodeon to Picture Palaces.* New York: Doubleday, 1952.

Sorrentino, Paul. *Stephen Crane: A Life of Fire.* Cambridge: Harvard University Press, 2014.

Thomas, Evan. *The War Lovers: Roosevelt, Lodge, Hearst, and the Rush to Empire, 1898.* New York: Little, Brown, 2010.

Tone, John Lawrence. *War and Genocide in Cuba, 1895–1898.* Chapel Hill: University of North Carolina Press, 2006.

Trask, David F. *The War with Spain in 1898.* New York: Free Press, 1981.

Tuchman, Barbara W. *The Proud Tower: A Portrait of the World Before the War, 1890–1914.* New York: Macmillan, 1966.

Vincent, George E., ed. *Theodore W. Miller, Rough Rider: His Diary as a Soldier Together with the Story of His Life.* Akron: Privately printed, 1899.

Walker, Dale L. *The Boys of '98: Theodore Roosevelt and the Rough Riders.* New York: Forge, 1998.

Wallace, Mike. *Greater Gotham: A History of New York City from 1898 to 1919.* New York: Oxford University Press, 2017.

Weigley, Russell F. *History of the United States Army.* New York: Macmillan, 1967.

Wells, J. O. *Diary of a Rough Rider.* St. Joseph, Mich.: A. B. Morse, n.d.

Westermeier, Clifford P. *Who Rush to Glory: The Cowboy Volunteers of 1898.* Caldwell, Idaho: The Caxton Printers. 1958.

Wheeler, Joseph. *The Santiago Campaign.* Boston: Lamson, Wolffe & Co., 1898.

Wiebe, Robert H. *The Search for Order, 1877–1920.* New York: Macmillan, 1967.

Wilkerson, Marcus M. *Public Opinion and the Spanish-American War: A Study in War Propaganda.* New York: Russell & Russell, 1932.

Wilson, Woodrow. *A History of the American People.* New York: Harper & Bros, 1902.

Wister, Owen. *Roosevelt: The Story of a Friendship, 1880–1919.* New York: The Macmillan Company, 1930.

Zacks, Richard. *Island of Vice: Theodore Roosevelt's Quest to Clean Up Sin-Loving New York.* New York: Anchor, 2012.

Articles

Anonymous. "Can the United States Afford to Fight Spain?" *The North American Review* 164, no. 483 (February 1897): 209–15.

Auxier, George W. "Middle Western Newspapers and the Spanish-American War, 1895–1898." *The Mississippi Valley Historical Review* 26, no. 4 (March 1940): 523–34.

———. "The Propaganda Activities of the Cuban Junta in Precipitating the Spanish-American War, 1895–1898." *The Hispanic-American Historical Review* 19, no. 3 (August 1939): 286–305.

Barton, Clara. "Our Work and Observations in Cuba." *North American Review* 166, no. 498 (May 1898): 552–59.

Bold, Christine. "Where Did the Black Rough Riders Go?" *Canadian Review of American Studies* 39, no. 3 (2009): 273–97.

Cordery, Stacy A. "The Precious Minutes Before the Crowded Hour: Edith and Theodore Roosevelt in Tampa, 1898." *Theodore Roosevelt Association Journal* 31, no. 1–2 (Winter–Spring 2010): 22–31.

Cortada, James W. "Economic Issues in Caribbean Politics: Rivalry Between Spain and the United States in Cuba, 1848–1898." *Revista de Historia de America* 86 (July–December 1978): 233–67.

Davis, Michelle Bray, and Rollie W. Quimby. "Senator Proctor's Cuban Speech: Speculations on a Cause of the Spanish-American War." *Quarterly Journal of Speech* 55, no. 2 (1969): 131–41.

Davis, Richard Harding. "The Rocking-Chair Period of the War." *Scribner's*, August 1898: 131–41.

———. "The Rough Riders' Fight at Las Guasimas." *Scribner's*, October 1898: 259–73.

———. "The Battle of San Juan." *Scribner's*, October 1898: 387–402.

———. "In the Rifle Pits." *Scribner's*, December 1898: 644–58.

De Santis, Hugh. "The Imperialist Impulse and American Innocence, 1865–1900," in *American Foreign Relations: A Historiographical Review.* Edited by Gerald K. Haines and J. Samuel Walker. London: Pinter, 1981.

Eggert, Gerald G. "Our Man in Havana: Fitzhugh Lee." *The Hispanic American Historical Review* 47, no. 4 (November 1967): 463–85.

Emerson, Edwin. "Life at Camp Wikoff." *Munsey's Magazine*, October 1898: 256–72.

Field, James A. "American Imperialism: The Worst Chapter in Almost Any Book." *The American Historical Review* 83, no. 3 (June 1978): 644–68.

Foner, Philip S. "Why the United States Went to War with Spain." *Science and Society* 32, no. 1 (Winter 1968): 39–65.

Frates, Kent. "The Great McGinty." *True West*, November 14, 2014. https://truewestmagazine.com/the-great-mcginty (accessed January 1, 2019).

Gatewood, Willard B., Jr. "Negro Troops in Florida 1898." *The Florida Historical Quarterly* 49, no. 1 (July 1970): 1–15.

Gibson, George H. "Opinion in North Carolina Regarding the Acquisition of Texas and Cuba, 1835–1855," *The North Carolina Historical Review* 37, no. 2 (April 1960): 185–201.

BIBLIOGRAPHY

Gillette, Howard, Jr. "The Military Occupation of Cuba, 1899–1902: Workshop for American Progressivism." *American Quarterly* 25, no. 4 (October 1973): 410–25.

Gleijeses, Piero. "1898: The Opposition to the Spanish American War." *Journal of Latin American Studies* 35, no. 4 (November 2003): 681–719.

Grenville, John A. S. "American Naval Preparation for War with Spain, 1896–1898." *Journal of American Studies* 2, no. 1 (April 1968): 33–47.

Harrington, Fred H. "The Anti-Imperialist Movement in the United States, 1898–1900." *The Mississippi Valley Historical Review* 22, no. 2 (September 1935): 211–30.

Holbo, Paul S. "The Convergence of Moods and the Cuban-Bond 'Conspiracy' of 1898." *The Journal of American Society* 55, no. 1 (June 1968): 54–72.

Huse, Harry. "On the Gloucester After the Battle." *The Century*, May 1899: 115–16.

James, Henry. "Theodore Roosevelt and the National Consciousness." *Literature*, April 23, 1898. Reprinted in Henry James, *Literary Criticism*, Vol. 1: *Essays, English and American Writers*. New York: Library of America, 1984, pp. 663–67.

Kennan, George. "George Kennan's Story of the War." *Outlook*, July 30, 1898: 769–74.

La Motte, Henry. "With the Rough Riders." *St. Nicholas*, July 1899: 832–40.

Latane, John H. "Intervention of the United States in Cuba." *The North American Review* 166, no. 496 (March 1898): 350–61.

Lee, Arthur. "The Regulars at El Caney." *Scribner's*, October 1898: 403–13.

Maass, Matthias. "When Communication Fails: Spanish-American Crisis Diplomacy 1898." *American Studies* 52, no. 4 (2007): 481–93.

Marshall, Edward. "A Wounded Correspondent's Recollections of Guasimas." *Scribner's*, September 1898: 273–76.

McClernand, E. J. "The Santiago Campaign." *Infantry Journal* 21 (1922): 280–302.

Miles, Nelson A. "The War with Spain." *The North America Review* 168, no. 510 (May 1899): 513–29.

Morgan, H. Wayne. "William McKinley as a Political Leader." *The Review of Politics* 28, no. 4 (October 1966): 417–32.

O'Connor, Nancy Lenore. "The Spanish-American War: A Re-Evaluation of Its Causes." *Science and Society* 22, no. 2 (Spring 1958): 129–43.

Offner, John L. "McKinley and the Spanish-American War." *Presidential Studies Quarterly* 34, no. 1 (March 2004): 50–61.

Patterson, Thomas G. "United States Intervention in Cuba, 1898: Interpretations of the Spanish-American-Cuban-Filipino War." *The History Teacher* 29, no. 3 (May 1996): 341–61.

Peabody, George Foster. "Why Should We Interfere?" *The Advocate of Peace* 60, no. 5 (May 1898): 114–15.

Pérez, Louis A. Jr. "The Meaning of the Maine: Causation and the Historiography of the Spanish-American War." *Pacific Historical Review* 58, no. 3 (August 1989): 293–322.

Pratt, Julius W. "American Business and the Spanish-American War." *The Hispanic-American Historical Review* 14, no. 2 (May 1899): 163–201.

Prentice, Royal. "The Rough Riders." *New Mexico Historical Review* 26, no. 4 (October 1951): 261–76.

————. "The Rough Riders—Concluded." *New Mexico Historical Review* 27, no. 1 (January 1952): 29–50.

Ramsden, Frederick W. "Diary of the British Consul at Santiago During the Hostilities." *McClure's*, October 1898: 580–90.

Ranson, Edward. "British Military and Naval Observers in the Spanish-American War." *Journal of American Studies* 3, no. 1 (July 1969): 33–56.

Rayburn, John C. "The Rough Riders in San Antonio, 1898." *Arizona and the West* 3, no. 2 (Summer 1961): 113–28.

Tarrago, Rafael E. "The Road to Santiago: Cuban Separatism and United States Americanism and How They Converged in 1898." *Iberoamericana* 1, no. 3 (September 2001): 61–89.

Taylor, Hannis. "A Review of the Cuban Question in Its Economic, Political, and Diplomatic Aspects." *North American Review* 165, no. 492 (November 1897): 610–35.

Walker, Dale. "Arizona's Buckey O'Neill and the Rough Riders." *Montana: The Magazine of Western History* 21, no. 1 (Winter 1971): 60–71.

————. "Last of the Rough Riders." *Montana: The Magazine of Western History* 23, no. 3 (Summer 1973): 40–50.

Whitney, Caspar. "The Santiago Campaign," *Harper's* 97, no. 581 (October 1898): 795–818.

Yockelson, Mitchell. "'I Am Entitled to the Medal of Honor and I Want It': Theodore Roosevelt and His Quest for Glory." *Prologue* 30, no. 1 (Spring 1998). https://www.archives.gov/publications/prologue/1998/spring/roosevelt-and-medal-of-honor-1.html (accessed January 1, 2019).

Index

INDEX

Cuba (*cont.*)
American planning for invasion of, 67–79
American pride over first major victory in, 214–15
American tariff on sugar cane in, 29
anti-American riot in, 13–14, 47
Cleveland's neutrality toward, 24–25
concerns about conditions in, 40, 44, 50–51
debates over type of military activity against, 41–43
declaration of war against Spain by, 58
desire for war against Spain in, 41, 51–52, 55, 87
Dewey's Manila victory and pressure for invasion of, 67
early revolts against Spain in, 6, 7
Fifth Corps' route to, map, xi
humanitarianism approach to, 42, 45, 137, 189, 281
independence achieved by, 284–85
insurrection over tariffs in, 29–32
Junta support for, 7, 30, 34, 35
lack of plan for capture cities from Spanish control in, 218
length of Rough Riders' stay in, 249
McKinley's initial noninterventionist policy toward, 25, 43–44
McKinley's letters to Cuba demanding peace in, 44
newspaper coverage of rebels in, 35–39
newspapers' influence on attitudes toward intervention in, 7–8, 35, 39–40
opposition to intervention in, 45, 51, 52, 53
Platt Amendment and, 285
popular support for independence of, 7, 30–31, 34, 42, 53, 55, 134, 277
reaction to *Maine* sinking and push for war on Spain in, 49–55, 187
Roosevelt's push for intervention in, 41, 45, 52–53
Rough Riders' departure from, 249

Senator Proctor's speech on intervention in, 50–51
Spain's refusal to voluntarily leave, 44
Spanish colonial control of, 5–6, 27–29, 43–45
Spanish fleet in Havana as sign of control over, 225
Treaty of Paris and, 275
Wood's reforms in, as military governor of, 284
Cuba in War Time (Davis), 39, 40
Cuban rebels
American food distributed to, 228
American men among rebels in, 30
American support pledged by, 185
American treatment of, as allies, 241
criticism of lack of effort by, 186
García as leader of, in eastern Cuba, 140
García on American treatment of, 186
García on condition of, 241
García's resignation after Spain's surrender and, 241
landing at Santiago and, 142, 144, 145–46, 147
move inland in Cuba by, 249
newspaper reports on assistance from, 185, 186
opinions about American army arrival held by, 184–85
physical appearance of, 147
possible participation in American efforts by, 184–86
private Americans' assistance to, 30–31, 110
Rough Riders on, 147–48
San Juan Heights battle with, 198, 199, 213, 227
Santiago's roads blocked by, 188
Shafter's relationship with, 183, 185–86, 241
Spanish civilian government of Santiago after surrender, 241
Spanish General Weyler's campaign against, 32–34
surrender of Santiago and continuing fighting by, 241
Ten Years' War between Spain and, 28–29, 31, 110, 141

on his troops' condition, 241
military background of, 141
move inland in Cuba by, 249
resignation of, after Spain's
surrender, 241
Shafter's visit with, 140–41, 175
Gatewood, Willard B. Jr., 119
Geronimo, 26, 80, 81–82, 84, 88
Gómez, Máximo, 31
Goodrich, David "Dade"
cousin Miller enlistment and, 107,
108
cousin's wounding and, 210
Las Guasimas battle and, 165–66
later career of, 286
Roosevelt's morning routine with, 251
San Juan Heights battle and, 208,
209, 210, 219
Gosling, Fred, 269
Gould, Helen, 255
Gould, Jay, 18, 255
Greenway, John Campbell, 86, 208,
251, 286, 314n
Grindell, Thomas C., 88
Guam, 275
Guantánamo Bay, Cuba, 139, 142, 175

Hagedorn, Hermann, 45, 89, 98, 172
Hagood, Johnson, 64–65
Hall, Tom, 88, 91, 93, 94, 98, 109, 143,
147, 234, 286
Hamilton, Alexander, 64, 246
Hamiltonian ideal of standing armies
and preparedness, 63, 64, 74,
281, 282
Hamner, George, 180, 288, 289
Hanna, Mark, 53
Hardy, Alexander, 187
Harrison, Benjamin, 19, 45
Harvard University, Rough Riders
from, 74–75, 86, 92, 115
Havana, Cuba
anti-American riot in, 13–14
deaths in, during Weyler's campaign
against the rebel insurrection, 33
naval blockade around, 58, 66, 71,
87, 187–88, 224–25, 249
proposed American campaign
against, 245

Spanish control of, 27, 225
Spanish fleet's dash for safety
through blockade in, 225–27
Hawaii, 1, 22, 25, 52, 275, 279
Hawkins, Hamilton, 207
Hay, John, 5, 20, 24, 25
Hayes, Frank P., 98, 130, 172–73
Haywood, Henry, 201
Hearst, William Randolph 104, 147
Davis's reporting on Cuban rebels
and, 36–37, 38–39, 50
Maine sinking and, 49
readers' demand for sensational
stories and, 35, 38
Roosevelt and, 157
Spanish consul's memo on
McKinley printed by,
40–41
Heffner, Harry, 162
Herrig, Fred, 19, 74, 96, 171
Hersey, Henry, 86
Hobart, Garret, 267
Hobson, Richmond, 121, 235–36
Hofstadter, Richard, 6, 63
Holderman, Bert, 238
holding camp. *See* Montauk, Long
Island, holding camp
Hollister, Stanley, 360
Holt, Harrison Jewell, 210
Horn, Tom, 88
hospitals. *See also* field hospitals
Montauk holding camp with,
260
wounded soldiers' return home to,
253, 260
hospital ships, 131, 150, 224
Howard, Charles, 288
Hughes, David L., 92, 147–48, 208
Hull, John A. T., 70, 168
humanitarianism approach to Cuba, 42,
45, 137, 189, 281
Huse, Harry P., 227

Independent Brigade, 144
Independents (political party), 259,
274, 275
Indiana (ship), 238
Infanta María Teresa (carrier),
225–27

337

INDEX

military preparedness belief, 23–24, 72

move to Santiago front, 190–91, 192

national profile of, as wartime leader, 2–3

New York City victory parade, 2, 267–68

newspaper reporters on Roosevelt's battlefield action, 160–61

on land crabs at Sevilla camp, 178

on rations, 130, 180–81

plan for attack on Santiago, 121–22, 124

political campaigns' use of battlefield experience, 169, 234, 254, 256–57, 278

popular culture celebrity of Roosevelt, 10, 58–59, 116, 124

praise for black soldiers, 212–13

preparing regiment for fighting, 73–74, 132

Puerto Rican invasion suggestions, 242

reaction to deaths of soldiers, 172, 173

relationship with troops, 95–96

Roosevelt on his "crowded hour," 4–5, 205

San Juan Heights battle significance, 194

Shafter's council of war on Santiago, 190

Tampa embarkation camp, 109, 114, 115–16, 120

train journey to Tampa embarkation point, 103, 104, 106

transport of his horses, 149

uniform with pince-nez, 73, 77, 93, 94, 95, 195

voyage home from Santiago, 250–52

voyage to Santiago, 127, 128, 130, 131–32, 140

War Department criticism, 243, 244–46, 252

war hero status, 2, 59, 62, 234, 253, 254

weaponry, 95

PERSONAL LIFE

author of books, articles, and essays, 17, 19, 20, 24, 259–60, 278–79, 284, 286

belief in imperialistic manhood concept, 3, 10

connection to the West, 18

cowboy imagery, 96, 273

Dakotas ranching venture, 18–19, 96, 252, 288

death of first wife, 18

family background and education, 16–18

hero worship of his father, 16

health and physical ailments, 16

on his "crowded hour" in Cuba, 4–5, 205

hobbies, 16–17

hunting trips, 17, 18, 19, 155, 212, 252, 278, 284

intellectual development, 3

leadership qualities, 2–3, 75–76, 98–99, 232–33

Long Island home, 19, 259, 264, 284

physical activities and love of sports, 16, 17, 20, 26

physical appearance, 16, 17, 114, 195, 273

pince-nez for poor eyesight, 77

pistol salvaged from the *Maine*, 95, 212

relationship with wife Edith, 114–15

reputation among peers, 17, 18, 21

second marriage and children, 19

speaking style and vocal qualities, 14

strenuous life philosophy, 3, 279–80

wildlife and wilderness conservation interests, 19, 116

POLITICAL CAREER. *See also* New York State governorship

America as emergent world power and intervention in Cuba, 40

Civil Service Commission member, 19, 20

desire for intervention in Cuba, 41, 45, 49, 50

Maine sinking reaction, 49–50, 52–53

345

ABOUT THE AUTHOR

Clay Risen is the deputy op-ed editor at the *New York Times* and the author of *Single Malt: A Guide to the Whiskies of Scotland*; *The Bill of the Century: The Epic Battle for the Civil Rights Act*, which was nominated for the PEN Galbraith Award and an NAACP Spirit Award; the bestselling *American Whiskey, Bourbon & Rye: A Guide to the Nation's Favorite Spirit*; and *A Nation on Fire: America in the Wake of the King Assassination*. He lives in Brooklyn with his wife and two children.